The Volitional Brain

ALSO OF INTEREST FROM IMPRINT ACADEMIC
Full details on: http://www.imprint.co.uk

Series Editor: Professor J.A. Goguen
Department of Computer Science and Engineering
University of California, San Diego

Thomas Metzinger, ed.
Conscious Experience

Francisco Varela and Jonathan Shear, ed.
The View from Within:
First-person approaches to the study of consciousness

Shaun Gallagher and Jonathan Shear, ed.
Models of the Self

Joseph A. Goguen, ed.
Art and the Brain

Rafael Núñez and Walter J. Freeman, ed.
Reclaiming Cognition: The primacy of action, intention and emotion

Published in the UK and USA by Imprint Academic
PO Box 1, Thorverton EX5 5YX, UK
World Copyright © Imprint Academic, 1999
No part of any contribution may be reproduced in any form without permission,
except for the quotation of brief passages in criticism and discussion.

ISBN 0 907845 50 9 (hardback)

ISSN 1355 8250 (*Journal of Consciousness Studies*, **6**, No.8–9, 1999)

British Library Cataloguing in Publication Data
A catalogue record for this book is available from the British Library

Cover illustration: Nicholas Gilbert Scott
Cover design: J.K.B. Sutherland

Printed in Exeter UK by Short Run Press Ltd.

The Volitional Brain

Towards a Neuroscience of Free Will

edited by
Benjamin Libet, Anthony Freeman
and Keith Sutherland

IMPRINT ACADEMIC

Contents

Philosophy

Comment

Contributors

Whit Blauvelt
406 7th Street #4, Brooklyn, NY 11211, USA

Jonathan Bricklin
89 Scribner Avenue, Staten Island, NY 10301, USA

Thomas W. Clark
34 Winslow Avenue, Somerville, MA 02144, USA

Guy Claxton
University of Bristol School of Education, 35 Berkeley Square,
Bristol BS8 1JA, UK

Anthony Freeman
Imprint Academic, PO Box 1, Thorverton, Devon EX5 5YX, UK

Chris D. Frith
Wellcome Department of Cognitive Neurology, Institute of Neurology,
University College London, QueenSquare, London WC1N 3BG, UK

Gilberto Gomes
CPRJ, R. Lopez Quintas 100–605–I, 22460–010 Rio de Janeiro, Brazil

David Hodgson
Supreme Court of New South Wales, Queens Square, Sydney,
NSW 2000, Australia

David H. Ingvar
Department of Clinical Neurophysiology, University of Lund,
University Hospital, S–221 85 Lund, Sweden

Jaron Lanier
Interactive Telecommunications Department, New York University,
721 Broadway, New York, NY 10003, USA

Benjamin Libet
Department of Physiology, University of California, San Francisco,
San Francisco, CA 94143–0444, USA

Jonathan Lowe
Department of Philosophy, University of Durham, 50 Old Elvet,
Durham, DH1 3HN, UK

John McCrone
10 Sterry Drive, Thames Ditton, Surrey KT7 0YN, UK

Ulrich Mohrhoff
Sri Aurobindo Ashram, Pondicherry 605 002, India

Wolfram Schultz
Institute of Physiology and Program in Neuroscience,
University of Fribourg, CH–1700 Fribourg, Switzerland

Jeffrey M. Schwartz
UCLA Department of Psychiatry, 760 Westwood Plaza, Room 67–468,
Los Angeles, CA 90024–1759, USA

Sean A. Spence
Neuroscience Section, Imperial College School of Medicine,
MRC Cyclotron Unit, Hammersmith Hospital, London W12 0NN, UK

Henry P. Stapp
Lawrence Berkeley National Laboratory, University of California,
Berkeley, CA 94720, USA

Keith Sutherland
Imprint Academic, PO Box 1, Thorverton, Devon EX5 5YX, UK

David Wilson
Department of Biology, University of Miami,
PO Box 249118, Coral Gables, FL 33124–0421, USA

Benjamin Libet, Anthony Freeman and Keith Sutherland[1]

Editors' Introduction: The Volitional Brain

Towards A Neuroscience of Free Will

The much-debated 'hard problems' in the emerging field of consciousness studies revolve around the difficulty in reconciling our first-person 'folk psychology' account of ourselves with our scientific understanding of the world. Despite the occasional dissident voice (for instance Anthony **Freeman**),[2] most people are agreed that we all 'know' that we have some degree of volitional control over the sort of experiences that we undergo. But when we try to reconcile this with our physics- and biology-based understanding of the world, we run into a number of serious and well-documented problems.

Free Will and Causality: Historical Background

Our sense of free will (volitional control) depends upon a balance between reliability and flexibility in relation to cause-and-effect. Without the former, all outcomes would be arbitrary; without the latter, all outcomes would be predetermined. In neither case would there be any way of putting one's will into effect. So much is clear, yet establishing that precarious balance has proved so difficult that Kant himself declared 'freedom of the will' to be one of only three metaphysical problems which lie beyond the powers of the human intellect (Kant, 1788).[3] Western debate on this topic reflects a complex ethical and religious inheritance. Insights from Greek philosophy and Hebrew scripture were combined and filtered through Christian and Jewish traditions which developed in late antiquity and through the middle ages. These formed the context for the Enlightenment, whose dominant thinkers in turn provide the backdrop against which today's scholars act and react.

---

[1] The editors wish to thank Susan Blackmore, Jean Burns, Tom Clark, David Hodgson and Jonathan Shear for substantial assistance in the preparation of this introduction.

[2] In this Introduction, names in bold type without a date refer to contributions to this volume.

[3] His other two intractable problems were God and Immortality.

Journal of Consciousness Studies, **6**, No. 8–9, 1999, pp. ix–xxiii

The major problem for Christian doctrine in this area was to find room for any flexibility. How could belief in an all-knowing God be compatible with the genuinely 'open' future necessary for meaningful human choice? Augustine (354–430AD) argued that God foreknows whether I shall freely choose to do good or evil, rather as I can predict what my wife will freely choose to have for breakfast, but this proved unconvincing, especially when combined with his teaching on original sin.[4] More influential has been the proposal of Boethius (480–524AD) that God has knowledge of the 'future' which is of a quite different order from human prediction, because he is 'outside time'. But this is to land us out of the frying pan straight into the fire, amidst a whole complex of problems relating to time (see, e.g., Atmanspacher & Ruhnau, 1997, and Jaron **Lanier**'s essay in this volume).

Just as damaging for the prospects of human freedom as an omniscient God was an all-powerful God, sovereign lord of all. Mediaeval theologians attempted to square this circle with a judicious blend of Aristotle and scripture. They taught that everything has both an 'efficient cause' (that which brings it about) and a 'final cause' (the purpose for which it is brought about).[5] Both types of 'cause' could have more than one step, so if P causes Q, and Q causes R, then P is the 'remote efficient cause' of R, and Q is the 'immediate efficient cause' of R. This enabled them to say that God (as creator of all things) was the ultimate efficient cause of everything and also (as the one for whose sake everything exists) the final cause of everything. That safeguarded his absolute sovereignty. Then, without contradiction, they could look to human agents as the immediate or intermediate causes, both efficient and final.

A minority Christian approach, associated particularly with the reformer John Calvin (1509–1564), cut the knot by taking Augustine's teaching on divine foreknowledge while abandoning his insistence on human freedom. Calvin combined a doctrine of 'double predestination' (in which, by God's sovereign will, a few are predestined for eternal bliss and the rest of humanity to eternal torment) with a completely 'hands on' view of God's agency in creation: 'Not a drop of rain falls without the express command of God.' Such an extreme form of 'theological determinism' posed problems — such as whether it is meaningful to talk about moral responsibility — which foreshadowed those posed today by the 'physical determinism' of scientists like Colin Blakemore (1988). This suggests that old theological controversies still have more relevance than one might think. For instance, Anthony Kenny (1987) says, 'The actual logical moves which somebody in the twentieth century will use to reconcile physical determinism with our experience of freedom will be, as often as not, the same steps gone through by people in the fourteenth century trying to reconcile divine predestination with human freedom' (p. 74).

A contemporary philosophical reconciliation of physical determinism and and genuine freedom of action for individual agents is offered by Jonathan **Lowe**. He argues that it is 'metaphysically possible' to discover a train of physical causes that *could* provide a complete causal expalnation for an action without ruling out the pos-

---

[4] The doctrine of original sin holds that 'fallen' humanity has an inbuilt tendency towards evil. Consequently there is an absolute necessity for divine grace to over-rule this tendency if the human will is to choose rightly.

[5] For example, the efficient cause of my car's stopping is the pressure of my foot on the brake pedal; the final cause might be the fact that the lights are set at red, or that a child has run out in front of the car, or that I have arrived home.

sibility that in fact they *do not* do so. Since he denies that mental states are physical states, he can then claim, at least as a possibility, that an action that is apparently completely physically caused does in fact have a mental, non-physical, element in its causal chain. Where Lowe speaks of a metaphysical possibility, psychiatrist Jeffrey **Schwartz** points to actual clinical examples where, in his opinion, patients have achieved a change in behaviour by the application of a non-physical 'mental force'. However, neurobiologist David L. **Wilson** is far more representative of current opinion when he concludes that violations of fundamental physical laws would occur if a non-physical mind were able to influence brain or behaviour.

Today's attitudes can be traced to the sixteenth century, when mediaeval consensus based on a 'baptized Aristotle' began to crumble under the combined pressure of Protestant views such as Calvin's and a growing unease at the idea that everything, even in the inanimate world, must have a purpose (Aristotle's 'final cause'). Surely, it was increasingly said, clouds form and rain falls and things get wet *according to the laws of nature*. Such things happen, and there are consequences, but they do not happen for a predetermined purpose. In this changing climate of opinion, theists still maintained that the underlying laws of nature carried out the purposes of a personal God, but an increasing number of people no longer believed in such a God.

The final blow came from David Hume (1740), who pointed out that *not only* is there no evidence for *final* causes (purposes) in inanimate nature, there is no evidence for *efficient* causes either. We may say that P causes Q and that Q causes R, as if the latter *necessarily* followed from the former, but the most we can actually *know* is that Q and R followed P in all observed cases. The so-called 'laws of nature' are no more than descriptions of observed regularities in the way things happen. David **Hodgson** calls this 'Hume's Mistake' and claims that the argument only appears to work because its conclusion (or something very like it) is assumed from the outset. It is true that we all tend at the practical level to continue acting 'as if' some things caused other things, and there will always be those who challenge Hume's claims about an absence of necessity in relation to events, but nonetheless he did change for ever the theoretical landscape regarding causality and, by extension, volition.

The Influence of Science

Immanuel Kant once credited Hume with having awoken him from his 'dogmatic slumbers' but, as we have seen, even Kant gave up when it came to understanding free will. The Newtonian science of his day was completely deterministic and he naturally felt this was incompatible with freedom of action; and without freedom of action there could be no moral responsibility, no ethics. But Kant was quite clear that we all *experience* moral dilemmas and make choices. He therefore concluded that while physical determinism held sway in the world of appearances (the world of which we have empirical knowledge), there might still be room in the (hidden) world of things-in-themselves for free will and choice. He could not prove this to be the case, but he could show it was not impossible (although it would remain entirely vacuous). And that enabled him to reconcile the theory of deterministic science with the personal experience of moral choice.

Kant's analysis has not prevented science from continuing to be unfriendly to free will, as can be seen from the perspective of Albert Einstein in the following extract:

If the moon, in the act of completing its eternal way around the earth, were gifted with self-consciousness, it would feel thoroughly convinced that it was travelling its way of its own accord on the strength of a resolution taken once and for all. So would a Being, endowed with higher insight and more perfect intelligence, watching man and his doings, smile about man's illusion that he was acting according to his own free will.

This is my belief, although I know well that it is not fully demonstrable. If one thinks out to the very last consequence what one exactly knows and understands, there will be hardly any human being who will be impervious to this view, provided his self-love does not ruffle up against it. Man defends himself from being regarded as an impotent object in the course of the Universe. But should the lawfulness of events, such as unveils itself more or less clearly in inorganic nature, cease to function in front of the activities in our brain?

Leaving aside the inconsistency of such a view, the influence of alcohol and other sharply controllable factors on our thoughts, feelings and activities should show very distinctly that determinism does not stop before the majesty of our human will (Einstein, 1931, quoted in Home and Robinson, 1995).

Although Einstein was using uncharacteristically flowery language for this passage (it was taken from a book dedicated to the Indian poet, Rabindranath Tagore), it provides a good summary of our current understanding of free will. So far as the physical sciences are concerned, the universe still appears to be a thoroughly deterministic system, even if it is not totally predictable.[6]

Quantum Theory

The model of physics that underlies this viewpoint of strong determinism is essentially classical. Einstein famously rejected the new quantum theory on account of its 'basic positivistic attitude' and rejection of ontological questions. However a number of scientists have claimed that the philosophical debate on volition is taking place within an old-fashioned view of science, and that a full acceptance of quantum theory will have radical entailments for the free will debate (cf. Beck & Eccles, 1992; Penrose, 1994). Towards the end of his life even Einstein grudgingly admitted that 'the contemporary quantum theory . . . constitutes an optimum formulation of the [statistical] connections.' (Einstein, 1951, p. 87).

Within the current debate on quantum theory there is no consensus over the role of the conscious observer — if any. However, Henry **Stapp**, continuing his development of the von Neumann/Wigner interpretation of quantum mechanics, takes the view that quantum theory is to do with human knowledge, the choice of question that we put to Nature. The increase in knowledge — the 'wave-packet reduction' — takes place in the brain/mind of the observer, who is an integral part of the quantum system. Stapp goes on to discuss how the conscious intentions of a human being can influence the activities of his brain. This approach makes no recourse to randomness and attempts to refute the argument that quantum events are ruled out in warm, wet 'classical' brains.

Ulrich **Mohrhoff** also discusses the mind–brain relation from the standpoint of physics and sets his face against two commonly voiced opinions: that conservation laws make mind/matter interaction impossible and that quantum indeterminism pro-

---

[6] Heisenberg's uncertainty principle and chaos theory (in which a small change in a parameter can make a major change in the behaviour of a system) would make it impossible to track all events predictably.

vides a physical correlate of free will. His own view is that electromagnetic interaction might provide a vehicle for mental causation, but that any departures from physical laws caused by (non-physical) mental events would not be amenable to mathematical description.

Ethics and Personal Responsibility

In reaching the view given above, Henry Stapp makes specific reference to personal responsibility, which is also a major concern of David Hodgson and Whit **Blauvelt**. One of the core principles of our notions of human rights and justice is the principle that, as a general rule, the State should not forcibly interfere with the freedom of its citizens. Only when the citizen has committed an *offence*, defined as voluntarily acting in breach of a reasonable and publicly promulgated law, does it then become *fair* that he or she be coerced or punished to an extent proportionate to the degree of guilt involved. The accused had the choice of either complying or not complying with the law, and chose not to comply; so punishment to an appropriate extent is just. However, when a citizen has not committed any offence it is not fair or just that he or she be coerced simply on the ground that his or her freedom is considered disadvantageous to other persons or to the State.

It can be argued that denial of free will undermines this principle by removing the concept of personal responsibility (see Hodgson, 1998). If a citizen who commits an offence does not have a real choice about the matter, but is simply acting out the inevitable consequences of things that occurred before he or she was born, how can it be any more fair or just to restrict the freedom of this citizen than it is to restrict the freedom of another whose similarly-caused actions, not involving any crime or misdemeanour, make that person's freedom seem desirable?

If the distinction between things we do through choice and necessity has no scientific validity, then the consequences need to be addressed as a matter of urgency. The problem is starting to move beyond the scope of armchair philosophers and concerns the future shape of society and civilization. Already scientists are starting to draw some very radical conclusions as to how our legal system could be recast on a more scientific basis (Blakemore, 1988; Crick, 1994).[7] But many would say that such a fundamental change should grow out of a major debate in which philosophy, sociology, ethics, religion, law and political considerations all had a voice.

Philosophy: Libertarianism and Compatibilism

Historically, the philosophical debate on free will has only rarely intruded into public awareness, but the exponential increase in scientific understanding of the human organism is likely to make it the successor to the 'death of God' controversies of the 1950s and '60s carried out in the popular press. At the centre of the debate is the

---

[7] The legislation being drafted in the UK in response to the Macpherson enquiry into the Metropolitan Police, with its claims of (implicit) 'institutionalized racism', and Home Office proposals for the preventive detention of certain types of psychopath, shows the extent to which the changing philosophical climate has already started to influenced jurisprudence. Both of these are examples of 'thought crimes' in the Orwellian sense. And the claim by Blakemore and Crick that our developing understanding of brain science will enable the pharmacological treatment of prisoners has echoes of Stanley Kubrick's *Clockwork Orange*.

scientific threat to what philosophers have traditionally called the *libertarian* conception of free will, defined by Robert Kane as 'the power of agents to be the ultimate creators (or originators) and sustainers of their own ends and purposes' (Kane, 1996, p. 4). Because such power — sometimes characterized as the capacity to have done or willed otherwise under identical internal and external conditions — is normally thought to be impossible in a world governed by deterministic physical, biological, psychological, and social forces, it is often called 'incompatibilist' free will, that is, incompatible with determinism. It is assumed by many in philosophical circles that this sort of free will corresponds more or less to the prevailing popular conception of human freedom (however inarticulate or unarticulated), but of course this is an empirical claim needing research. Both Richard Double (1991) and Ted Honderich (1993) have argued that there may well not be a monolithic, unitary, and universally held conception of free will, but rather a miscellany of conflicting intuitions, only some of which would count as libertarian.

More commonly held by philosophers, if not the unpolled public, is the *compatibilist* conception of free will, which in various guises attempts to reconcile a robust sense of agency, especially moral agency, with determinism (cf. Gilberto **Gomes**; Thomas **Clarke**). Here the will is free just in so far as it is unconstrained by factors external to the willing self, but the self or agent is not imagined to be *ultimately* responsible for itself, or its ends and purposes. Rather, the self is entirely a function of environment and genetics, even though many selves acquire a high degree of non-ultimate autonomy (see for instance Waller, 1998, for an entirely naturalistic account of autonomy). Freedom for such a self is a matter of being *free from* outside constraints and abnormal internal compulsions.

Given the rise of the empirical sciences, and the underlying impulse to include mankind in an objective description of nature, it is perhaps not surprising that philosophers, largely insulated from public scrutiny, have been willing to consider compatibilist alternatives that many in the lay community might consider impolitic or even dangerous. A common reaction, after all, to the suggestion that we are *not* ultimate self-originators — that we could *not* have willed otherwise in a given situation — is to suppose that morality, responsibility, justice, fairness, and the social order itself are deprived of a necessary foundation. Some, like Daniel Dennett (1984), have taken great pains to show that the seemingly perilous implications of denying libertarian free will are just so many 'bugbears', childish fears that will dissipate upon sufficient reflection. Dennett argues that the only sort of free will 'worth wanting' is compatibilist, and that it can indeed support moral intuitions about praise, blame, punishment and responsibility.

But middle-ground compatibilists such as Dennett get flack from two sides: libertarians such as Kane (1996; 1999), Van Inwagen (1983) and Hodgson (1998; this volume) strongly believe that responsibility and justice can only derive from personal choices that are radically free from determining influences, hence the effort by some, such as Kane, to establish *indeterminism* as the essential ingredient of free will. On the other side, 'hard determinists' such as Waller, Honderich, Double and Clark (1990; 1996; 1998; this volume) urge oppositely that some revisions of our moral intuitions (e.g., the appropriateness of retributive punishment) may be in order to align them better with our burgeoning scientific self-understanding. Libertarians complain that compatibilists don't offer the sort of freedom most of us want, and that compatibilist rationales for moral judgments are too weak to prevent 'creeping exculpation' (Dennett's term) and social anarchy. Hard determinists, along with most compatibilists, find libertarian freedom — that of the self-chosen, unmoved mover — either conceptually incoherent or empirically unfounded, or both (e.g., Strawson, 1998) and accept the burden of showing that Western culture can survive, even prosper, without assuming that we are exceptions to natural causality. Eastern cultures are perhaps less burdened with this assumption (see **McCrone**).

If and when the debate over free will moves into the mainstream, it will likely be in terms of naturalistic science vs. a more or less supernaturalist conception of the self, something radically independent of the rest of nature. Humans, after all, have always fancied themselves privileged denizens of the universe, and the assumption of contra-causal free will is perhaps the last bastion of anthropoid specialness left to defend. This contrasts with the philosophical debate, which is largely cast *within* naturalism.

The challenge to libertarians who remain committed to naturalism is to find in scientific method and ontology evidence for something within the person analogous to a supernatural god's self-creative power. Kane (1996), Stapp, Hodgson and Libet (all in this volume) seem willing to accept the deliverances of science on the question of agency, although they clearly expect their side to be vindicated.

The challenge to compatibilists, hard determinists, and other species of non-libertarian naturalists is to develop a philosophical account of agency broadly consistent with science which also saves enough of our pre-theoretical intuitions about the self and morality (or changes them smoothly and safely enough) to ensure social stability, personal freedoms, justice and democracy. In the very long run, perhaps, the tension among various philosophical and 'folk' conceptions of free will may be resolved, either by scientific discoveries which validate libertarian freedom (the dominant folk conception, perhaps), or by a deep revision, in a compatibilist direction, of the commonly accepted notion of the freedom we actually have and need.

Volition and Free Will in Neuroscience

The great neuroscientist Charles Sherrington made lengthy arguments, using physiological and anatomical data, that brain processes simply cannot account for or explain mental subjective phenomena including conscious free will (Sherrington 1940; 1947). He noted examples of processes that must occur in the 'mental sphere', without any cerebral connections or processes that could be involved, later to be supported by Libet's (1992, p. 267) experimental evidence for the subjective referrals of sensory timings backwards in time. Sherrington defended his dualist-interactionism, writing: 'that our being should consist of two fundamental elements offers I suppose no greater inherent improbability than that it should rest on one only'(1947, p. xxiv).

John Eccles was a pupil of Sherrington and held similar views (as did the philosopher Karl Popper; see Popper and Eccles, 1977). Eccles sought to devise actual mechanisms for mediating the brain/mind interactions, including that for free will. As a pre-eminent experimental contributor to understanding the mechanisms of synaptic transmission, Eccles (1994) proposed a highly organized structural arrangement of the synaptic vesicles (containing neurotransmitter substance) at the terminal of the presynaptic nerve fibre. He further proposed that the probability of release of a vesicle could be a function of quantum mechanical behaviour, and that this probability can be changed without infringing the law of conservation of energy. But how does the spiritual self affect this process? Eccles proposed the existence of units of mental experience called 'psychons'. Psychons interact with the cerebral nerve fibres so as to affect synaptic transmission and provide a basis for the action of free will. However, the psychon interaction part of this theory is not testable, as Eccles himself admitted.

Roger Sperry's study of 'split-brain' patients led to the fundamental discovery that the left and right cerebral hemispheres could each gain knowledge not available to the other and could produce different behavioural responses thereby. Early on, Sperry espoused a philosophical position that mind was indeed not reducible to the properties of the brain's constituents. He argued that the mind emerged as a unique attribute of the brain's processes, and he proposed that the emerging mental phenomenon could in turn causally determine neural activities (Sperry, 1976). This provided a basis for free will, but Sperry argued that mind could only 'supervene' on, not directly determine, neural activities, and that there still remained a deterministic aspect in all this. However, during the last years of his life, Sperry altered that position and argued in favour of the option that mind could causally affect neural functions in a *non-determined* manner (as related by Doty, 1998); that would produce the fully humanistic nature of mind–brain interaction that Sperry sought.

Benjamin Libet's (1994) proposed field nature for the conscious mind is also based on the concept of 'emergence'. The 'conscious mental field' could both unify subjective experience and potentially intervene in neural activities to provide a basis for free will. Libet provided an experimental design that could potentially test this field feature that no other mind–brain theories had provided. This difficult experiment still awaits execution.

Meanwhile the work of neuroscientists making use of ever more sophisticated techniques, carries on at the practical level to provide experimental evidence for the various theories. David **Ingvar** has 'mapped' brain activity during both actual willed movements and the willed inner imagination of the same movements. Significant differences were found, which he interprets as indicating that deliberately willed actions are first formulated in one part of the brain and then activated in another. **Spence & Frith** report similar work researching which brain regions contribute to the performance of consciously willed actions. Their contribution to this volume is concerned especially with the voluntary selection of one possible action rather than another, and the use of brain-imaging to make clinical investigations related to this in cases as diverse as schizophrenia, Parkinsonism and 'alien limb' syndrome.

Much of the contemporary case for the illusory nature of free will is derived from the experimental work of **Libet** and his colleagues, who found that volitional acts were preceded by a readiness potential (RP) which arose in the brain some 350 milliseconds before the conscious decision to act was experienced. On face value this appears to be a straightforward experimental refutation of free will, though only of its initiation. However, Libet's experiments have arguably generated more controversy and conflicting interpretations than any other work in cognitive neuroscience, including an extended symposium in *The Behavioral and Brain Sciences* (1985) and a long discussion in Dennett's (1991) *Consciousness Explained*. Furthermore, it is worth noting that Libet himself (in this volume) does not conclude that his work necessarily leads to a jettisoning of the idea of free will, as he feels that consciousness could (and does) act as a veto over volitional activity. Conscious will, although delayed after the brain (RP) starts the process, does appear 200 msec before the muscle acts. There is also the point that Libet's experiments do not exclude a role for free will in *shaping* our actions — as for example in the case of the concert pianist whose fingers are programmed by practice to hit certain notes, but who concentrates intensely so as to convey the feelings of the instant in the *way* these notes are played (see Hodgson, 1996).

Libet's use of EEG, rather than more recent scanning techniques such as PET and fMRI, allows him to make very precise timings of brain activity. Wolfram **Schultz** employs a method that permits an even more specific investigation, recording the electrical state of individual neurones. He reports work on goal-directed behaviour in primates, which indicates that the activity of a single neurone might be the physical correlate of the mental anticipation of a reward. He observes that 'these activations might reflect the evaluation of outcome before the behavioural reaction is executed', but cautiously refrains from drawing firm conclusions concerning free will in his subjects.

Monistic Approaches

Some scientists and philosophers have chosen to take the bull by the horns with a far more robust approach to the problem, and have ended up with some outrageous conclusions. Erwin Schrödinger, one of the founders of quantum theory, pondered on the problem in the tantalising epilogue of his classic *What Is Life?* (Schrödinger, 1993).

Schrödinger encapsulated the problem of consciousness in the form of two premises:

• My body functions as a pure mechanism according to the laws of nature.

• Yet I know, by incontrovertible direct experience, that I am directing its motions, of which I foresee the effects, that may be fateful and all-important, in which case I feel and take full responsibility for them.

To avoid a contradiction here, he said, 'The only possible inference from these two facts is, I think, that I — I in the widest meaning of the word, that is to say, every conscious mind that has ever said or felt "I" — am the person, if any, who controls the "motion of the atoms" according to the laws of nature.' And this would lead you to say, Schrödinger provocatively suggested: 'Hence I am God Almighty'.

Though even today to many western ears such a statement sounds both 'blasphemous and lunatic' — and in 1943 it caused the rejection of *What is Life?* by its original (Catholic) publisher — the idea is hardly new. As its author noted, this 'grandest of all thoughts' was recorded in the Upanishads more than 2,500 years ago, and has long been considered the deepest insight in Indian philosophy. Surely, said Schrödinger, the singularity of consciousness is more intuitively convincing than the western idea of a plurality of consciousnesses, which leads inevitably to the invention of souls — as many as there are bodies — and to unhelpful questions such as whether the soul survives death and whether animals (and bacteria) have souls? (Robinson, 1996).

Ivan Havel (1995, p. 49.) points out that Schrödinger's viewpoint was remarkably consistent over a period of almost forty years:[8] Schrödinger refers to the ancient Vedantic vision, according to which consciousness is only one, singular, identifiable

---

[8] Note that Schrödinger is referring to the *observed* multiplicity of conscious minds as just an illusion. We may feel it is hardly scientific to call *observable* facts illusory in favour of a *non-observable* universal entity, whose existence is also not testable.

with its universal source (*Brahman*). The perceived spatial and temporal plurality of consciousnesses or minds is just an appearance or illusion. He writes in 1925 (p. 21), '. . . knowledge, feeling and choice (which you call *your own*) are essentially eternal and unchangeable and numerically one in all men, nay in all sensitive beings.' Nineteen years later: 'Consciousness is a singular of which the plural is unknown; that there *is* only one thing and that what seems to be a plurality is merely a series of different aspects of this one thing, produced the deception.' (Schrödinger, 1993, p. 89.) Thirty years later: 'There is obviously only one alternative, namely the unification of minds or consciousnesses. Their multiplicity is only apparent, in truth there is only one mind.' (p. 129.) And thirty-six years later, shortly before his death, he writes again (as a comment to a line in the Upanishads) '. . . the plurality of sensitive beings is mere appearance (*maya*); in reality they are all only aspects of the *one* being.' (Schrödinger, 1983, p. 101.)

Schrödinger's view has striking parallels with the philosophy of Benedict de Spinoza (1632–77). Spinoza's monist philosophy echoes the Upanishadic view even more closely than Schrödinger's, despite the fact that he knew nothing of the Upanishads themselves. For Spinoza, like the Upanishads, ultimately there is only one thing in the universe, God or substance, 'that which is in itself and conceived through itself' (Spinoza, 1964). Spinoza also held, like the authors of the Upanishad and the later sages of Yoga and Vedanta, that all individual consciousnesses are simply this one ultimate substance perceiving through the diverse orientations of individual body/minds.

How do these monisms relate to the questions of free will? Schrödinger, as we saw, reasoned monisticly from the real experience of will and the (apparently conflicting) existence of objective universal laws of causality to the conclusion that — to avoid contradiction — the 'I' of the individual and that of the universe must be one and the same. But the monisms of Spinoza and the Upanishads imply that free will is actually an illusion. For, as Spinoza put it, once one's physiology has become integrated enough to see everything 'under the gaze of eternity' — that is, once one has become 'enlightened' — one recognizes that the free will was only an illusion produced by one's prior inadequate perceptual and conceptual perspective: in Upanishadic terms, a product of *maya*. If there is in reality only *one* existent, all distinctions of beings, states and actions can only be appearances and not realities, and — from the enlightened state — all willing, and therefore all freedom of the will, is only 'as if'.

It is noteworthy that this sort of monistic philosophy arose within a religious context, and some would argue that it cannot be simply abstracted from its original setting. Both East and West have among their traditions those which teach that it is only at the end of the spiritual journey (when 'enlightenment' or the 'unitive way' is reached) that one becomes aware that 'all is one'. Prior to that, and especially in the early stages, obedience — the subjection of the individual personal will to that of the spiritual master, the guru, the abbot, etc., and thereby to the divine will — is the chief and necessary means of making progress. The paradox is that one is only really 'free' when one becomes, in the words of Hildegard of Bingen, a 'feather on the breath of God'. On such a view, to sacrifice one's personal freedom at the altar of one's god, that is, to align one's own will perfectly with the divine Will, becomes the highest religious goal. The phenomenological record indicates that the change is in the *ownership* of the volition act, not a disappearance of volition.

Most of us, having the experience of being in control of our *own* volition, draw a firm distinction between ourselves and other agents with whom we interact. This is highlighted in the monisms of Spinoza and the Upanishads, which emphasize that there is no problem with agency *per se*, because it does not really exist (at the level of the individual). The problem is purely phenomenological. So how can we reconcile the non-existence of individual beings and their actions and willings with our obvious everyday experience? Their response is that what is needed is a *change of state of consciousness* in which the monistic reality does become apparent. This, of course, is not of much use for those of us who remain in the mere, ordinary waking state of consciousness. Another puzzle would be that of distinguishing will from other apparent causes, whether those of other people or even inanimate things (or laws).

Ambiguous Phenomenology

It is interesting to note how even the contributors to this volume can come to quite opposite conclusions from from a common phenomenological approach. As already noted, Jeffrey **Schwartz** places great emphasis on will-power and effort to generate the mental force in his patients that is necessary for them to adapt their behaviour. As he makes clear, Schwartz draws heavily in his work upon the 'mindfulness' traditions of meditation that are found especially in Buddhism. Yet Jonathan **Bricklin**, steeped in a similar meditation tradition, concludes in his examination of William James' understanding of free will that 'effort' contributes no energy to any of our action. And Guy **Claxton**, also in the Buddhist tradition, concludes that what seems at first sight to be an excercise of volitional control, reveals itself on closer inspection to be an illusion.

To examine further the question of the validity of mystical experience, let's take a leaf out of current practices in cognitive neuropsychology and see whether the exception can cast any light on the rule. Forman (1998), following Maslow, has argued that if it is considered valid for pathological cases — the men who mistake their wife for a hat — to illuminate the standard case, then why should we not take the reports of highly self-actualized people in the same way. The following is a report from Krishnamurti, widely felt to be highly 'self-actualized':

> On the first day while I was in that state and more conscious of the things around me, I had the first most extraordinary experience. There was a man mending the road; that man was myself; the pickax he held was myself; the very stone which he was breaking up was a part of me; the tender blade of grass was my very being, and the tree beside the man was myself. I also could feel and think like the roadmender and I could feel the wind passing through the tree, and the little ant on the blade of grass I could feel. The birds, the dust and the very noise were a part of me. Just then there was a car passing by at some distance; I was the driver, the engine, and the tires; as the car went further away from me, I was going away from myself. I was in everything, or rather everything was in me, inanimate and animate, the mountain, the worm and all breathing things. All day long I remained in this happy condition. (Krishnamurti, quoted in Forman, 1998.)

But just compare this with a pathological case:

> Here are two other cases, on which I would very much like your comments. Last November on a conference in the psychiatric institute of the Universitätsklinik in Frankfürt am Main two patients were described and discussed, who represent every single event in their phenomenal model of the world as caused by their own volitional acts. One of them stood at the window the whole day, looking up and was consciously moving the sun

across the sky all day long. The other one was observing traffic all day long — driving the cars around each other, walking the pedestrians around, turning the traffic lights from red to yellow to green and back again. What do you make of this? (Metzinger, 1997.)

So is the passage from Krishnamurti to be taken as an example of self-actualization or brain pathology?[9] Mystical experiences have long been associated with the temporal lobes of the brain. For example temporal lobe epileptics sometimes report *déjà-vu* experiences, the sense of presence, or feelings of intense meaningfulness, as part of their seizures. Also temporal lobe activity is implicated in the effects of anoxia in producing near-death experiences which are often mystical in nature (Blackmore, 1993).

Some theorists, such as Michael Persinger, argue that religious and mystical experiences are nothing more than artefacts of temporal lobe function (Persinger, 1983). Using both electroencephalographic methods and questionnaires, Persinger has shown that mystical experiences, psychic experiences and paranormal beliefs are associated with unstable temporal lobes, or high 'temporal lobe lability' (Persinger and Makarec, 1987; Persinger and Valliant, 1985). He has also been able to induce out-of-body and other experiences by applying rapidly fluctuating weak magnetic fields across the temporal lobes of subjects in the laboratory (Persinger, 1995).

Others disagree. For example, Blackmore (1993) argues that neurological changes can bring about not only tunnels, lights, and out-of-body experiences, but the dissolution of the normal sense of self which lies at the heart of a mystical experience. In ordinary life we hold the false notion of a persisting inner self that has consciousness and free will — the audience in Dennett's (1991) 'Cartesian Theatre'. In certain circumstances, such as mystical experiences and near death, this illusion breaks down, giving rise to a new sense of self as one with the universe, or to a state of no-self.

With this dissolution of self comes a sense of vivid realness, clarity of consciousness, and a loss of the normal sense of volition. Actions happen without the sense of a person doing them, or, as the Buddha once put it 'actions do exist, and also their consequences, but the person that acts does not' (Parfit, 1984). This state can arise spontaneously or can be developed by training in meditation or mindfulness (Blackmore, 1986). To those who have never experienced this state it seems both paradoxical and a threat to morality, but when it arises it seems the most natural and easy way to be. And, as Claxton (1994) points out, people seem to become nicer rather than nastier when they live this way.

On Persinger's view Krishnamurti may have been suffering solely from excessive temporal lobe activity. On Blackmore's view Krishnamurti had dropped, or begun to drop, the false sense of self and was living with the insight that self and other are not separate. On the other hand there is also a psychiatric literature (e.g. Sass, 1992; Chadwick, 1992; 1997) which claims that the division between the schizophrenic and the self-actualized is more a question of cultural interpretation than substance. The neurologist Oliver Sacks (1994), commenting on the visions and migraines of Hildergard of Bingen, saw no reason why both the clinical and mystical evaluations should not be accepted side by side: 'I certainly think that physical states can exist as porters to the spiritual' (p. 239). The psychology of creativity and genius is also of relevance, with the study of Van Gogh as the classic case.

---

[9] It has been pointed out that the beliefs reported by the psychiatric patients contain an alleged element of causality, which offers the possibility of refutation (e.g. by asking the subject causally to alter the pattern of activity being observed). The Krishnamurti extract contains no comparable testable claim.

Conclusion

So where do we go from here? Present-day physics does not provide for the possibility of free will, but neither does it rule it out — unless one subscribes to the view that presently known physics is final and complete. Given the immense complexity of the brain, it probably is not feasible to demonstrate unequivocally the presence or absence of free will through analysis of neurophysiological processes. But further experiments can give us insight as to the way it presumably works, if it exists. Perhaps the only conclusion one can draw is that we need a lot more careful studies, including the parallel tracking of phenomenal experience (subjectively reported), brain events and volitional acts. The extraordinary pace of development of non-invasive imaging techniques should give us some hope that science may soon be able to provide a much better handle on subjective experience.[10] However the results will always be interpreted in terms of the dominant paradigm. If it is just *assumed* that free will is an illusion and folk psychological reports are only of interest to anthropologists then our science will just underline this pretheoretical position. However, as Libet and some of the other authors in this study point out, there really is no evidence available to draw such a strong conclusion. Seeing as our experience is one of agency and free will, and seeing as the entire religious, ethical, cultural and legal system of the western world is based on such an assumption, then it might be much better to assume that this is the position until science tells us, unequivocally, that this is not the case. That way we should all be 'innocent until proven guilty'.

One post-modern religious view is that while there may well be no god 'out there', human beings (both individually and socially) still have need of the concept of God and find value in the practice of religion. This being the case, it is argued that religion can and should continue, although the jury is still out as to whether it has any ultimate substance (cf. Freeman, 1993). Perhaps we should adopt a similar approach to the problem of free will. As Steven Pinker (1997) says, when he likens it to geometry, 'Free will is a fictional construction but it has applications in the real world.'[11]

References

Atmanspacher, H. and Ruhnau, E. (ed. 1997), *Time, Temporality, Now* (Heidelberg: Springer Verlag).
Beck, F. & Eccles, J.C. (1992), 'Quantum aspects of brain activity and the role of consciousness', *Proceedings of the National Academy of Science USA*, **89**, pp. 11357–61.
Blackmore,S.J. (1986), 'Who am I?: Changing models of reality in meditation',in *Beyond Therapy: The impact of Eastern religions on psychological theory and practice*, ed. G.Claxton (London: Wisdom).
Blackmore, S.J. (1993), *Dying to Live. Science and the Near Death Experience* (London: Grafton).
Blakemore, C. (1988), *The Mind Machine* (London: BBC Publications).
Chadwick, P.K. (1992), *Borderline: A Psychological Study of Paranoia and Delusional Thinking* (London and New York: Routledge).
Chadwick, P.K. (1997), *Schizophrenia: The Positive Perspective* (London and New York: Routledge).
Clark, T. (1990), 'Free choice and naturalism', *The Humanist*, **50** (3), pp. 18–24.
Clark, T. (1996), 'The freedom of Susan Smith', *The Humanist*, **56** (2), pp. 8–12.
Clark, T. (1998), 'Materialism and morality: the problem with Pinker', *The Humanist*, **58** (6), pp. 20–25.
Claxton,G. (1994), *Noises from the Darkroom* (London: Aquarian).

[10] It should be noted, however, that these non-invasive techniques (PET and functional MRI) only tell us *where* a change in neural activity occurs. They do not inform us about *timings* of events when the times are shorter than seconds.

[11] Constraints on the length of this book have led to two papers that have been accepted for publication being held over to the October 1999 issue of the *Journal of Consciousness Studies*: 'Volition and Physical Laws', by Jean Burns, and 'The Libertarian Imperative', by Undo Uus.

Crick, F.H.C. (1994), *The Astonishing Hypothesis* (London: Simon & Schuster).

Dennett, D.C. (1984), *Elbow Room* (Cambridge, MA: MIT Press).

Dennett, D.C. (1991), *Consciousness Explained* (Boston, MA: Little, Brown).

Doty, R.W. (1998), 'Five mysteries of the mind, and their consequences', in *Views of the Brain – A Tribute to Roger W. Sperry,* ed. A. Puente (Washington, DC: American Psychological Association, in press).

Double, R. (1991), *The Non-Reality of Free Will* (Oxford: Oxford University Press).

Eccles, J.C. (1994), *How the Self Controls its Brain* (Berlin, etc.: Springer Verlag).

Einstein, A. (1931), 'About free will', in *The Golden Book of Tagore* (cited in Home and Robinson, 1995).

Forman, R.K.C. (1998), 'What does mysticism have to teach us about consciousness?', *Journal of Consciousness Studies,* **5** (2), pp. 185–201.

Freeman, A. (1993), *God In Us: A case for Christian humanism* (London: SCM Press).

Hameroff, S., Kaszniak, A., Scott, A. (1998), *Toward a Science of Consciousness II* (Cambridge, MA: MIT).

Havel, I.M. (1995), 'Remarks on Schrödinger's concept of consciousness', *Consciousness at the Crossroads of Philosophy and Cognitive Science* (Exeter: Imprint Academic).

Hodgson, D. (1994), 'Neuroscience and folk-psychology — an overview', *JCS,* **1** (2), pp. 205–16.

Hodgson, D. (1996), 'The easy problems ain't so easy', *Journal of Consciousness Studies,* **3** (1), pp. 69–75.

Hodgson, D. (1998), 'Folk psychology, science and the criminal law', in Hameroff *et al.* (1998).

Home, D. and Robinson, A. (1995), 'Einstein and Tagore', *JCS,* **2** (2), pp. 167–79.

Honderich, Ted (1993), *How Free Are You?* (Oxford: Oxford University Press).

Hume, D. (1740), *A Treatise of Human Nature,* Book I, Part III, Sections 1–7, 14–16.

Kane, R. (1996), *The Significance of Free Will* (New York: Oxford University Press).

Kane, R. (1999), 'Responsibility, luck and chance: Reflections on free will and determinism', *Journal of Philosophy,* **96** (5), pp. 217–40.

Kant, I. (1788), *Critique of Practical Reason,* ed. and tr. L.W. Beck (Macmillan).

Kenny, A. (1987), 'Mediaeval philosophy', in *The Great Philosophers,* ed. Bryan Magee (Oxford: OUP).

Libet, B. (1985), 'Unconscious cerebral initiative and the role of conscious will in voluntary action', *Behavioural and Brain Sciences,* **8**, pp. 529–66.

Libet, B. (1992), 'The neural time-factor in perception, volition and free will', *Revue de Metaphysique et de Morale,* pp. 255–72.

Libet, B. (1994), 'A testable field theory of mind–brain interaction', *JCS,* **1** (1), pp.119–126.

Metzinger, T. (1997), 'Volition and NCC (clearing up some misunderstandings)', *Thalamocortical Foundations of Conscious Experience* (ASSC E-seminar),
http://www.phil.vt.edu/ASSC/newman/metzinger2.html

Parfit, D. (1984), *Reasons and Persons* (Oxford: Oxford University Press).

Penrose, R. (1994), *Shadows of the Mind* (Oxford: Oxford University Press).

Persinger, M.A. (1983), Religious and mystical experiences as artifacts of temporal lobe function: A general hypothesis', *Perceptual and Motor Skills,* **57**, pp. 1255–62.

Persinger, M.A. (1995), 'Out-of-body-like experiences are more probable in people with elevated complex partial epileptic-like signs during periods of enhanced geomagnetic activity: A nonlinear effect', *Perceptual and Motor Skills,* **80**, pp. 563–9.

Persinger, M.A. and Makarec, K. (1987), 'Temporal lobe epileptic signs and correlative behaviors displayed by normal populations', *Journal of General Psychology,* **114**, pp. 179–95.

Persinger, M.A. and Valliant, P.M. (1985), 'Temporal lobe signs and reports of subjective paranormal experiences in a normal population', *Perceptual and Motor Skills,* **60**, pp. 903–9.

Pinker, S. (1997), 'In search of humanity', Interview in *The Times* (London: 29 December 1997), p.15.

Popper, K.R. and Eccles, J.C. (1977), *The Self and Its Brain* (Berlin, London, New York: Springer Verlag).

Robinson, A. (1996), 'Science's inner frontier', *Times Higher Education Supplement,* 5 April 1996, Consciousness Supplement, p. i.

Sacks, O. (1994), 'An anthropologist on Mars', Interview in *JCS,* **1** (2), pp. 234–40.

Sass, L. (1992), *Madness and Modernism* (New York: Basic Books).

Schrödinger, E. (1983), *My View of the World* (Woodbridge, CT: Ox Bow Press). This book includes two essays, *Seek for the Road,* written in 1925 and *What is Real?,* written in 1960.

Schrödinger, E. (1993), *What is Life?* with *Mind and Matter* and *Autobiographical Sketches* (Cambridge: Cambridge University Press; original edition: 1944).

Sherrington, C.S. (1940), *Man on his Nature* (Harmondsworth: Penguin Books).

Sherrington, C.S. (1947), *The Integrative Action of the Nervous System* (Cambridge: CUP).

Sperry, R.W. (1976), 'Mental phenomena as causal determinants in brain function', in *Consciousness of the Brain,* ed. Globus, Maxwell and Savodnik (New York: Plenum).

Spinoza, B. (1964), 'Ethics, Part I', in *From Descartes to Locke,* ed. T.V. Smith and Majorie Grene (Chicago: University of Chicago Press/Phoenix Books).

Strawson, G. (1986), *Freedom and Belief* (Oxford: Oxford University Press).

Strawson, G. (1998), 'Luck swallows everything', *Times Literary Supplement,* 26 June, pp. 8–10.

Van Inwagen (1983), *An Essay on Free Will* (Oxford: Clarendon Press).

Waller, B. (1998), *The Natural Selection of Autonomy* (Albany: State University of New York Press).

David H. Ingvar

On Volition

A Neurophysiologically Oriented Essay

During the last decades, the enigmatic field of volition has been the object of quantitative brain mapping studies. In this essay, emphasis will be given to brain mapping observations during overt or imagined willed acts in conscious normal individuals. The findings suggest that such acts are 'formulated' in the frontal/prefrontal cortex as neuronal programs for future motor, behavioural, verbal, or cognitive acts. During imagined movements or speech, brain mapping reveals important prefrontal activations which contrast to perirolandic activations during overt willed acts. In psychiatric disorders with symptoms of a 'sick will', like in schizophrenia, affective disorders, and organic dementia, reductions of the resting prefrontal activity have been recorded. The relationship between will and prefrontal activity is compatible with the view that frontal/prefrontal (efferent) parts of the cortex are involved in the serial temporal programming of motor behaviour, speech, and cognition. In addition, there are unconscious mechanisms participating in volition. Electrophysiological evidence presented by Libet (1985 et seq.) supports this view.

I: Introduction

Willed movements, verbal performance, and certain types of cognition, are carried out either consciously or unconsciously. The latter form will only briefly be considered here, due to the fact that cerebral neuronal mechanisms underlying unconscious mental activity are by and large unknown. On the contrary, the cerebral prerequisites of conscious awareness are, in principle, relatively well known (Schmidt, 1951; Magoun, 1963; Ingvar and Lassen, 1975; Edelman, 1989; Searle, 1990).

In accordance with the opinion of Libet (1985 *et seq.*), the state of *consciousness* is here understood as the well-known subjective experience of being a human individual with a mental activity separate from that of other individuals. This includes an awareness of one's own body, its sensory milieu, and one's cognitive capacity, as well as an awareness of the continuous temporal 'flow' of consciousness (Davidson and Davidson, 1980) with a past, a present, and a future (Ingvar, 1985). *Will* is defined as the common experience that one can produce inner concrete or abstract goals for

Journal of Consciousness Studies, **6**, No. 8–9, 1999, pp. 1–10

one's future behaviour and/or cognition. Then, with the aid of one's will, one tries to achieve the goal conceived of. It should be recognized that the borderlines between conscious wilful acts, shorter reflex-like responses and unconscious behaviour or cognitive actions are diffuse. One may claim that most responses of the organism include a component of volition, pure perceptual phenomena being the only non-volitional cerebral events (cf. Sechenov, 1863). However, there are here epistemological problems which lie outside the scope of the present paper.

The views expressed in this essay have been presented briefly in a preliminary version (Ingvar, 1994).

II: Methods

The present essay focuses on brain mapping techniques in which the regional distribution of cerebral activity (blood flow) has been recorded with isotope techniques during overt or imagined willed acts. The principles of the most important brain mapping methods are presumed to be known to the reader. They are based upon 2-D extracranial measurements of the regional cerebral (cortical) blood flow (rCBF) using 133 Xenon clearance (Lassen and Ingvar, 1961; Ingvar and Lassen, 1975; Lassen *et al.*, 1963; 1991). Some studies using different tracers with the 3-D SPECT technique (Stokely *et al.*, 1980), as well as with the 3-D positron emission tomography (PET) will also be considered. PET techniques enable measurements of functional changes in the whole brain with a very high spatial resolution (Frackowiak *et al.*, 1997, Part One).

Comparing the low resolution 2-D and 3-D rCBF studies with high resolution PET observations, an important difference should be pointed out. PET techniques usually emphasize statistically highly significant activity changes in circumscribed brain regions (Frackowiak *et al.*, 1997). This emphasis of focal activity changes may cause an underestimation of global activity alterations. Background changes in the cerebral (cortical) rCBF may appear more clearly in 2-D rCBF measurements. This difference might be taken into account, especially in studies of complex cortical global brain functions like will.

Electrophysiological techniques include DC recordings of cortical potentials during willed acts. They yield so-called 'readiness potentials'. Deecke *et al.* (1997) have compared such potentials with electromagnetic recordings (MEG) from the cortex, as well as findings with magnetic resonance methods (FMRI). Finally, reference must here be made to the fundamental observations of Libet (1985 *et seq.*) who studied temporal aspects of cortical potentials preceding conscious willed movements and their relations to the actual awareness of the intention to carry out a willed act.

III: Neuropsychological Aspects of Will

One may define three separate steps behind a willed act. Here, mainly purposeful intentional goal-directed willed motor acts will be taken as examples. In *step 1*, there is an awareness of the necessity to achieve a future goal. Behind this urge there may be a cognitive operation, an event in the surrounding, etc. The primary urge most often emanates from a cognitive analysis of sensory messages, often with an emotional colour, which leads to an awareness of *causality*. This line of argument is especially considered below (section VIII; Ingvar, 1997). The inner representation of this goal may be formulated, processed, and optimized cognitively in order to secure the success of the willed act. The goal formulation takes place, one may assume, with the aid of memories and emotions of varying complexity and origin. Subcortical structures, notably the basal ganglia, participate in this process (Lou *et al.*, 1989; Damasio *et al.*, 1990; Posner and Raichle, 1994). Attention mechanisms must also be included, especially of the goal-directed type (Baddeley, 1983). The primary formulation of the goal appears closely related to the establishment of a more or less firm 'mental set' as defined by Shachow (1967), a concept for which intention appears to be a synonym in the present context (Searle, 1990).

Electrophysiological studies of willed acts indicate that *step 1* takes a certain time. Deecke and Lang (1996) have reported that readiness potentials which precede a willed finger movement may take several seconds. These findings on *preplanned* willed movements appear at variance with those of Libet (1992), who studied *spontaneous* willed finger movements. Libet found that the electrocortical potential began about 550 msec before an actual finger movement took place. During the initial 350 msec of this time period the subjects were not consciously aware of having willed to carry out the movement. In other words, Libet's observations (1985; 1989; 1992) suggest that this initial event of a willed act may include information processing at an unconscious level in neuronal brain structures.

A formulation of a goal in accordance with the assumptions above includes an active suppression of thoughts and representations which do not contribute to the chosen willed activity. Such an inhibition of irrelevant thoughts may emanate from the prefrontal cortex (Fuster, 1989; 1995; Frith *et al.*, 1991). There is also evidence that the cingulate gyrus may participate in the suppression of irrelevant representations (Posner and Raichle, 1994; cf. section IV).

The formulation of goals for intentional, willed behaviour may vary considerably. They may concern short-lasting simple motor acts, as well as long-lasting complex verbal, behavioural, or cognitive activity. Furthermore, the inner goals may be retained in time for use in the immediate future or later, perhaps years ahead. Programs for a goal-directed willed behaviour may thus be retained in what has been termed 'memory of the future' (Ingvar, 1985), or 'prospective memory' (Brandimonte *et al.*, 1996). Such memorized programs for willed acts may thus be included in the conscious awareness of the future and, one may assume, like most memories and action plans, be continuously rehearsed and optimized over time (Ingvar, 1979; 1985).

At present, no concrete description can be given in neuronal terms of the plans or programs which underlie will. It has been speculated that they, like other cognitive events, depend upon the activity in complex parallel neuronal networks (Edelman, 1989; Mesulam, 1990; Searle, 1990). As will be shown below, overt automatic willed movements are controlled by perirolandic structures related to the extremity moved. Imagined 'inner' movements activate prefrontal cortex especially (see fig.1).[1]

Step 2 includes the performance of the actual willed act, such as a movement, a behavioural reaction, verbal response, or a cognitive change, all carried out in accordance with the primary action plan formulated in step 1. It is self-evident that willed activity may be of shorter or longer duration, as pointed out above. During this time period, feedback and feed-forward control may be exerted from prefrontal mechanisms and postrolandic structures (Fuster, 1989). In this way, the future con-

---

[1]   Figures 1 and 2 are reproduced in colour on the back cover — Editor.

sequences of one's intentional, willed acts can normally be anticipated, often unconsciously. *Step 2* is accompanied by specific cortical potential changes in the vertex
region which vary according to the methods used (Libet, 1985 *et seq.*; Deecke *et al.*,
1997).

Step 3 follows the achievement of the goal of the willed act. This final step is
accompanied by a dissolution of the inner representation of the completed act.
There can also be a general assessment of the success or failure of the act, accompanied by well known emotional reactions such as satisfaction or dismay, respectively. Most likely, subcortical mechanisms pertaining to the higher control of
emotions are involved in this evaluation (Damasio *et al.*, 1990; Frith *et al.*, 1991;
Posner and Raichle, 1994).

IV: Brain Mapping of Willed Acts

Our early studies with low resolution rCBF techniques showed that most types of
mental activation, during, for example, reasoning tests, problem solving, etc., were
accompanied by a moderate general rCBF increase dominating in frontal / prefrontal
structures (Ingvar and Risberg, 1965; 1967; Risberg and Ingvar, 1973; Ingvar, 1979;
Risberg, 1986). The prefrontal ('hyperfrontal') rCBF increase appeared related to the
mental effort induced by the tests performed. The experimental paradigm of these
studies was relatively complex due to the combination of cognitive and verbal performance. At the time we did not fully realize that brain mapping during memorizing,
reasoning, and other tests included a definite component of will (see section I).

The first dedicated study of cortical effects of a willed imagination of a motor act
was made by Ingvar and Philipson (1977; fig 1). They demonstrated the principally
important difference of the cortical activity landscape during (A) overt automatic
willed unilateral rhythmic hand clenching movements and (B) the willed inner imagination of the same movement. In the latter situation, the subjects were not exposed to
any deliberate verbal or other sensory stimulation, and EMG controls did not show
any muscular activity. Situation B may thus be taken to represent a 'pure' wilfully
induced cognitive representation in the cortex of a movement, uninfluenced by ongoing sensory feedback, other afferent signals, or verbal activity. The result was clear-
cut in spite of the low resolution technique used. The actual overt hand movement A
gave a fairly focal rCBF increase dominating in the rolandic hand area (Olesen,
1971). The inner imagination of the same movement B activated prefrontal cortical
regions mainly, and did not appreciably change the activity in the hand area. In both
situations A and B, there were other, less prominent postrolandic activations, possibly representing memory and other sensory mechanisms active in controlling the
hand movement A as well as the concept of the hand movement B (Baddeley, 1983;
Fuster, 1995).

Subsequent experiments have confirmed the principal finding described by Ingvar
and Philipson (1977). Thus, handwriting movements and other overt or imagined
behavioural acts, including speech, gave rise to different cortical activation patterns
during A, the actual behavioural act and B, during imagination of the same act
(Decety *et al.*, 1990; Decety and Ingvar, 1990; Ryding *et al.*, 1996). Related observations of differences between actual movements and motor imagery have been made
by Lang and Deecke (1997) in electrophysiological studies.

The findings concerning speech (Ryding *et al.*, 1996; fig 2) are especially noteworthy. *Counting aloud* gave a bilateral activation dominating in lower perirolandic and
upper temporal regions with a notable absence of frontal/prefrontal activation. (This
does not mean that prefrontal structures were inactive, only that they did not change
their activity level significantly.) *Counting silently* (the same series of numbers at the
same rate) gave a totally different pattern with bilateral, but asymmetrical prefrontal
activations (fig 2). Apparently, overt automatic speech is related to perirolandic activation which emanates from sensorimotor activity including sensory feedback from
the auditory input, and from oral/laryngeal muscles and soft tissues. In this way the
subject is 're-minded' of what he is actually saying and thus controls his verbal performance. When the oral and auditory feedback is lacking during *silent speech,* prefrontal representations from the inner behavioural repertoire of memorized action
programs take over the control. Here one may raise the question, to what extent the
neuronal control of overt and silent speech are equivalent. There is an obvious well-
trained automaticity in overt counting of numbers. This does not mean that higher
controls of the aloud speech are excluded. They may only be less prominent than in
overt speech when the perirolandic feedback systems dominate (cf. Raichle, 1995).
Silent speech, on the other hand, requires an inner control of the cognitive representations of the number series. Apparently, this control is located in prefrontal structures
where they show an asymmetrical distribution of focal high activity regions.

Focal prefrontal activations by imagined willed acts have been reported and elaborated in high resolution PET studies of speech and motor paradigms in various combinations. Petersen *et al.* (1990) and Posner and Raichle (1994) demonstrated that
wilful choice of semantically meaningful words gave circumscribed prefrontal activations. A related finding was made by Frith *et al.* (1991) who established asymmetrical prefrontal and other activations during both willed choice of words, and willed
finger movements. Some of the studies showed that the specific content of the willed
act put an imprint upon the prefrontal cortical activation landscape. Apparently, in the
silent speech study by Ryding *et al.* (1996; cf. fig 2), the inner representations controlling the willed acts have a complex multifocal — and asymmetrical prefrontal
organization. This finding appears compatible with the studies in monkeys
(Goldman-Rakic, 1988; cf. Fuster, 1995). They found a complex, but precise and stable, organization of mnemonic neuronal traces in the prefrontal region.

Frith *et al.* (1991) made another important observation. Willed acts caused a dimi-
nution of activity in certain brain regions. Such decreases possibly represent a suppression of alternative action plans, irrelevant for the chosen willed performance. In
this connection it is pertinent to remind that increase of regional cerebral activity
(blood flow) cannot always be equated with an increased neuronal excitatory activity.
It is likely, although as yet not clear, that inhibitory neuronal activity may also influence regional cerebral blood flow. However, here one approaches as yet unsolved
problems concerning the metabolic effects of excitatory and inhibitory neuronal
events, a field which has to await further research.

The 2-D and 3-D rCBF studies, as well as the PET observations, suggest a relationship between the cortical patterns of volition and the dorsolateral prefrontal cortex on
the left side (DLPFC; Broadmann's area 46; cf. fig.2). This area has a well-known
importance for the performance of so-called delayed responses and also for working
memory (Goldman-Rakic, 1988; Mesulam, 1990; Baddeley, 1983; Fuster, 1995). It is

pertinent to recall here that the DLPFC area appears involved in the 'hypofrontality', the subnormal prefrontal activity, recorded in schizophrenics with symptoms of a 'sick will', i.e. inactivity and autistic behaviour (Ingvar and Franzén, 1974; see section VI).

The present discussion on prefrontal cortical activity changes during imagined willed acts might include a reference to Eccles (1982). He suggested that the supplementary motor area (SMA) might especially be involved in the production of willed motor acts (cf. Damasio and Van Hoesen, 1980; Frackowiak *et al.*, 1997, chapter 11). The SMA could act as the interface between mind and body, the region in the cortex where inner mental events were transformed into neuronally controlled overt behaviour. This view has been criticized by Fuster (1995) amongst others. It is of interest, though, that electrophysiological findings of Deecke and his collaborators (Lang and Deecke, 1997) appear to demonstrate that cortical potentials (readiness potentials) during willed movements dominating in the anterior vertex region most likely emanate from the SMA. Our rCBF brain mapping studies indicate that inner concepts coupled to imagined silent speech are located more anteriorly in the prefrontal cortex (fig 2). The discrepancy between the brain mapping findings and the electrophysiological observations might be related to methodological differences. Electrophysiological studies focus upon cortical events during a few seconds at the most before and after a willed act, while brain mapping techniques may average cortical metabolic/circulatory changes during several seconds or even a few minutes.

In 3-D SPECT measurements. we found that the *cerebellum* is also activated during overt, as well as imagined, motor acts and speech (Decety *et al.*, 1990; Ryding *et al.*, 1996; cf. Decety and Ingvar, 1990). Apparently, the cerebellum participates in both overt and imagined serial temporal programming of motor acts and speech. Cerebellar mechanisms may thus contribute to the mental activity which underlies the serially organized inner programs upon which willed acts are based.

V: Consciousness and Will

It is a common experience that low levels of conscious awareness in drowsiness, exhaustion, lack of sleep, boredom, etc. exemplify states in which willed acts may be difficult to perform. Similar experiences of lack of so-called 'will power' may accompany the malaise pertaining to a common cold. At even lower levels of brain activity, in deep sleep, during stupor or coma, the capacity to perform willed acts disappears completely.

At abnormally high levels of conscious awareness, during excitation, severe anxiety, pain with intense emotional stress, the realm of will is also reduced. Possibly anxiety and / or pain diminish one's ability to direct a constant attention and to establish a firm mental set (Shachow, 1967). However, the important aspects of will and stress, emotions, etc. cannot further be considered here.

States of the type mentioned, both below and above the normal level of conscious awareness, can be defined quantitatively in terms of a subnormal, respectively supranormal, level of global mean cerebral metabolism and blood flow (Ingvar and Lassen, 1975). It therefore appears possible to define a level of global brain activity at which the volitional capacity of a given individual is optimal.

VI: Clinical observations

There are several clinical states in which abnormalities of will can be seen in the form of lack of volitional control of movements and behaviour, as well as lack of will in general.

The ADHD syndrome in children (Attention-Deficit/Hyperactivity Disorder) may exemplify a specific lack of the volitional control of behaviour. It is of great interest that children of this type, with their prominent distractibility and restlessness, have deep seated bilateral frontal lesions including defects in the basal ganglia (Lou *et al.*, 1989). Some patients with the contrary type of symptomatology, i.e. autism, have also shown frontal (and temporal) abnormalities (Gillberg and Coleman, 1992). Other states in adults, often termed psychopathic, may show sudden explosive irresistible — willed? — bursts of violent behaviour, with an incomplete insight into the future consequences of their behaviour. Such patients are at present the object of a clinical and criminological research project with PET technique (Ingvar *et al.*, in preparation).

It is a well known clinical fact that several psychiatric disorders show signs of a subnormal volition. Patients with depression (Baxter *et al.*, 1991), and some types of organic dementia (Risberg, 1986; Risberg *et al.*, 1990; cf Frackowiak *et al.*, 1997, chapter 14) may show a general lack of initiative and ambition, as well as a general inactivity and symptoms of autism. Brain mapping studies have shown a low prefrontal resting activity in such cases. Finally, Ingvar and Franzén (1974; cf. Ingvar, 1980, 1985; Weinberger *et al.*, 1991; Frackowiak *et al.*, 1997, chapter 16) demonstrated that certain schizophrenic patients showed a low resting level of activity in the prefrontal cortex (possibly related to an abnormality in the basal ganglia). The prefrontal rCBF reduction correlated significantly to symptoms of inactivity, mutism, and autistic behaviour, i.e. to symptoms of a 'sick will'. This finding was interpreted as a fundamental abnormality in some schizophrenic patients which could be caused by a defective temporal organization of conscious awareness and behaviour. As a result, the schizophrenic patients could not establish a normal 'memory of the future', which is a prerequisite for normal will (see section VIII).

Here a note on Parkinson's disease should be added. This disorder is characterized by transmitter abnormalities within the basal ganglia. It appears possible, although at present not yet clear, that such subcortical mechanisms are related to the specific abnormalities of volition which are often evident in Parkinson's disease (Frackowiak *et al.*, 1997, chapter 14). However, the Parkinson findings indicate clearly that subcortical mechanisms play an important role in the control of willed motor acts, and perhaps also speech and cognition in general. However, the role of the basal ganglia and other subcortical structures for volition is still insufficiently clarified.

VII: Discussion

This essay has been given a simplified form. This may be of heuristic value for future studies of will. The main concepts presented can briefly be summarized thus:

> Willed acts concern the future. They include a program or an inner concept of how to reach a specific goal. Goals of this type are retained as 'memories of the future' which constitute an inherent component of consciousness (Ingvar, 1985).

Overt willed movements or speech give rise to expected perirolandic cortical — as well as cerebellar — activation patterns. By contrast, inner, imagined willed acts, motor or speech ideation, show a clear-cut prefrontal and also cerebellar (and some postrolandic) activations. These structures, especially the prefrontal ones, apparently house serially organized action programs for willed acts. They can be revealed by brain mapping in studies which eliminate the important auditory, sensorimotor, and other forms of sensory (afferent) feedback flow which dominate overt willed acts.

It is of interest that patients with symptoms of a 'sick will', i.e. inactivity, lack of ambition, autistic behaviour, depressive motor and behavioural inhibition, show a subnormal activity in prefrontal regions. Symptoms of this type are encountered in chronic schizophrenia, depression, and organic dementia.

There are important similarities between brain mapping and electrophysiological findings in experiments on will. It is difficult to relate them to brain mapping findings. The main hindrance is that the nature and location of the generators for wilfully induced electrocortical events is not known. However, it appears evident that electrophysiological techniques are suited for studies of unconscious cerebral components of volition (Libet, 1985 *et seq.*).

VIII: Addendum: Will and Causality

In a recent analysis of the phenomenon of consciousness (Ingvar, 1997), concepts originally developed by Immanuel Kant (1724–1804) were applied. These concepts pertained to what Kant called categories which we use to interpret the surrounding world. The three most important categories were *space*, *time* and *causality*. The model for consciousness developed from Kant's ideas emphasized that sensory parts of the cerebral cortex, located in the postrolandic regions, in parietal, occipital, and temporal cortex, handle the analysis of *spatial* characteristics of the world. Powerful and rapid phylogenetically young transcortical connections are then assumed to transmit 'packages' of complex supramodal sensory messages to precentral frontal and prefrontal cortex. Here the *temporal* organization of the sensory input — from all modalities — is identified. From this temporal analysis, *causalities* in the sensory input can be recognized. The postrolandic (sensory/spatial) and the prerolandic (motor/temporal) division of the hemisphere cortex has been inspired by the work of Luria (1966) and of Fuster (1995; cf. Ingvar, 1985).

Once causality has been established and evaluated emotionally, as well as reached consciousness, one may furthermore assume that the individual 'understands' the survival value of the causal relationships observed. Such a series of events may, as a consequence, then induce behavioural, verbal, or cognitive responses of the type we call intentional, willed acts. In this manner will is used by the organism in order to avoid, or search for, certain situations compatible with survival. It appears possible that this biological — and teleological — line of argument may contribute to the discussion of whether man has a free will or not.

Acknowledgements

The author is indebted to Drs. B. Libet, A. Lundberg, J. Risberg, E. Ryding and L. Widén for valuable criticism and suggestions. The author has been supported by the Swedish Medical Research Council and by the Wallenberg Foundation in Stockholm.

References

Baddeley, A. (1983), 'Working memory', *Philos Trans Soc London (Biol)*, **323**, pp. 311–24.

Baxter, L.R., Guze, B.H., Schwartz, J.M., Phelps, M.E., Mazziotta, J.C. and Szuba, M.P. (1991), 'PET studies of cerebral function in major depression and related disorders', in *Brain Work and Mental Activity*, ed. N.A. Lassen, D.H. Ingvar, M.E. Raichle and K.Friberg (Copenhagen: Munksgaard).

Brandimonte, M., Einstein, G.O. and McDaniel, M.A. (1996), *Prospective Memory* (Mahwah, NJ: Erlbaum).

Damasio, A.R. and Van Hoesen, G.W. (1980), 'Structure and function of the supplementary motor area', *Neurology*, **30**, p. 359.

Damasio, A.R., Tranel. D. and Damasio, H. (1990), 'Individuals with sociopathic behavior caused by frontal damage fail to respond autonomically to social stimuli', *Behav. Brain Res.*, **41**, pp. 81–94.

Davidson, J.M. and Davidson, R.J. (1980), *The Psychobiology of Consciousness* (New York: Plenum).

Decety, J. and Ingvar, D.H. (1990), 'Brain Structures Paricipating in Mental Simulation of Motor Behaviour', *Acta Psychol.*, **73**, pp. 13–34.

Decety, J., Sjöholm, H., Ryding, E., Stenberg, G. and Ingvar, D.H. (1990), 'The cerebellum participates in mental activity. Tomographic measurements of regional cerebral blood flow', *Brain Research*, **535**, pp. 313–17.

Deecke, L. and Lang, W. (1996), 'Generation of movement-related potentials and fields in the supplementary senorimotor area and the primary motor area', *Advances in Neurology*, **70**, *Supplementary Sensorimotor Area*, pp. 127–46.

Deecke, L., Lang, W., Beisteiner, R., Uhl, F., Lindinger, G. and Cui, R.Q. (1997), 'Experiments in movement using DC-EEG, MEG, SPECT and FMRI', *Proceedings of the Int Symposium on Brain Mapping*, Oiso/Japan 13–15 Sept 1996 Nishimura Publ. (in press).

Eccles, J.C. (1982), 'The initiation of voluntary movements by the supplementary motor area', *Archiv.Psychiatr.Nervenkrankh.*, **231**, pp 423–41.

Edelman, G.M. (1989), *The Remembered Present: A Biological Theory of Consciousness* (New York: Basic Books).

Frackowiak, R.S.J., Friston, K.J., Frith, C.D., Dolan, R.J. and Mazziotta, J.C. (1997), *Human Brain Function*, (San Diego, CA: Academic Press).

Frith, C.D., Friston, K., Liddle, P.E. and Frackowiak, R.S.J. (1991), 'Willed action and the prefrontal cortex in man. A study with PET', *Proc. R.Soc.Lond. (B)*, **244**, pp 241–6.

Fuster, J.M. (1989), *The Prefrontal Cortex*. 2nd ed. (New York: Raven Press).

Fuster, J.M. (1995), *Memory in the Cerebral Cortex* (Cambridge, MA: MIT Press).

Gillberg, Ch. and Coleman, M. (1992), *The Biology of the Autistic Syndromes*, 2 ed. (Oxford: Blackwell Sci. Publ.).

Goldman-Rakic, P.S. (1988), 'Topography of cognition. Parallel distributed networks in primate association cortex', *Ann. Rev. Neurosci.*, **11**, pp.137–56.

Ingvar, D.H. (1979), ''Hyperfrontal' distribution of the cerebral grey matter flow in resting wakefulness: on the functional anatomy of the conscious state', *Acta Neurol. Scand.*, **60**, pp. 12–25.

Ingvar, D.H. (1980), 'Abnormalities of activity distribution in the brain of schizophrenics', in *Perspectives in schizophrenia,* ed.D. Baxter and B. Melnechuk (New York: Raven).

Ingvar, D.H. (1985), 'Memory of the future: An essay on the temporal organization of conscious awareness', *Human Neurobiol.*, **4**, pp.127–36.

Ingvar, D.H. (1994), 'The will of the brain: Cerebral correlations of wilful acts', *J. Theor. Biol.*, **171**, pp. 7–12.

Ingvar, D.H. (1997), 'A "Kantian" model of consciousness', *Proc. Italian Ass. of Philosophy*, Naples (in press).

Ingvar, D.H. and Franzén, G. (1974), 'Abnormalities of regional cerebral blood flow distribution in patients with chronic schizophrenia', *Acta Psychiatr.Scand.*, **50**, pp. 425–62.

Ingvar, D.H. and Lassen, N.A. (ed. 1975), *Brain Work: The Coupling of Function, Metabolism, and Blood Flow in the Brain* (Copenhagen: Munksgaard).

Ingvar, D.H. and Philipson, L. (1977), 'Distribution of cerebral blood flow in the dominant hemisphere during motor ideation and motor performance', *Ann. Neurol.*, **2** (3), pp. 230–7.

Ingvar, D.H. and Risberg, J. (1965), 'Influence of mental activity upon regional cerebral blood flow in man', *Acta Neurol. Scand.* (Suppl 14), pp. 183–6.

Ingvar, D.H. and Risberg, J. (1967), 'Increase of regional cerebral during mental effort in normals and in patients with focal brain disorders', *Exp.Brain Res.*, **3**, pp.195–211.

Lang, W. and Deecke, L. (1997), 'Psychophysiologie der Motorik', in *Ergebnisse und Anwendungen der Psychophysiologie*, ed. F. Rösler (Göttingen: Hogrefe).

Lassen, N.A., Hoedt-Rasmussen, K., Sörensen, S.C., Skinhöj, E., Cronqvist, S., Bodforss, B. and Ingvar, D.H. (1963), 'Regional cerebral blood flow in man determined by Krypton-85', *Neurology*, **13**, pp. 719–27.

Lassen, N.A. and Ingvar, D.H. (1961), 'The blood flow of the cerebral cortex determined by radioactive Krypton-85', *Experientia*, **17**, pp. 42–3.

Lassen, N.A., Ingvar, D.H., Raichle, M.E. and Friberg, L. (ed 1991), *Brain Work and Mental Activity: Quantitative Studies with Radioactive Tracers* (Copenhagen: Munksgaard).

Libet, B. (1985), 'Unconscious cerebral initiative and the role of conscious will in voluntary action', *Behav. Brain Sci.*, **89**, pp. 567–615.

Libet, B. (1989), 'Conscious subjective experience and unconscious mental functions', in *Models of Brain Functions*, ed. R.M.J. Cotterill (Cambridge: Cambridge University Press).

Libet, B. (1992), 'The neural time-factor in perception, volition and free will', *Revue de Métaphysique et de la Morale*, **2**, pp. 255–72.

Libet, B. (1993), 'The neural time-factor in conscious and unconscious events', in *Experimental and Theoretical Studies of Consciousness*, Ciba Foundation Symposium # 174 (Chichester: Wiley).

Libet, B. (1994), 'A testable field theory of mind-brain interaction', *Journal of Consciousness Studies*, **1** (1), pp.119–26.

Libet, B. (1996), 'Solutions to the hard problem of consciousness', *Journal of Consciousness Studies*, **3** (1), pp. 33–5.

Lou, H.C., Henriksen, L., Bruhn, P., Börner, H. and Bieber Nielsen, J. (1989), 'Striatal dysfunction in attention deficit and hyperkinetic disorder', *Arch. Neurol.*, **46**, pp. 48–52.

Luria, A.R. (1966), *Higher Cortical Functions in Man* 2nd ed. (New York: Basic Books).

Magoun, H.W. (1963), *The Waking Brain* (Springfield, IL: Charles C. Thomas).

Mesulam, M.M. (1990), 'Large scale neurocognitive networks and distributed processing for attention, language, and memory', *Ann. Neurol.*, **28**, pp. 597–613.

Olesen, J. (1971) 'Contralateral focal increase of cerebral blood flow in man during arm work', *Brain*, **94**, pp. 635–46.

Petersen, S.E., Fox, P.T., Snyder, A.Z. and Raichle, M.E. (1990), 'Activation of extrastriate and frontal cortical areas by visual words and word-like stimuli', *Science*, **249**, pp. 1041–4.

Posner, M.I. and Raichle, M.E. (1994), *Images of Mind* (New York: W.H. Freeman and Company).

Raichle, M.E. (1995), 'Language and the brain', in *Of Thoughts and Words*, ed. S.Allén (London: Imperial College Press).

Risberg, J. (1986), 'Regional cerebral blood flow', in *Experimental Techniques in Human Neuropsychology*, ed. H.J. Hannay (Oxford: Oxford University Press).

Risberg, J., Gustafson, L. and Brun, A. (1990), 'High resolution regional cerebral blood flow measurements in Alzheimer's disease and other dementia disorders', in *Alzheimer's Disease,* ed. K.Maurer, P. Riederer and H. Beckmann (Vienna: Springer).

Risberg, J. and Ingvar, D.H. (1973), 'Patterns of activation in the grey matter of the dominant hemisphere during memorizing and reasoning: A study of regional cerebral blood flow changes during psychological testing in a group of neurologically normal patients', *Brain*, **96** (4), pp. 737–59.

Ryding, E., Brådvik, B. and Ingvar, D.H. (1996), 'Silent speech activates prefrontal cortical regions asymmetrically', *Brain Lang.*, **52**, pp. 435–51.

Schmidt, C.F. (1951), *The Human Brain in Health and Disease* (Springfield, IL: Charles C. Thomas).

Searle, J.R. (1990), 'Consciousness, explanatory inversion, and cognitive science', *Behav. Brain Sci*, **13**, pp. 585–642.

Sechenov I. (1863, repr.1965), *Reflexes of the Brain* (Cambridge, MA: MIT Press).

Shachow, D. (1967), 'Some psycho-physiological aspects of schizophrenia', in *The Origins of Schizophrenia*, ed. J. Romano (Amsterdam: Exerpta Medica).

Stokely, E.M., Sveinsdottir, E., Lassen, N.A. and Rommer, P. (1980), 'A single photon dynamic computer assisted tomograph (DCAT) for imaging brain function in multiple cross-sections', *J. Comput. Assist. Tomogr.*, **4**, pp. 230–40.

Weinberger, D.R., Berman, K.F., Daniel, D.G., Zigun, J.R., Gorey, J., Handel, S., Jones, D.W. and Coppola, R. (1991), 'Studies of rCBF during cognitive activation in patients with schizophrenia and affective disorders', in *Brain Work and Mental Activity*, ed. N.A. Lassen, D.H. Ingvar, M.E. Raichle and L.Friberg (Copenhagen: Munksgaard).

Sean A. Spence and Chris D. Frith

Towards a Functional Anatomy of Volition

In this paper we examine the functional anatomy of volition, as revealed by modern brain imaging techniques, in conjunction with neuropsychological data derived from human and non-human primates using other methodologies. A number of brain regions contribute to the performance of consciously chosen, or 'willed', actions. Of particular importance is dorso-lateral prefrontal cortex (DLPFC), together with those brain regions with which it is connected, via cortico-subcortical and cortico-cortical circuits. That aspect of free will which is concerned with the voluntary selection of one action rather than another critically depends upon the normal functioning of DLPFC and associated brain regions. Disease, or dysfunction, of these circuits may be associated with a variety of disorders of volition: Parkinson's disease, 'utilization' behaviour, 'alien' and 'phantom' limbs, and delusions of 'alien control' (the passivity phenomena of schizophrenia). Brain imaging has allowed us to gain some access to the pathophysiology of these conditions in living patients. At a philosophical level, the distinction between 'intentions to act', and 'intentions in action' may prove particularly helpful when addressing these complex disturbances of human cognition and conscious experience. The exercise and experience of free will depends upon neural mechanisms located in prefrontal cortex and associated brain systems.

Introduction

'I say, beware of all enterprises that require new clothes . . .'
H.D. Thoreau, 'By Walden Pond'

We will consider the following question: can 'free will' be localized in the brain, using modern functional neuroimaging techniques? This question immediately betrays a range of assumptions, some of which are the following: (1) that free will exists; (2) that it will have a neural correlate; (3) that the latter will be 'localizable' within the brain, rather than distributed throughout the central nervous system; and (4) that such a 'freedom' may be adequately studied in an experimental setting (confined to the study of a single subject in a brain scanner).

The new brain imaging techniques provide an indirect, but remarkably sensitive, index of neuronal activity in the brain. The regional distribution of activity so revealed is strongly associated with the mental state of the volunteer when the meas-

Journal of Consciousness Studies, **6**, No. 8–9, 1999, pp. 11–29

ures were being taken, whether or not any overt behaviour was occurring. Imagining making a movement, imagining the sound of someone's voice, or keeping in mind the image of a face, are all associated with detectable and characteristic patterns of brain activity. It follows that brain imaging is ideally suited for identifying patterns of brain activity associated with those mental states in which we have the *subjective experience* of exerting our 'will': deciding for ourselves whether or not to perform an action, or choosing which, of a number of actions, to perform.

Brain imaging alone, however, cannot answer questions as to whether our subjective experience of free will is justified, or whether the existence of free will is compatible with scientific materialism.

Freedom of the will may be a subjective phenomenon, experienced by the subject (when not experiencing coercion), but nevertheless purely subjective. Freedom may be a 'quale' of the first-person mental state, although a third-person observer might, given sufficient information regarding the functioning of the subject's brain, *predict* what they are about to do (and hence, conclude that a given act was inevitable, even prior to the subject's conscious 'intention'). In this example the subject experiences one reality (their freedom 'to choose'), while another, material reality, coincides with (and indeed pre-empts) their experience. A neuropsychiatric perspective on this form of freedom has been provided by Spence (1996; and see commentaries by Frith, 1996; and Libet, 1996).

In a similar way, there are practical constraints upon the degree of 'freedom' which a given neuroimaging experiment can be said to be imaging. Central to the practice of functional neuroimaging is the experimental protocol, wherein the subject performs tasks given to them by the experimenter. Such tasks may be, of necessity, rather simple, and of limited 'ecological' relevance. The subject agrees to do as the experimenter asks, and complies with the experimental conditions. In the case of studies of movement or word generation (as described below) the tasks may be paced by the experimenter, and may comprise repetitive exercises which few would regard as existentially challenging in their 'real lives'. Thus, although the subjects taking part in such experiments may be said to be performing voluntary movements, in so far as they intend to move their limbs or mouths, they can only be said to be performing 'actions' in a very limited (philosophical) sense. If an action is defined philosophically as being the result of a conscious choice by an agent ('the one who acts'; Macmurray, 1991) then it is clear that the 'agent' has only a very limited choice in most brain imaging studies (for instance moving a joystick in one of four directions, or saying a word beginning with the letter 'S'). Hence, we may study the functional neuroanatomy of voluntary movement in the context of limited behavioural outputs, but it would be premature indeed to consider this to be the same as studying free will. A conservative interpretation might be the following: that brain imaging techniques serve to indicate those structures and systems that might subserve 'freedom' in a normal (unconstrained) environment (outside the scanner).

Functional Neuroimaging

A number of techniques, now available to neuroscientists, allow the study of the human brain (Frackowiak *et al.*, 1997). In this paper we will be mostly concerned with studies using positron emission tomography (PET). Central to PET is the relationship between neuronal synaptic activity and regional cerebral blood flow (rCBF). When local synaptic activity increases so does rCBF. Thus, if rCBF changes can be 'imaged', they may provide an index of regional synaptic activity. The former is achieved using trace doses of short-acting radioisotopes (e.g. oxygen[15] labelled water or carbon dioxide) administered to the subject (intravenously or by inhalation) while they perform a cognitive task. The subject lies with their head in a PET camera, and the latter detects activity emitted from the cerebral circulation. The data acquired undergo a series of computational reconstructions and transformations so that the brain activity from each subject, under each experimental condition, may be compared and further analysed, in a standardised 'stereotactic' brain space (an account of the methodology used in our laboratories is provided by Friston *et al.*, 1995). The use of short-acting radioisotopes allows the subject to be studied under more than one experimental (behavioural) condition during a single scanning session, and also (potentially) on more than one occasion. In other words each subject may be used as their own experimental control. The advent of functional magnetic resonance imaging (fMRI) opens up the opportunity for more intensive, repeated studies, as the technique involves no radiation exposure, but instead uses magnetic field manipulations to detect changes in cerebral blood flow.

We will not deal further with the methodology of scanning, but it will be apparent that there are practical constraints upon the study of humans in the PET or fMRI camera. The volunteer must lie on his back for the duration of the scanning session while keeping his head as still as possible throughout. In order to interpret the pattern of blood flow the experimenter must be able to control, as far as possible, the mental state of the volunteer during each scan. This is usually achieved by giving the volunteer appropriate tasks to perform.

Although these techniques provide an image of regional brain activity in spatial terms, it is also possible to image the *temporal* characteristics of brain activity, using electroencephalography (EEG). The study of the timing of regional brain activity during the performance of movements may inform our knowledge of how the brain generates action (within the constraints noted above). It may also elucidate the temporal relationship between conscious 'intentions' to act and the acts to which these intentions refer (Libet, 1993; Spence, 1996).

The fundamental assumption behind the interpretation of brain imaging studies is that different brain regions have different functions. Identification of these functions cannot be achieved by brain imaging alone. On one side of the 'divide' between mind and brain we require information about the discrete cognitive components of mental activity revealed by cognitive psychology and the study of patients with brain injuries. On the other side of the divide we need information from studies of animal neurophysiology which identify discrete brain regions, their interconnections, and something about the flow of information through the system.

In keeping with this observation we will present the following account within the framework of information available from other fields where relevant, and bearing in mind the philosophical constraints referred to above. Descriptions of brain-damaged humans will inform our knowledge of the genesis of actions, especially when these patients are studied outwith the constraints of the laboratory. Studies of non-human primates may inform our knowledge of functional anatomy, but will be of limited applicability to the problem of 'action', in view of the inaccessibility of their 'intentions'.

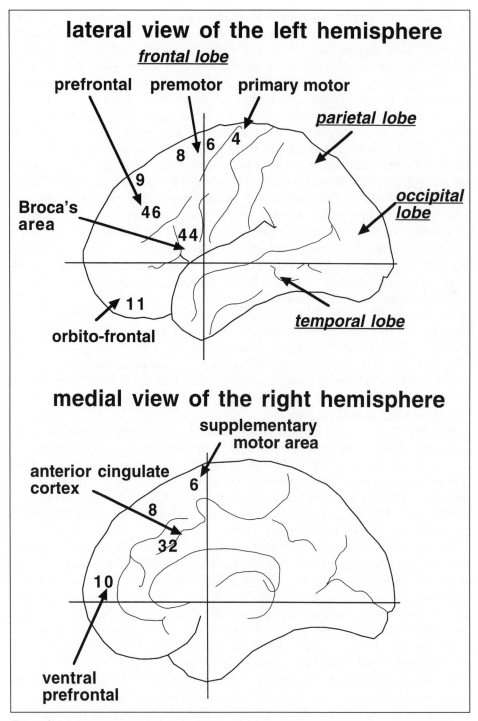

Figure 1.

Schematic view of the human brain showing the four lobes and the major subdivisions of the frontal cortex. The numbers refer the regions delineated by Korbinian Brodmann on the basis of a detailed study of neural architecture. Only a subset of these Brodmann areas are shown. The dorsolateral prefrontal cortex (DLPFC) consists of the regions labelled 9 and 46.

The Frontal Lobes

The major functional division in the brain is between the front (anterior) regions and the back (posterior). The anterior regions (the frontal lobes) are concerned with response generation, while the posterior regions (occipital, parietal, and temporal lobes) are concerned with the analysis of incoming sensory data. The frontal lobes account for at least a third of the total area of cortex in the brain.

The frontal lobes are heterogeneous in terms of neuronal (cyto-)architecture and functional specificity (figure 1). Thus, the most posterior frontal regions bilaterally are the primary motor cortices (Brodmann's Area 4). Anterior to these lie the pre-motor cortices (BA 6 and 8). Primary motor cortices are 'low level' output regions, whereas premotor regions engage in the programming of motor acts. It is the 'prefrontal' regions which are thought to initiate such acts (see below). Prefrontal regions do not project directly to primary motor cortices, but instead project to the intervening premotor regions. In most right handed subjects the 'speech centres' are located in the left cerebral hemisphere, and Broca's area (BA 44) is the motor (speech) output region, located in the left inferior frontal gyrus.

Elsewhere, the functions of the frontal regions are more complex and multimodal. Medially, near to the midline, are the anterior cingulate (BA 32) and supplementary motor area (SMA; BA 6). Both have roles in the generation of motor responses: the former involved in attention to, and selection of, 'information for action', the latter involved in the sequencing and programming of motor acts to fit a 'motor plan'. The SMA plays an important role in the coordination of the two hands and in movements which are self-paced. It receives projections from the prefrontal cortices. Lesions of SMA may lead to akinetic mutism in which the patient shows neither spontaneous movement or speech. The anterior cingulate is a complex region concerned with emotion, pain, and possibly (as proposed by Crick) consciousness.

The region of the frontal lobes lying over the orbits of the eyes (the orbito-frontal region), and extending medially towards the anterior cingulate (the ventral prefrontal cortex) has attracted recent interest because it has been hypothesised to play a role in the modulation of action by reward and social context. This brain region was lesioned in the famous case of Phineas P. Gage, a man whose personality was radically altered by a railroad explosion, when a tamping iron was driven through his skull. He lived, but was 'no longer Gage', such was the change in his personality. He deteriorated in terms of his self-care and his adherence to social convention. His language and his behaviour became coarse, and he went from being a respected member of his community to becoming a vagrant, eventually dying in penury (Damasio, 1994). It has been proposed that deficits of this nature (a lack of responsiveness to social cues and consequences) may underpin the neurobiology of psychopathy (Damasio, 1994).

Reviews of the contribution of specific frontal lobe regions to action are provided by Passingham (1993), and Jeannerod (1997). The region of the prefrontal cortex that we shall be most concerned with in this paper is the dorsolateral prefrontal cortex (DLPFC; BA 9 and 46, see figure 1). This comprises the lateral convexity of the frontal lobes bilaterally, and is an area of multimodal association cortex reaching its apogee in humans. This brain region is implicated in working memory (Goldman-Rakic & Selemon, 1997), the form of memory that is engaged when we keep information 'in mind', as with a newly heard telephone number. Working memory allows such information to be manipulated within consciousness, and to serve as a guide to ongoing behaviour. Dorsolateral prefrontal cortex has been implicated in response selection and the 'internal generation' of action.

Dorsolateral Prefrontal Cortex

Damage to the dorsolateral prefrontal cortex in humans leads to a lack of spontaneous activity, distractibility by environmental cues, and the repetitive, stereotypic use of inappropriate behavioural responses (perseveration). These phenomena may indicate an inability to *choose* or initiate the correct course of action. Patients with large, diffuse lesions involving this region can show 'utilization' behaviour (Lhermitte, 1983). Such patients make stereotyped responses to objects in their environment; putting on spectacles or eating food simply because these are placed in front of them. Such patients might be said to have a major impairment of free will since they have become slaves to their environment. Neuropsychological studies have reported disturbed initiation of action *sequences* in the presence of left DLPFC lesions (Petrides & Milner, 1982), and experimental studies in primates have produced congruent findings (Passingham, 1993). Frontal lesions may lead to the 'release' of primitive reflexes, suggesting that inhibitory control of 'lower' brain regions has been lost in these cases. In consequence, perseverations have been termed 'defaults' by Goldman-Rakic and Selemon (1997).

In normal subjects, studied with PET, left DLPFC activation has been found during word generation and finger movement tasks (Frith *et al.*, 1991; and see figure 2). In both these tasks subjects were called upon to choose their responses. The 'activations' detected in such studies are relative to a control, or contrast, condition. An example is the following.

The word generation protocol: Subjects are scanned under two experimental conditions. In each case they are lying in a darkened room, with their eyes closed, and their head in the PET camera. In the first condition (A) the subject hears the experimenter read a list of words at a rate of one word every three seconds. The subject repeats each word aloud. Hence, in this condition, the response is entirely predicated upon the environmental stimulus. In the terms of Frith *et al.* (1991) it is 'externally specified'. In the second condition (B) the experimenter provides a letter (e.g. 'S') at

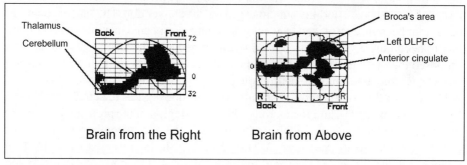

Brain from the Right   Brain from Above

Figure 2.
Brain regions showing a significantly greater neuronal response to the word generation condition compared with the repetition of words spoken by the experimenter (in normal subjects). These figures show statistical parametric maps thresholded at P < 0.05 (corrected for multiple comparisons). Abbreviation: DLPFC = dorsolateral prefrontal cortex

a rate of 1 every 3 seconds, and the subject responds with one word beginning with that letter (e.g. 'Sugar'). In this condition the response is not entirely predicated upon the stimulus, and the subject may choose (within constraints) which response to make. This response is 'internally generated' (Frith *et al.*, 1991). At the superficial level of stimulus and response the two conditions are matched since, in both cases, the subject hears a sequence of words and speaks a sequence of words. Any difference in brain activity should therefore relate to the additional requirement in the second condition of choosing which word to say. A similar pattern of activation was observed in a study by Deiber *et al.* (1991) in which subjects had to choose movements rather than words.

In the study by Frith *et al.* (1991) the result of subtracting activations seen in condition A from those in condition B (the 'cognitive subtraction') was an area of increased activation in left DLPFC and the anterior cingulate region (see figure 2). This was interpreted as being due to the 'internal generation' of the response required in condition B. Hence, this was compatible with neuropsychological reports described above. However, it remains uncertain whether such increased activation in condition B is a correlate of the internal generation of action, and/or the greater working memory demand of this task. It might be argued that there is minimal working memory demand involved in passively repeating a given word (the stimulus in condition A). But when called upon to generate novel words beginning with the letter 'S' (as in condition B) the subject must avoid repetition. Thus, he must retain some awareness of his *previous* responses. This awareness might constitute a greater working memory load.

In a subsequent study Spence *et al.* (1997) studied normal subjects under three conditions on two occasions (4–6 weeks apart). While in a similar scanning environment to that described above, subjects heard a pacing tone at a rate of 1 every 3 seconds. They held a joystick in their right hand. In the first condition (A) they responded by moving the joystick in one of four possible directions (they were instructed to make to pattern of movements as random as possible). In the second condition (B) they moved the joystick in a stereotypic sequence (over successive moves) at the same rate. In the third condition (C) they remained at rest.

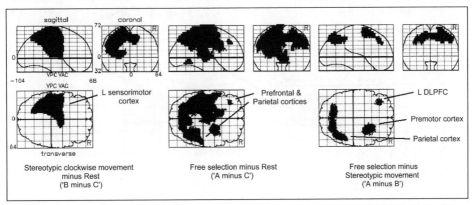

Figure 3.
Brain regions showing significant neuronal responses to the performance of movements of a joystick with the right hand, in normal subjects. These figures show statistical parametric maps thresholded at P < 0.05 (corrected for multiple comparisons). Abbreviation: L DLPFC = left dorsolateral prefrontal cortex. Conditions A, B, and C refer to 'Freely selected movement', 'Stereotypic movement', and 'Resting state' conditions respectively.

Cognitive subtractions on both occasions revealed a replicable pattern of cerebral activation. Whereas stereotypic movement (relative to rest; 'B minus C') revealed contralateral sensorimotor cortex activation (figure 3), freely selected movement ('A minus C') revealed greater activation in a number of brain regions (figure 3) including prefrontal and parietal cortices. The differential response of these regions to free selection (or 'internal generation') of joystick movements was clarified by subtracting the stereotypic from the free selection condition ('A minus B'). The cerebral regions specifically activated by choosing the sequence of movements (rather than performing a sequence of hand movements *per se*) were: left prefrontal cortex, right premotor, and bilateral parietal cortices (figure 3; Spence *et al.*, 1997). Again, the working memory demands of the tasks may constitute a confounding variable (since A and B are not completely identical in this respect), but the requirement to produce *sequences* of movements is likely to have made some demands upon working memory in both conditions. A recent study used a very different paradigm in which subjects had to complete word stems (Desmond *et al.*, 1998). This task does not involve working memory since there is no need to keep track of previous responses. Nevertheless, greater activity was observed in DLPFC in conditions where selection between many different possible completions was required (e.g. STA . . . : stamp, stand, stack, station, etc.).

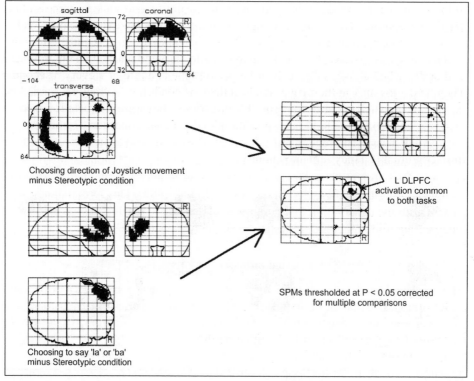

Figure 4.
Brain regions showing a significant neuronal response to the selection of movement independent of the mode of movement (by arm or by mouth). These figures show statistical parametric maps thresholded at P < 0.05 (corrected for multiple comparisons). Abbreviation: L DLPFC = left dorsolateral prefrontal cortex. The latter is activated by each mode of action selection.

Spence and colleagues (1998) also considered the question of whether any brain region might be activated by choice of movement independent of the precise mode of motor output. Combining data from the joystick study (above) with those obtained from a mouth movement protocol (performed at the same rate, in normals) they found activation within an area of left DLPFC (BA 9) to occur whether subjects chose sequences of limb or mouth movements (figure 4).

In the studies reviewed so far subjects had to select for themselves which movements to make, but were constrained to make these movements at a particular time by having to follow a pacing signal. In an alternative paradigm (as in the experiment by Libet, 1993) subjects are told which movement to make, but are free to make the movement whenever they wish. Jahanshahi *et al.* (1995) showed that when subjects selected the time at which to make their movements this was also associated with activation of DLPFC. Again, it is important to acknowledge the limited nature (in philosophical terms) of the 'action' being described. Yet we may conclude that left DLPFC plays a substantial role in the generation of novel movement sequences and in the free selection of responses.

These studies demonstrate that there is an increase in activity in DLPFC when actions are being selected and initiated. A converse observation has been made in psychiatric patients who, as a consequence of depression or chronic schizophrenia have 'poverty of action' and, in particular, a marked reduction of spontaneous speech. When scanned at rest these patients have a specific reduction of activity in left DLPFC, which is associated with clinical ratings of poverty of speech rather than diagnosis (Dolan *et al.*, 1993).

The evidence accumulated thus far supports a specific role for this brain region (DLPFC) in the spontaneous generation of action. A plausible account is that the DLPFC formulates action 'goals', while specific motor commands are 'delegated' to premotor regions (Passingham, 1993). This notion is compatible with data from single unit recording in animals revealing movement-related DLPFC activity which precedes that seen in premotor and subcortical regions (Goldman-Rakic *et al.*, 1992). By what mechanism does prefrontal cortex select one of a number of possible actions? One possibility is that most behavioural outputs are inhibited so that one 'single appropriate act' is selected (Goldman-Rakic, 1987). This formulation is consistent with the observation that patients with damage to prefrontal cortex are often unable to inhibit inappropriate responses to their environment.

Cortico-subcortical Circuits

Having established a possible role for DLPFC in the generation of action it is important to emphasize that the brain is an integrated unit, with spatially distributed regions 'co-operating' in the execution of cognitive tasks. Thus, it is important to consider the functional connections of DLPFC with other brain regions.

Dorsolateral prefrontal cortex participates in one of the five basal ganglia thalamo-cortical circuits or 'loops' described by Alexander *et al.* (1986; see figure 5). Lesions in any part of this DLPFC circuit may disturb executive function (Masterman & Cummings, 1997). The SMA also participates in such a loop. These semi-closed circuits project between specific thalamic nuclei and circumscribed regions of the frontal lobe. They are 'funnelled' through the basal ganglia (Alexander *et al.*, 1986).

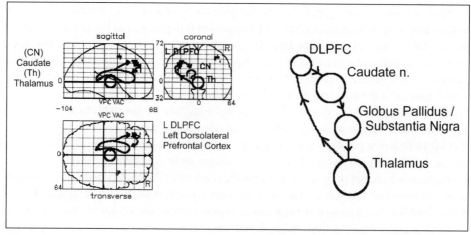

Figure 5.
A cartoon diagram illustrating one of the prefrontal-subcortical circuits; this one involves the dorsolateral prefrontal cortex, caudate nucleus, globus pallidus / substantia nigra, and thalamus. The 'loop' is closed by projections from the thalamus to the DLPFC. Similar loops involve the supplementary motor area and the anterior cingulate cortex. See text for references.

Disordered basal ganglia function (as in Parkinson's disease) may affect the execution of movement directly but may also exert indirect effects upon distant frontal regions, and their instantiated cognitive functions.

Passingham (1997) has contrasted the roles of prefrontal cortex (DLPFC and ACC) with more posterior regions such as SMA and premotor cortex, and subcortical structures such as basal ganglia and cerebellum. The prefrontal areas are active when subjects pay attention to their actions and make conscious decisions about them. These regions are also active when subjects simply imagine making movements as originally demonstrated by Ingvar & Philipson (1977). However, these areas are not active when subjects perform movements that are routine, or when a new skill is being learned without awareness (implicit learning). In contrast, the posterior cortical regions and the subcortical structures continue to be active even when movements have become routine, and are also active during implicit learning. These observations suggest that the prefrontal areas have a specific role in modifying the behaviour of the cortico-subcortical circuits when non-routine actions have to be selected.

The anatomy of the local circuits found within the basal ganglia is complex. In consequence, damage to different components of the system can result in very different kinds of movement disorder. For example, the loss of nigrostriatal dopamine in Parkinsonism leads to excessive inhibition of SMA and DLPFC. This produces the rigidity and bradykinesia (slowed movement) of Parkinson's disease. Subjectively, such patients find that all actions require much more effort than before, and movements will often fail to reach their target. In some circumstances the patient will 'freeze'. He knows precisely what action he wants to perform, but is unable to initiate it. An appropriate external (environmental) signal can sometimes trigger the initiation of the action in this state ('paradoxical kinesis').

PET activation studies in Parkinson's disease have demonstrated hypoactivation of SMA, DLPFC, and anterior cingulate cortex (each one a cortical projection site for a basal ganglia loop), with preservation of primary motor, and lateral premotor cortical activity (Brooks, 1995). Jenkins *et al.* (1992) demonstrated recovery of SMA activity when Parkinson's patients were 'activated' using the dopaminergic drug apomorphine. Thus, loss of dopaminergic function in the basal ganglia may lead to (potentially reversible) hypo-activation of distant cortical regions receiving thalamocortical 'loop' projections.

In contrast, idiopathic dystonic disorders, characterized by abnormal posturing during voluntary movement, may result from disinhibition within these loops, as opposed to the inhibitory state of Parkinsonism (above). When such patients are studied using functional neuroimaging the results have shown that dystonic movements are accompanied by characteristic abnormalities of cortical activation, namely hyperactivation of SMA and DLPFC (Playford *et al.*, 1992; Ceballos-Baumann *et al.*, 1995; see Brooks, 1995, for review). In this sense their profiles appear to be the opposite of Parkinson's patients (who exhibit hypo-activation of the same cortical regions).

We may conclude that although DLPFC plays a role in the selection of action, the performance of the action itself is facilitated by 'lower' motor regions, such as SMA and the basal ganglia. The functional integrity of such circuits underpins 'higher' motor programming, and disease affecting these regions adversely affects the performance parameters of the 'intended' act.

Cortico-cortical Circuits

As well as projections to subcortical brain regions DLPFC has multiple connections with anatomically, and functionally, discrete cortical regions. It receives its greatest input from the posterior parietal cortex (see figure 1), a complex area of association cortex involved in diverse cognitive functions. Posterior parietal cortex (PPC) integrates information from multiple sensory modalities (vision, touch and balance); contributes to the direction of attention and visual gaze; encodes the spatial coordinates of the body and objects (in terms of egocentric, body-space); is involved in spatial working memory; and appears to store 'motor memories' of movements, such as grasping and reaching, and meaningful gesture. Destruction of the parietal regions may reveal asymmetries of function, with right-sided lesions giving rise to (greater) visuospatial neglect (failure to attend to the left side of space), and left-sided lesions causing deficits in the serial performance of actions and deficits of motor symbolism (apraxia). It is the 'mental image' of an act which appears to be lost in the latter lesions. The functions of these complex regions have been reviewed by: Critchley (1953), McCarthy and Warrington (1990), Roland (1993), Andersen *et al.* (1997), Jeannerod (1997) and Maguire (1997).

Apraxia is defined as the inability to carry out a purposeful movement, the nature of which the patient understands, in the absence of severe motor paralysis, sensory loss, or ataxia (tremor). Apraxia may involve any movement normally voluntarily initiated: movement of the eyes, face, muscles of articulation, chewing and swallowing, manipulation of objects, gestures with the upper limb, walking, or sitting down (Bannister, 1985). In the current context it is worth considering what apraxia reveals of the normal performance of actions. Jeannerod (1997) reviewed cases in which PPC lesions gave rise to a failure in grasping by the affected (contralateral) hand (despite preservation of muscle tone). Under normal conditions the precise deformations in hand configuration, e.g. the precise articulation of the fingers required to pick up a cup by its handle, occur unconsciously. The subject may be aware of the goal, but not the intervening motor commands required for its successful execution: these are implicit. In some, automatic tasks the subject may be only minimally aware of the 'goal'. Yet complex computations are occurring, the significance of which is revealed when PPC is damaged by pathology. Studies in primates reveal that some PPC neurons may specifically represent 'intended' actions, independent of other features such as attention (Andersen *et al.*, 1997).

But of course, the use of the word 'intention' with respect to such findings may be problematic, if by this we mean a *conscious* intention to act. Animal data would be inadmissible in this regard (we don't *know* if they're conscious or not), and in apraxic humans conscious awareness of the act may only arise after movement has failed. A useful distinction has been made by Searle (1983) between an 'intention in action' (the implicit step that precedes an overtly executed act), and a 'prior intention' to act (the conscious desire to do something). It may be most parsimonious at this stage to regard the 'intentions' localized to some PPC neurons as being components of the former, implicit, variety. The distinction we are making between 'prior intention' and 'intention in action' does not have any implications for the temporal ordering of the brain activity associated with these processes. Activity corresponding to 'intention in action' might be elicited in PPC by the appearance of a graspable object (such as a door knob) in the subject's field of view. In the absence of a 'prior intention' this activity would not, in the normal case, be followed by an action. It would be possible for activity associated with 'intention in action' to precede the conscious 'prior intention' to act.

Most actions we perform occur within (external) space, and hence, it is clear that fronto-parietal circuits are vital to their unimpeded execution. In the joystick task of Spence *et al.* (1997; 1998), reported above, it was seen that bilateral parietal activation was a feature of the free selection of joystick movement (cf. the stereotypic sequence; figure 3), although it was not seen with a freely selected mouth movement task (figure 4). Hence, parietal activation was confined to freely selected movements in space. (In this regard it is also interesting that *oral* apraxia, affecting mouth movements, is associated not with parietal but with left inferior frontal lesions; McCarthy and Warrington, 1990.)

A Consideration of Normal Action

So far, we have focused upon the performance of movements by normal subjects under experimental conditions. Such movements, especially when they require novelty, or a degree of 'internal generation' by the subject, involve the activation of distributed brain regions, some of which appear to make specific contributions to motor performance. Hence, we have made a case for DLPFC contributing to the selection of a movement, which may be held 'on line' in working memory in prefrontal cortex, but may also exist as a motor symbol or 'intention in action' in posterior parietal regions. The latter contribute to the programming of movements in space, whereas the SMA may be particularly important in the programming of movements in time (bimanual coordination and self-pacing). Both SMA and the basal ganglia facilitate the execution of movements, perhaps after selection by DLPFC, but before their 'delegation' to the motor cortex and spinal cord (Brooks, 1995).

Therefore, despite our comments regarding the limited nature of the 'actions' that may be elicited in the PET camera, it is clear from an integrated reading of PET experiments, and human and non-human-primate neuropsychological data, that even the most simple motor procedures require complex (and distributed) neuronal activity. This serves to emphasize the prematurity of pondering the 'localization of free will'!

The Possession of Action

Notwithstanding the above comments, there are 'natural experiments' in human neurology and psychopathology which may inform our understanding of the normal phenomenology of action. Whether we believe in 'free will' or not, it is clear that most of us experience our actions as self-determined (in the absence of coercion). But there are patients who are not so fortunate.

Alien limbs

Goldstein (1908; in Feinberg *et al.*, 1992) described a 57 year old woman who felt her left hand had a will of its own. The hand 'behaved' as if it was out of her control, and at one point attempted to strangle her. A post-mortem examination revealed multiple brain lesions, one of which involved the corpus callosum (the fibre bundle connecting the left and right cerebral hemispheres). A similar case involving self-strangulation has been reported in modern times by Banks *et al.* (1989), also implicating callosal pathology. A number of 'alien hand syndrome' or 'anarchic hand syndrome' cases now exist in the world literature, and it is clear that there may be at least two forms of this disorder (Feinberg *et al.*, 1992; below). (In the following, we shall assume that we are referring to right-handed subjects unless otherwise stated.)

Essentially, the affected patient complains that they cannot control one of their hands. When describing the hand they may say it has a 'mind of its own', but in most cases they continue to regard it as belonging to their body. A lesion of the left medial prefrontal region, extending to the SMA, anterior cingulate and anterior corpus callosum, produces a (contralateral) right-sided alien hand. The 'behaviour' of the latter, characteristically includes: reflexive grasping, groping, and the compulsive manipulation of tools. Feinberg *et al.* (1992) interpret this as the release of exploratory behaviour which is normally inhibited by the dominant (left) hemisphere. Referred to as 'magnetic apraxia' by Denny-Brown (1958), such behaviours may emanate from the parietal lobes. It is as if irrelevant stimuli, such as door knobs and pencils, activate 'intentions in action' in the parietal lobe which are no longer inhibited by the impaired frontal regions. Similar behaviours are seen in primates with SMA lesions (Denny-Brown, 1965), and in the so-called 'utilization' syndrome in humans, characterized by bilateral (rather than unilateral) grasping of common objects following diffuse frontal lobe lesions (Lhermitte, 1983).

When corpus callosal lesions occur alone, the non-dominant (left) hand may become 'anarchic'. In this case the condition is characterized by intermanual conflict, wherein the patient's hands may struggle with each other to produce opposite effects. Hence, there are patients who report one hand attempting to lift a cup while the other puts it down, or one hand fastening a button while the other undoes the same. The proposed cause is the disinhibition of the non-dominant (right) hemisphere, as the callosal lesion interrupts the (normal) inhibitory tone from the dominant left (Feinberg *et al.*, 1992). Hence, the left hand is released from inhibitory control.

To return to the subject of 'intentions', it is clear from the above that the patient may have conscious 'intentions to act', but that these are thwarted by the implicit 'intentions in action' of the abnormal, alien, hand ('intentions' to which the patient does not experience conscious access). Again, it would be consistent with the above material to contend that these 'alien intentions' emanate from the parietal lobes, and that the latter are somehow disinhibited. Also, these conditions provide a contrast with Parkinson's disease where the patient may have 'intentions to act' but these fail to occur through the absence, or limitation, of 'intentions in action', due to subcortical pathology.

A strange variation on this theme is a case reported by Hari *et al.* (1998). They describe a patient with an abnormal corpus callosum and damage to the right SMA. This patient experiences the presence of a 'phantom' left arm which occupies a different position in space from her actual left arm. This phantom arm follows the movements of the right arm (suggesting some form of collateral activity) but only when the right arm is moved actively by the patient (not passively by an examiner: hence, implying a relationship to volition). However, the phantom disappears when the left arm is touched or looked at, implying modulation of right parietal activity by sensory afferents.

Alien limbs may also be reported in the presence of pathology intrinsic to the parietal lobes. Here there may be an additional dimension in that the limb is not only behaviourally disinhibited, but may also be regarded as 'truly' alien, i.e. belonging to another. Thus, in the presence of epileptic activity in a right-sided parietal lesion, Leiguarda *et al.* (1993) report a woman who experienced an intermittent, left-sided, alien limb: 'She said: "Suddenly I had a strange feeling on my left side; later I could not recognise the left arm as my own; I felt it belonged to someone else and wanted to hurt me because it moved towards me . . ."' (Leiguarda *et al.*, 1993)

Thus, in this case both the intentions and the identity of the alien limb are disturbed.

Other automatic 'intentions'

The veracity of a distinction between conscious 'intentions to act' and implicit 'intentions in action' is further supported by other unusual neurological phenomena.

In the Foix-Chavany-Marie syndrome (FCMS) the patient exhibits a so-called 'automatic voluntary dissociation' with respect to facial expression (Weller, 1993). Simply stated, the patient may smile spontaneously, but cannot (consciously) imitate a smile. Such a disorder may be caused by stroke or developmental abnormality, and appears to 'require', in most cases, bilateral lesions of the operculum (those regions of the frontal and parietal lobes which are covered by the temporal lobes, bilaterally). In these disorders implicit intentions are intact, but conscious intentions ('to act') are unsuccessful.

Schizophrenic delusions of alien control

One of the most characteristic symptoms of schizophrenia is the belief, expressed by the patient, that their actions or thoughts are under the direct control of an-Other. Such beliefs have been termed delusions of alien control, and may refer to movements, emotions, or thoughts. If the 'agent' is the one 'who acts', then the schizophrenic patient experiences their agency as being interfered with in a most direct (and distressing) way. It is as if the subject not only experiences their own conscious 'intentions' as being interfered with, but also partakes, at a conscious level, in the intentions of another ('their' thoughts, 'their' actions). Such reports throw up a host of philosophical problems addressed elsewhere by Fulford (1995).

Frith (1992) has hypothesized that, in cognitive neuropsychological terms, the deficit in such patients is of the 'internal monitoring' of action: the patient has no representation of the prior intention to act. Thus, when an 'act' occurs the patient fails to recognise it as his own and attributes it to an-Other. Consistent with such a deficit of internal monitoring are studies which have reported failure by such patients to correct their own motor errors (in the absence of visual feedback; Frith and Done, 1989), and impaired memory for the patient's own motor acts (Mlakar *et al.*, 1994).

To discover the possible biological substrate of this symptom, Spence *et al.* (1997) used PET to study schizophrenic patients with and without delusions of alien control, and normal subjects, while they performed a joystick task on two occasions over time. In this study the index patients were compared with themselves as they recovered, and with each of the other (normal and schizophrenic) control groups. Freely selected joystick movement in the presence of delusions of alien control was consistently associated with overactivity of the right inferior parietal lobule and foci within the cingulate gyrus. The parietal region in question is an area of heteromodal association cortex, unique to humans, involved in the processing of information about the body, and the programming of movements, in space. Hence, when this region is overactive, the conscious intention to move may be qualitatively, experientially, abnormal and mis-attributed to forces outside the 'self': a disorder of both identity and spatial processing. One of the patients reported that he 'felt like an automaton, guided by a female spirit who had entered [him] during it' (the moving of the joystick; Spence *et al.*, 1997).

Schizophrenic phenomenology is unlikely to be explained by localized damage in one brain region. It is more likely that these strange experiences arise from disorder in a widely distributed system of inter-connected brain regions. For instance, in both groups of schizophrenic patients referred to above there was also under-activity in the prefrontal cortices while patients were at their most symptomatic (Spence *et al.*, 1997; 1998). This might explain the disinhibited behaviour of the parietal region.

Disordered Action

We infer from the above examples taken from neurological and psychiatric disorders that both the objective execution, and the subjective experience, of action, may be highly abnormal in the presence of dysfunctional brain systems. Frontal and parietal regions seem repeatedly to be implicated, with frontal disorders impairing the selection and execution of movement, and parietal disorders producing highly abnormal experiences of the self during movement. Further work in this field is likely to increase our knowledge of these disorders *in vivo*, and might, hopefully, lead to more rational forms of treatment. The implication of these observations is that the exercise and experience of free will depends upon neural mechanisms which are located in prefrontal cortex and the brain regions with which this brain region is linked.

A Reconsideration of Normal Action

We have been circumspect in our assessment of the extent to which normal action may be said to be accessed during brain imaging. Partly this is due to the limited nature of the tasks undertaken by subjects in the scanner. Moving a joystick in one of four directions, or producing words beginning with the letter 'S', appear simple in comparison to deciding what to write in a paper, or which road to take in an unfamiliar town. But it may be that the constituent 'chunks' of information, regarded as alternatives in everyday life, themselves comprise only a limited, finite, set of options. We do not have space to pursue this line of enquiry at length, but two examples may serve to prompt the reader.

Few 'real life' situations would appear to require more inventiveness, or spontaneity, than improvising on a musical instrument, playing jazz, in front of a live audience. In his account of that branch of the music called 'Bebop', the musicologist Owens (1995) analyses the recorded solos of the alto-saxophonist Charlie Parker (1920–1955). The latter is one of the seminal figures in music, and indeed fragments of his solos continue to be heard in the improvisations of others who follow after him. Yet, when Parker's own, hundreds, of (recorded) solos are analysed, there is a pattern which emerges, when the solos are broken down into their constituent parts. Owens provides examples of 16 recurring phrases, the most prevalent of which occurs once in every eight or nine measures of each of Parker's solos. Parker achieved the highest levels of creativity by selecting from a small number of basic units and applying subtle variations of intonation, volume and timing.

Similarly, other creative productions are built from limited numbers of characteristic elements, otherwise academics would not be able to analyse the 'style' of a given author, painter, or composer. Linguistic studies of glossolalic schizophrenic speech (comprising newly made-up, 'neologistic', words), and the utterances of those ('charismatics') who 'speak in tongues', reveal that here also, patterns eventually emerge, and the same sequences of motor (speech) acts tend to recur (Lecours, 1995) although usually without the subtle variations which are the hallmark of creativity.

These characteristic and (ultimately) stereotyped sequences of action may arise because the optimum route for achieving a goal can never be unequivocally specified. There are usually many different ways of achieving the same goal. I may pick up my glass of beer with my left or my right hand. I can hold it by the handle or, more likely, I can thread my fingers through the handle and hold the body of the glass. In a more formal experiment, Ward and Allport (1997) studied a planning task ('The Tower of London') in which a goal has to be reached in the minimum number of moves, and measured the time taken to make each move. The longest times occurred at points where two different moves were equally good for achieving the goal. This clearly reflects a strategy in which moves are selected on the basis of their likely value. The selection is most difficult when the values of the choices are essentially the same. In such cases it does not matter which one is chosen and there is no need to waste time deciding. The easiest way to overcome the problem is to make an arbitrary, but stereotyped, choice at such points. Our sense of making a choice remains whenever we are faced with novel alternatives which need to be contrasted. The *process* may be essentially the same whether we are deciding to move the joystick left or right in the PET camera, or deciding which cup to use in the kitchen, to have a cup of tea.

Conclusions

Brain imaging studies show that a characteristic pattern of activity is associated with the subjective experience of deciding when to act and which action to perform. DLPFC seems to be uniquely involved in this kind of mental activity. Other regions — anterior cingulate, SMA, basal ganglia, and parietal cortex — are also necessary, but are sufficient on their own when actions are carried out routinely and without thought. Thinking about what we are going to do before we do it clearly requires some form of mental representation of intended actions, and indeed the pattern of brain activity associated with imagining making a movement is very similar to the pattern of activity associated with preparing to make a movement (Jeannerod, 1997).

The parietal lobe probably contains representations of intended actions such as the intended position of a limb or an eye. DLPFC seems to be involved in keeping possible actions in mind before they are executed, and selecting which one will be performed. Damage to different parts of this system disrupts the experience of selecting between actions. Limbs may perform actions against our will (alien hand) or we may have the experience of being passively controlled by an external agent (delusions of alien control). These experiences are both disturbing and debilitating.

Rather than asking whether our experience of freedom in choosing different actions is justified, we consider that the important question to be answered is: what advantage does this experience of free choice confer upon us? The evolution of these complex brain systems must have resulted from pressure to develop such an advantage.

One possibility is that the experience of choice is necessary for us to make the distinction between us, as agents, and the outside world upon which we act. A second, and related, advantage concerns our ability to recognize other agents in the world and to understand something of the basis of the decisions which seem to guide their behaviour. In a complex environment our experience of choice is associated with our execution of non-routine (non-stereotypic) procedures. Our unique behaviours may characterize 'ourselves' ; they may make us who we feel we are.

Acknowledgements
SAS is supported by the Medical Research Council (UK); CDF is supported by the Wellcome Trust.

References

Alexander, G.E., DeLong, M.R., Strick, P.L. (1986), 'Parallel organization of functionally segregated circuits linking basal ganglia and cortex', *Ann. Rev. Neurosci.*, **9**, pp. 357–81.

Andersen, R.A., Snyder, L.H., Bradley, D.C., Xing, J. (1997), 'Multimodal representation of space in the posterior parietal cortex and its use in planning movements', *Ann. Rev. Neurosci.*, **20**, pp. 303–30.

Banks, G., Short, P., Martinez, J. *et al.* (1989), 'The alien hand syndrome: Clinical and post mortem finding', *Arch. Neurol.*, **46**, pp. 456–9.

Bannister, R. (1985), *Brain's Clinical Neurology* (Oxford: Oxford University Press).

Brooks, D.J. (1995), 'The role of the basal ganglia in motor control: contributions from PET', *J. Neurol. Sci.*, **128**, pp. 1–13.

Ceballos-Baumann, A.O., Passingham, R.E., Warner, T., Playford, E.D. *et al.* (1995), 'Overactive prefrontal and underactive motor cortical areas in idiopathic dystonia', *Ann. Neurol.*, **37**, pp. 363–72.

Critchley, M. (1953), *The Parietal Lobes* (New York: Hafner Press).

Damasio, A.R. (1994), *Descartes' Error* (New York: Putnam).

Deiber, M-P., Passingham, R.E., Colebatch, J.G., Friston, K.J., Nixon, P.D. & Frackowiak. (1991), 'Cortical areas and the selection of movement. Experimental Brain research', **84**, pp. 393–402.

Denny-Brown, D. (1958), 'The nature of apraxia', *J. Nerv. Ment. Dis.*, **126**, pp. 9–32.

Denny-Brown, D. (1965), 'Positive and negative aspects of cerebral cortical functions', *North Carolina Med. J.*, **17**, pp. 295–303.

Desmond, J.E., Gabrieli, J.D.E. & Glover, G.H. (1998), 'Dissociation of frontal and cerebellar activity in a cognitive task: Evidence for a distinction between selection and search', *Neuroimage*, **7**, pp. 368–76.

Dolan, R.J., Bench, C.J., Liddle, P.F., Friston, K.J. *et al.* (1993), 'Dorsolateral prefrontal cortex dysfunction in the major psychoses; symptom or disease specificity?', *J. Neurol. Neurosurg. Psychiatry*, **56**, pp. 1290–4.

Feinberg, T.E., Schindler, R.J., Flanagan, N.G., Haber, L.D. (1992), 'Two alien hand syndromes', *Neurology*, **42**, pp. 19–24.

Frackowiak, R.S.J., Friston, K.F., Frith, C.D., Dolan, R.J., Mazziotta, J.C. (1997), *Human Brain Function* (San Diego, CA: Academic Press).

Friston, K.J., Holmes, A.P., Worsley, K.J., Poline, J-B. *et al.* (1995), 'Statistical parametric maps in functional imaging: a general linear approach', *Hum. Brain Mapp.*, **2**, pp. 189–210.

Frith, C.D. (1992), *The Cognitive Neuropsychology of Schizophrenia* (Hove: Lawrence Erlbaum).

Frith, C.D. (1996), 'Commentary on "Free Will in the Light of Neuropsychiatry"', *Philos. Psychiatr. Psychol.*, **3**, pp. 91–4.

Frith, C.D., Done, D.J. (1989), 'Experiences of alien control in schizophrenia reflect a disorder in the central monitoring of action', *Psychol. Med.*, **13**, pp. 779–86.

Frith, C.D., Friston, K., Liddle, P.F., Frackowiak, R.S.J. (1991), 'Willed action and the prefrontal cortex in man: A study with PET', *Proc. R. Soc. London B.*, **244**, pp. 241–6.

Fulford, K.W.M. (1995), 'Thought insertion, insight and Descartes' cogito : Linguistic analysis and the descriptive psychopathology of schizophrenic thought disorder', in *Speech and Language Disorders in Psychiatry*, ed. A. Sims (London: Gaskell).

Goldman-Rakic, P.S. (1987), 'Motor control function of the prefrontal cortex', in *Motor Areas of the Cerebral Cortex*, Ciba Foundation Symposium 132 (Chichester: Wiley).

Goldman-Rakic, P.S., Bates, J.F., Chafee, M.V. (1992), 'The prefrontal cortex and internally generated motor acts', *Current Opinion Neurobiology*, **2**, pp. 830–5.

Goldman-Rakic, P.S., Selemon, L.D. (1997), 'Functional and anatomical aspects of prefrontal pathology in schizophrenia', *Schizophrenia Bulletin*, **23**, pp. 437–58.

Ingvar, D.H. & Philipson, L. (1977), 'Distribution of cerebral blood flow in the dominant hemisphere during motor ideation and motor performance', *Annals of Neurology*, **2**, pp. 230–7.

Hari, G., Hanninen, R., Makinen, T., Jousmaki, V. *et al.* (1998), 'Three hands: fragmentation of bodily awareness', *Neurosci. Lett.*, **240**, pp. 131–4.

Jahanshahi, M., Jenkins, I.H., Brown, R.G., Marsden, C.D., Passingham, R.E., Brooks, D.J. (1995), 'Selfinitiated versus externally-triggered movements. I. An investigation using regional cerebral blood flow and movement-related potentials in normals and Parkinson's disease', *Brain*, **118**, pp. 913–33.

Jeannerod, M. (1997), *The Cognitive Neuroscience of Action* (Oxford: Blackwell).

Jenkins, I.H., Fernandez, W., Playford, E.D., Lees, A.J. *et al.* (1992), 'Impaired activation of the supplementary motor area in Parkinson's disease is reversed when akinesia is treated with apomorphine', *Ann. Neurol.*, **32**, pp. 749–57.

Lecours, A.R. (1995), 'Schizophasia: The glossomanic and glossolalic subtypes', in *Speech and Language Disorders in Psychiatry*, ed. A. Sims (London: Gaskell).

Leiguarda, R., Starkstein, S., Nogues, M., Berthier, M., Arbelaiz, R. (1993), 'Paroxysmal alien hand syndrome', *J. Neurol. Neurosurg. Psychiatry*, **56**, pp. 788–92.

Lhermitte, F. (1983), '"Utilization Behaviour" and its relation to lesions of the frontal lobes', *Brain*, **106**, pp. 237–55.

Libet, B. (1993), 'The neural time factor in conscious and unconscious events', in *Experimental and Theoretical Studies of Consciousness*, Ciba Foundation Symposium 174 (Chichester: Wiley).

Libet, B. (1996), 'Commentary on "Free Will in the Light of Neuropsychiatry"', *Philos. Psychiatr. Psychol.*, **3**, pp. 95–6.

Macmurray, J. (1991), *The Self as Agent* (London: Faber & Faber: first published 1957).

Maguire, E.A. (1997), 'The cerebral representation of space: insights from functional imaging data', *Trends Cog. Sci.*, **1**, pp. 62–8.

Masterman, D.L., Cummings, J.L. (1997), 'Frontal-subcortical circuits: the anatomic basis of executive, social and motivated behaviours', *J. Psychopharmacol.*, **11**, pp. 107–14.

McCarthy, R.E., Warrington, E.K. (1990), *Cognitive Neuropsychology* (San Diego, CA: Academic Press).

Mlakar, J., Jensterle, J., Frith C.D. (1994), 'Central monitoring deficiency and schizophrenic symptoms', *Psychol. Med.*, **24**, pp. 557–64.

Owens, T. (1995), *Bebop* (Oxford: Oxford University Press).

Passingham, R. (1993), *The Frontal Lobes and Voluntary Action* (Oxford: Oxford University Press).

Passingham, R.E. (1997), 'Functional organisation of the motor system', in *Human Brain Function*, ed. R.S.J. Frackowiak *et al.* (San Diego, CA: Academic Press).

Petrides, M., Milner, B. (1982), 'Deficits in subject-ordered tasks after frontal and temporal lobe lesions in man', *Neuropsychologia*, **20**, pp. 249–62.

Playford, E.D., Jenkins, I.H., Passingham, R.E., Nutt, J., Frackowiak, R.S.J., Brooks, D.J. (1992), 'Impaired mesial frontal and putamen activation in Parkinson's disease: A positron emission tomography study', *Ann. Neurol.*, **32**, pp. 151–61.

Roland, P.E. (1993), *Brain Activation* (New York: Wiley-Liss).

Searle, J. (1983), *Intentionality. An essay in the philosophy of mind* (Cambridge: CUP).

Spence, S.A. (1996), 'Free Will in the Light of Neuropsychiatry', *Philos. Psychiatr. Psychol.*, **3**, pp. 75–90.

Spence, S.A., Brooks, D.J., Hirsch, S.R., Liddle, P.F., Meehan, J., Grasby, P.M. (1997), 'A PET study of voluntary movement in schizophrenic patients experiencing passivity phenomena (delusions of alien control)', *Brain*, **120**, pp. 1997–2011.

Spence, S.A., Hirsch, S.R., Brooks, D.J., Grasby, P.M. (1998), 'PET studies of prefrontal activity in schizophrenics and normals: Evidence for remission of "hypofrontality" with recovery from acute schizophrenia', *Br J. Psychiat.*, in the press.

Ward, G., Allport, A. (1997), 'Planning and problem-solving using the five-disc tower of London task', *Q.J.E.P. A*, **50**, pp. 49–78.

Weller, M. (1993), 'Anterior opercular cortex lesions cause dissociated lower cranial nerve palsies and anarthria but no aphasia: Foix-Chavany-Marie syndrome and "automatic voluntary dissociation" revisited', *J. Neurol.*, **240**, pp. 199–208.

Wolfram Schultz

The Primate Basal Ganglia and the Voluntary Control of Behaviour

This review summarizes recent experiments on neuronal mechanisms underlying goal-directed behaviour. We investigated two basic processes, the internally triggered initiation of movement and the processing of reward information. Single neurons in the striatum (caudate nucleus, putamen and ventral striatum) were activated a few seconds before self-initiated movements in the absence of external triggering stimuli. Similar activations were observed in the closely connected cortical supplementary motor area, suggesting that these activations might evolve through build up in fronto-basal ganglia loops. They may relate to intentional states directed at movements and their outcomes. As a second result, neurons in the striatum were activated in relation to the expectation and detection of rewards. Since rewards constitute important goals of behaviour, these activations might reflect the evaluation of outcome before the behavioural reaction is executed. Thus neurons in the basal ganglia are involved in individual components of goal-directed behaviour.

Control of Voluntary Behaviour By Intentions and Goals

The roles of intentions and goals in voluntary behaviour can be displayed in a simplified diagram (Fig. 1). The origin of most forms of voluntary behaviour would involve some intentional processes. An initial wish to obtain a particular object determines which goal could be potentially pursued and thus serve as a kind of definition of the goal. This is related to the belief that when action a is taken, goal x may be obtained. This belief would in most forms be based on some kind of experience with the action, the goal and the relationship between them. Having established an at least potentially accessible goal would lead to the formation of a general intention of obtaining goal x, or the intention to undertake action a in order to obtain goal x. The three mental processes wish, belief and intention all possess intentionality, as they are 'about' something, like a goal. Together they constitute the initial, intentional phase of goal-directed behaviour. These processes may not evolve in the strict, temporal succession described here but occur partly in parallel, depending on the particular behavioural situation studied.

Journal of Consciousness Studies, **6**, No. 8–9, 1999, pp. 31–45

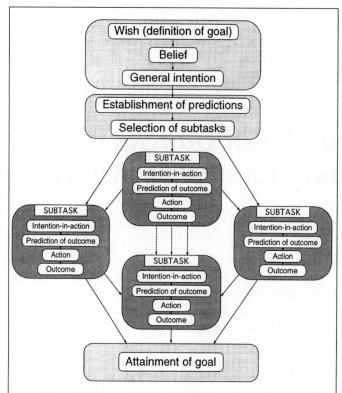

Figure 1

A simplified scheme of component processes for the voluntary control of behaviour. About four consecutive phases are shown, namely the initial intentional phase comprising wishes, beliefs and intentions, a more specific task-related phase comprising cognitive prediction and selection processes, a number of subtasks with individual structures, and the final attainment of the goal.

In order to put the general intention into action, a number of subsequent processes are required which concern the planning of action and the preparation of individual steps towards obtaining the goal. In particular, it would be important to assess in a predictive manner the positive and negative consequences of pursuing the goal. Choosing a particular goal over alternatives usually leads to interruption of ongoing activity and the loss of advantages from an alternative. The behaviour would involve leaving the present situation and going through a number of sequential or parallel subtasks. Each of these subtasks would have its own internal structure, comprising an intention-in-action towards a 'local' outcome, predictions about the next small steps, and an action hopefully resulting in the intended outcome. If the whole sequence is successful, the condition of satisfaction of the initial general intention may be fulfilled and the overall goal attained.

Behavioural Deficits After Lesions of Basal Ganglia

As with many brain structures, the functions of the basal ganglia have classically been defined by the deficits arising after lesions of their component structures. The prominent motor deficits of patients suffering from Parkinsonism, chorea or hemiballism suggest that the basal ganglia are importantly involved in the initiation and execution of voluntary limb and eye movements, and in particular the initiation of spontaneous movements. One of the most serious deficits in Parkinsonian patients and experimentally lesioned animals consists in the reduction of spontaneous movements (Fig. 2) (for review, see Schultz, 1982; 1988). These deficits are due to the

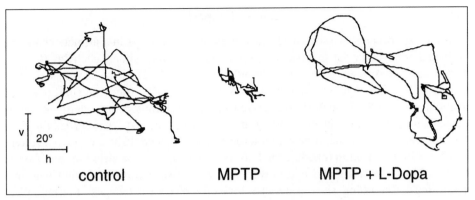

Figure 2

Reductions of spontaneous eye movements in monkey after destruction of the nigrostriatal dopamine system. Two-dimensional plots of eye movements were collected while the animal scanned the laboratory with its eyes in the absence of phasic external stimuli and while not performing any task. Data are shown from left to right for 3 situations: a control period in the normal animal, 10 days after destruction of its nigrostriatal dopamine system by the neurotoxine MPTP, and after L-Dopa was orally administered for restoring dopamine in the striatum to normal levels. Data are displayed from the position of the animal: eye movements to the right are represented by deflections to the right, and upward movements are shown upwards. Each of the three data displays comprises 14 s of continuous recording of eye positions. Reprinted from Schultz *et al.,* (1989) with permission by Springer Verlag.

degeneration of neurons which use the neurotransmitter dopamine and project to the striatum, a part of the basal ganglia. The basal ganglia are closely connected with the frontal lobe through several, partly segregated, partly converging loops (Selemon and Goldman-Rakic, 1985; Alexander *et al.,* 1986; Flaherty and Graybiel, 1994). This would infer a role of the basal ganglia in the cognitive organization of behaviour, including the preparation of movement. Correspondingly, the investigation of neuronal activity in behaving primates revealed activity in many basal ganglia structures related to the preparation of movements, the expectation of task events and the coding of reward (Hikosaka *et al.,* 1989b; Alexander and Crutcher, 1990; Apicella *et al.,* 1992). Furthermore, lesion studies and psychopharmacological experiments revealed that ventral parts of the basal ganglia, namely the ventral striatum and ventral globus pallidus, are involved in neuronal mechanisms underlying important motivational aspects of behaviour, including approach behaviour and reward-directed learning (Fibiger and Phillips, 1986; Robbins and Everitt, 1996). The ventral striatum receives the majority of limbic inputs from cortical and subcortical structures (Russchen *et al.,* 1985; Selemon and Goldman-Rakic, 1985; Haber *et al.,* 1995). Taken together, these data suggest that the basal ganglia process important components of voluntary behaviour, namely the initiation of voluntary movement and the pursuit of reward as a behavioural goal.

This review summarizes recent experiments in our laboratory which investigated how single neurons in the basal ganglia and closely associated cortical structures coded basic aspects of goal-directed behaviour. Given the deficits following basal ganglia lesions, we were particularly interested in two of the processes mentioned above, the initiation of movement and the processing of reward information. We studied how neurons were activated in relation to an internally triggered movement and in which manner they coded information about a future or past reward.

Technical Aspects

In these experiments, we seated Macaca fascicularis monkeys in a primate chair and trained them to carry out specific behavioural tasks for a few hours each day (for further details see Apicella *et al.*, 1992; Schultz *et al.*, 1992). These tasks were designed to test internally triggered movements and the reception of food and fluid rewards. Animals were partly food or fluid deprived and received most of their daily intakes as rewards for performing the task. While they performed the task we recorded the electrical activity of single neurons with microelectrodes that could be moved to different positions in the striatum (caudate nucleus, putamen and ventral striatum) and frontal cortex. Muscle activity and eye movements were also monitored during neuronal recordings. Recording sites were histologically reconstructed post mortem from small electrolytic marker lesions on coronal brain sections. All experiments were conducted in compliance with the Swiss law of animal protection and supervised by the cantonal veterinary office in Fribourg.

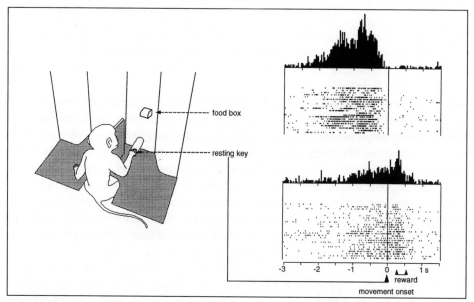

Figure 3

Neuronal activity in the primate striatum during the internally generated preparation of self-initiated arm movements.

Left: Behavioural task. The animal sits in a completely enclosed primate chair and faces a response panel with a touch-sensitive, immovable resting key and a food box. The cover mounted in front of each box prevents vision into the interior while permitting manual access from below. At a self-chosen moment, the animal releases the resting key without any phasic external stimuli and performs a reaching movement into the food box for obtaining a small morsel of apple as reward.

Right: Activation in a caudate neuron terminating before movement onset (top) and in a different caudate neuron terminating with manual contact with reward (bottom). Perievent time histograms are composed of neuronal impulses shown as dots below them. Each dot denotes the time of a neuronal impulse, and distances to instruction onset correspond to real-time intervals. Each line of dots shows one trial. The original sequence of trials is preserved from top to bottom. Movement onset is defined by release of resting key. Reprinted from Schultz *et al.*, (1997b) with permission by Harwood Academic Publishers.

Neuronal Activity During Self-Initiated Movements

Neuronal mechanisms underlying internally triggered behaviour were investigated with self-initiated arm movements in the absence of explicit movement-inducing stimuli. Monkeys reached out and entered with their hand into a food box at self-chosen moments (Fig. 3 left) (Romo and Schultz, 1990; Schultz and Romo, 1992). These movements were performed in order to obtain reward and therefore were not fully spontaneous. However, the animal was free to choose the time of the movement. Thus, movements were triggered internally by the animal and not by external imperative stimuli. Several months of training assured that the individual movements started from a well defined hand position with the muscles relaxed and were not performed in a rhythmic or automatic manner. Intervals between movements were irregular and >5 s (usually 7–40 s). All other behavioural parameters were constrained, including the use of a single, spatially constant target and a single kind of food reward.

The severe impairments in self-initiated movements in Parkinsonian patients are associated with degeneration of the nigrostriatal dopamine system which projects from the pars compacta of substantia nigra to the striatum. We therefore expected to find activity related to self-initiated movements in the dopamine neurons of substantia nigra. However, these neurons very rarely showed such activity (Romo and Schultz, 1990). By contrast, eleven per cent of a studied sample of 683 neurons in the striatum, the target area of nigrostriatal dopamine neurons, were activated 0.5–5 s before the onset of such self-initiated reaching movements (Schultz and Romo, 1992). The activity usually began slowly with a few irregularly spaced impulses, built up over several hundreds of milliseconds toward movement onset, and abruptly ended either with movement onset or with obtainment of food from the box (Fig. 3 right). Continuous monitoring of arm muscle activity and eye movements suggested that these premovement activations were not related to uncontrolled muscle contractions or eye movements. One-third of the neurons showing such activity failed to show any activity during the preparatory period preceding movements triggered by external imperative stimuli. This suggests a partial selectivity of striatal neurons for the internal movement initiation process. These data illustrate how the striatum is

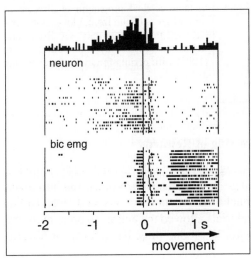

Figure 4

Activity of a single neuron in the supplementary motor area preceding self-initiated arm movements. In the absence of any phasic external cue, neuronal activity starts about 1 s before the monkey releases the resting key and reaches into the food box to collect a hidden morsel of apple (same task and animal as for Fig. 3). All data are referenced to movement onset (key release). Bic emg shows biceps muscle activity recorded simultaneously with neuronal activity. Reprinted from Romo and Schultz (1992) with permission by Springer Verlag.

engaged between an internal urge or decision to move and an overt behavioural action.

These results raise the question about the potential origin of such internally triggered activity. Activity preceding self-initiated movements also exists in the frontal cortex, namely the supplementary motor area, the pre-supplementary motor area, the supplementary eye field and the premotor cortex (Fig. 4) (Okano and Tanji, 1987; Romo and Schultz, 1987; 1992; Schlag and Schlag-Rey, 1987). All of these areas project to the anterior striatum (caudate and putamen). It is possible, albeit by no means proven, that such activity originates and subsequently builds up in such activity in cortico-basal ganglia loops. The axonal conduction and synaptic transmission times of neuronal connections add up to a maximal loop time of 40–50 ms, probably much less (Fig. 5). This may allow such activity to begin with a few impulses deviating from random background activity, be augmented through propagation in successive parts of the loop and reach the observed strength in 1–3 s after 20–150 turns of the loop (Romo and Schultz, 1992).

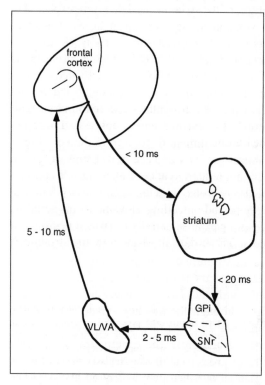

Figure 5

Processing times of activity in cortico-basal ganglia loops. Adding up conduction times in serially connected, individual monosynaptic connections established in electrophysiological experiments results in a total of maximally 40–50 ms, probably much less. Long lead premovement activity could be generated by initial small deviations from background activity in any part of the loop. A subsequent, synaptically mediated build up of activity through reverberations in the loop could lead to the full expression of such activity. With premovement times of 1 s, the short loop times would allow at least 20-50 reverberations to occur before movement onset. Arrows indicate directions of axonal projections without specifying exact anatomical paths; the thalamo-cortical projection is directed to several areas of the frontal lobe. For references to the original data, see Romo and Schultz 1992. Reprinted from Schultz (1995) with permission by Springer Verlag Tokyo.

Neuronal Processing of Rewards

Neuronal correlates related to the processing of reward information were studied in monkeys performing in so-called delayed go-nogo tasks. Depending on an initial visual instruction, animals executed or withheld movement reactions, and received liquid rewards. Different delays in individual trials allowed the animal to prepare for the behavioural reaction and expect the reward. We found three basic forms of reward-

-4   -3   -2   -1   0   1   2   3   4 s
                    ▲   ▲   ▲
                 Trigger   reward

Figure 6

Neuronal activations in primate striatum related to the expectation of reward. Activations develop between the last external signal predicting the liquid reward (trigger) and terminates shortly after reward is delivered at a spout at the mouth of the animal. The activation continues until reward is delivered, even when the trigger-reward delay is occasionally shortened (top) or increased (bottom). The original sequence of trials is preserved from top to bottom.

related neuronal activity, namely activations related to the expectation of reward, responses following the delivery of reward, and neuronal activity related to the preparation of movement which reflected the expected reward.

Reward expectation

A total of 210 neurons in a studied sample of 3,080 neurons (seven per cent) in the dorsal and ventral striatum showed sustained activations which began after one of the last signals predicting the liquid reward and ended immediately after the reward was delivered (Apicella *et al.*, 1992; Schultz *et al.*, 1992; Hollerman *et al.*, 1994). Similar prereward activations have been seen in the striatum during an oculomotor delay task (Hikosaka *et al.*, 1989b). Activations terminated earlier when reward was delivered before the usual time (Fig. 6 top) and continued even when reward was delayed beyond the usual time (Fig. 6 bottom). Although the monkeys made arm and eye movements on some occasions, the prereward activations did not begin or end in close temporal relation to movements. Apparently these activations were not explained by arm or eye movements. Prereward activations were also observed when reward was delivered in a predictable manner outside of any behavioural task. Some prereward activations distinguished between different types of liquid reward, e.g. apple juice vs. water, suggesting a relationship to the particular characteristics of the future reward. Most prereward activations were absent in trials reinforced with a conditioned sound rather than juice, suggesting that they did not simply reflect any upcoming reinforcement. Prereward activations occurred more frequently in ventral striatum, as compared to more dorsal regions of striatum.

These data suggest that striatal neurons were activated in relation to the expectation of primary reward which occurred predictably during the task and was known to

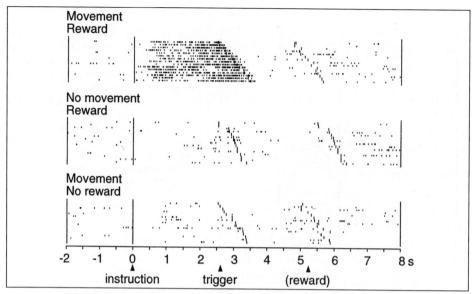

Figure 7

Movement preparatory activity of primate caudate neuron depends on delivery of liquid reward at the end of the trial. The instruction signal defines the onset of a period during which the behavioural reaction is being prepared, and the monkey performs an arm movement in reaction to the trigger stimulus in the top and bottom group of trials. The activation occurs during the preparatory period in rewarded movement trials (top) but not in rewarded non-movement trials (middle), suggesting that it is related to the preparation of movement. However, although a movement to the same target is being prepared in unrewarded movement trials, there is no activation during the preparatory period in these trials reinforced by a conditioned sound (bottom). Thus, the neuron is only activated during the preparation of a movement but not a non-movement reaction, and only when the movement is reinforced by an alimentary reward and not by a conditioned sound. The three trial types alternated randomly during the experiment and were separated for analysis. All trials are rank-ordered according to the instruction-trigger interval. Reprinted from Schultz *et al.*, (1997b) with permission by Harwood Academic Publishers.

the animal through its previous experience. Striatal neurons apparently have access to central representations of reward and thereby participate in the predictive processing of information important for the motivational control of goal-directed behaviour.

Reward detection

A total of 195 neurons in a studied sample of 3,080 neurons (six per cent) in the dorsal and ventral striatum were activated following the reception of liquid rewards with various latencies and durations (Apicella *et al.*, 1991; Hollerman *et al.*, 1994). Similar striatal responses have been seen in an oculomotor delay task (Hikosaka *et al.*, 1989b). Responding neurons were twice as frequent in ventral as compared to dorsal striatal areas. Reward responses were mostly limited to alimentary rewards and largely failed to occur after secondary auditory reinforcers, suggesting that they constituted a reward signal and were unrelated to the end of trial information contained in this event. Responses were directly related to the delivery of primary liquid reward and not to simultaneous auditory stimuli associated with it, as shown by the absence of responses when liquid delivery was interrupted while maintaining the associated solenoid noise. In most reward-responsive neurons, responses also occurred when reward was delivered outside of the task, suggesting that they were not specific for reinforcing an established task. Reward responses were independent of arm, mouth and eye movements. They could be differentiated from movement-related activity in the face area of posterior putamen where activity varied synchronously with individual mouth movements. Taken together, reward responses constituted an entirely different mechanism than the reward expectation-related activations. Rather than occurring on the basis of internally stored information about upcoming events, reward responses reflected the detection of the actual reception of the reward delivered by the experimental protocol.

Reward dependency

The two forms of striatal reward processing described occurred in close temporal contiguity with the rewarding event. In the third form of reward signal observed in 160 neurons in a studied sample of 1,487 neurons (eleven per cent) in the dorsal and ventral striatum, activations related to various behavioural events other than rewards appeared to be dependent on the reward being obtained at the end of the behavioural trial. In the delayed go-nogo task described above, different types of relationships to behavioural processes were observed, such as the detection of behaviourally significant signals, expectation of task events, and the preparation, initiation and execution of movements. In the anterior striatum, the majority of these activations only occurred under the condition that a primary reward was predicted but were absent in unrewarded movement trials in which the secondary auditory reinforcer constituted the predicted trial outcome (Hollerman et al., 1994). For example, striatal activations occurred during the preparation of movement between the initial instruction and the movement trigger signal, subsiding with movement onset several seconds before reward delivery (Fig. 7). These activations were not observed in movement trials performed with the secondary auditory reinforcer as outcome. Similar reward-dependent activations have been seen in response to movement-triggering signals and occasionally even during the execution of movement.

Of the three described striatal reward signals, reward-dependent activations related to various components of task performance represent the most complex form of reward signal. They indicate how predicted reward may influence behavioural reactions by interacting with neuronal activity related to individual behavioural components. These activations may reflect neuronal processes in which information acquired through past experience about the outcome may be used for directing the behaviour of the subject.

Correlates for a Large Spectrum of Task Events

A comprehensive account of neuronal activity in the striatum of awake monkeys revealed a relatively large spectrum of behavioural relationships. Neurons showed a spectrum of nearly continuous behavioural relationships in given task structures, from the expectation and detection of initial task signals via the preparation, initiation and execution of reactions to the expectation and detection of rewarding outcomes (Fig. 8). The activations during limb and eye movements occurred usually in parts of the striatum receiving inputs from skeletal and ocular motor cortical areas (Crutcher and DeLong, 1984; Hikosaka et al., 1989a). Thus, individual striatal neurons may

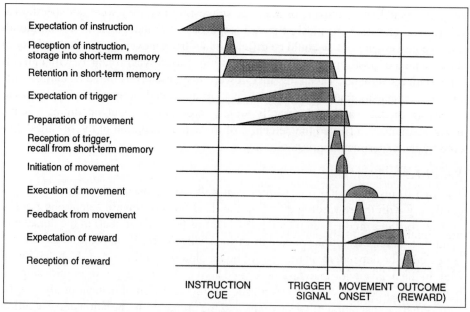

Figure 8

Schematic overview of behavioural relationships of neurons in primate striatum. These activities span the period between the initial expectation of the first task event and the detection of the final trial outcome. Striatal neurons respond to stimuli and events, such as an initial instruction cue, a movement-triggering signal or a drop of liquid reward, and are activated preceding these events, such as stimuli, movements and reward. These events are being expected or prepared following extended experience in the task. A given striatal neuron, if modulated in the task, shows usually only one or occasionally two of these changes. Reprinted from Schultz (1995) with permission by Springer Verlag Tokyo.

process, rather separately, the individual task events occurring between the initial cues and the final outcome of action. This indicates that the basal ganglia are involved when intentions to obtain goal objects lead to actions directed at these outcomes (Schultz *et al.*, 1995).

Neuronal Correlates For Intentions

The activities related to the preparation of movement and the expectation of task signals and reward demonstrate that striatal neurons have access to stored information about environmental events and the subject's own action. These activities may reflect internal states that are set according to information about the environmental context (task contingencies, position of movement target, reward). They are not directly driven by these events, rather they precede them and are directed at individual behavioural acts or concern forthcoming events. In the psychology and philosophy of mind, this 'aboutness' refers to intentionality as a basic property of mental states and events which are directed at or 'are about' an event in the world (Searle, 1983). Such mental states as beliefs, fears, desires and intentions have this property of intentionality in common. They are 'about' particular objects, events or actions, like believing, being afraid of, wanting or intending something. Mental states with intentionality directed at actions or goals may lead to goal-directed actions and are referred to as intentions. Intentions may concern a movement itself (an intention to move the arm forward) or a final reward (an intention to obtain reward) for which the movement is one of several means.

How, then, may the reported sustained activity preceding predictable task events reflect internal states of intention or components of such states? Suggestive examples are the activities in the striatum and frontal cortex preceding self-initiated movements, as they do not directly follow explicit external signals. Consider the case of a partly food-deprived monkey sitting in its home cage and anxiously awaiting the time of daily experimentation where it will be fed with highly appetitive pieces of fruit. The animal certainly desires the food and could be said to have the intention to do whatever action is necessary to get into the laboratory and obtain the food, a procedure it knows very well through daily routine. However, the animal is not free to intentionally move to the laboratory, because the experimenter will fetch him. Its intentional acts are limited to performing in a task in the laboratory where it can only reach out with the arm and collect a morsel of food. Already in its home cage, the animal may have formed a general prior intention to do the hundreds of reaching movements each morning. However, every single movement may not be done with a separate intention behind. The intention for a simple reaching movement may arise at the moment of the action itself. Searle (1983) has well distinguished between these forms of prior intention and 'intention-in-action'. The intention-in-action might be the major form of intention when repeated trials of self-initiated or cue-instructed movements are performed. A general prior intention may not even exist or be required in this externally imposed situation without choices for the subject. The observed neuronal premovement activity of 1–3 s duration may be within the time frame of such an intention-in-action. A somewhat comparable conclusion was reached by Heyes and Dickinson (1990) which argued that even simple lever pressing behaviour fulfilled basic criteria of intentionality, namely belief (that approach will lead to food) and desire (to obtain food). Aside from these arguments, it might be questioned whether monkeys have prior intentions at all, as the degree of spontaneity in behaviour may be quite limited, even in apes (Terrace, 1985).

However, not all internally generated activity may reflect intentional states, in particular, rhythmic, automated movements or pacemaker activity should not do so. As an extreme example, the slowly depolarizing membrane potentials in heart pacemaker cells are certainly not correlates of intentions because there is no internal mental state necessarily related to them, nor is heart action directed at anything particular that can be fulfilled. Heart action thus lacks intentionality.

The intentions involved in the studied self-initiated movements may be directed at the movement itself. Alternatively, they may be directed at the reward, and the movement is just one possible means for obtaining it. Satisfaction for the movement intention is obtained when the movement actually occurs, whereas satisfaction for the reward intention is obtained when the reward is collected. There might be separable neuronal correlates for such different intentions. In some neurons, premovement activity stops before or at the movement, suggesting a relationship to the movement per se. By contrast, other neurons show reward expectation-related activity which continues until the reward is touched or respond to the delivery of reward, thus signalling the primary appetitive outcome of the task. Activations following the reward indicate the obtainment of the goal of behaviour and thus the fulfillment of the intention. Neuronal mechanisms related to the intention of obtaining an important object would be compatible with the general role of the basal ganglia and frontal cortex in determining and mediating goal-directed behaviour. Activity reflecting intentions of individual actions as means of obtaining a goal could be components of such mechanisms.

In our attempt to relate the observed neuronal activity to intentional states, we may be confronted with an even more complex issue, the question of conscious behaviour. We will not discuss the degree of conscious action in animals, and we are also aware that the cited notions of intention are largely derived from human behaviour. Nevertheless, humans performing the described tasks would not necessarily have conscious intentions for every single movement, although these reward-directed movements are certainly not unintentional. Searle (1983) notes quite clearly that relatively simple intentional behaviour can be performed with very low degrees of awareness or no awareness at all. It might be that entering an overall behavioural situation involves a conscious general intention, but the intention-in-action for each individual movement may not be accompanied by a state of high awareness. Quite in agreement with his argumentation, simple, self-initiated movements in humans become aware only a few hundred milliseconds after the onset of brain potentials underlying each movement. These spontaneous movements were basically initiated without awareness (Libet *et al.*, 1983).

If we suppose that the observed activities preceding self-initiated movements or task signals reflect neuronal processes related to intentional states, we imply that correlates of such complex states are expressed in the activity of single neurons. Quite in contrast to Lashley's concept of mass action, which argued against an explicit expression of perceptual or mental events in the activity of single neurons, research in recent years has revealed correlates of surprisingly complex percepts in single neurons. The activity of some neurons in the visual association cortex of monkeys matches the perception of objects independent of their physical properties, such as viewing illusionary contours (Von der Heydt *et al.*, 1984), detecting coherent motion in moving random dot patterns (Newsome *et al.*, 1989) or viewing competing movement directions between the two eyes (Logothetis and Schall, 1989). Apparently individual neurons show high degrees of perceptual specificity in their activity. These neurons are distributed and connected over wide areas of the brain, each area elaborating and contributing a particular aspect of the treated event. Correlates of similarly specific processes might exist in single neurons of the motor system, such as the preparation of action, the expectation of events and the intention to move or obtain objects. Would single neuron correlates exist also for other mental states with intentionality, like desires, beliefs or fears?

If correlates for intentional states are found in single neurons, and if such neurons are distributed and connected over different brain areas, the cited cortico-basal ganglia loops might be among the sites where intentions are elaborated and put into action. The presence of relatively long lasting activities preceding movements and events, the possibility that such activities circulate in these highly connected loops and the fact that these loops involve brain structures known to be importantly involved in determining, selecting and pursuing goals for behaviour would all be consistent with this view. It could be difficult to imagine or even name a single brain structure where intentions 'reside', rather they may evolve through loop activity and involve both the frontal cortex and the basal ganglia. The role of the dopamine input to these loops would also be interesting to investigate. Dopamine neurons are activated by primary rewards occurring at unpredicted moments before and during learning (Schultz *et al.*, 1997a). They report the outcome of previous behaviour and the sudden satisfaction of an intention. This may lead to an immediate focusing of behaviour and a longer term learning effect. Dopamine neurons are also activated by reward-predicting stimuli. With this response, they predict the outcome of future behaviour and signal the condition of satisfaction of intentions directed at that goal. The dopamine input to the striatum and frontal cortex could serve in this way as a dynamic modulator or selector of intention-related activity.

Neuronal Correlates For Goal-Directed Behaviour

Rewards have three different basic functions. In their first function, rewards elicit approach and consummatory behaviour. This is due to the objects being labeled with appetitive value through innate mechanisms or, in most cases, following learning. In their second function, rewards increase the frequency and intensity of behaviour leading to such objects (learning), and they maintain learned behaviour by preventing extinction. Rewards serve as 'positive reinforcers' of behaviour in classical and instrumental conditioning procedures. In general 'incentive' learning, environmental stimuli acquire appetitive values following classically conditioned stimulus-reward associations and induce approach behaviour (Bindra, 1968). In instrumental conditioning, rewards 'reinforce' behaviours by strengthening associations between stimuli and behavioural responses (Law of Effect: Thorndike, 1911). This is the essence of 'coming back for more' and is related to the common notion of rewards being obtained for having done something good. In an instrumental form of incentive learning, rewards are 'incentives' and serve as goals of behaviour following associations between behavioural responses and outcomes (Dickinson and Balleine, 1994). In their third function, rewards induce subjective feelings of pleasure (hedonia) and positive emotional states. Aversive stimuli function in opposite directions. They induce innate withdrawal responses, and increase and maintain avoidance behaviour upon repeated presentation (negative reinforcement), thereby reducing the impact of damaging events. Furthermore, they induce internal emotional states of anger, fear and panic. Taken together, rewards subserve several functions and among them constitute goals of voluntary behaviour, usually as a consequence of associations with environmental stimuli and actions.

At least two requirements need to be fulfilled in order to call behavioural actions 'goal-directed' (Dickinson and Balleine, 1994). First, subjects should perform behavioural actions with the knowledge about a close relationship between the action and the outcome of the action. This knowledge may comprise the belief that a particular action will lead to a particular outcome, involving the explicit expectation that the outcome will occur as a consequence of the behavioural action. In animal learning theory (Dickinson, 1980), the association between behavioural action and outcome constitutes the basis for an instrumental form of incentive learning, according to which the outcome provides the incentive for the behavioural action. Thus, actions will be knowingly linked with particular outcomes. The second requirement concerns the representation of the outcome at the time of the action. Subjects perform an action, knowing at this moment that the particular outcome will be obtained should the action succeed. With both requirements fulfilled, subjects will be able to perform particular actions *in order to* obtain particular outcomes.

This description of goal-directed behaviour suggests that actions are linked to goals on the basis of representations involving logical inferences. Although it appears difficult to imagine that the activity of single neurons provides correlates for this level of cognitive operation, some of the described neurophysiological data seem to point in this direction. In particular, neuronal activity in the striatum precedes reward delivery during several seconds, apparently reflecting the expectation of reward. This suggests that neurons have access to representations of this important behavioural event. This neuronal 'knowledge' has been obtained through the experience of the subject in the particular task situation with its contingencies and temporal sequence of events. The task stimuli would evoke the representations of the reward before the reward actually occurs. Such brain activity would allow the subject to perform an action with the knowledge of the outcome present during the action. An even stronger case for neuronal correlates of goal-directed behaviour exists in the form of reward-dependent activity in striatal neurons. These neurons are activated during the preparation and execution of movements only in trials in which reward is predicted at the end of the trial, as opposed to auditory reinforcement. The expectation of the outcome appeared to be present at the time the neurons were engaged in the preparation and execution of the behaviour leading to the outcome. Taken together, these data suggest that neurons in the striatum code basic components for the control of goal-directed behaviour.

Acknowledgements

The experiments were conducted together with P. Apicella, J. R. Hollerman, T. Ljungberg, R. Romo and L. Tremblay. The work was supported by the Swiss National Science Foundation, the Fyssen Foundation (Paris), the Fondation pour la Recherche Médicale (Paris), the Roche Research Foundation (Basel), the National Institutes of Mental Health (Bethesda) and the Fonds pour la Recherche Scientifique du Quebec (FRSG).

References

Alexander, G.E., DeLong, M.R. and Strick, P.L. (1986), 'Parallel organization of functionally segregated circuits linking basal ganglia and cortex', *Ann. Rev. Neurosci.*, **9**, pp. 357–81.

Alexander, G.E. and Crutcher, M.D. (1990), 'Preparation for movement: Neural representations of intended direction in three motor areas of the monkey', *J. Neurophysiol.*, **64**, pp. 133–50.

Apicella, P., Ljungberg, T., Scarnati, E. and Schultz, W. (1991), 'Responses to reward in monkey dorsal and ventral striatum', *Exp. Brain Res.*, **85**, pp. 491–500.

Apicella, P., Scarnati, E., Ljungberg, T. and Schultz, W. (1992), 'Neuronal activity in monkey striatum related to the expectation of predictable environmental events', *J. Neurophysiol.*, **68**, pp. 945–60.

Bindra, D. (1968), 'Neuropsychological interpretation of the effects of drive and incentive-motivation on general activity and instrumental behaviour', *Psychol. Rev.*, **75**, pp. 1–22.

Crutcher, M.D. and DeLong, M.R. (1984), 'Single cell studies of the primate putamen. I. Functional organization', *Exp. Brain Res.*, **53**, pp. 233–43.

Dickinson, A. (1980), *Contemporary Animal Learning Theory* (Cambridge: Cambridge University Press).

Dickinson, A. and Balleine, B. (1994), 'Motivational control of goal-directed action', *Animal Learning and Behaviour*, **22**, pp. 1–18.

Fibiger, H.C. and Phillips, A.G. (1986), 'Reward, motivation, cognition: psychobiology of mesotelencephalic dopamine systems', in *Handbook of Physiology —The Nervous System IV*, ed. F.E. Bloom (Baltimore, MA: Williams and Wilkins).

Flaherty, A.W. and Graybiel, A. (1994), 'Input-output organization of the sensorimotor striatum in the squirrel monkey', *J. Neurosci.*, **14**, pp. 599–610.

Haber, S., Kunishio, K., Mizobuchi, M. and Lynd-Balta, E. (1995), 'The orbital and medial prefrontal circuit through the primate basal ganglia', *J. Neurosci.*, **15**, pp. 4851–67.

Heyes, C. and Dickinson, A. (1990), 'The intentionality of animal action', *Mind and Language*, **5**, pp. 105–20.

Hikosaka, O., Sakamoto, M. and Usui, S. (1989a), 'Functional properties of monkey caudate neurons. I. Activities related to saccadic eye movements', *J. Neurophysiol.*, **61**, pp. 780–98.

Hikosaka, O., Sakamoto, M. and Usui, S. (1989b), 'Functional properties of monkey caudate neurons. III. Activities related to expectation of target and reward', *J. Neurophysiol.*, **61**, pp. 814–32.

Hollerman, J.R., Tremblay, L. and Schultz, W. (1994), 'Reward dependency of several types of neuronal activity in primate striatum', *Soc. Neurosci. Abstr.*, **20**, p. 780.

Libet, B., Gleason, C.A., Wright, E.W. and Pearl, D.K. (1983), 'Time of conscious intention to act in relation to onset of cerebral activities (readiness-potential): The unconscious initiation of a freely voluntary act', *Brain*, **106**, pp. 623–42.

Logothetis, N.K. and Schall, J.D. (1989), 'Neuronal correlates of subjective visual perception', *Science*, **245**, pp. 761–3.

Newsome, W.T., Britten, K.H. and Movshon, J.A. (1989), 'Neuronal correlates of a perceptual decision', *Nature*, **341**, pp. 52–4.

Okano, K. and Tanji, J. (1987), 'Neuronal activities in the primate motor fields of the agranular frontal cortex preceding visually triggered and self-paced movement', *Exp. Brain Res.*, **66**, pp. 155–66.

Robbins, T.W. and Everitt, B.J. (1996), 'Neurobehavioural mechanisms of reward and motivation', *Cur. Op. Neurobiol.*, **6**, pp. 228–36.

Romo, R. and Schultz, W. (1987), 'Neuronal activity preceding self-initiated or externally timed arm movements in area 6 of monkey cortex', *Exp. Brain Res.*, **67**, pp. 656–62.

Romo, R. and Schultz, W. (1990), 'Dopamine neurons of the monkey midbrain: Contingencies of responses to active touch during self-initiated arm movements', *J. Neurophysiol.*, **63**, pp. 592–606.

Romo, R. and Schultz, W. (1992), 'Role of primate basal ganglia and frontal cortex in the internal generation of movements. III. Neuronal activity in the supplementary motor area', *Exp. Brain Res.*, **91**, pp. 396–407.

Russchen, F.T., Bakst, I., Amaral, D.G. and Price, J.L. (1985), 'The amygdalostriatal projections in the monkey. An anterograde tracing study', *Brain Res.*, **329**, pp. 241–57.

Schlag, J. and Schlag-Rey, M. (1987), 'Evidence for a supplementary eye field', *J. Neurophysiol.*, **57**, pp. 179–200.

Schultz, W. (1982), 'Depletion of dopamine in the striatum as experimental model of Parkinsonism: Direct effects and adaptive mechanisms', *Prog. Neurobiol.*, **18**, pp. 121–66.

Schultz, W. (1988), 'MPTP-induced Parkinsonism in monkeys: Mechanism of action, selectivity and pathophysiology', *Gen. Pharmacol.*, **19**, pp. 153–61.

Schultz, W. (1995), 'The primate basal ganglia between the intention and outcome of action', in *Functional Linkages Between the Cerebral Cortex and Basal Ganglia In the Functional Control Of Movement*, ed. M. Kimura and A.M. Graybiel (Tokyo: Springer).

Schultz, W., Apicella, P., Romo, R. and Scarnati, E. (1995), 'Context-dependent activity in primate striatum reflecting past and future behavioural events', in *Models Of Information Processing In the Basal Ganglia*, ed. J.C. Houk, J.L. Davis and D.G. Beiser (Cambridge, MA: MIT Press).

Schultz, W., Apicella, P., Scarnati, E. and Ljungberg, T. (1992), 'Neuronal activity in monkey ventral striatum related to the expectation of reward', *J. Neurosci.*, **12**, pp. 4595–610.

Schultz, W., Dayan, P. and Montague, R.R. (1997a), 'A neural substrate of prediction and reward', *Science*, **275**, pp. 1593–9.

Schultz, W. and Romo, R. (1992), 'Role of primate basal ganglia and frontal cortex in the internal generation of movements. I. Comparison with instruction-induced preparatory activity in striatal neurons', *Exp. Brain Res.*, **91**, pp. 363–84.

Schultz, W., Romo, R., Scarnati, E., Sundström, E., Jonsson, G. and Studer, A. (1989), 'Saccadic reaction times, eye-arm co-ordination and spontaneous eye movements in normal and MPTP-treated monkeys', *Exp. Brain Res.*, **78**, pp. 253–67.

Schultz, W., Tremblay, L., Hollerman, J.R. and Mirenowicz, J. (1997b), 'Delayed responding and reward signals: Neurons coding component processes of goal-directed behaviour in primate basal ganglia and orbitofrontal cortex', in *The Association Cortex — Structure and Function*, ed. H. Sakata, A. Mikami, J.M. Fuster (Amsterdam: Harwood).

Searle, J.R. (1983), *Intentionality* (Cambridge: Cambridge University Press).

Selemon, L.D. and Goldman-Rakic, P.S. (1985), 'Longitudinal topography and interdigitation of corticostriatal projections in the rhesus monkey', *J. Neurosci.*, **5**, pp. 776–94.

Terrace, H.(1985), 'Animal cognition: thinking without language', *Phil. Trans. Roy. Soc. B*, **308**, pp. 113–28.

Thorndike, E.L. (1911), *Animal Intelligence: Experimental Studies* (New York: MacMillan).

Von der Heydt, R., Peterhans, E. and Baumgartner, G. (1984), 'Illusory contours and cortical neuron responses', *Science*, **224**, pp. 1260–2.

Benjamin Libet

Do We Have Free Will?

*I have taken an experimental approach to this question. Freely voluntary acts are preceded by a specific electrical change in the brain (the 'readiness potential', RP) that begins 550 ms before the act. Human subjects became aware of intention to act 350–400 ms **after** RP starts, but 200 ms. before the motor act. The volitional process is therefore **initiated** unconsciously. But the conscious function could still control the outcome; it can veto the act. Free will is therefore not excluded. These findings put constraints on views of how free will may operate; it would not initiate a voluntary act but it could **control** performance of the act. The findings also affect views of guilt and responsibility.*

But the deeper question still remains: Are freely voluntary acts subject to macro-deterministic laws or can they appear without such constraints, non-determined by natural laws and 'truly free'? I shall present an experimentalist view about these fundamental philosophical opposites.

The question of free will goes to the root of our views about human nature and how we relate to the universe and to natural laws. Are we completely defined by the deterministic nature of physical laws? Theologically imposed fateful destiny ironically produces a similar end-effect. In either case, we would be essentially sophisticated automatons, with our conscious feelings and intentions tacked on as epiphenomena with no causal power. Or, do we have some independence in making choices and actions, not completely determined by the known physical laws?

I have taken an experimental approach to at least some aspects of the question. The operational definition of free will in these experiments was in accord with common views. First, there should be no external control or cues to affect the occurrence or emergence of the voluntary act under study; i.e. it should be endogenous. Secondly, the subject should feel that he/she wanted to do it, on her/his own initiative, and feel he could control what is being done, when to do it or not to do it. Many actions lack this second attribute. For example, when the primary motor area of the cerebral cortex is stimulated, muscle contractions can be produced in certain sites in the body. However, the subject (a neurosurgical patient) reports that these actions were imposed by the stimulator, i.e. that he did not will these acts. And there are numerous clinical disorders in which a similar discrepancy between actions and will occurs. These include

Journal of Consciousness Studies, **6**, No. 8–9, 1999, pp. 47–57

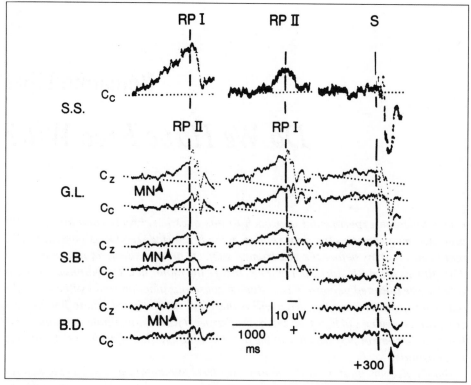

Figure 1

Readiness potentials (RP) preceding self-initiated voluntary acts. Each horizontal row is the computer-averaged potential for 40 trials, recorded by a DC system with an active electrode on the scalp, either at the midline-vertex (C_z) or on the left side (contralateral to the performing right hand) approximately over the motor/premotor cortical area that controls the hand (C_c).

When every self-initiated quick flexion of the right hand (fingers or wrist) in the series of 40 trials was (reported as having been) subjectively experienced to originate spontaneously and with no pre-planning by the subject, RPs labelled type II were found in association. (Arrowheads labelled MN indicate onset of the 'main negative' phase of the vertex recorded type II RPs in this figure; see Libet *et al.* 1982. Onsets were also measured for 90% of the total area of RP). When an awareness of a general intention or preplanning to act some time within the next second or so was reported to have occurred before some of the 40 acts in the series, type I RPs were recorded (Libet *et al.*, 1982). In the last column, labelled S, a near-threshold skin stimulus was applied in each of the 40 trials at a ran-domized time unknown to the subject, with no motor act performed; the subject was asked to recall and report the time when he became aware of each stimulus in the same way he reported the time of awareness of wanting to move in the case of self-initiated motor acts.

The solid vertical line through each column represents 0 time, at which the electromyogram (EMG) of the activated muscle begins in the case of RP series, or at which the stimulus was actually delivered in the case of S series. The dashed horizontal line represents the DC baseline drift.

For subject S.S., the first RP (type I) was recorded before the instruction 'to let the urge come on its own, spontaneously' was introduced; the second RP (type II) was obtained after giving this instruction in the same session as the first. For subjects G.L., S.B. and B.D., this instruction was given at the start of all sessions. Nevertheless, each of these subjects reported some experiences of loose preplanning in some of the 40-trial series; those series exhibited type I RPs rather than type II. Note that the slow negative shift in scalp potential that precedes EMGs of self-initiated acts (RP) does not precede the skin stimulus in S series. However, evoked potentials following the stimulus are seen regularly to exhibit a large positive component with a peak close to +300 ms. (arrow indicates this time); this P300 event-related potential had been shown by others to be associated with decisions about uncertain events (in this case, the time of the randomly delivered stimulus), and it also indicates that the subject is attending well to the experimental conditions.

the involuntary actions in cerebral palsy, Parkinsonism, Huntington's chorea, Tourette's syndrome and even obsessive compulsions to act. A striking example is the 'alien hand syndrome'. Patients with a lesion in a fronto-medial portion of premotor area may find that the hand and arm on the affected side performs curious purposeful actions, such as undoing a buttoned shirt when the subject is trying to button it up; all this occurs without or even against the subject's intention and will. (Cf. Spence & Frith, 1999, p. 23.)

Timing of Brain Processes and Conscious Will

Performance of 'self-paced' voluntary acts had, surprisingly, been found to be preceded by a slow electrical change recordable on the scalp at the vertex (Kornhuber & Deecke, 1965). The onset of this electrical indication of certain brain activities preceded the actual movement by up to 1 sec or more. It was termed the 'Bereitschaftpotential' or 'readiness potential' (RP). To obtain the RP required averaging the recordings in many self-paced acts. Subjects were therefore asked to perform their acts within time intervals of 30 sec. to make the total study manageable. In our experiments, however, we removed this constraint on freedom of action; subjects performed a simple flick or flexion of the wrist at any time they felt the urge or wish to do so. These voluntary acts were to be performed capriciously, free of any external limitations or restrictions (Libet *et al.*, 1982). RPs in these acts began with onsets averaging 550 msec. before activation of the involved muscle (fig. 1).

The brain was evidently beginning the volitional process in this voluntary act well before the activation of the muscle that produced the movement. My question then became: *when* does the *conscious* wish or intention (to perform the act) appear? In the traditional view of conscious will and free will, one would expect conscious will to appear before, or at the onset, of the RP, and thus command the brain to perform the intended act. But an appearance of conscious will 550 msec. or more before the act seemed intuitively unlikely. It was clearly important to establish the time of the conscious will relative to the onset of the brain process (RP); if conscious will were to *follow* the onset of RP, that would have a fundamental impact on how we could view free will.

To establish this temporal relation required a method for measuring the time of appearance of the conscious will in each such act. Initially, that seemed to me an impossible goal. But after some time it occurred to me to try having the subject report a 'clock-time' at which he/she was *first aware* of the wish or urge to act (fig. 2) (Libet *et al.*, 1983a). The clock had to be much faster than the usual clock, in order to accommodate time differences in the hundreds of msec. For our clock, the spot of light of a cathode ray oscilloscope was made to revolve around the face of the scope like the sweep-second hand of an ordinary clock, but at a speed approximately 25 times as fast. Each of the marked off 'seconds' around the periphery was thus equivalent to about 40 msec. When we tried out this method we were actually surprised to find that each subject reported times for *first awareness of wish to act* (W) with a reliability of 20 msec., for each group of 40 such trials. A test for the accuracy of such reports was also encouraging. In this, the subject remained relaxed and did *not* perform any voluntary act. Instead, a weak electrical stimulus was delivered to the skin of the same hand. The stimulus was applied at random times in the different trials. The experi-

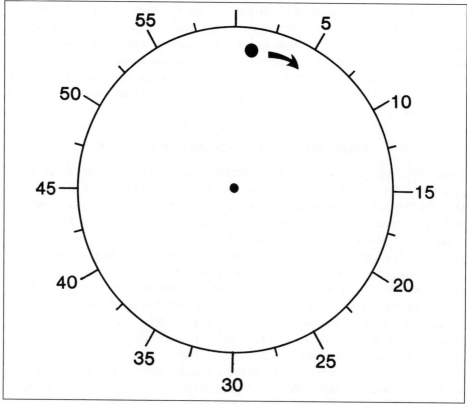

Figure 2
Oscilloscope 'clock'. Spot of light revolves around periphery of screen, once in 2.56 sec. (instead of 60 sec. for a sweep-second hand of a regular clock). Each marked off 'second' (in the total of 60 markings) represents 43 msec. of actual time here. The subject holds his gaze to the centre of the screen. For each performed quick flexion of the wrist, at any freely chosen time, the subject was asked to note the position of the clock spot when he/she first became aware of the wish or intention to act. This associated clock time is reported by the subject later, after the trial is completed.

mental observers knew the actual time for each stimulus. The subject did not know this actual time but was asked to report the clock-time at which he felt each such stimulus. Subjects accomplished this with an error of only –50 msec.

The experiment

In the actual experiment, then, each RP was obtained from an averaged electrical recording in 40 trials. In each of these trials the subject performed the sudden flick of the wrist whenever he/she freely wanted to do so. After each of these trials, the subject reported W, the clock-time associated with the first awareness of the wish to move (Libet *et al.*, 1983a).

Brain initiates voluntary act unconsciously

The results of many such groups of trials are diagrammed in fig. 3. For groups in which all the voluntary acts were freely spontaneous, with no reports of rough pre-planning of when to act, the onset of RP averaged –550 msec. (before the muscle was activated). The W times for first awareness of wish to act averaged about –200 msec.,

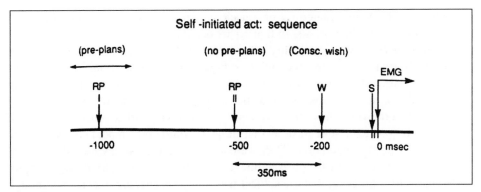

Figure 3
Diagram of sequence of events, cerebral and subjective, that precede a fully self-initiated voluntary act. Relative to 0 time, detected in the electromyogram (EMG) of the suddenly activated muscle, the readiness potential (RP)(an indicator of related cerebral neuronal activities) begins first, at about −1050 ms. when some pre-planning is reported (RP I) or about −550 ms. with spontaneous acts lacking immediate pre planning (RP II). Subjective awareness of the wish to move (W) appears at about −200 ms., some 350 ms. after onset even of RP II; however, W does appear well before the act (EMG). Subjective timings reported for awareness of the randomly delivered S (skin) stimulus average about −50 ms. relative to actual delivery time. (From Libet, 1989.)

for all groups. This value was the same even when subjects reported having pre-planned roughly when to act! If we correct W for the −50 msec. error in the subjects' reports of timings of the skin stimuli, we have an average corrected W of about −150 msec. Clearly, the brain process (RP) to prepare for this voluntary act began about 400 msec. before the appearance of the conscious will to act (W). This relationship was true for every group of 40 trials and in every one of the nine subjects studied. It should also be noted that the actual difference in times is probably greater than the 400 msec; the actual initiating process in the brain probably starts before our recorded RP, in an unknown area that then activates the supplementary motor area in the cerebral cortex. The supplementary motor area is located in the midline near the vertex and is thought to be the source of our recorded RP.

Any Role for Conscious Will?

The initiation of the freely voluntary act appears to begin in the brain unconsciously, well before the person consciously knows he wants to act! Is there, then, any role for conscious will in the performance of a voluntary act? (see Libet, 1985). To answer this it must be recognized that conscious will (W) does appear about 150 msec. before the muscle is activated, even though it follows onset of the RP. An interval of 150 msec. would allow enough time in which the conscious function might affect the final outcome of the volitional process. (Actually, only 100 msec. is available for any such effect. The final 50 msec. before the muscle is activated is the time for the primary motor cortex to activate the spinal motor nerve cells. During this time the act goes to completion with no possibility of stopping it by the rest of the cerebral cortex.)

Potentially available to the conscious function is the possibility of stopping or vetoing the final progress of the volitional process, so that no actual muscle action ensues. *Conscious-will could thus affect the outcome* of the volitional process even though the latter was initiated by unconscious cerebral processes. Conscious-will might block or veto the process, so that no act occurs.

The existence of a veto possibility is not in doubt. The subjects in our experiments at times reported that a conscious wish or urge to act appeared but that they suppressed or vetoed that. In the absence of the muscle's electrical signal when being activated, there was no trigger to initiate the computer's recording of any RP that may have preceded the veto; thus, there were no *recorded* RPs with a vetoed intention to act. We were, however, able to show that subjects could veto an act planned for performance at a pre-arranged time. They were able to exert the veto within the interval of 100 to 200 msec. before the pre-set time to act (Libet *et al.*, 1983b). A large RP preceded the veto, signifying that the subject was indeed *preparing* to act, even though the action was aborted by the subject. All of us, not just experimental subjects, have experienced our vetoing a spontaneous urge to perform some act. This often occurs when the urge to act involves some socially unacceptable consequence, like an urge to shout some obscenity at the professor. (Incidentally, in the disorder called Tourette's syndrome, subjects do spontaneously shout obscenities. These acts should not be regarded as freely voluntary. No RP appears before such an act. A quick reaction to an unwarned stimulus also lacks a preceding RP, and it is not a freely voluntary act.)

Another hypothetical function for conscious will could be to serve as a 'trigger' that is required to enable the volitional process to proceed to final action. However, there is no evidence for this, such as there is for a veto function, and the 'trigger' possibility also seems unlikely on other grounds. For example, voluntary acts that become somewhat 'automatic' can be performed with no reportable conscious wish to do so; the RP is rather minimal in amplitude and duration before such automatic acts. Automatic acts clearly go to completion without any conscious trigger available.

Does the conscious veto have a preceding unconscious origin?

One should, at this point, consider the possibility that the conscious veto itself may have its origin in preceding unconscious processes, just as is the case for the development and appearance of the conscious will. If the veto itself were to be initiated and developed unconsciously, the choice to veto would then become an unconscious choice of which we *become* conscious, rather than a consciously causal event. Our own previous evidence had shown that the brain 'produces' an awareness of something only after about a 0.5 sec. period of appropriate neuronal activations (see reviews by Libet, 1993; 1996).

Some have proposed that even an unconscious initiation of a veto choice would nevertheless be a genuine choice made by the individual and could still be viewed as a free will process (e.g. Velmans, 1991). I find such a proposed view of free will to be unacceptable. In such a view, the individual would not consciously control his actions; he would only become aware of an unconsciously initiated choice. He would have no direct conscious control over the nature of any preceding unconscious processes. But, a free will process implies one could be held consciously responsible for one's choice to act or not to act. We do not hold people responsible for actions performed unconsciously, without the possibility of conscious control. For example, actions by a person during a psychomotor epileptic seizure, or by one with Tourette's syndrome, etc., are not regarded as actions of free will. Why then should an act unconsciously developed by a normal individual, a process over which he also has no conscious control, be regarded as an act of free will?

I propose, instead, that the conscious veto may *not* require or be the direct result of preceding unconscious processes. The conscious veto is a *control* function, different from simply becoming aware of the wish to act. There is no logical imperative in any mind–brain theory, even identity theory, that requires specific neural activity to precede and determine the nature of a conscious control function. And, there is no experimental evidence against the possibility that the control process may appear without development by prior unconscious processes.

Admittedly, to be conscious of the decision to veto does mean one is aware of the event. How may one reconcile this with my proposal? Perhaps we should re-visit the concept of awareness, its relation to the content of awareness, and the cerebral processes that develop both awareness and its contents. Our own previous studies have indicated that *awareness* is a unique phenomenon in itself, distinguished from the contents of which one may become aware. For example, awareness of a sensory stimulus can require similar durations of stimulus trains for somatosensory cortex and for medial lemniscus. But the *content* of those awarenesses in these two cases is different, in the subjective timings of sensations (Libet *et al.*, 1979). The content of an unconscious mental process (e.g. correct detection of a signal in the brain *without any awareness* of the signal) may be the same as the content *with awareness* of the signal. But to become aware of that same content required that stimulus duration be increased by about 400 msec. (see Libet *et al.*, 1991).

In an endogenous, freely voluntary act, awareness of the intention to act is delayed for about 400 msec. after brain processes initiate the process unconsciously (Libet *et al.*, 1983a; Libet, 1985). Awareness developed here may be thought of as applying to the whole volitional process; that would include the content of the conscious urge to act and the content of factors that may affect a conscious veto. One need not think of awareness of an event as restricted to one detailed item of content in the whole event.

The possibility is not excluded that factors, on which the decision to veto (control) is *based*, do develop by unconscious processes that precede the veto. However, the *conscious decision to veto* could still be made without direct specification for that decision by the preceding unconscious processes. That is, one could consciously accept or reject the programme offered up by the whole array of preceding brain processes. The *awareness* of the decision to veto could be thought to require preceding unconscious processes, but the *content* of that awareness (the actual decision to veto) is a separate feature that need not have the same requirement.

What Significance Do Our Findings Have for Voluntary Acts In General?

Can we assume that voluntary acts other than the simple one studied by us also have the same temporal relations between unconscious brain processes and the appearance of the conscious wish/will to act? It is common in scientific researches to be limited technically to studying a process in a simple system; and then to find that the fundamental behaviour discovered with the simple system does indeed represent a phenomenon that appears or governs in other related and more complicated systems. For example, the charge on a single electron was measured by Milliken in one isolated system, but it is valid for electrons in all systems. It should also be noted that RPs have been found by other investigators to precede other more complex volitional acts, such as beginning to speak or to write; they did not, however, study the time of appearance of the conscious wish to begin such acts. We may, therefore, allow ourselves to consider what general implications may follow from our experimental findings, while recognizing that an extrapolation to encompass voluntary acts in general has been adopted.

We should also distinguish between *deliberations* about what choice of action to adopt (including pre-planning of when to act on such a choice) and the final intention actually 'to act now'. One may, after all, deliberate all day about a choice but never act; there is *no voluntary act* in that case. In our experimental studies we found that in some trials subjects engaged in some conscious pre-planning of roughly when to act (in the next second or so). But even in those cases, the subjects reported times of the conscious wish to actually act to be about −200 msec.; this value was very close to the values reported for fully spontaneous voluntary acts with no pre-planning. The onset of the unconscious brain process (RP) for preparing to act was well before the final conscious intention 'to act now' in all cases. These findings indicated that the sequence of the volitional processes 'to act now' may apply to all volitional acts, regardless of their spontaneity or prior history of conscious deliberations.

Ethical Implications of How Free Will Operates

The role of conscious free will would be, then, not to initiate a voluntary act, but rather to *control* whether the act takes place. We may view the unconscious initiatives for voluntary actions as 'bubbling up' in the brain. The conscious-will then selects which of these initiatives may go forward to an action or which ones to veto and abort, with no act appearing.

This kind of role for free will is actually in accord with religious and ethical strictures. These commonly advocate that you 'control yourself'. Most of the Ten Commandments are 'do not' orders.

How do our findings relate to the questions of when one may be regarded as guilty or sinful, in various religious and philosophical systems. If one experiences a conscious wish or urge to perform a socially unacceptable act, should that be regarded as a sinful event even if the urge has been vetoed and no act has occurred? Some religious systems answer 'yes'. President Jimmy Carter admitted to having had urges to perform a lustful act. Although he did not act, he apparently still felt sinful for having experienced a lustful urge.[1] But any such urges would be initiated and developed in the brain unconsciously, according to our findings. The mere appearance of an intention to act could not be controlled consciously; only its final consummation in a motor act could be consciously controlled. Therefore, a religious system that castigates an individual for simply having a mental intention or impulse to do something unacceptable, even when this is not acted out, would create a physiologically insurmountable moral and psychological difficulty.

---

[1] President Carter was drawing on a Christian tradition deriving from the following two verses in the 'Sermon on the Mount': '[Jesus said], "Ye have heard that it was said by them of old time, Thou shalt not commit adultery: But I say unto you, That whosoever looketh on a woman to lust after her hath committed adultery with her already in his heart"' (*Matthew*, 5.27–8).

Indeed, insistence on regarding an unacceptable urge to act as sinful, even when no act ensues, would make virtually all individuals sinners. In that sense such a view could provide a physiological basis for 'original sin'! Of course, the concept of 'original sin' can be based on other views of what is regarded as sinful.

Ethical systems deal with moral codes or conventions that govern how one behaves toward or interacts with other individuals; they are presumably dealing with actions, not simply with urges or intentions. Only a motor act by one person can directly impinge on the welfare of another. Since it is the performance of an act that can be consciously controlled, it should be legitimate to hold individuals guilty of and responsible for their acts.

Determinism and Free Will

There remains a deeper question about free will that the foregoing considerations have not addressed. What we have achieved experimentally is some knowledge of how free will may operate. But we have not answered the question of whether our consciously willed acts are fully determined by natural laws that govern the activities of nerve cells in the brain, or whether acts and the conscious decisions to perform them can proceed to some degree independently of natural determinism. The first of these options would make free will illusory. The conscious feeling of exerting one's will would then be regarded as an epiphenomenon, simply a by-product of the brain's activities but with no causal powers of its own.

First, it may be pointed out that free choices or acts are *not predictable*, even if they should be completely determined. The 'uncertainty principle' of Heisenberg precludes our having a complete knowledge of the underlying molecular activities. Quantum mechanics forces us to deal with probabilities rather than with certainties of events. And, in chaos theory, a random event may shift the behaviour of a whole system, in a way that was not predictable. However, even if events are not predictable in practice, they might nevertheless be in accord with natural laws and therefore determined.

Let us re-phrase our basic question as follows: *Must* we accept determinism? Is non-determinism a viable option? We should recognize that both of these alternative views (natural law determinism vs. non-determinism) are unproven theories, i.e. unproven in relation to the existence of free will. Determinism has on the whole, worked well for the physical observable world. That has led many scientists and philosophers to regard any deviation from determinism as absurd and witless, and unworthy of consideration. But there has been no evidence, or even a proposed experimental test design, that definitively or convincingly demonstrates the validity of natural law determinism as the mediator or instrument of free will.

There is an unexplained gap between the category of physical phenomena and the category of subjective phenomena. As far back as Leibniz it was pointed out that if one looked into the brain with a full knowledge of its physical makeup and nerve cell activities, one would see nothing that describes subjective experience. The whole foundation of our own experimental studies of the physiology of conscious experience (beginning in the late 1950s) was that externally observable and manipulable brain processes and the related reportable subjective introspective experiences must be studied simultaneously, as independent categories, to understand their relationship. The assumption that a deterministic nature of the physically observable world (to the extent that may be true) can account for subjective conscious functions and events is a speculative *belief*, not a scientifically proven proposition.

Non-determinism, the view that conscious-will may, at times, exert effects not in accord with known physical laws, is of course also a non-proven speculative belief. The view that conscious will can affect brain function in violation of known physical laws, takes two forms. In one it is held that the violations are not detectable, because the actions of the mind may be at a level below that of the uncertainty allowed by quantum mechanics. (Whether this last proviso can in fact be tenable is a matter yet to be resolved). This view would thus allow for a non-deterministic free will without a perceptible violation of physical laws. In a second view it may be held that violations of known physical laws are large enough to be detectable, at least in principle. But, it can be argued, detectability in actual practice may be impossible. That difficulty for detection would be especially true if the conscious will is able to exert its influence by minimal actions at relatively few nerve elements; these actions could serve as triggers for amplified nerve cell patterns of activity in the brain. In any case, we do not have a scientific answer to the question of which theory (determinism or non-determinism) may describe the nature of free will.

However, we must recognize that the almost universal experience that we can act with a free, independent choice provides a kind of *prima facie* evidence that conscious mental processes can causatively control some brain processes (Libet, 1994). As an experimental scientist, this creates more difficulty for a determinist than for a non-determinist option. The phenomenal fact is that most of us feel that we do have free will, at least for some of our actions and within certain limits that may be imposed by our brain's status and by our environment. The intuitive feelings about the phenomenon of free will form a fundamental basis for views of our human nature, and great care should be taken not to believe allegedly scientific conclusions about them which actually depend upon hidden *ad hoc* assumptions. A theory that simply interprets the phenomenon of free will as illusory and denies the validity of this phenomenal fact is less attractive than a theory that accepts or accommodates the phenomenal fact.

In an issue so fundamentally important to our view of who we are, a claim for illusory nature should be based on fairly direct evidence. Such evidence is not available; nor do determinists propose even a potential experimental design to test the theory. Actually, I myself proposed an experimental design that could test whether conscious will could influence nerve cell activities in the brain, doing so via a putative 'conscious mental field' that could act without any neuronal connections as the mediators (Libet, 1994). This difficult though feasible experiment has, unfortunately, still to be carried out. If it should turn out to confirm the prediction of that field theory, there would be a radical transformation in our views of mind–brain interaction.

My conclusion about free will, one genuinely free in the non-determined sense, is then that its existence is at least as good, if not a better, scientific option than is its denial by determinist theory. Given the speculative nature of both determinist and non-determinist theories, why not adopt the view that we do have free will (until some real contradictory evidence may appear, if it ever does). Such a view would at least allow us to proceed in a way that accepts and accommodates our own deep feeling that we do have free will. We would not need to view ourselves as machines that act in a manner completely controlled by the known physical laws. Such a permissive option has also been advocated by the neurobiologist Roger Sperry (see Doty, 1998).[2]

I close, then, with a quotation from the great novelist Isaac Bashevis Singer that relates to the foregoing views. Singer stated his strong belief in our having free will. In an interview (Singer, 1968) he volunteered that 'The greatest gift which humanity has received is free choice. It is true that we are limited in our use of free choice. But the little free choice we have is such a great gift and is potentially worth so much that for this itself life is worthwhile living'.

References

Doty, R.W. (1998) 'Five mysteries of the mind, and their consequences', in: *Views of the Brain-A Tribute to Roger W. Sperry*, ed. A. Puente (Washington, DC: American Psych. Assoc. ; in press).

Kornhuber, H., Deecke, L. (1965), 'Hirnpotentialanderungen bei Willkurbewegungen und passiven Bewegungen des Menschen: Bereitschaftspotential und reafferente Potentiale', *Pfluegers Arch Gesamte Physiol Menschen Tiere*, **284**, pp. 1–17.

Libet, B. (1985), 'Unconscious cerebral initiative and the role of conscious will in voluntary action', *Behav. and Brain Sciences,* **8**, pp. 529–66.

Libet, B. (1989), 'Conscious subjective experience vs. unconscious mental functions: A theory of the cerebral processes involved', in *Models of Brain Function*, ed. R.M.J. Cotterill (New York: Cambridge University Press).

Libet, B. (1993), 'The neural time factor in conscious and unconscious mental events', in Ciba Foundation Symposium #174, *Experimental and Theoretical Studies of Consciousness* (Chichester: Wiley).

Libet, B. (1994), 'A testable field theory of mind-brain interaction', *JCS*, **1** (1), pp. 119–26.

Libet, B. (1996), 'Neural time factors in Conscious and Unconscious Mental Function', in *Toward a Science of Consciousness*, ed. S.R. Hameroff, A. Kaszniak, A. Scott (Cambridge, MA: MIT Press).

Libet, B., Gleason, C.A., Wright, E.W. and Pearl, D.K. (1983a), 'Time of conscious intention to act in relation to onset of cerebral activity (readiness potential): The unconscious initiation of a freely voluntary act', *Brain*, **106**, pp. 623–42.

Libet, B., Wright, E.W. and Gleason, C.A. (1983b), 'Preparation — or intention-to-act, in relation to pre-event potentials recorded at the vertex', *Electroenceph. & Clin. Neurophysiology*, **56**, pp. 367–72.

Libet, B., Pearl, D.K., Morledge, D.E., Gleason, C.A., Hosobuchi, Y., Barbaro, N.M. (1991), 'Control of the transition from sensory detection to sensory awareness in man by the duration of a thalamic stimulus. The cerebral time-on factor', *Brain*, **114**, 1731–57.

Libet, B., Wright, E.W., Jr., Feinstein, B., Pearl, D.K. (1979), 'Subjective referral of the timing for a conscious sensory experience: A functional role for the somatosensory specific projection system in man', *Brain*, **102**, pp. 191–222.

Libet, B., Wright, E.W. and Gleason, C.A. (1982), 'Readiness potentials preceding unrestricted spontaneous pre-planned voluntary acts', *Electroenceph. & Clin. Neurophysiology*, **54**, pp. 322–5.

Singer, I.B. (1968), Interview by H. Flender, in *Writers at Work* (1981), ed. G. Plimpton (New York:Penguin Books).

Spence, S.A. And Frith, C.D. (1999), 'Towards a functional anatomy of volition', *Journal of Consciousness Studies*, **6**, 8–9, pp. 11–29.

Velmans, M. (1991), 'Is human information processing conscious?', *Behavioral and Brain Sci.,* **3**, pp. 651–69.

---

[2] The belief by many people that one's fate is determined by some mystical reality or by divine intervention produces a difficult paradox for those who also believe we have free will and are to be held responsible for our actions. Such a paradox can arise in the Judeo-Christian view that (a) God is omnipotent, knows in advance what you are going to do and controls your fate, while (b) also strongly advocating that we can freely determine our actions and are accountable and responsible for our behaviour. This difficulty has led to some theological attempts to resolve the paradox. For example, the Kabbalists proposed that God voluntarily gave up his power to know what man was going to do, in order to allow man to choose freely and responsibly, and to possess free will.

Gilberto Gomes

Volition and the Readiness Potential

I: Introduction

The readiness potential was found to precede voluntary acts by about half a second or more (Kornhuber & Deecke, 1965). Kornhuber (1984) discussed the readiness potential in terms of volition, arguing that it is not the manifestation of an attentional processes. Libet discussed it in relation to consciousness and to free will (Libet *et al.*, 1983a,b; Libet, 1985; 1992; 1993). Libet asked the following questions: Are voluntary acts initiated by a conscious decision to act? Are the physiological facts compatible with the belief that free will determines our voluntary acts? What is the role of consciousness in voluntary action? In this paper I will discuss these questions and the answers that Libet gave to them.

Libet conducted experiments in which he tried to determine the timing of the conscious intention to act, in relation to the readiness potential and to the act itself (Libet *et al.*, 1983a,b). His results suggested that the conscious intention to act occurs *after* the beginning of the readiness potential and *before* the neural command that determines the muscular contraction. He also found that a conscious decision could abort the movement, even in the presence of the initial phases of the readiness potential. He concluded that voluntary acts are unconsciously initiated but are subject to conscious control. He proposed that a conscious mental field (that cannot be studied by physical means) causes neural events in the brain that either promote the culmination in action of the unconsciously initiated process or prevent its progress to action by a veto (Libet, 1993; 1994). So, free will does not initiate the neural process that leads to action but is able to control it.

I have elsewhere made an extensive critical analysis and reinterpretation of Libet's results, both on the timing of conscious sensations and on the timing of conscious intentions (Gomes, 1998b). But, as I will argue later in more detail, I believe we can agree with Libet's conclusion that voluntary acts are nonconsciously initiated. We can also agree that the process leading to action can often be aborted by a conscious veto. However, I will propose alternative views on the bearing of these experiments on free will, on the role of consciousness in voluntary action and on the concepts of conscious intention and conscious control themselves.

Journal of Consciousness Studies, **6**, No. 8–9, 1999, pp. 59–76

II: Voluntary Acts, Free Will and Causality

Voluntary acts may be defined as acts that are felt by the subject to have been determined by himself or herself and to have been caused by a conscious decision. This definition depends explicitly on the first-person perspective. From the third-person perspective, one can also regard an act by someone else as voluntary, based on its appearance. In this case, one believes the person in question will also have the feeling that he or she determined the act by a conscious decision. Suppose someone is undergoing brain surgery, in an awake state. He suddenly raises his arm. Someone who is looking on will probably take this to be a voluntary act, because raising one's arm usually is. But she asks the patient: 'Why did you raise your arm?', and he answers: 'I didn't. My arm moved by itself.' And in fact the movement has been caused by the surgeon's having applied an electrical stimulus on the patient's motor cortex.[1] The patient was not conscious of any decision by himself to perform the movement, so he does not experience it as a voluntary act.

A person's usual conception of his or her own voluntary acts seems to be in conflict with the idea that all events in the world are causally determined. According to classical physical theory, everything that happens is wholly determined by previous events. So, if one thinks one has done something because one has chosen to do so, one will not easily accept the idea that in fact this act was already completely determined before one's decision. The idea of choice itself implies that one could as well have chosen to do something different.

The evolution of physical theory has changed this deterministic view of the world. At the quantum level, events are now considered to be, up to a certain point, undetermined, that is, subject to probabilistic (and not strictly deterministic) laws. And, according to modern theories, a series of random events, at the microscopic level, can initiate a causal chain that produces an event that is observed at the macroscopic level. However, this change in physical theory brings no solution to the problem of causation of voluntary acts, as considered from the first-person perspective. The idea that one's voluntary acts are in fact determined by chance is no more akin to the intuition we have of our free actions than the idea that they are strictly determined by previous events. When I do something voluntarily, the impression I have is that I do it because I have chosen to do so for some reason, and this does not seem compatible with the idea that my action was the result of random fluctuations of quantum or other microscopic events in my brain. Reasons and choice seem as different from chance as from causes.

It is difficult, then, to reconcile our naturalistic view of the physical world with the idea that we ourselves, as voluntary agents, are part of this physical world. The dualist thesis is of course a solution to this dilemma. According to this view, purely physical events, including those of our bodies, are wholly determined by causes and chance, but our minds are not a part of the physical world. Mind is something of a completely different nature, and when the mind chooses to do something, this act of will is purely spontaneous, that is, it is not caused by anything else. The difficulty with the dualist position, however, is that it brings a whole series of other, unsolved and well-known

---

[1] The feeling that the movement had not been made by oneself was systematically reported by the patients studied by W. Penfield and others with electrical stimulation of the motor cortex (Penfield, 1975).

problems. In relation to voluntary actions, too, the dualist thesis has to face a specific problem. Some people (schizophrenic people) sometimes have the impression that they are not the agent of some of their actions. They do not feel these acts to be determined by themselves or to be the result of a conscious decision of theirs. They believe them to be controlled by someone else. This condition, however, can be eliminated by the introduction of certain chemical substances (neuroleptic drugs) in their brain. So it seems that the feeling itself that gave our initial definition of voluntary acts is dependent on chemical events in the brain.

If we switch now to the materialist monist position, we may be led into thinking that, since our decisions will in any case be determined by the causal factors that are present and by random fluctuations in probabilistic events, we should not worry about them at all. We should not try to think which is the best thing to do, we had better just let the events happen in our brains, and do whatever these events determine. There would be no sense in considering an action to be right or wrong, good or evil. Nobody should be considered guilty or responsible, for whatever they do will have been determined by causal processes in their brain, over which they have no control.

A certain amount of reflection, however, will show us that these conclusions are unfounded. They do not really follow from the monist position. The materialist monist position maintains that the mind is identical with complex states and processes of the brain. It is based on the third-person perspective. It concerns explanation, so there is no place in it for prescription. In an explanation, there is no place for 'should'. When it was said, in the previous paragraph, that we should not try to choose our actions, there is an inherent contradiction in this. This prescription itself supposes the capacity of choosing — paradoxically, choosing not to choose, for the reason of considering that there is no real choice! If we say: 'we *had better* just *let* the events happen', we are assuming the capacity to choose and to do what we freely decide.

However, from the third-person perspective — which is anyway the proper perspective for explanation — there is not so much difficulty in considering choice, decision and action as part of the natural world. Even other people's first-person perspective on their free decisions and action, when I consider it from my third-person perspective — in fact, even my own first-person perspective, when I consider myself 'as someone else' — is compatible with a naturalistic view of the world. All we need is to suppose that there is, in human beings, a decision system that can represent actions and action sequences before their performance, that can select among them, and the output of which is not fully determined by its input, but also by its internal state, by representations of aims to be achieved, by internal criteria that affect its activity (moral and other personal values), and also by a certain degree of randomness (which gives the arbitrary character that our choices often have).

It is reasonable to think, then, that since we are made up this way, we will always be choosing and acting upon our choices. Even if we abstain from choosing, we will only be choosing to abstain from other choices. As an existentialist thinker once said, 'we are condemned to be free'. Being free is simply in our nature, as a consequence of the way in which our brain functions. It is clear that, from this point of view, being free is not incompatible with natural causality. However, from the first-person perspective, I can have no access to the causal determination of my choices, thence the impression that they are not caused at all. We may recall here a statement by Max Planck (1945, quoted by Kornhuber, 1992) : 'From the outside, objectively considered, the will is causally tied; from the inside, subjectively considered, the will is free.'[2] But I argue that from the third-person (objective) perspective we can also apply a concept of freedom to the will, though one that does not imply absence of causality.

Some will say that, on this account, free will is an illusion. But I do not think this is a necessary conclusion. When I feel my acts to be free, I feel that they are not caused by external factors, but that they are determined *by me*. ('External factors' here means: factors external *to me*, to my *self*.) This need not be considered an illusion. If the 'I' is such a system as we have roughly described above, we can consider this intuition to be essentially correct. It all depends of the concept we have of the self, of the 'I'. When we see our actions as determined *by ourselves*, this can be considered to be right. It is when we consider our *self* to be pure spontaneity — a being that is not subject to causality — that we are in illusion.

'Why did you do this?', someone asks me. 'Because I chose to do it', I answer. 'Why did you choose to do it?', she asks, and I give my reasons. (Of course, these reasons can be true or false — and even if true, they may give only a partial justification for my action.) 'But why did your reasons lead you to choose to do this?', she asks. If I am not to give further reasons, which would only lead to the question being asked again, then from the first-person perspective the answer can only be: 'I do not know'. Only from the third-person perspective can we try to find the causes for our reasons and our choices.

From the first-person perspective, *I* am the cause of my actions. But what am I? The incompatibility between free will, as seen from the first-person perspective, and natural causation dissolves if we adopt the 'astonishing hypothesis' (to use Crick's phrase; Crick, 1994) that we ourselves, as free agents, are brain systems capable of choice, decision and action. This is the 'compatibilist' position concerning free will, that is, one that considers free will as compatible with natural causality.

III: The Readiness Potential and the Initiation of Voluntary Action

Let's now consider the readiness potential. In 1964, using a new method of reverse computation of stored electroencephalographic (EEG) data, Kornhuber and Deecke discovered that self-paced voluntary hand or foot movements are preceded by a slow negative cortical potential (Kornhuber & Deecke, 1965). Movements were voluntarily performed by the subjects, following the instructions given, at moments that were determined by the subjects themselves, independently of any external stimulus. The potential preceding the movement was called *'Bereitschaftspotential'* or 'readiness potential' (RP), this term implying a process of preparation for the movement. The interval between the beginning of the potential and the start of muscle activity varied from 0.4 to 4 s, being on the average 1–1.5 s (Kornhuber & Deecke, 1965, pp. 4–5). In a later series of experiments, average onset of RPs was 750 ms prior to finger flexion (Standard Deviation, 360), but it could start as early as 1.5 s or more prior to movement onset (Deecke *et al.*, 1976, p. 101). As the authors remark, such an early onset time rules out the possibility that the readiness potential corresponds to the motor command, so they take it to indicate a process of preparation of the movement (p. 113).

---

[2] My translation of 'Von aussen, objektiv betrachtet, ist der Wille kausal gebunden; von innen, subjektiv betrachtet, ist der Wille frei.'

Libet and his colleagues made RP measurements in which they tried to minimize any process of conscious or nonconscious preparation of the movement. Each trial was an independent event and there was no limitation on the time in which to perform the act. Furthermore, an additional instruction was introduced, asking the subjects 'to let the urge to act appear on its own at any time without any pre-planning . . . i.e., to try to be "spontaneous"' (Libet *et al.*, 1982, p. 324). In series in which the subjects reported no pre-planning, RPs were shorter (what the authors described as 'type II' or 'type III', with mean onset time 577 ms and 240 ms prior to movement onset, respectively; S.D. 151 and 47, respectively; *ibid.*, table I, p. 326).

What kind of preparation is then indicated by the readiness potential? And what is the temporal relation between the voluntary decision to perform the movement and the RP? If these acts are determined by a conscious decision of the subject, must this conscious decision precede the brain events reflected in the RP? If, on the contrary, the RP starts before the conscious decision to act, one could ask how the brain can start preparing an action before the mind decides to make it. How could the brain know in advance that the mind was going to decide to perform the movement at that precise moment?

Let us consider that these acts are determined by the self (or the 'I') or by free will. Let us use here the term 'the free agent'. Now, we have two alternative possibilities. First, we may consider free will to be the activity of a brain system (see the previous section). We may consider the free agent to be a brain system, or the activity of some brain structures, according to the materialist theory of mind-brain relation. If so, the readiness potential, since it always precedes these voluntary acts, will be seen as an expression of the workings of this free agent itself (or of processes derived therefrom).

Second, we may consider free will as the activity of an immaterial mind. According to the interactionist dualist theory of mind–brain relation, the free agent is not a brain system, but something that acts on the brain to make it perform the actions that this free agent decides. In this case, we get a temporal problem. Since the RP always precedes these voluntary acts, it certainly reflects the brain activity that prepares the performance of these acts. Now, if these acts are determined by something that is external to the brain, then the mental decision that determines the act must *precede* any preparation of it, so that it may in fact *cause* it. So the conscious decision must precede the RP. And since the RP often lasts half a second or more, before initiation of the muscle contraction, there would be a gap of this duration between the mental decision to act and the motor act.

However, we have seen that an essential constituent of our intuition about voluntary acts is that they are caused by a *conscious* decision. And *we are not conscious of such a long gap between our conscious decision to act and the act itself.* On the contrary, in situations such as those in which the RPs were recorded, we consciously perceive the motor act as *immediately* following the conscious decision. One should recall that subjects were not instructed to decide the moment of performing the movement, wait for about half a second, and then move. Clearly, they performed the movement as soon as they decided to do so. So how could there be such a long interval between the conscious decision, preceding the RP, and the movement? The experimental fact seems to pose a serious difficulty for the dualist hypothesis.

Eccles, a supporter of interactionist dualism concerning mind–brain relation (Popper & Eccles, 1977/1983), tried to surmount this difficulty with an ingenious hypothesis. According to this hypothesis, there are spontaneous fluctuations in cortical activity (not visible in the EEG) and 'there is a tendency for the initiation of the movements to occur during the excitatory phases of the random spontaneous activity' (Eccles, 1985, p. 542). The earlier phase of the RP (up to about 200 ms before the movement) would then reflect this spontaneous activity, of which the immaterial mental event then takes advantage in order to produce the voluntary action. The hypothesis thus preserves the essential character of interactionist dualism (*ibid.*, pp. 542–3). This hypothesis implies that spontaneous fluctuations in the global activity of large populations of cortical neurons, such as those reflected in the earlier part of the RP, should regularly occur, independently of any intention or movement, so as to allow the production of voluntary acts. In fact, the supposition that the earlier part of the RP reflects a spontaneous fluctuation, that is not necessarily linked to the preparation of an action, is a viable specific hypothesis, and it is not necessarily dependent on Eccles' dualist theory of action determination by an immaterial agent. This specific hypothesis would be very difficult to test, due to the absence of a common reference time from which to average different EEG tracings of subjects at rest. In fact, in a single EEG tracing the RP itself is not visible. As explained above, one needs to average many EEG tracings to obtain the RP, and a common reference time is necessary for this (in the case of voluntary acts, it is the movement onset time). At present, there seems to be no way of testing this hypothesis, but in principle it should be testable.

Libet, faced with the available experimental evidence, preferred to accept the conclusion that voluntary acts are nonconsciously initiated. For him, this in fact implies that they are not initiated by free will. 'Clearly, free will or free choice of whether "to act now" could not be the initiating agent, contrary to one widely held view' (Libet, 1992, p. 269). However, he was not willing to consider free will as a complete illusion. He argued that, even if voluntary actions are not initiated by free will, they might still be controlled by free will. According to his data, consciousness of the intention to act seemed to precede the muscle contraction by about 200 ms. Libet argued that during this period, the subject might either veto the act or allow it to proceed to motor completion. 'The findings should therefore be taken not as being antagonistic to free will but rather as affecting the view of how free will might operate' (Libet, 1985, p. 538). He considers that for this conscious 'veto' or 'trigger' to be really free it must not be decided by neural events that precede it. 'For *control* of the volitional process to be exerted as a *conscious initiative*, it would indeed seem necessary to postulate that conscious control functions can appear without prior initiation by unconscious cerebral processes, in a context in which conscious awareness of intention to act has already developed' (*ibid.*).

However, it must be emphasized that this supposition, whatever its intrinsic value, does not give us back the intuition that the *initiation* of the act itself is free. As Bittner remarks, 'his hypothesis does not give us back a recognizable concept of voluntary movements nor vindicate our feelings of being in conscious control' (Bittner, 1994). According to Libet, actions such as the voluntary wrist flexions performed by his subjects when they decided to do it are free because the subject could have vetoed them. But what about what we are conscious of as being a free decision that really *initiates* the voluntary action? What about the intuition we have that our actions are really *initiated*, and not only controlled, by ourselves, and not by something else? What about our feeling of being the true cause of our actions? Libet's account gives no explanation of this intuition. If one accepts his interpretation, one will be obliged to consider this intuition as an illusion. According to him, there is no free will for creating actions, there is free will only for censoring them — allowing some to pass and forbidding others.

IV: Problems with the Concept of Intention

There is an ambiguity in the usual meaning of the word 'intention'. In discussions of action, the word is often employed in relation to the mental event that is considered directly to cause the voluntary act. However, one can also have an intention to do something at some time in the future, without deciding to do it now. In this case, the word merely indicates a representation of an action to be performed in the future. In the first sense, the intention is what effectively causes the action. In the second sense, the intention is a mental state that predisposes the subject to the action but is not sufficient to produce it *now*. The final decision to act is still needed. For the first sense, we may prefer to use the word 'decision', as I did in the last sentence. But we must recognize that this word in fact also has the same ambiguity, since we may decide to do something without doing it now. To completely avoid ambiguity, it would perhaps be necessary to say: 'the irrevocable decision to act now'. I believe that our usual concept of voluntary acts imply that these are caused by a free irrevocable decision to act now. (The concepts of wish, desire, wanting or urge, just as the intention in the second sense above, do not imply an irrevocable decision to act now.)

However, as I will explain later in greater detail, I believe there is another distinction to be made. Libet's observations of aborted actions show the need for such a distinction. His subjects sometimes reported that they had experienced an urge or intention to act *now* that was not in the end followed by a movement (see section 5). So we should distinguish three different mental events: the intention to act at some time in the future, the intention to act now (which may still fail to lead to an action) and the irrevocable decision to act now.

I believe we should admit that every voluntary action is preceded by an intention to act now, in the sense of a representation of the action that precedes its performance. But I argue that this intention does not always become conscious as a separate event. For it to become conscious as a separate event, it must become conscious before performance is started. If it does not, consciousness of the intention to act now merges with consciousness of the action itself. As noted in the previous paragraph, I also argue that it should be distinguished from the decision to act that immediately causes the action. How do we experience this decision that immediately causes the action? I argue that we do not experience it as a separate event, but as a part of our experience of the action itself. We distinguish very clearly between an involuntary movement and a voluntary one, even if it is made so suddenly and spontaneously that we have no consciousness of intention prior to the action itself. We feel that the voluntary movement was caused by a decision of our own (sometimes also called 'intention', see previous paragraph), so this decision is experienced as something that precedes the movement, but this experience does not occur before the experience of the movement. It is integrated into the experience of the movement itself.

In order to appreciate the distinction between a voluntary and an involuntary act, take the case of a person who has a tic and at a certain moment decides to imitate his own tic. If he succeeds in the performance, he will feel the movement itself to be essentially the same in the two cases. However, he will also be conscious of a clear difference between them. He will feel that, in the first case, the movement 'happened' to him, whereas in the second, *he made* the movement. In the second case, he will be conscious that the act was caused by a decision to make it.

The word 'intention' may also be used in a third sense, to indicate the aim or purpose of an action. The question 'What was your intention in doing that?', for instance, implies that before the action the subject wanted to reach a certain end and performed the action as a means towards this end. In this case, 'intention' denotes not a prior representation of the action, but a prior representation of the end to be reached through the action.

V: Libet's Solution to the Problem of the Free Determination of Voluntary Acts

Some subjects told Libet that, on some occasions, they felt as if they were going to perform a movement but in fact did not. It seemed they had the wish to make the movement but then aborted it. Libet tried to reproduce this phenomenon in a way that allowed the study of RPs. Of course, in spontaneous instances, the presence of an RP cannot be determined, for there is no time reference from which to average different tracings. So Libet instructed the subjects to prepare to make a movement at a pre-set moment, as indicated by the position of the revolving spot they were looking at, and veto the movement about 100–200 ms before this pre-set time (Libet *et al.*, 1983b). The pre-set time served then as the zero-time for the backward computation of the RP. It was shown that this procedure produced RPs that were to begin with similar to those obtained with real movements. Then, about 200 ms before the pre-set moment, this potential started to fall, contrary to what happened with real movements.

Libet interprets this as indicating that the conscious decision to veto the movement can in fact abort it after the subject has become conscious of the intention to move. And, since he thinks that a decision cannot be regarded as free if it is made unconsciously, he concludes that it is here that free will may operate. The experimental facts had imposed on him the idea that the initiation of an action is not caused by free will, since it precedes consciousness of the 'decision' to act. So the real decision, for him, comes after consciousness of the illusory decision, in allowing the action to proceed or vetoing it. '[W]e arrive at a conscious specific "action intention" (to move now) *and* a subsequent "decision" (whether or not to carry out the action-intention), both processes occurring in sequence just before the time of action' (Libet, 1987, p. 320). So it seems he wants to keep the word 'decision' for what happens *consciously* (and not *before* consciousness). We must note, however, that it is only the decision *not* to carry out the action-intention that may be experienced as a discrete event. As I argued in the previous section, conscious experience of the irrevocable decision to act now is incorporated into consciousness of the action itself.

The possibility of vetoing the action after becoming conscious of an intention to act is thus essential to Libet's conception of free voluntary acts. And he takes this conscious veto to be a purely spontaneous event, not determined by causes. 'The potential for such conscious veto power, within the last 100–200 ms before an anticipated action, was experimentally demonstrated by us' (Libet, 1993 p. 134). Of course, it is only the *potential* for such conscious veto power, and not this kind of conscious veto power itself, that was experimentally demonstrated. Libet himself admits: 'There is nothing in our new evidence to entail that a conscious veto or trigger is not itself initiated by preceding cerebral processes, as correctly noted by a number of commentators' (Libet, 1985, p. 563). The only argument he has in favour of his conception is that 'there is presently no directly applicable evidence *against* the appearance of a conscious control function without prior unconscious cerebral processes' (*ibid.*).

Of course, everybody has already had the experience of giving up the intention of doing something at the last moment, that is, of having almost done something before aborting the action. Retrospectively, one experiences that one 'had almost started' the act and then refrained from carrying it out. Of course, 'having almost started' means not having started. But besides this negative meaning, what is its *positive* content, so that it may be experienced as something that really happened? It can only be an intention to act now involving a real preparation for action, that in this case is dissociated from the irrevocable decision to act, since the performance of the action itself is not triggered. This does not mean, however, that in the case of effective action the subject necessarily experiences first this kind of preparation to act (an intention to act *now* that is not yet a *decision* to act now). Nor does it mean that the irrevocable decision to act now can only occur after consciousness of this intention to act now (that, according to Libet, is non-chosen). In *some* cases, we *may* experience a prior intention to act now, but we do not have the additional experience of triggering or 'not vetoing' this intention, as a discrete experience that precedes the experience of the act itself. As I have already said, experience of deciding to act is an integral part of the experience of the action itself. And very often the prior experience of an intention is absent; we experience only the suddenly decided and performed action.

Indeed, even in the case in which the subject experiences that an impending action has been aborted, it is debatable whether the word 'veto' is a good description of his experience. In some of the spontaneous cases, a more suitable description is perhaps that the final decision to move simply did not occur, although the subject has the experience that it almost occurred. It seems it is more a case of *not* having decided than of positively vetoing an impending event. In other cases, and in the experimental case of the 'pre-set veto' (Libet *et al.*, 1983b), subjects reported having experienced the intention to act and the active process of stopping the intention. However, the situation seems to be different from that of opposing, for instance, the felt impulse to sneeze or burp (Bittner, 1994), since one feels not only the active opposition but the process itself that is being opposed as caused by one's own will.

Libet is right in saying that when we are conscious of an intention to act before performing the act, we feel we can stop ourselves from performing it (Libet, 1993, p. 134). But this is not the only basis for our common intuition that our voluntary acts are free. In the case of a purely voluntary act, such as the hand movement performed by Libet's subjects at an arbitrary moment, we also feel that we could have had no intention to perform it in the first place. In other words, we feel it is up to us also to initiate the action, and not only to stop ourselves from performing it (Bittner, 1994, chapter 3, section III). The intention to act now that precedes the act is not experienced as an autonomous event that is independent of our free will. On the contrary, *it is experienced as an expression of our free will.* Trying to give a verbal expression to these experiences, the intention to act now is experienced as something like 'I am going to do this now'. It is not passively experienced as something like 'Here comes the intention to do this'. It is also different from a wanting or wish, which is something like 'I would like to do this now'. The 'veto' experience would be something like 'I am going to do this now . . . no, not really'. The decision that causes the action, on the other hand, is not experienced as something like 'I am deciding now that I am going to do this'. It is experienced as something like 'I am doing this because I have decided to'.

The importance of Libet's pre-set 'veto' experiments, to my mind, is not that of demonstrating the possibility of giving up a conscious intention to act. We already knew of this possibility from common experience. I believe the new and important fact revealed by these experiments is that an RP may occur in the absence of any act. Libet has shown that the RP is not a sufficient condition for an act to occur. Thus, it should not be identified with the irrevocable decision to act of which we are conscious as being the cause of our voluntary acts.

VI: What Are Voluntary Acts, Conscious Acts and Conscious Decisions?

In order further to discuss the relations between volition and consciousness, we must first discuss the concepts of voluntary acts, conscious acts and conscious decisions, since these terms may be used in different senses and be associated with different theoretical and philosophical presuppositions.

1. A conscious act may be conceived as:

1a An act of which we are conscious. This simple definition is compatible with two very different concepts of consciousness (Rosenthal, 1986; see also Gomes, 1982; 1995). According to the first one, consciousness is an intrinsic property either of all mental states or of some of them. A mental state (or a conscious mental state) is conscious in itself, it does not need anything else to be conscious, and a person is conscious of a mental state simply by having one (or by having one of this conscious sort). According to the second concept, what makes a mental state conscious is the presence of another mental state, which is a sort of internal perception of the first one or else a special kind of thought about it. The person who has this second-order mental state is then conscious of the first-order mental state. Proposition (1a) is also compatible with either an identity-theory or a dualist view of the mind–brain relation.

1b An act that is decided after consciousness of the intention to act or after consciously imagining the act. One first consciously thinks about an act and then makes it, so one is fully conscious of the act before making it, and this consciousness participates in the decision to make it. Although this use of the terms 'conscious act' or 'conscious action' is very common, I prefer to use here the term 'deliberate act'. The reason is the need for a term to indicate simply the acts of which the person is conscious (proposition 1a).

2. A voluntary act may be conceived as:

2a An act that is felt by the subject to have been caused by a conscious decision. This raises the question of what a conscious decision should be considered to be.

2b An act that is decided after consciousness of the intention to act or after consciously imagining the act. In this sense, 'voluntary act' is synonymous with 'conscious act' in sense (1b). As I have already said, I propose to use the term 'deliberate act' in this sense.

3. A conscious decision may be conceived as:

3a A decision of which we become conscious, but which may exist and produce effects before that.

3b A decision that is intrinsically conscious, and so can only produce effects after we are conscious of it. Two alternative possibilities may complement this proposition:

3b$_1$ This intrinsically conscious decision is not determined by causes. This is in accordance with the conception that a mental event that is fully determined by natural antecedent causes cannot be considered as really free. Free will is considered incompatible with causal determination.

3b$_2$ This intrinsically conscious decision is caused by prior neural events.

Of course, there may be other concepts or hypotheses about conscious acts, voluntary acts and conscious decisions. I have just indicated those that are relevant to the present discussion.

VII: What Is the Relationship Between Voluntary Acts and Conscious Acts?

If one adopts propositions (1b) and (2b), 'voluntary acts' and 'conscious acts' are two ways of saying the same thing.

If one adopts propositions (1a) and (2a), voluntary acts are conscious, but they may be either thoughtlessly spontaneous or deliberate. In the first case, one is conscious of both the act and the decision that caused it, but only after its performance has already started. In the case of a deliberate act, by contrast, one is also conscious of the intention to act now before starting its performance. On the other hand, conscious acts may be voluntary or involuntary. A tic is involuntary but the subject is conscious of performing it.

If one adopts propositions (1a) and (2b), then conscious acts may be voluntary (that is, deliberate) or non-voluntary. In this case, an impulsive or thoughtlessly spontaneous act is considered as non-voluntary, although conscious. This position fails to differentiate between non-deliberate acts and truly involuntary acts such as tics. In the case of an impulsive act, for example, one feels that it was caused by one's will, even though one started it without consciously thinking that one was going to do it. In the case of a tic, on the contrary, one feels that the act was not caused by one's will.

If one adopts proposition (3b), the distinction between (2a) and (2b) disappears. So rejecting (2b) in favour of (2a) implies adopting (3a). If one adopts (1b) and (2a), rejecting (2b) and so adopting (3a), then conscious (i.e. deliberate) acts are voluntary, but voluntary acts may be conscious or not. Impulsive or thoughtlessly spontaneous acts are now called voluntary, but they are not considered as conscious acts. In this case, the adjective 'conscious' is used differently when it qualifies acts and when it qualifies decisions. If a conscious decision is just a decision of which we become conscious (according to (3a)), it would seem more coherent to define a conscious act as just an act of which we become conscious (proposition (1a)).

My own preference is for propositions (1a), (2a) and (3a). According to these, conscious acts may be voluntary or involuntary, and voluntary acts are conscious, but not all are deliberate. Some are impulsive or else just thoughtless, but they are nonetheless voluntary and conscious. In those non-deliberate acts, we are not conscious of the intention to act now before acting. One is not conscious of what one is going to do before doing it. But during the act or after it, one has nevertheless the feeling that it was caused by a decision of one's own.

VIII: What Is the Role of Consciousness of the Intention in Voluntary Acts?

If one adopts propositions (2a) and (3a), consciousness of the intention to act now has a role only in deliberate actions. In these, since the subject is conscious of the intention to act now before starting performance, this consciousness of intention may affect his or her final decision. In the case of non-deliberate acts, there is no prior consciousness of an intention to act now. (This is not to say that consciousness itself has no role at all in the determination of non-deliberate acts, since they derive from conscious experience of the situation in which the subject is.)

If one accepts (2b), consciousness of the intention has a role in all voluntary acts and it becomes difficult to explain the difference between deliberate and non-deliberate acts. And, as we have already noted, if one accepts (3b), one also accepts (2b).

What about consciousness of the irrevocable decision that immediately causes the action? I argue that we should not only accept (3a) but also admit that this decision in fact causes the action *before we become conscious of it*. Thus, consciousness of this decision has no role in the causation of this very same action, since it only occurs after performance has already started. Again, this is not to say that consciousness has no role in voluntary action, since consciousness of the intention is important in deliberate actions, and consciousness of the situation is determinant in both deliberate and non-deliberate voluntary actions. Besides, consciousness of the final decision, as a part of the experience of the action itself, may have an important role in the subsequent correction of the action or in the causation or avoidance of other actions. It is essential, among other effects, for the occurrence of guilt feelings, which typically do not occur with truly involuntary acts.

IX: Are Conscious Actions Nonconsciously Initiated?

I think we should agree with Libet that conscious actions are nonconsciously initiated, in the sense that the subject is not conscious of the beginnings of the neural activity that eventually produces the motor act. Three facts converge to justify this conclusion. First, the long gap between the beginning of the RP and the beginning of muscular contraction (about half a second). Second, the fact that we can only become conscious of performing the act after the beginning of muscular contraction or at least after the final motor commands that occur very shortly before it. Third, the fact that we are not conscious of any gap of similar duration between the decision that causes the act and the act itself, nor, in the case of deliberate acts, between the intention to act now and the act.

Of course, one could program oneself to perform the motor act only about half a second after the conscious intention. That is, one could time the movement so as to have the conscious experience of an interval of half a second between the decision to move and the movement itself. But in the usual case of a deliberate act, the subject has the conscious experience of performing the movement immediately after the conscious intention to act now. However, the RP indicates that neural activity had already started about half a second before the movement. Even though we should recognize that it takes some time to proceed from consciousness of the intention to the consciousness of the movement, it certainly does not take half a second. In half a second, for instance, we can see several individually perceived flashes, or hear several beeps, but we would not be able to see or hear them between the moment when we become conscious of the intention to act now and the moment when we become conscious of making the movement (if we make it immediately after the conscious intention). So, the onset of the RP cannot be the correlate of the conscious intention to act now.

We conclude that the first part of the RP manifests neural processes that are not reflected in conscious experience. Bittner makes the opposite claim. For him, the neural events measured by the RP are identical to the conscious decision (Bittner, 1996, p. 337). Accepting Libet's measure of the time of occurrence of the conscious intention (350 ms after onset of the RP), he interprets the interval between onset of the RP and occurrence of conscious intention as the time that is necessary for the decision to become conscious. 'The subject becomes aware of the whole of the decision; though as with every causal-physical process, time is needed for the relevant events to occur' (*ibid.*, p. 338). His reasoning is based on a theory of consciousness as a higher-order mental state. The decision is the first-order state and consciousness of the decision is a second-order state caused by the former. It is reasonable then to suppose that the latter occurs some time after the former.

I agree with a great part of Bittner's reasoning. I also view consciousness as a higher-order mental state (Gomes, 1982; 1995; 1998a,c) and I also believe there is reason to assume the presence of a latency for conscious experience of a first-order state (Gomes, 1998b). However, his interpretation does not take into account the fact that in usual cases we are not conscious of an interval of about half a second between consciousness of the intention and consciousness of the movement. If we assume a latency for consciousness of the intention, we should also assume a latency for consciousness of the movement, and the interval between the conscious experiences should be roughly equivalent to the interval between the first-order states. We are forced to conclude that the neural events that correspond to the intention to act now must occur much nearer the time of the movement itself. Those that correspond to the decision that causes the movement must occur still nearer in time to the movement. The first part of the RP must then correspond to a process of preparation of the decision that causes the movement. (The distinction I have made between the intention and the decision and the consideration of cases in which there is no conscious intention are also absent from Bittner's analysis.)

But why suppose, as Bittner does, that since its very beginning the RP must correspond to the intention of which we become conscious? Bittner believes it is necessary to make this assumption in order to preserve the intuition that our conscious decision (and not something else) causes the action. He considers there is a problem of agency here. '[T]he conscious decision, if it occurs at a moment . . . after the onset of the RP events . . . cannot be the cause of the movement' (Bittner, 1994). Why not? Is this idea not a consequence of the assumption that a free personal decision that causes an action cannot be itself determined by causal factors? Why not consider the initial RP events as *a cause* (or a set of causes) *of the cause* of the movement? In my view, the initial RP events are a cause (or a set of causes, among others) of the intention to act now, or a parallel effect of the processes that cause it; this intention to act now is a cause (among others) of the final decision to act; and this final decision is the event of which we are conscious as being the cause of our action. The case of spontaneously aborted movements, in which no movement follows a conscious intention to act now, and the case of aborted movements in the presence of RPs, in Libet's 'pre-set veto' experiments, show that neither the initial RP events nor the conscious intention to act now are sufficient to cause the movement.

I believe we could picture the sequence of events thus: First, the neural events manifested in the initial part of the RP correspond to a process of preparation or formation of the intention to act. Then, at a certain point in time, comes the intention to act now (as a representation of the impending motor commands). Next, in the case of deliberate acts, comes consciousness of this intention to act now. After this, or directly after the nonconscious intention to act now in the case of non-deliberate acts, comes the final decision to act, which causes the action. After the final motor commands, or after the movement itself, comes consciousness of the action as caused by a decision of one's own.

A testable empirical prediction of this way of picturing the events is that the RP should be longer in the case of deliberate actions than in the case of non-deliberate actions.

In a different sense, however, we could say that voluntary acts are *consciously* initiated, since they are necessarily created on the basis of a *conscious* experience of the situation the subject is in. From this point of view, there is after all an intimate relationship between consciousness and voluntary action, even if the subject is not conscious of the first events in the causal chain that leads to an action, and even if in many actions he is not conscious of an intention to act now before the final decision occurs. Even in non-deliberate voluntary acts, causation of the act depends on consciousness — consciousness of something in relation to which the act is prepared. If the perception of an event in the environment does not reach conscious experience, one cannot undertake a voluntary action directly related to this event. Consider the case of blindsight patients, for instance, in which the responses given in the forced choice situation are evidence of a nonconscious perception of the stimuli presented in the blind field. The voluntary action of giving a response is instigated not by the nonconscious perception itself but by the conscious acceptance of the instructions for 'guessing'. It is only the content of this 'guessing' that is influenced by the nonconscious perception. In this sense, consciousness is indispensable for voluntary action.

Although consciousness is thus intimately linked with voluntary action, and even more with deliberate action, consciousness should be distinguished from the 'acts of will' or volitional mental events. And these should not be considered to be made *by* consciousness. As Bittner remarks, being the subject of conscious experiences 'is not all we are; besides the passive receiver of experiences we are also the one who decides and wills. . . . Libet's subjects are not able to report their own acts of will, but only their experiences of these acts' (Bittner, 1996, pp. 338–9).

X: Are Voluntary Acts Free?

According to Libet, the initiation of voluntary acts is not free, since it is determined by neural events that are not conscious. For him, an action can only be free if it is the result of a conscious decision. As we have seen, for Libet it is only the control of intentions to act, after they have arisen, that may be free. This free control of actions depends on conscious decisions, conceived according to proposition (3b₁).

For many thinkers, there is an incompatibility between freedom and causal deter-mination of the will.[3] From this perspective, the neural events that initiate an action might well be naturally caused events, if we consider that it is only the subsequent control of intentions that is free. This free conscious control of intentions would not itself be caused by prior neural events.[4]

In section II, I have presented an alternative view of what it is for an action to be free. A free action is an action that is not automatically determined by external events, but is determined by the subject himself, by his will. But what is the subject? What is his will? If we admit that his will is the functioning of some brain systems of his, there is no incompatibility between an action being free and its being causally determined. *I* make my actions, it is not something else that makes them. But what am I? If I am a functioning body, there is no incompatibility between my agency and its causal deter-mination. My mind is free to choose whether to accomplish a voluntary action or not. This means that the final decision is not determined by anything external to my mind. But what is my mind? If it is the working of some brain systems, the incompatibility concerns only causal processes external to these systems, not the causal processes that determine the functioning of these systems themselves. The subject feels that his or her actions are caused by himself or herself and that he or she may choose what he or she will do. Is this an illusion? According to this view, no, this is not an illusion. The illusion is to think that his or her mind is not subject to causality. And this is an understandable illusion, since there is no access to these causal processes from the first-person perspective. Even the feeling one has that one's choices could not be pre-dicted with certainty, even if all the relevant facts were known, can be considered to be true, since, according to modern science, natural events do not always obey strictly

---

[3] See, for instance, Campbell (1957).

[4] Libet does not commit himself to the view that initiation of voluntary acts is determined by neural events that obey natural causality (personal communication, 1999). But he seems to commit himself to the view that free conscious decisions cannot be caused by prior neural events, since he states that '[f]or *control* of the volitional process to be exerted as a *conscious initiative*, it would indeed seem necessary to postulate that conscious control functions can appear without prior initiation by unconscious cerebral processes . . .' (Libet, 1985, p. 538). He postulates this even though he recognizes, in response to criticism, that '[t]here is nothing in our new evidence to entail that a conscious veto or trigger is not itself initiated by preceding cerebral processes' (Libet, 1985, p. 563).

deterministic laws. But the main point here is that the subject can have no first-person access to the causal determination of his or her own mind.[5]

One of the main concepts used to characterize free will is the possibility of doing otherwise (see, for instance, Taylor, 1974). An act is considered free when we think that the subject could have done otherwise in the same circumstances. But what are 'the same circumstances'? These include, of course, all external events affecting the subject at that moment. We could also include here all the 'somatic' states of the person, that is, all states of his or her body external to the nervous system, or external to those systems of the nervous system involved in mental events. We could even include in these circumstances many mental states, such as desires, beliefs and emotions. One could say, for example, that even having the same belief about X, even having the same desire concerning Y and even feeling the same emotion Z, the subject could have chosen to do otherwise. However, one could not include the activity of the deciding system itself in the list of circumstances. This would amount to saying that, even if the subject had decided to do the same thing, he could have decided to do otherwise, which is self-contradictory. When we think about the possibility of deciding to do otherwise in the same circumstances, the deciding agent is necessarily external to the circumstances. And if one says that the subject could have chosen to do otherwise even if all the preceding physical events had been the same, one is begging the question against the hypothesis that the subject itself is a physical system.

One could say that free will does not exist because our actions are determined by the world of causes and effects (which includes our brain) and not by our will. Or, from the opposite point of view, one could say that free will is not causally determined, because our free actions are determined by our will and not by the world of causes and effects. But in both cases one is admitting that the will is not or could not be a part of the world of causes and effects, and this is not a necessary assumption. One is implicitly putting the self outside the natural world. Philosophically, this is an effect of the Cartesian heritage. And perhaps this is also part of our natural folk psychology. However, we can consider that in fact the self is part of the world of causes and effects. From this point of view, when we say that the subject could have done otherwise in the same circumstances, this should be interpreted to mean that, had the causal factors internal to the self (a subsystem in the brain) been different, this self would have exerted a different causal action on the rest of the world, even in the presence of the same external causal factors. Instead of thinking of a self facing the world and acting upon it, we should rather think of a self facing *the rest of* the world and acting upon it. We are part of the world. We, as agents that freely decide to do so or otherwise, are part of the physical world of causes and effects.

Another important concept for the characterization of free will is the concept of choice. Free actions are actions that are not only determined but *chosen* by the subject. For an action to be considered free, the subject must have chosen to do it, and this implies having chosen not to do otherwise. This means that the possibility of doing otherwise should not be just an abstract possibility, it should not be just a possibility that exists from the point of view of someone who considers the case from the outside. Rather, it should be a possibility for the subject himself or herself. The subject must

---

[5] Since Hume (1739/1965), some philosophers have argued for the causal determination of free choices, while others have argued against it (see Kenny, 1989). A useful discussion of the subject is given by Patricia S. Churchland (1996).

be able to consider this possibility before the final decision to act. This means that the subject must be conscious of the intention to act now before acting. We conclude that only what we have called *deliberate* acts should be considered as really free.

Acts that are voluntary but non-deliberate would then manifest an intermediate degree of free will. They are determined by the subject, we consider that the subject could have done otherwise in the same circumstances, they derive from a conscious experience of the situation in which the subject is, but they were not consciously chosen, in the sense that they and the possibility of doing otherwise were not consciously considered by the subject before starting their performance.

Acknowledgements
I am grateful to Rüdiger Vaas, Rimas Čuplinskas and Henrik Walter for inspiring conversation on the subject, to Keith Sutherland for having stimulated me to write this paper and to Benjamin Libet,[6] Patricia Churchland, Michael Pauen and Georg Northoff for their comments on the first version of it. I am indebted to the CNPq — Conselho Nacional de Desenvolvimento Científico e Tecnológico (Brasilia, Brazil) for financial support.

References

Bittner, T. (1994), *Timing Conscious Intentions: An experimentally-based paradox about free action* (Doctoral Dissertation, University of Washington).

Bittner, T. (1996), 'Consciousness and the act of will', *Philosophical Studies*, **81**, pp. 331–41.

Campbell, C.A. (1957), *On Selfhood and Goodhood* (London: George Allen).

Churchland, Patricia S. (1996), 'Feeling reasons' in *The Neurobiology of Decision-Making*, ed. A. Damasio *et al.* (Berlin: Springer); reprinted in Churchland, P.M. & Churchland, P.S., *On the Contrary: Critical Essays (1987-1997)* (Cambridge, MA: The MIT Press, 1998).

Crick, F. (1994), *The Astonishing Hypothesis* (London: Simon & Schuster).

Deecke, L., Grözinger, B & Kornhuber, H.H. (1976), 'Voluntary finger movement in man: cerebral potentials and theory', *Biological Cybernetics*, **23**, pp. 99–119.

Eccles, J.C. (1985), 'Mental summation: The timing of voluntary intentions by cortical activity', *Behavioral and Brain Sciences*, **8** (4), pp. 542–3.

Gomes, G. (1982), *O Problema Mente-Corpo, o Problema do Reducionismo e o Conceito de Energia Psíquica* (Dissertation. PUC, Rio de Janeiro).

Gomes, G. (1995), 'Self-awareness and the mind-brain problem', *Philosophical Psychology*, **8** (2), pp. 155–65.

Gomes, G. (1998a), 'Consciousness as higher-order representation' (paper presented at the conference 'Toward a Science of Consciousness III', Tucson, Arizona, April 27—May 2, 1998). Abstract in *Consciousness Research Abstracts (a service from the Journal of Consciousness Studies): Toward a Science of Consciousness 1998*.

Gomes, G. (1998b), 'The timing of conscious experience: a critical review and reinterpretation of Libet's research', *Consciousness and Cognition*, **7**, pp. 559–95.

Gomes, G. (1998c), *Contribution à la Théorie de la Conscience, Conçue comme Activité du Cerveau* (Thesis, Université Paris 7).

Hume, David (1739/1965), *A Treatise of Human Nature* (Oxford : Clarendon).

Kenny, A.J.P. (1989), *The Metaphysics of Mind* (Oxford: Clarendon).

Kornhuber, H.H. (1984), 'Attention, readiness for action, and the stages of voluntary decision — some electrophysiological correlates in man', *Experimental Brain Research*, **9** (suppl.), pp. 420–9.

Kornhuber, H.H. (1992), 'Gehirn, Wille, Freiheit', *Revue de métaphysique et de morale*, **97** (2), pp. 203–23.

[6] There remain elements in this paper that Dr Libet does not accept. He will be responding to the present author's criticisms in a forthcoming paper in *Consciousness and Cognition*, responding in particular to Gomes (1998b) — Editor.

Kornhuber, H.H. & Deecke, L. (1965), 'Hirnpotentialänderungen bei Willkürbewegungen und passiven Bewegungen des Menschen: Bereitschaftspotential und reafferente Potentiale', *Pflügers Arch. ges. Physiol.*, **284**, pp. 1–17.

Libet, B. (1985), 'Unconscious cerebral initiative and the role of conscious will in voluntary action', *Behavioral and Brain Sciences,* **8** (4), pp. 529–66.

Libet, B. (1987), 'Awareness of wanting to move and of moving', *Behavioral and Brain Sciences*, **10** (2), pp. 320–1.

Libet, B. (1992), 'The neural time-factor in perception, volition and free will', *Revue de métaphysique et de morale*, **97** (2), pp. 255–71.

Libet, B. (1993), 'The neural time factor in conscious and unconscious events', *Experimental and Theoretical Studies of Consciousness* (Ciba Foundation Symposium, **174**), pp. 123–46.

Libet, B. (1994), 'A testable field theory of mind-brain interaction', *Journal of Consciousness Studies*, **1** (1), pp. 119–26.

Libet, B., Wright, Jr., E.W. & Gleason, C.A. (1982), 'Readiness-potentials preceding unrestricted "spontaneous" vs. pre-planned voluntary acts', *Electroencephalography and clinical Neurophysiology*, **54**, pp. 322–35.

Libet, B., Gleason, C.A., Wright, Jr., E.W. & Pearl, D.K. (1983a), 'Time of conscious intention to act in relation to onset of cerebral activity (readiness-potential)', *Brain*, **106**, pp. 623–42.

Libet, B., Wright, Jr., E.W. & Gleason, C.A. (1983b), 'Preparation- or intention-to-act, in relation to pre-event potentials recorded at the vertex', *Electroencephalography and clinical Neurophysiology*, **56**, pp. 367–72.

Plank, M. (1945), *Vom Wesen der Willensfreiheit*, 4, Aufl. (Leipzig: Barth), p. 21 (quoted in Kornhuber, 1992).

Penfield, W. (1975), *The Mystery of Mind* (Princeton, NJ: Princeton University Press).

Popper, K.R. & Eccles, J.C. (1977/1983), *The Self and Its Brain* (London: Routledge & Kegan Paul).

Rosenthal, D. M. (1986), 'Two concepts of consciousness', *Philosophical Studies,* **49**, pp. 329–59.

Taylor, R. (1974), *Metaphysics* (Englewood Cliffs, NJ : Prentice-Hall).

Jonathan Bricklin

A Variety of Religious Experience
William James and the Non-Reality of Free Will

Free will does not exist, nor can it be explained, outside the confines of subjective experience. William James, whose talent for depicting subjective experience was equal to his brother Henry's, desperately wanted to believe in free will. But his introspections did not support it.

'It was . . . through meditating on the phenomenon [of willing] in my own person that I first became convinced of the truth of the doctrine which these pages present . . .' (II, p. 525),[1] James wrote in *The Principles of Psychology*. Much of this classic text, perhaps the best-known book in all psychology,[2] is made up of James' personal introspections, but only when he came to the experience of will did he use the more intensified word, 'meditating,' to describe the process. Although James himself considered this meditation 'to contain in miniature form the data for an entire psychology of volition' (II, p. 525), it has, curiously, been largely ignored or, even worse, casually dismissed. Rollo May, after quoting it in its entirety in his 1969 best-seller, *Love and Will*, rejects it as 'unfinished' (May, 1969, pp. 221–2); but he does so without reflecting upon the basic, irreducible nature of James' subjective account. Gerald Meyers, in his 1989 biography, says that the conclusion James drew from his meditation conflicted with his (James') 'typical common-sense defences of free will,' as if challenging common sense were not as essential a duty of a philosopher as defending it.

Certainly James' conclusion did challenge common sense, at least the sense common to mainstream Western thought. To a Zen Buddhist, or even a Christian Quietist, on the other hand, James' conclusion follows naturally from the method he used to reach it. Indeed, given that the form of his meditation, an exercise in 'direct experience,' was similar to the 'bare attention' of Buddhist meditation, it is hardly surprising that the key insight he derived from it should be the same that Buddhist practitioners derive from theirs.

---

[1] For simplicity, in this paper all references to *The Principles of Psychology* (James, 1890) are to volume and page number only.

[2] According to the *Oxford Companion to the Mind* (See Gregory, 1987, p. 395).

Journal of Consciousness Studies, **6**, No. 8–9, 1999, pp. 77–98

Yet it came as a surprise to him. For so radical was James' insight, undermining the very belief in free will he was seeking to uphold, that he himself recoiled from it. Despite openly supporting the Buddhist conception of the non-reality of self, James never accepted the non-reality of will that his meditation revealed, and he never fully integrated it into his other observations about the experience of will or the experience of self.

James' Meditation

James' meditation on will posed the question: how do we get out of bed? He could, of course, have used any act of deliberation that culminates in an apparent triumph of will. What is especially apt about this example, however, is that it is usually the first deliberate act we make in our day, following, as it does, a long period of passivity.

Often, to be sure, getting out of bed does not feel mediated by will. It feels, rather, like an automatic response — we are *jolted* upwards — whether this jolt is prompted by the sound of an alarm clock, or the feeling of pressure in our bladder, or the flash of the image of our bus pulling out without us. At other times, however, our movement does indeed seem to resolve a deliberation on whether or not to abandon the cosy environment in which we lay; we have looked at two alternatives and feel we have *chosen* one of them. *There is no feeling of will (let alone verification of its ultimate reality) without such a feeling of having chosen.*

James' meditation served as his paradigm of the feeling of having chosen, of having made a decision and acted upon it, in a word — of having willed.

> We know what it is to get out of bed on a freezing morning in a room without a fire, and how the very vital principle within us protests against the ordeal. Probably most persons have lain on certain mornings for an hour at a time unable to brace themselves to the resolve. We think how late we shall be, how the duties of the day will suffer; we say, 'I *must* get up, this is ignominious,' etc.; but still the warm couch feels too delicious, the cold outside too cruel, and resolution faints away and postpones itself again and again just as it seemed on the verge of bursting the resistance and passing over into the decisive act. Now how do we *ever* get up under such circumstances? If I may generalize from my own experience, we more often than not get up without any struggle or decision at all. We suddenly find that we *have* got up. A fortunate lapse of consciousness occurs; we forget both the warmth and the cold; we fall into some reverie connected with the day's life, in the course of which the idea flashes across us, 'Hollo! I must lie here no longer' — an idea which at that lucky instant awakens no contradictory or paralysing suggestions, and consequently produces immediately its appropriate motor effects. It was our acute consciousness of both the warmth and the cold during the period of struggle, which paralysed our activity then and kept our idea of rising in the condition of *wish* and not of *will*. The moment these inhibitory ideas ceased, the original idea exerted its effects.

> (II, pp. 524–5.)

As we said, James considered his example to 'contain in miniature form the data for an entire psychology of volition.' The data can be broken down into three parts. First, thoughts arise. Second, insofar as thoughts have an impulsive power, that power is directly linked to our motor operations. And third, the feeling of will and effort is derivable from the interplay between opposing thoughts.

The Stream of Thoughts

'When man studies himself with honest impartiality, he observes that he is not the conscious and voluntary artisan either of his feelings or of his thoughts, and that his feelings and his thoughts are only phenomena which happen to him.'

Hubert Benoit (1990, p. 29)

'I conceive a man as always spoken to from behind, and unable to turn his head and see the speaker.'

Emerson (1849, p. 129)

Thoughts arise. This becomes strikingly clear if you sit still and bring your awareness to only the movement of your breathing, as in meditation. No matter how hard you try to keep this exclusive focus, you very soon find yourself watching random thoughts, arriving unescorted to consciousness. These thoughts are experienced more as happening to us than as being made by us. The arising nature of thoughts is so manifest in meditation, in fact, that sitting still with the breath may seem not to be revealing this fundamental truth so much as concocting it. Yet it does not take a still inner environment to experience the arising nature of thoughts. It is, rather, our everyday experience, even if we don't everyday assess it as such. Does Mark Twain not speak for us all when he describes his thought process as 'racing along from subject to subject — a drifting panorama of ever-changing, ever-dissolving views manufactured by my mind without any help from me — why, it would take me two hours to merely name the multitude of things my mind tallied off and photographed in fifteen minutes . . .' (Twain quoted in Brooks, 1933, p. 264).

Even when you seem to be directing the flow of your thoughts — such as when you are explaining something to someone — you don't know the next word out of your mouth until you say it. And even when you *do* know the next word out of your mouth — such as when you are reciting something — you still don't know the thought that will accompany it. (Actors, for example, who repeat the same lines every night, can never repeat precisely the same thoughts to go along with them.)[3] As the British philosopher Gilbert Ryle says: 'One thing that I cannot prepare myself for is the next thought that I am going to think' (Ryle, 1949, p. 197). We may believe that so-called 'deliberate choices' constitute an exception — that *they*, at least, are not so much received as made. James, however, could find nothing in experience that confirmed the 'making' of any thought — a deciding thought or otherwise — nothing that confirmed anything other than — as our idiom expresses it — thoughts *occur*. 'If we could say in English "it thinks", as we say "it rains" or "it blows"', he wrote, 'we should be stating the fact most simply and with the minimum of assumption' (I, pp. 224–5).

And James *was* careful to use such minimum of assumption whenever he characterized the will experience, utilizing such egoless phrases as 'things are really being decided from one moment to another' and 'mental spontaneity . . . selects' etc.[4] Despite his belief in free will, James had no problem reconciling himself to this

---

[3] Nor would they want to, since the illusion of undergoing an original experience is paramount to their success.

[4] By contrast, Rollo May, in his account of will, repeatedly leaps from the experience of intention 'in consciousness' to an 'I' intending.

impersonality of the thought process. Several times throughout *The Principles of Psychology* he derides the attempts of others to establish an independent 'I' — an abiding *subject* or 'soul' in which experience inheres:

> It is . . . with the word Soul as with the word Substance in general. To say that phenomena inhere in a substance is at bottom only to record one's protest against the notion that the bare existence of the phenomena is the total truth. A phenomenon would not itself be, we insist, unless there were something *more* than the phenomenon. To the more we give the provisional name of Substance. So . . . [accordingly] we ought certainly to admit that there is more than the bare fact of coexistence of a passing thought with a passing brain-state. But we do not answer the question 'What is that more?' when we say that it is a 'Soul' which the brain-state affects. This kind of more *explains* nothing . . . The phenomena are enough, the passing Thought [capitalized by James to mean 'the present mental state'] itself is the only *verifiable* thinker . . . (I, p. 346).

To affirm that 'every thought tends to be part of a personal consciousness' (I, p. 225), is not to affirm that personal consciousness generates thoughts. Instead of saying 'I make thoughts,' we must simply say *'thoughts go on'* (I, p. 225).

Indeed, not only is James' will paradigm absent a deciding 'I,' it is absent a deciding *moment*. James went looking for such a moment but could not find it. Instead of the moment of decision, he found a 'lapse of consciousness'. Out of this lapse 'we suddenly find that we *have* got up'. Since awareness of the decision came only *after* it had already occurred, consciousness of the decision was not simultaneous with its generation. The decision, the actual deciding moment, occurs, as he says, 'without any . . . decision at all'. James dilutes this startling discovery with the phrase 'more often than not', but obviously, if he had been able at any time to catch himself in the act of *making* a deciding thought, rather than receiving it (as the words 'flashes across' indicate), he would not have presented this particular example as his paradigm of the will experience.

Now it may be argued that James' meditation has a design flaw: If you are trying to witness an act of will, 'you' are occupied by the 'trying to witness' and thus miss the role of 'you' in the act of will. Such a criticism, however, begs the question that any meditation on will ultimately poses — namely, whether an active, agent 'I' exists in the first place. The only proof of an agent 'I' is what can be inferred from the experience of agency. As Nietzsche clearly saw, will is not an afterbirth of 'I,' an autonomous agent; 'I' is an afterbirth of will, the experience of autonomy.[5] 'Trying to witness' is, itself, ostensibly, an act of will. Thus, referring the action of 'trying to witness' to an 'I' *assumes* what needs to be proven. Obviously, we experience something like will. The *experience* is not in question; the question is: what does this experience entail? To answer this question it matters not whether the experience be trying to do something (such as getting out of bed on a cold morning) or trying to witness the trying. What matters is that some moment of trying be revealed for what it is, stripped of assumptions.

---

[5]   Of . . . [the] three 'inward facts' which seem to guarantee causality, the first and most persuasive is that of the will as cause. The conception of a consciousness ('spirit') as a cause, and later also that of the ego as cause (the 'subject'), are only afterbirths: first the causality of the will was firmly accepted as given, as empirical.

   Meanwhile we have thought better of it. Today we no longer believe a word of all this. The 'inner world' is full of phantoms and will-o'-the-wisps: the will is one of them (Nietzsche, 1976, p. 494).

The Gap Between Thoughts

In 1921, Karl Marbe, of the University of Wurzburg, devised an experiment in which subjects attempted to 'catch themselves' in the act of choosing between two impressions. The experiment was concerned with judgement not will, but, like James' meditation, it was, at bottom, an attempt to detect the onset of a decision between two options. As described by Julian Jaynes in his *The Origin of Consciousness in the Breakdown of the Bicameral Mind*, the subjects were asked to lift two (small) weights in front of them and decide which one was heavier. They indicated their choice by placing the heavier object in front of them. The results startled both Marbe and his subjects, all of whom were trained in introspective psychology. For, contrary to their own expectation, they discovered that, while the feeling of the two weights was conscious, as well as the placing of the heavier one in front of them, *the moment of decision was not*. Jaynes offers a home-kit version of this experiment:

> Take any two unequal objects, such as a pen and pencil or two unequally filled glasses of water, and place them on the desk in front of you. Then, partly closing your eyes to increase your attention to the task, pick up each one with the thumb and forefinger and judge which is heavier. Now introspect on everything you are doing. You will find yourself conscious of the feel of the objects against the skin of your fingers, conscious of the slight downward pressure as you feel the weight of each, conscious of any protuberances on the sides of the objects, and so forth. And now the actual judging of which is heavier. Where is that? Lo! the very act of judgement that one object is heavier than the other is not conscious. *It is somehow given to you by your nervous system* (Jaynes, 1976, p. 37: emphasis added).

Marbe's experiment thus corroborated James' meditation on will. The gap before the 'deciding' thought exists. This gap, that both Marbe and James discovered before the 'deciding' thought, meditation reveals to exist before all thoughts. 'If you watch very carefully,' says Krishnamurti, 'you will see that, though the response, the movement of thought, seems so swift, there are gaps, there are intervals between thoughts. Between two thoughts there is a period of silence which is not related to the thought process' (Krishnamurti, 1954, p. 226).

Stream of Consciousness

James used the phrase 'lapse of consciousness' to describe the gap before the 'deciding' thought, but the use of the word 'consciousness' can mislead. If we look at his paradigm, we see that it was not his consciousness *per se* that lapsed, but consciousness of thoughts. James did not black out just prior to his 'deciding moment';[6] he simply witnessed a gap between thoughts. This gap, however, was nonetheless part of the uninterrupted flow of his 'stream of consciousness' (James' most famous phrase). In fact, it is precisely because the stream of consciousness is an uninterrupted continuity that this gap between thoughts can be perceived as such. James illustrates this point well:

> Into the awareness of the thunder itself, the awareness of the previous silence creeps and continues; for what we hear when the thunder crashes is not thunder *pure*, but thunder-breaking-upon-silence-and-contrasting-with it. Our feeling of the same objective thunder, coming in this way, is quite different from what it would be were the thunder a continuation of previous thunder. The thunder itself we believe to abolish and exclude the

---

[6] And perhaps blackouts are actually black*ins*, in which only the last moment of blackness is recalled as one 'comes to'.

silence; but the feeling of the thunder is also a feeling of the silence as just gone; and it would be difficult to find in the actual concrete consciousness of man a feeling so limited to the present as not to have an inkling of anything that went before (I, pp. 240–1).

By this analogy, consciousness without thoughts would be the silence, and consciousness with thoughts would be the 'thunder-breaking-upon-silence-and-contrasting-with-it'. While thoughts tumble by so quickly one upon the other as to seem contiguous, their perceived distinction from each other implies something other than thoughts in which this distinction plays out. This 'something other' is consciousness.

Consciousness, even 'actual concrete consciousness', abides; thoughts arise within it. James, like many, sometimes interchanges the words 'consciousness' and 'thought'. His well-worn phrase, 'stream of consciousness', for example, is found within a chapter titled 'Stream of Thoughts'. Watch how he substitutes one word for the other in the following passage from that chapter:

> The transition between the thought of one object and the thought of another is no more a break in the *thought* than a joint in a bamboo is a break in the wood. It is a part of the *consciousness* much as the joint is a part of the *bamboo* (I, p. 240: emphases in original).

What else can 'the *thought*' in the phrase 'no more a break in the *thought*' mean other than '*consciousness*', as used in the last sentence? The two italicized words are, here, equivalent; James begins with the word 'thought' but switches to the word 'consciousness' by way of clarification. If the transition between the 'thought of one object and the thought of another' is analogous to the *joints* in the bamboo, then it is not an 'unbroken *thought*' that is the bamboo itself but, as James amends it, 'consciousness'.

In the East, this distinction between breaking thoughts and 'unbroken' consciousness is well known. Indeed, the most respected of all Indian metaphysicians, the advaitin Sankara, came to prominence because of the perceived failure of the Buddhists to adequately distinguish between the arising nature of thoughts and the abiding nature of consciousness in which the movements or moments (the word 'moment' is derived from the word 'movement') of thought occur. But the distinction is there for anyone who has either a heightened gift for introspection, like James, or a perseverance in meditation. For it is precisely the existence of this underlying, abiding, 'unbroken', witnessing consciousness that the practice of meditation helps make manifest.[7]

James' interchanging of the two terms 'thought' and 'consciousness' as in the example above, helps account for why, in his meditation, he called a lapse of thought a lapse of consciousness. Nonetheless, his discovery of a lapse before the 'deciding' thought forms the centre of his paradigm on will. James himself never downplayed the significance of this lapse, or suggested, as May and others have, that it left his meditation incomplete. Seeking neither to disprove or to substantiate it by other methods, James, the 'radical empiricist' of 'pure experience', let the lapse remain in

---

[7]   According to Hindu scholar Georg Feuerstein:

> . . . Witness-Consciousness, or 'Seer' (drashtri) is the pure Awareness (cit.) that abides eternally beyond the senses and the mind, uninterruptedly apperceiving all the numerous and changeable contents of consciousness. All schools of Hinduism agree that the ultimate Reality is not a condition of stonelike stupor but superconsciousness.
>
> This assertion is not mere speculation but is based on the actual realization of thousands of yogins, and their great discovery is corroborated by the testimony of mystics in other parts of the world (Feuerstein, 1989, p. 13).

place at the centre of his paradigm on will; a period of silence between two thoughts, not related to the thought process.

Ghostbuster

'. . . no one knows how or by what means the mind moves the body, nor how many various degrees of motion it can impart to the body, nor how quickly it can move it. Thus, when men say that this or that physical action has its origin in the mind, which latter has dominion over the body, they are using words without meaning, or are confessing in specious phraseology that they are ignorant of the cause of the said action, and do not wonder at it.'

Spinoza (1677, p. 131)

In James' paradigm, there were several instances of attention being paid to getting out of bed, but only the one that got him up was considered to be a possible instance of will. As he said, the original idea to get out of bed was, until it got him out, a wish not will. Such a distinction between wishing and willing is commonplace. Our sense of autonomous empowerment comes not from what we think but from what we do. This is why most discussions of free will do not focus on free thoughts but on free actions. It is in *doing*, not in *thinking* about doing, that belief in free will is based.

This is true despite the fact that few of our movements feel consciously guided. We are forever discovering the movements we are making only after we have begun to make them. When, for example, we are reading, we may feel, as we get to the bottom of a page, that it is time to move on, but we rarely detect the specific impulse to turn the page. Instead, we find that we *have turned* or *are turning* the page. Similarly, on a hot summer's day, we get a mental picture of a watermelon in our refrigerator and *the next thing we know*, we're on the way to the kitchen. Even complicated tasks, such as playing a waltz on the piano, often proceed without a semblance of conscious guidance, since our 'nervous system grows to the modes in which it has been exercised' (W.B. Carpenter, quoted by James, I, p. 112). After sufficient practice, in fact, the amount of attention required to perform complicated tasks becomes almost nil. While beginning pianists must focus on what their fingers are actually doing, accomplished pianists can play a Chopin Waltz while watching TV.

'Consciousness', says James, 'deserts all processes where it can no longer be of use' (II, p. 496). And, since most of our movements are habitual, consciousness is often missing in action. If consciousness is hanging around, *being of use*, then the movement is likely to be either novel or difficult, or at least made in a way that it has not been made before — such as when a newly appointed judge tries to sit with a newly-acquired dignity, or when a condemned person, awaiting a last minute pardon, tries to sit on the electric chair as slowly as possible. To sit 'with dignity', or 'as slowly as possible' is not simply to move but to *attempt* to move in a specified way. The sense of this attempt to move in a specified way is the sense of conscious guidance all the way down: Pause! Keep head erect! Place hands lightly on knees!, etc.

Such guidance, like a novel or difficult movement, feels conscious, but of what does any conscious guidance actually consist? To what extent does the guidance of any movement penetrate into the movement itself? As James puts it, 'Whoever says that in raising his arm he is ignorant of how many muscles he contracts, in what order of sequence, and in what degrees of intensity, expressively avows a colossal amount of unconsciousness of the processes of motor discharge' (II, p. 499). That we can, and do, consciously guide our movements is a widely believed generalization, but we cannot 'see farther into a generalization than . . . [our] own knowledge of details extends' (James, 1920, Vol. I, p. 65).[8] In James' paradigm, instead of finding any details confirming the conscious initiation of a movement, we find, instead, a blind spot. The movement, *as it is being enacted*, no less than the 'decision' to move, feels more like something that *has happened* rather than something that one does.

Like the moment of decision, a movement, immediately after it has been made, is easily construed as *having been* generated by a self-in-charge. But as the movement *is being* initiated, what we believe to be the execution of our will over our motor responses is no more than automatic reactions to the thoughts that prompt them. 'The first point to start from,' says James, 'in understanding voluntary action and the possible occurrence of it with no fiat or express resolve, is the fact that consciousness is *in its very nature impulsive*' (II, p. 526). By impulsive, James does not mean 'capricious' but 'capable of producing an impulse'. 'We do not have a sensation or a thought and then have to *add* something dynamic to it to get a movement. Every pulse of feeling which we have is the correlate of some neural activity that is already on its way to instigate a movement' (II, p. 526). Thus, twenty years before the philosopher Gilbert Ryle referred to volition as a 'ghost in the machine' (Ryle, 1949, p. 63), James had concluded that nothing stands between the thought of an act and the act itself except 'a supernumerary phenomenon depending on executive ganglia whose function lies outside the mind' (II, p. 560). Between the thought to move and the movement itself no 'third order of mental phenomenon' intervenes (II, p. 501).

Not all thoughts of action lead to action. Many thoughts of performing an action — from momentary flashes to extended scenarios — refer to an action not possible in one's immediate circumstance. And even thoughts of actions that *are* possible to be undertaken in one's immediate circumstance do not necessarily lead to actions. As James' example of trying to get out of bed shows, the arising of one thought can inhibit the movement about to be instigated by another. The inhibiting thought need not be antagonistic. It need merely distract. But once a thought to make a movement '*fills* the mind' unchallenged (II, p. 564), or '*stings* us in a certain way' (II, p. 568), says James, the rest is automatic: 'We may . . . lay it down for certain that *every representation of a movement awakens in some degree the actual movement which is its object; and awakens it in a maximum degree whenever it is not kept from so doing by an antagonistic representation present simultaneously to the mind* (II, p. 526).

James' use of the word 'sting' — a word that denotes a distinct bodily feeling — is not poetic license when applied to thoughts. The experience of will is obviously the experience of a convergence of thought and feeling. But, as James repeatedly observed, thought itself converges with feeling since ' . . . whatever elements an act of cognition may imply besides, it at least implies the existence of a *feeling*' (1909, p. 833). No thought enters consciousness other than as a feeling. 'Feelings', says James, 'are the germ and starting point of cognition, thoughts the developed tree' (I, p. 222). Regardless of how plain-feeling a thought may be, such as the thought of a number, it is a feeling nonetheless, a feeling distinctly its own. The thought of the number '3492,' for example, *feels* differently than the thought '3493.' Some thoughts may seem more neutral than other thoughts, but, depending on their context, all

---

[8] From a letter to his father in praise of the zoologist, Louis Agassiz, whom he was accompanying on an expedition to Brazil. James credits Agassiz with teaching him 'the difference between all possible abstractionists and all livers in the light of the world's concrete fullness . . .' (James, 1920, Vol. I, p. 56).

thoughts — all words and images — can register as neutral or otherwise. The feeling, for instance, that registers with the thought of my sister as the answer to a query about whether I have any siblings has a plainer feeling than the feeling that registers with the thought of my sister as someone who can lend me money. But this second thought of my sister is not a neutral feeling/thought composite (like the first) *to which I add* the feeling of relief. Each thought is its own distinct mix. My sister-as-a-fact-of-relation is a *different* thought/feeling composite than my sister-as-benefactor; they each form the composite peculiar to their context. So, too, the word 'Yes' strikes consciousness with a different feeling than 'Yes?' or 'Yes!' Neither 'Yes?' or 'Yes!' is experienced as a chord, one of whose notes is the neutral word 'Yes' (the word, say, as flashed on TV during Sesame Street). Rather, just as the neutral word 'yes' itself, each is experienced as its own note.

For James, the feeling aspect of thoughts was especially evident in relation to conscious movements. '*Movement*', he says, '*is the natural immediate effect of feeling, irrespective of what the quality of feeling may be. It is so in reflex action, it is so in emotional expression, it is so in the voluntary life*' (II, p. 527, emphasis in original). To illustrate a thought's feeling's 'immediate effect' on a movement, try writing your name backwards so that you have the same 'beginner's' attention to writing that you had in grammar school. From the thought of writing your name backwards to the actual production of letters, myriad responses (of neurons, chemicals, and muscles) come into play. All such responses help relay the thought to the movement. But however co-ordinated this relay may be, however *directed*, where is the consciousness of the relay itself? All that consciously affects the shaping of the letters on the page is the 'stinging' thought of writing them. This thought, the conscious thought of writing letters, consists of 'certain digital sensations, certain alphabetic sounds, of certain appearances on the paper and no others' (II, p. 500). But the work of guiding or *prompting* the movement ends, is 'absolutely completed', with the thought of the movement itself — what James calls the 'stable state of the idea' (II, p. 560).

As introspection reveals, in all movement the last 'mental cue' — the last conscious, 'psychic' antecedent — is never more than the stinging feeling of the kinaesthetic thought of the movement (II, p. 496). Whatever outward effect such feeling may have in our muscles — from waving our arms to wriggling our toes — there is no consciousness of an outgoing *surge* on its way to making the connection. Whether we move our arms away from us or toward us, the feeling in our muscles is always an incoming feeling *after the fact*. James quotes what he calls the 'admirably acute' observation of the physician/philosopher Rudolph Lotze on this critical distinction between an outgoing movement and the incoming sensation that *accompanies, but does not precede*, it: the feeling of the movement in our muscles is not the '*force* on its way to produce an effect . . . but only . . . the *sufferance* already produced in our . . . muscles, after the force has, in a manner unobservable to us, exerted upon them its causality' (II, p. 523).

No matter how difficult or challenging a movement, no matter what strain of muscles it entails, its only conscious agency is the impulsive power of the thought itself. A woman who struggles for three minutes to weightlift a hundred pounds may well lift twenty times that amount in an instant if a car should pin her son under its front wheel. This instantaneous response is not the result of a strong will but a pervasive thought — so pervasive that what James refers to as the 'familiar' though 'mysterious' 'distinction between thought as such, and what it is "of" or "about"' (I, pp. 296–7) collapses. Regardless of what she may have been thinking about just prior to the accident, as soon as her child is pinned she has no other thought than to come to his aid. What fills her mind completely, without a margin, even the margin of the immediate future, is the unified thought/feeling complex to lift the car off her son. The responder has become the response.

That evening, the mother may return to her weights to test her new found strength, but she won't find it. She will lift, she will feel resistance, and a dialogue with that resistance will ensue. An exclusive, peremptory, unchallenged thought will not fill her mind. And, in the absence of the instantaneous impulsive power that came with that thought earlier in the day, no 'superadded "will-force"' (II, p. 526) will make up the difference.

Later, we will look at the *feeling* of effort and will that accompanies some (but by no means all) of our movements. For now, though, it is enough to note that, despite the feeling of an active will moving things along, no movement, from lifting the front end of a car to lifting its hood, need be, indeed *can* be, referred to any activating agency beyond the impulsive power of the thought itself. James, in agreement with Spinoza, points out that this impulsive power of a thought, the immediate electrical connection it makes to our 'motor centres', is 'a mysterious tie', 'behind which we cannot go' (II, pp. 551, 564).

The Half-Second Delay

Since James' time, our capacity to measure neurological responses has, of course, vastly increased. If we cannot go behind the mysterious tie between the thought of movement and its connection to our motor centre, we can now at least go behind the skull, into the cerebral cortex, to detect the first impulses of electrical energy that precede all motor activity. We can and we have, but, as with James' meditation on will, and Marbe's experiment on the moment of judgement, the light it has shed on intention has darkened its overall mystery.

Until recently, if we knew nothing else about the electrical connection that a thought makes to our motor centre, we knew that the thought of movement preceded the movement. Now, thanks to a series of startling experiments, we no longer can be sure.

In 1964, two German neurophysiologists, Hans Kornhuber and Luder Deecke, using an EEG, discovered that, before every conscious movement, the electrical pattern in the cerebral cortex shifts (Norretranders, 1998, pp. 213–4). This shift, which they called the readiness potential, is the first detectable physical manifestation of a movement. But it is detectable only by the EEG. The subjects who are doing the movements have no awareness of it. The average time from the first detection of the movement by the EEG to the actual movement is 0.8 of a second (Norretranders, p. 215). The delay between the readiness potential and the actual movement is thus a measurable gap between the physical inception of a movement and its actualization.

Prior to the onset of the readiness potential, one would naturally expect to find the onset of the thought to make the movement — the sequence being:

(1) Thought to move (conscious)
(2) Readiness Potential, preceding all movement (*non*-conscious)
(3) Movement (conscious)

Given that the readiness potential is non-conscious, however, there is only one way to verify this sequence: compare the precise moment the subject felt that he or she had initiated or 'willed' the movement, with the precise moment the cerebral cortex's electrical energy was initiated (the non-conscious readiness potential). Benjamin Libet, a professor at the University of California, devised an experiment fifteen years ago to make such a comparison, and published his results in the journal *Brain*, with the title: 'Time of Conscious Intention to Act in Relation to Onset of Cerebral Activity (Readiness-potential)'. The experiment, accounts of which have been widely published,[9] went like this: The subjects, hooked to an EEG, sat in a chair, facing a clockface with a rotating dot. Their instructions were to move their finger at random, while still observing the rotating dot. They were then to report the time they felt themselves initiate the finger movement. Like James, in his meditation on will, Libet held that the moment of willing, if it existed at all, existed as an irreducible subjective conscious experience. No amount of wires and gadgets could replace subjective, personal testimony. Where Libet's experiment enhanced the subjective aspect of James' meditation was the addition of the clock. For it allowed each subject to pinpoint a precise temporal moment for when the initiation of the movement first became conscious — that is, to assign a time, less vague than 'now' — for the moment of willing.

Since the subjects had been instructed to move their finger, it is a condition of the experiment that some thought or thoughts of moving their finger preceded the movement itself. But what of *the* thought credited with triggering the actual movement?

James, as we saw, emphasized the impulsive power of a thought, but by that he meant only that no other conscious agency influencing the movement comes between the thought to move and the movement itself. Moreover, it is not clear from his will paradigm whether the thought to get up preceded, was simultaneous with, or followed, the actual movement to get up. His first description puts the consciousness of the action before the consciousness of the decision: 'We suddenly find that we *have* got up.' His second, longer description, both elaboration and commentary, restores the common sense temporal order of decision . . . action. The sequence discrepancy between these two descriptions renders the actual sequence ambiguous.

Such ambiguity might seem to be a flaw in his description, but, as it turns out, ambiguity is always precisely what introspection reveals. A drill sergeant barks 'touch your toes' to his soldiers, and his words seem to both precede and instigate their bending movement; but tell yourself to bend your finger, and this sequence is not so apparent. The precise moment you will act on your command is held in suspension for a moment or two if not longer; during this interval there will be one or more thoughts of bending your finger. But what happens when your finger first begins to bend? What of the actual thought associated with the actual movement? Can you truly tell whether the thought triggered the movement or the movement triggered the thought? Even if you shorten the command to 'Now!', there are various response times to that word, suggesting the intervention of an additional guiding impulse. You can, of course, establish a strict, repetitive sequence of 'Now!' [Bend finger], 'Now!' [Bend finger] . . . , all of which have the same response time. But in such a strict, rhythmical sequence the additional impulse is either suppressed or subsumed by the rhythmical 'Now!'s, whose even, metered repetition ceases to feel like an experience

---

[9]   See, most recently, *The User Illusion*, by Tor Norretrander (1998).

of willing an action. Not 'Now!' [Bend finger], 'Now!' [Bend finger] 'Now!' [Bend finger] . . . so much as 'Now!' [Bend finger], 'Now!' [Bend finger], 'Now!' [Finger bends], 'Now!' [Finger bends]. Only the first few movements, in which the response time to the 'Now!' is being established, would feel actively willed. But, like all seemingly willed movements, whether or not the movement precedes or follows the precise conscious impulse to move is, from the evidence of introspection, ambiguous.

In a sense this ambiguity could not be otherwise, since watching for the beginning of a willed moment is like watching for the green flag and the chequered flag to drop together. The green flag drops with the it's-*now*-going-to-happen conscious impulse to move, but it is only when the actual movement begins that the chequered flag — marking the transformation from 'the condition of wish' to the 'condition of will' — drops with it. Thus, while Libet's subjects *were* able to report a conscious initiating impulse at a time that proved to be 0.2 seconds before the movement began, they were also able to stop the movement *after* that conscious impulse. They had no way to distinguish a moment of wishing a movement from a moment of willing a movement *until* the movement began.

Whenever the subjects did abort an it's-*now*-going-to-happen impulse to move, the non-conscious readiness potential was still activated, even though 'it looked different toward the end (as action approached) from when the action had been carried out' (Norretranders, 1998, p. 243). But to his astonishment, Libet discovered that, whether a movement was actualized or not, the non-conscious process always began *before* (often a full half-second before) *any* conscious sense that the movement was being initiated. The appearance of the readiness potential did not dictate that an action would follow, but nonetheless any conscious sense of initiating a it's-*now*-happening movement always followed the *non*-conscious process. As Libet explains: 'Some neuronal activity associated with the eventual performance of the act has started well before any (recallable) conscious initiation or intervention is possible' (Libet, 1985, p. 536).

This startling result (which has since been repeated by others)[10] comes as less of a surprise when we consider James' data for a psychology of volition. For, if we accept that the 'willed' thought, like all thoughts, arises, that it is 'somehow given' to consciousness, it follows that it may indeed have a formation of its own prior to the added-on sense of being our own personal thought. If we further accept that thought is, in itself, impulsive, then it may well be, as Libet's experiment suggests, that the initiation of even so-called voluntary movements begins 'unconsciously'.

To say that our actions begin unconsciously is to say one of two things: either (1) they are initiated by an un- (or at least sub-) conscious thought, or (2) they are initiated by no thought at all. If the latter interpretation of Libet's results is correct, then thoughts of making a movement do not initiate movements but merely attach themselves to a movement-in-progress as it passes into consciousness — like a rodeo cowboy jumping down on a horse as soon as it emerges from the corral. But, given how smoothly and seamlessly the conscious intention to move fits with the movement itself, the former interpretation seems more plausible: that the unconscious neuronal activity of the readiness potential originates with some sort of submerged or preconscious thought just before it surfaces into consciousness.

---

[10] See Keller & Heckhaursen (1990).

What it means for any thought to be sub- or pre- conscious has yet to be resolved. James did not believe that a thought could exist other than as conscious (I, pp. 162–76). Thoughts *could* occur so 'quickly and inattentively that no *memory* of them remains' (I, p. 165), one moment 'consciously there but the next instant forgotten' (I, p. 166), but that is not the same as being subconscious. Since Freud it has become customary to speak of subconscious thoughts as repressed conscious thoughts.[11] But, as Sartre, among others, has pointed out, the notion of subconscious thoughts as repressed conscious thoughts raises the question of how someone can repress something that they are not conscious of (Sartre, 1956, p. 52). Are sub- or pre- conscious thoughts completely unacknowledged or are they just infinitesimally fleeting, communicating in an ellipsis of a very few words or a partial image, our knowledge of them obscured by the reactions they trigger — one dim moment of consciousness lost in the glare of the next few brighter ones?

Just such an infinitesimally conscious thought may have passed unnoticed by Libet's subjects. At any rate, the onset of neuronal activity that was detected in their brains was clearly not initiated by an agent 'I', since the sense of agency arose only after the initiating impulse began. Thus, when James, in his paradigm of how we will ourselves to get up out of bed, says ' . . . we more often than not get up without any struggle or decision at all. We suddenly find that we *have* got up', he was anticipating Libet's results.

The Feeling of Effort

'Effort is a distraction from what *is*.'

Krishnamurti (1954, p. 68)

As we have said, despite the evidence of his own introspection, James did not abandon his belief in will. He granted that thoughts arose impersonally; he granted that thoughts themselves had impulsive power; but those two facts, for him, did not add up to the non-reality of free will. The moment of will, he believed, transpired somewhere in between: after the thought arises but before it has an effect. The possibility of such an in-between positioning — revealed to him by the French philosopher Renouvier twenty years before he wrote *The Principles of Psychology* — had helped to rouse him from a prolonged depression. In his twenties, having just graduated from Harvard Medical School, James spent the summer in his parent's hammock, swaying to this refrain: 'I'm swamped in an empirical philosophy. I feel that we are Nature through and through, that we are wholly conditioned, that not a wiggle of our will happens save as the result of physical laws' (James, 1920, Vol. I, p. 152). Less than a year later, he wrote in a journal:

> I think that yesterday was a crisis in my life. I finished the first part of Renouvier's second 'Essais' and see no reason why his definition of Free Will — 'the sustaining of a thought *because I choose to* when I might have other thoughts' — need be the definition of an illusion. At any rate, I will assume for the present — until next year — that it is no illusion (James, 1920, Vol. I, p. 147).

---

[11] Freud himself never used the term subconscious, preferring, instead, 'preconscious'.

Twenty years later, when he had new reason to suspect that free will might be an illusion after all, this distinction between generating a thought and sustaining it loomed large for him:

> . . . [E]ven though there be a mental spontaneity, it can certainly not create ideas or summon them *ex abrupto*. Its power is limited to *selecting* amongst those . . . already introduced. If it can emphasize, reinforce, or protract for a second one of these, it can do all that the most eager advocate of free will need demand . . . (I, p. 594).

The power to 'emphasize, reinforce, or protract' certain thoughts among those 'introduced' to consciousness, James identified with 'attention', finding there the mental spontaneity commonly associated with will. The question of will thus became, for him, not how the thought I have now got there, or where 'other thoughts' 'I might have' come from, but *how much attention* is paid to thoughts once they arise. Indeed, he declared, 'Volition is nothing but attention' (I, p. 447).

James, of course, meant by attention something more than a particular focus at a particular moment, a focus that would hardly be distinguishable from consciousness. Rather, he meant something active (as is implied by attention's root meaning 'to stretch toward'). It is the stretch toward (or what he calls the 'strain of attention') (II, p. 564) for which James claimed the power of 'selecting amongst' thoughts 'already introduced'. This position has been echoed by Benjamin Libet as well, who held that even though the nonconscious readiness potential occurs before the conscious thought to move, *another* thought to *block* the move can still prevent the movement from being actualized. 'Processes associated with individual responsibility and free will,' he writes, 'would operate not to initiate a voluntary act but to select and control volitional outcomes' (Libet, 1985, p. 538).

But to define free will as attention and selection is simply to give more discernible names to a still indiscernible process. For the ultimate source of the selection — attention's power to 'emphasize, reinforce, or protract' one thought over another — is no less mysterious than the ultimate source of the thoughts themselves. To acknowledge attention's 'mental spontaneity' is to acknowledge *its* ultimate freedom, but not, thereby, 'mine'. If 'it thinks' is 'stating the fact most simply and with the minimum of assumption' then so is 'it sustains'. Just as you cannot know the next thought that will arise, what 'it thinks' will think, you cannot know how long any thought that does arise will stay. You can close your eyes and try to concentrate on the image of a full moon, but whether your attention holds that image easily, or whether the glow of the moon begins to fade, or whether thoughts and images gather, like clouds, in front of it, cannot be controlled. Once attention is engaged (by whatever means to whatever thought), there is no way to predict how long before it becomes disengaged. As Twain says: 'The mind? — man has no control over it; it does as it pleases. It will take up a subject in spite of him; it will stick to it in spite of him; it will throw it aside in spite of him. It is entirely independent of him' (Brooks, 1933, p. 264). To paraphrase Ryle, one thing I cannot prepare myself for is *when* the next thought that I am going to think will appear. Even James, who proclaimed that 'Volition is nothing but attention', allows that 'Attention *per se*, the *feeling* of attention, need no more fix and retain the ideas than it need bring them' (I, p. 450).

This is not to deny that attention, at times, rather than being part of a drifting thought process, feels like an active assertion of will against such drift. Nor is to deny the veto power (stressed by both James and Libet) that attention can have over any act-about-to-happen.[12] Instead of coming into consciousness as just another arising thought, the thought to attend, to *pay* attention,[13] seems to intervene against the whole arising thought process itself. But despite its effect of dispersing all other thoughts and images, the thought 'to attend' is itself just another arising thought, following the same protocol as all other thoughts and feelings in being introduced to consciousness. On what grounds can we assert that a rebuking thought to 'pay attention' is a stage director, controlling the on-stage action from offstage, in the house, rather than merely another on-stage actor, playing the role of a director, who makes an entrance and yells 'cut'? Is there, in fact, anything in consciousness akin to such an offstage director, standing in a darkened house, watching all that takes place 'before the foot-lights of consciousness'? (I, p. 450) (A permanent 'witnessing consciousness,' a wit-ness with no emotional involvement or even identification with the various thoughts, feelings and moods which parade in front of it, would, obviously, be no director at all. Its perspective would be closer to the architect of the theatre building who watches a rehearsal from the back of the house without any special interest or even curiosity in the proceedings.)

While the 'stretching toward' 'strain of attention' is real, what does this reality consist of? To begin with, the strain — anything from a barely conscious beat of focusing to a formal rebuke addressed to one*self* — is felt only when attention is a problem, either in starting up (amidst distractions) or in returning once it has 'strayed'. Only in such situations do we feel attention *as something distinct from consciousness*. In James' will paradigm, his attending to the thought to get up was a prob-lem because it was juxtaposed with the thought to stay in bed. The two thoughts rotated. Nothing in his paradigm suggested otherwise than that the 'strain of atten-tion' he felt was a result of this juxtaposition rather than its own original force. The split or division in his consciousness was a division of *energy*, a '. . . partial neutrali-zation of the brain energy that would otherwise be available for fluent thought' (I, p. 451).[14] Rather than being an original force, the strain of attention, by this analy-sis, is nothing more than an effect on one thought of a contrary ('inhibitory') thought (or thoughts) 'pulling back'. What can *feel* like an original force, such as the surge of will-force that James felt in the 'lucky instant' when he got out of bed, would be no more than the release of energy from the blocking thought, to stay in bed, into the original thought, to get up. In cases of 'antagonistic thoughts', says James, '[w]hen the blocking is released, we feel as if an inward spring were let loose, and this is the additional impulse or *fiat* upon which the act effectively succeeds' (II, p. 527).

---

[12] 'Thou shalt refrain, renounce, abstain!' This often requires a great effort of will power, and, physio-logically considered, is just as positive a nerve function as is a motor discharge' (James, 1899, p. 26). For Libet on will as veto power, see Norretranders, pp. 242–50. Libet's enthusiasm for the veto as the reality of free will is not yet as infectious as he might want. As one of his colleagues puts it: '. . . Libet has shown that the experienced intention to perform an act is preceded by cerebral initiation. Why should the experienced decision to veto that intention, or to actively or passively promote its comple-tion, be any different?' (Velmans, 1991, p. 705.)

[13] A curious phrase, suggesting not making or creating but somehow giving over that which is there.

[14] Although this quote is logically linked with the quote at the end of this paragraph, it appears in his ear-lier section on the passive model of attention, 'fitted to carry conviction,' but not to his liking. How-ever, by the time James revisits the passive model, he has embraced it as a description of 'what happens in deliberative action,' albeit 'warning the reader' that this 'introspective account of symptoms and phenomena' does not address the issue of causal agency (II, pp. 528–9).

At the end of his chapter on Will, James, in what threatens to be the start of an infinite regress, writes 'that although attention is the first and fundamental thing in volition, *express consent to the reality of what is attended to* is often an additional and quite distinct phenomenon involved' (II, p. 568). James does not define what this 'additional phenomenon' is, and 'freely confesses' that he is 'impotent' to do so (II, p. 568). Rather, it is an 'experience *sui generis* . . . which we can translate into no simpler terms' (II, p. 568). Presumably, this experience had already been translated into simplest terms by his paradigm of the will experience and the discussion that followed. His last-minute aside on the concept 'express consent' has, perhaps, more to say about his resistance to the implications of that discussion than to a deepened understanding of it.

By the evidence of introspection alone, neither attention or 'express consent to the reality of what is attended to' can be proven to be an active, original force. Nothing in direct experience refutes the passive model of attention, subscribed to by many of James' contemporaries, including his esteemed colleague F.H. Bradley, who wrote: 'Active attention is not primary, either as being there from the first or as supervening, but is a derivative product' (Bradley, 1886, p. 305). James himself, in one of his most poetic passages, again evoking a stream metaphor, expressed the passive model this way:

> The stream of our thought is like a river. On the whole easy simple flowing predominates in it, the drift of things is with the pull of gravity, and effortless attention is the rule. But at intervals an obstruction, a setback, a log-jam occurs, stops the current, creates an eddy, and makes them temporarily move the other way. If a real river could feel, it would feel these eddies and setbacks as places of effort. 'I am here flowing', it would say, 'in the direction of greatest resistance, instead of flowing, as usual, in the direction of least. My effort is what enables me to perform this feat.' Really, the effort would only be a passive index that the feat was being performed. The agent would all the while be the total downward drift of the rest of the water, forcing *some* of it upwards in this spot; and although, *on the average*, the direction of least resistance is downwards, that would be no reason for its not being upwards now and then. Just so with our voluntary acts of attention. They are momentary arrests, coupled with a peculiar feeling, of portions of the stream. But the arresting force, instead of being this peculiar feeling itself, may be nothing but the processes by which the collision is produced (I, pp. 451–2).

James offers this passive model of attention early on in his *The Principles of Psychology,* in his chapter on Attention. He acknowledges such a model to be 'a clear, strong, well-equipped conception . . . fitted to carry conviction' (I, p. 452). Nonetheless, he states his bias against it, in words recalling the crisis of will he suffered in his youth:

> . . . the whole drama of the voluntary life hinges on the amount of attention, slightly more or slightly less, which rival motor ideas may receive. But the whole feeling of reality, the whole sting and excitement of our voluntary life, depends on our sense that in it things are really being decided from one moment to another, and that it is not the dull rattling off of a chain that was forged innumerable ages ago (I, p. 453).

Such a statement is, of course, less an argument than a plea. By itself — and James offers no other refutation in his chapter on Attention — this plea for the 'excitement of our voluntary life' is hardly 'fitted to carry conviction'. James himself acknowledges this by stating that his reason for rejecting the passive model of attention is 'ethical', and, as such, 'hardly suited for introduction into a psychological work'

(I, p. 454). Moreover, when James returns to a consideration of attention in his later chapter on Will, he is unable to 'equip' an active model. On the contrary, his own paradigm, as well as his other introspective evidence, served instead to equip the already 'well-equipped' passive model.

His paradigm uncovered no active control of 'the amount of attention, slightly more or slightly less' which the 'rival ideas received', but rather a passive witnessing of a neutral process: '. . . resolution [not, in this meticulous introspection, 'my' or 'our' resolution] faints away and postpones itself again and again just as it seemed on the verge of bursting the resistance and passing over into the decisive act' (II, p. 524). His rendering of an impersonal, non-'I'-controlled resolution conforms to his overall sense of the impersonal, arising nature of thoughts. In his paradigm, two conflicting thoughts (or sets of thoughts), defined in relation to each other as resolve and resistance to resolve, battled for predominance like a dogfight in the sky watched by consciousness on the ground below. The dogfight ended when one side dropped out long enough so that the other side, no longer neutralized, 'exerted its effects'.

Nothing in James' paradigm suggested that the predominance in consciousness of one thought over another was *generated* by the power of attention; rather, the predominance in consciousness was *itself* the attention. The first Western psychiatrist trained in Zen meditation, Dr Hubert Benoit, confirmed this essential aspect of James' paradigm. Calling will an 'illusory notion', Benoit, too, could find no 'I' *influencing* the battle between resolve and resistance to resolve, no 'special inner power . . . exercising a kind of police supervision' over feelings and thoughts. If, for example, I fail to stick to a diet, I might say 'My greed was stronger than I was', but all that can be substantiated, says Benoit, is 'My greed was stronger than my wish to be beautiful' (Benoit, 1990, p. 203). To say otherwise, to suggest that there is some power of attention that proceeds from an 'I' conveys, as Bradley says, nothing that can be found 'in fact' (Bradley, 1886, p. 315). James all but concedes as much when, at the end of his chapter on Will, he states that 'for scientific purposes' one need not give up the view whereby the identification of effort and resistance with our *self* is an 'illusion and trick of speech' (II, p. 576).[15]

Making an Effort: Physical Exertion

All of us, to be sure, have moments, even extended moments, when we feel that not only our feelings and thoughts but even our actions are being transmitted through us rather than being generated by us. Dancing can feel this way, as can any improvised

---

[15] Schopenhauer, in an amusing illustration, depicts the illusion this way:

> . . . let us imagine a man who, while standing on the street, would say to himself: 'It is six o'clock in the evening, the working day is over. Now I can go for a walk, or I can go to the club; I can also climb up the tower to see the sun set; I can go to the theatre; I can visit this friend or that one; indeed, I also can run out of the gate, into the wide world, and never return. All of this is strictly up to me, in this I have complete freedom. But still I shall do none of these things now, but with just as free a will I shall go home to my wife.' This is exactly as if water spoke to itself: 'I can make high waves (yes! in the sea during a storm), I can rush down hill (yes! in the river bed), I can plunge down foaming and gushing (yes! in the waterfall), I can rise freely as a stream of water into the air (yes! in the fountain), I can, finally, boil away and disappear (yes! at a certain temperature); but I am doing none of these things now, and am voluntarily remaining quiet and clear water in the reflecting pond (1985, p. 43).

activities, such as doodling, or playing a bongo. At such times, our movements feel like nothing more than reactions to arising stimuli not of our own making; in a word, they feel effortless. The deeper we 'lose ourselves' in these activities, the less we experience anything resembling effort and will. Yet no one — besides, perhaps, an enlightened Tai Chi master — routinely lives in such a state. Whatever obscures the absolute beginning of the emergence of a thought, whatever significance one gives to the 'lapse of consciousness' that precedes a decision, even granting that a decision has no more epistemological status than an arising stimulus, feelings of making an active, physical effort do exist. Mental exertion is one thing, but what of physical exertion? Can it, too, like the feeling of resolve that initiates some actions, be construed as a derivative product?

Before attempting to answer, we need to distinguish between the two words 'effort' and 'will'. While both words are used to describe the active feeling of influencing a goal ('It takes will,' 'It takes effort'), only 'effort' is used to describe the passive sensation of struggling with the goal ('What an effort this is'). Moreover, this passive meaning of effort is never completely absent from the active meaning. If I say 'It's going to be an effort', I mean both that I am going to have to make an effort and that I am going to *feel the sensation of struggle* when I do. Even in the command, 'Make an effort!', the meaning of the word 'effort' is blurred by its two usages. 'Make an effort!' means, for the most part, to actively make an effort, but it carries, at the same time, the passive sense: 'Put yourself in a situation whereby you will experience struggle'.

The word 'will', by contrast, both as noun and verb, has no dual meaning or even ambiguity. It has only an active sense. Yet curiously, if not significantly, the word is seldom unambiguously active in its usage. Zeus wills, and the universe responds as if it were a well-tuned Porsche he was driving; we, however, despite the instantaneously impulsive power of a thought, do not, in our language, acknowledge such a direct relationship to our will (whatever we believe it to be). Unlike Zeus, we don't will, we *use* will, suggesting assistance or collaboration — as in the phrase 'Use public transportation'. Our avoidance of the verb 'to will' in depicting our everyday experience, in favour of the less clearly active phrases, 'Make an effort' and 'Use your will', may, in fact, be a clue to the ultimate nature of will and effort.[16]

Returning to our first action of the day, we can see that, barring illness or injury, the physical effort of getting out of bed is negligible. Despite this negligible physical effort, however, we often find ourselves crawling out of bed as if we were battling gravity. Sometimes we seem to be fighting physical grogginess, but other times we seem to be fighting nothing more than our own inner reluctance, moment to moment, as we are rising (just as James felt before he rose). When this reluctance to move is experienced with the movement itself, the movement becomes an effort. The effort is not the feeling of energy going into the movement upward; nor is it the feeling of energy being siphoned away. Rather, it is both together — the feeling of the energy moving upward *as* it is being siphoned away. It is trying to drive a car with the foot on the accelerator and the brake. Accelerating does not feel like effort, nor does braking — only accelerating *while* braking.

---

[16] Gilbert Ryle lists it as his first objection against the reality of will: 'No one ever says such things as that at ten a.m. he was occupied in willing this or that, or that he performed five quick and easy volitions and two slow and difficult volitions between midday and lunch-time' (Ryle, 1949, p. 64).

If we leap out of bed because we smell the coffee brewing, or hear the doorbell ringing, or see a fresh field of snow outside our window, we are accelaerating without braking. But as long as the contradictory thought of staying in bed is present, and our consciousness is *split* between two courses of action, each one 'neutralizing' the 'fluent thought' of the other, we may not be able to move at all. When ideas, says James, '*do not* result in action . . . in every . . . case, without exception . . . it is because other ideas simultaneously rob them of their impulsive power' (II, p. 525).

With a simple experiment, James illustrates how this robbery takes place:

> Try to feel as if you were crooking your finger, whilst keeping it straight. In a minute it will fairly tingle with the imaginary change of position; yet it will not sensibly move, because *its not really moving* is also a part of what you have in mind. Drop *this* idea, think of the movement purely and simply, with all brakes off; and presto! it takes place with no effort at all (II, p. 527).

The dynamic of making a physical effort can thus be explained in the same impersonal terms as the dynamic of making a decision, *with the addition of the thought's impulsive power*.

James got up 'without any struggle . . . at all' since 'the moment . . . [the] . . . inhibitory ideas ceased, the original idea exerted its effects' (II, p. 525). But *had* he struggled, his active physical effort could still be interpreted as 'a passive index that the feat was being performed'. Just as the thought of staying in bed, if it arises immediately after the thought of getting up, can check the thought's initial impulsive power, so can it check the surge of energy that has begun to lift one upward, if it arises just after the movement has begun. If the thought of staying in bed (or any image or variation of this thought) remains before the 'footlights of consciousness' long enough, it can trigger an impulse that brings the upward movement-in-progress to a complete standstill. If it does not stay before the footlights of consciousness long enough, then the impulse it triggers will siphon off only *some* of the upward moving energy. It is at this point that continuing out of bed is felt to be a struggle; the feeling of effort has arisen.

Sustained Effort

Assuming, at the first feeling of (passive) effort, that you do not respond by 'giving up', relaxing the physical muscular contraction producing the movement, what can be said about the feeling of (active) effort by which you seem to persevere? Such sustained (active) effort is, perhaps, easier to reflect upon in relation to an outside force. James, in going from a mental 'period of struggle', when he is lying in bed with conflicting thoughts, to a physical movement made 'without any struggle', seems to have bypassed the experience of overcoming external pressure. After all, it wasn't the cold *itself* that kept James from getting out of bed, but only his attitude toward that cold. What if, it may be asked, someone had tied James' arms and legs to the bed while he was asleep? His struggle, then, would not have been with the inhibitory power of an internal thought, but rather the restraining force of ropes.

James himself did not give an example of using will and effort against an outside force. He didn't need to. The dynamic of will and effort remains the same whether the obstacle is internal (such as a feeling of reluctance) or external (such as a rope).

Whether the restraint is internal or external, the feeling of will and effort (rather than the sensation of mere muscular exertion) can always be explained as the interplay between contradictory ideas or images. An outside restraining force adds no essentially new information to the psychology of volition.

To illustrate, say you awoke one morning to find your arms and legs tied. Undoubtedly your first reaction would be to tug at the ropes. The contraction of your muscles notwithstanding, this first physical response would not be experienced as will or effort. It would feel, rather, like a reflex: an instantaneous reaction to the repugnant feeling of being bound. You would, at first, have had no idea of the actual degree of your bondage, or whether the ropes were even tied to anything else. It would only be after the initial tug, if it did not free you, that a moment of assessment would take place. This assessment would include both the fact of the actual restraint ('Hey, I really am tied down!') and your preliminary estimation of its force. Immediately following this assessment, two thoughts flash by in alternating succession so quickly as to be a whirl: an image of your (objectified) self as bound and an image of your (objectified) self as unbound. Neither of these arising thoughts would be witnessed in detachment, not even the relative detachment in which James witnessed the alternating thoughts of rising up or staying in bed. They would be experienced rather with an explosive emotional force. There would not be, as in James' paradigm, some sort of tennis volley going on between two opposing options. The repugnant thought of your present bound self and the liberating thought of your future unbound self, far from being opposed to each other, are, instead, complementary. The energy of one feeds into, rather than siphons off, the energy of the other. Instead of a volley back and forth there is a single smash stroke — the thought to break free — which, without any other mediation, produces a second, intensified physical response.

This second physical response, however, though intensified, would not necessarily feel like effort. The increased muscle contraction would not feel like active effort unless the ropes offered more resistance than anticipated. For the feeling of active effort is not a function of the muscle force being applied, but of the resistance being overcome. The feeling of active physical effort only arises in conjunction with the feeling of passive physical effort, of struggle — here the realization (however slight) that the muscle force required to complete the movement has been *underestimated*.Without a moment of *contradicted assessment*, in which your movement would be experienced as a struggle, the force being applied would not be experienced as a force of will.

In the absence of such contradicted assessment (or any other contradictory thought), your movement would not feel like effort, but like an easeful, flowing motion, even a motion *assisted* by an outside force — like walking with the wind at your back. If, for instance, after your initial tug, the ropes had, unknown to you, become unhitched, your next use of muscle force would not feel like active effort or a force of will; it would not, in fact, feel like you *were doing* anything at all. Your arms would simply fly up over your head as if by magic. This magical sense of ease would accompany the movement even though your muscle contraction would have been the same as if you had, in actuality, been bound. Likewise, a strong sustained pull that instantly began to loosen the ropes, so that less muscle force was required with each succeeding moment of the tugging, would feel less like a force of will than would a far weaker tug that produced no immediate effect, and required more muscle force in each succeeding moment of the tugging.

The Flickering Reality of Effort

Assuming that you do not let your arms drop back down at the first indication that you have underestimated the force required to break free, but instead increase the muscle force, such increase would clearly be a continuation of one sustained force. Yet the same cannot be said of the feeling of physical effort (active and passive) that accompanies it. For the feeling of physical effort is *always* repeated at intervals, however close together those intervals may be so as to seem like one sustained feeling. Unlike the *muscle* force, the feeling of effort *flickers* into consciousness with each assessment that the muscle force being applied is inadequate. Try any sustained muscular exertion and you will see that a continuous, unbroken feeling of effort does not exist.

But even a flickering feeling of effort is effort. And the feeling of adding some 'oomph' to an action is, like the experience of making a choice, so prevalent that it is seldom isolated for observation, let alone introspection. Nonetheless, any feeling of active effort can be explained in the same impersonal terms as the feeling of will: a unification of brain energy that had been divided — a flowing into one thought of energy that had been divided between two thoughts. As James reluctantly conceded, 'the feeling of effort' ['effort' in the sense of 'making' an effort, but also, as always, with the passive sense of 'undergoing' effort not entirely removed] may indeed be nothing more than 'an inert accompaniment and not the active element which it seems' (I, p. 432). No one, James believed, could ever prove that a feeling of effort was an 'original force': 'No measurements are as yet performed (it is safe to say none ever will be performed) which can show that it *contributes* energy to the result' (I, p. 452: emphasis added).

Conclusion

Having found no evidence for free will, James declared that the free will controversy was 'insoluble on strictly psychologic[al] grounds' (II, p. 572). This was not exactly an admission of defeat, since James believed that there was no psychological proof of determinism either. No psychological evidence, introspective or otherwise, suggests that there is an automatic 'push of the past' (James, 1907, p. 537) onto the present. Our actions, before they are made, are 'ambiguous or unpredestinate', in a word, 'indeterminate' (II, p. 571).

But, while James claimed that in 'common parlance' this was the equivalent of saying 'our wills are free' (II, p. 571), he himself knew better. That no external or internal stimulus commands a predictable sway over attention does not substantiate free will. To accept attention (active or passive) as 'an independent variable' (II, p. 571) is to acknowledge only a radical ignorance concerning it. On strictly psychological grounds (as opposed to 'ethical' grounds 'hardly suited for introduction into a psychological work'), the 'question of fact in the free-will controversy' (II, p. 571) is neither free will nor determinism. It is indeterminism. What we believe to be acts of will are automatic reactions to stimuli of unascertainable origin.

References

Benoit, Hubert (1990), *Zen and the Psychology of Transformation* (Rochester, Vermont: Inner Traditions International, Inc.).

Bradley, F.H. (1886), 'Is there any special activity of attention?', *Mind*, **43**.

Brooks, Van Wyck (1933), *The Ordeal of Mark Twain* (New York: E.P. Dutton & Co., Inc.).

Emerson, Ralph Waldo (1849), *The Method of Nature*, in *The Collected Works of Ralph Waldo Emerson*, Vol. I (Cambridge, MA: Belknap Press of Harvard University Press: 1971).

Feuerstein, Georg (1989), *Yoga: The Technology of Ecstasy* (Los Angeles: Jeremy Tarcher, Inc.).

Gregory, Richard L. (ed. 1987), *The Oxford Companion to the Mind* (Oxford and New York: Oxford University Press).

James, William (1890), *The Principles of Psychology*, Vols. I–II (New York: Henry Holt and Company).

James, William (1899), *Talks to Teachers on Psychology* (Cambridge, MA: Harvard University Press: 1983).

James, William (1907), *Pragmatism: A New Name for Some Old Ways of Thinking*, in William James: Writings 1902–1910 (New York: Library of America, 1987).

James, William (1909), 'The meaning of truth: A sequel to Pragmatism' in *William James: Writings 1902–1910* (New York: Library of America, 1987).

James, William (1920), *The Letters of William James*, Vols. I–II (Boston, MA: The Atlantic Monthly Press).

Jaynes, Julian (1976), *The Origin of Consciousness in the Breakdown of the Bicameral Mind* (Boston, MA: Houghton Mifflin Company).

Keller, I. and Heckhausen, H. (1990), *Electroencephalography and Clinical Neurophysiology*, **76**, pp. 351–61.

Krishnamurti, J. (1954), *The First and Last Freedom* (New York: Harper and Row).

Libet, Benjamin (1983), 'Time of conscious intention to act in relation to onset of cerebral activity (Readiness Potential)', *Brain*, **106**, pp. 623–42.

Libet, Benjamin (1985), 'Unconscious cerebral initiative and the role of conscious will in voluntary action', *The Behavioral and Brain Sciences*, **8**, pp. 529–66.

May, Rollo (1969), *Love and Will* (New York: W.W. Norton & Company, Inc.).

Nietzsche, Friedrich (1976), 'Twilight of the idols' in *The Portable Nietzsche* (New York: Penguin).

Norretranders, Tor (1998), *The User Illusion: Cutting Consciousness Down to Size* (New York: Viking Penguin).

Ryle, Gilbert (1949), *The Concept of Mind* (New York: Barnes & Noble).

Sartre, Jean-Paul (1956), *Being and Nothingness* (New York: Philosophical Library).

Schopenhauer, Arthur (1985), *On The Freedom of the Will* (Oxford: Blackwell).

Spinoza, Benedict de (1677), *Philosophy of Benedict de Spinoza* (New York: Tudor Publishing Co.; no date).

Velmans, Max (1991), 'Consciousness from a first-person perspective', *Behavioral and Brain Sciences*, **14**, pp. 702–19.

Guy Claxton

Whodunnit?

Unpicking the 'Seems' of Free Will

The cornerstone of the dominant folk theory of free will is the presumption that conscious intentions are, at least sometimes, causally related to subsequent 'voluntary' actions. Like all folk theories that have become 'second nature', this model skews perception and cognition to highlight phenomena and interpretations that are consistent with itself, and pathologize or render invisible those that are not. A variety of experimental, neurological and everyday phenomena are reviewed that cumulatively cast doubt on this comforting folk model. An alternative view, more consistent with the evidence, sees intentions and actions as co-arising in complex neural systems that are capable of (fallibly) anticipating the outcomes of their own ongoing processing. Such tentative predictions, when they become conscious, are appropriated by a 'self system' that believes itself to be instigatory, and reframed as 'commands'. This confusion between prediction and control is hypothesized to arise particularly in selves that are identified in terms of a complex proliferation of partially conflicting goal-states. Such a system routinely needs to carry out detailed and time-consuming analyses of the motivational character of situations, thus creating the conditions in which anticipatory neural states surface into consciousness. The experience of 'self control' occurs when the system successfully predicts the dominance of a 'higher', more long-term or a priori less likely goal state, over another that is seen as 'lower', short-term or more likely.

The Untrustworthiness of 'Seems'

When asked why people believed for so long that the sun went round the earth, Wittgenstein is reputed to have replied: 'How would it have looked, if it had looked as if the earth went round the sun?' The answer, of course, is: pretty much the same. Likewise, from most vantage points, and for many purposes, it certainly seems as if the earth is flat. Without the aid of a telescope, or the ability to take simultaneous observations from the tops and bottoms of cliffs, the disappearance of ships as they sail away can be as easily attributed to the limits of visual acuity as they can to their sinking below a hypothetical horizon.

Such 'folk theories' are resistant to being revised, or even questioned, for a number of reasons. First, they do a good job, to a first approximation, of accounting for the data. It is only by paying attention to an accumulation of details that are apparently trivial, hard to spot, or even invisible without the aid of specialized equipment or procedures, that their flaws become apparent, and the possibility, let alone the necessity,

Journal of Consciousness Studies, **6**, No. 8–9, 1999, pp. 99–113

of an alternative 'theory' can be entertained. Second, they account for the most obvious phenomena in a way that accords with 'common sense' — the existing collateral body of folk theory. In particular, they are congenial: they offer a comforting model of individuals, their tribes and species, and their place in the great scheme of things. The idea that the sun goes round the earth places us at the centre of creation. It is nicer to see humankind as the pinnacle of evolution, or 'God's chosen', than as the provisional outcome of a vast concatenation of historical accidents. Third, the contrary evidence to the consensual view may be not only intrinsically slight; it may become virtually hidden. Once such a view has been culturally adopted and become 'second nature', then perception itself becomes skewed and selective, so that inconsistent trifles become invisible, and persistent interpretations self-reinforcing.

The self-perpetuating nature of belief systems is blindingly obvious, except when one happens to be inside them (Stolzenberg,1984). To a culture that is inside one belief system, it is simply a fact that the crops failed because the gods were displeased, and there will be plenty of 'evidence' that makes this 'fact' self-evident. To a different culture, the gales and floods that ruined the corn are the effects of entomic activity in remote corners of the planet: those pesky butterflies recklessly flapping their chaotic wings. In one dominant worldview, it is obvious that hunger and malnutrition in Africa and Asia are caused by a shortage of food. It takes the meticulous research of an economics Nobel laureate, Amartya Sen, to show that this obviousness is in fact ill-founded. How things *seem* is, as we well know, an unreliable indicator of their actual provenance, especially when the phenomena in question are connected to what Tart (1980) calls a 'consensual trance', and when the dominant interpretation seems to offer its interpreters comfort or privilege. It takes sharp, disinterested observation to force a reluctant acknowledgement that the way things seem is not the way they are.

The Invisible Unconscious and the 'Seems' of Folk Psychology

The disparity between 'seems' and 'is' reveals itself in the way people construe their own experience — their 'folk psychology' — as well as in their 'folk cosmology'. Demonstrations abound. To a well-meaning informant in an innocent-looking consumer survey, it genuinely seems as if the rightmost pair of pantyhose in the shopping-mall display is finer or more elegant than the rest — though they are in fact all identical, and we can show that it is their position, and not their composition, that most strongly determines the choice (Nisbett and Wilson, 1977). To an observer of two hamsters in an Ames-room cage, it genuinely seems as if they are changing size as they run along the back wall, though, from the outside, we can clearly see how the geometrical illusion is created. To the average gambler, it seems unquestionable that the coin that has come up heads ten times in a row has got to be more likely to be tails next time, even though they may themselves have had the probability arguments explained to them umpteen times. Collections such as Nisbett and Ross's *Human Inference* (1980), Gilovich's aptly-titled *How We Know What Isn't So* (1991), or Blakeslee's more popular *Beyond the Mind* (1996) make unanswerable cases for the suspect status of a rich variety of psychological 'seems'.

One common cause of the disparities between folk psychology and cognitive reality is the general neglect, in the former, of the role played by unconscious mental processes in normal mental activity. Folk psychology admits odd cases in which 'the unconscious' seems to be at work, most obviously in psychopathology and hypnosis, and in such curiosities as sleep learning and subliminal advertising. But, in vernacular accounts of mundane cognition, the 'intelligent unconscious' is conspicuous by its absence. Yet we now know a great deal about the ubiquitous influence of subliminal stimulation and non-conscious mental processes on awareness and action: the conscious 'seems' (e.g. Marcel, 1983; Velmans, 1991). We are not privy to all the data. Phenomena such as memory, creativity and decision-making reflect such unconscious phenomena (Claxton, 1999). People who tend to 'comfort eat' can be induced to do so by the presentation of a threatening subliminal message, but not by the same message presented consciously (Patton, 1992). Split-brain patients can be encouraged to act in curious ways, for which they then give explanations that are convincingly confabulated but demonstrably false. More informally, a visual image, a snatch of a long-forgotten tune, a desire for a childhood food can emerge into consciousness without any apparent precursor, yet sometimes can be traced back to a thought or an event not, at the time, consciously registered. Here again, things are not always as they seem.

The 'Seems' of Free Will

The way people think about their 'will' — the folk model of the relationship between what we think or intend and what we actually do — is perhaps the area of human psychology where all the considerations illustrated in this preamble loom the largest and weigh most heavily. A fortiori, we have to approach the phenomena of 'free will' distrustful of observations that seem immediate and unequivocal, and construals that appear self-evident. It certainly seems as if each of us is a centre of volition, and that conscious deliberation plays a causal role in determining our plans and actions — albeit an intermittent one. And sophisticated theoretical superstructures can be built which seem to buttress, but which actually presuppose, this 'common sense' (e.g. Baars, 1997; Sperry, 1985). Even — perhaps especially — when in academic mode, we have to try to see where unexamined belief or self-interest might lead to a preference for one view over another, and how this might in turn result in an unconscious epistemological squint or a tendency to load the observational dice. What phenomena, within the consensual view, seem to be trivial or even invisible, or are explained away as insignificant aberrations — uninteresting 'noise' that adds up to nothing? What alternative positions — 'epiphenomenalism'?, 'mysticism'? — tend to be dismissed out of hand as transparently nonsensical or potentially dangerous? ('If we didn't have free will and self-control, we'd all run amok' and suchlike, presented as knockdown arguments). It is only with a stance that is as radically sceptical as we can make it that we can hope to pursue a disinterested inquiry into the phenomenology of free will.

The consensual view of free will presupposes a view of the human psyche in which there are self-evident distinctions between 'self' and 'other', and 'body' and 'mind', which naturally lead to questions about who or what is in charge. What is the source of action, and what is the functional relationship between conscious mental events on the one hand, and physical and physiological events on the other? In folk psychology, once these dualisms have been accepted, the instigator of action has to be either 'me' — identified as a centre of conscious intelligence — or something else, identified as 'not me'. If it is 'me', I possess, and exercise, free will. If it is 'not me', then — given the general neglect of unconscious influences — my actions are the effects of external causes and I am 'determined'. And if this latter option is construed, within that folk model, as aversive, then the idea that conscious intention is the source of 'voluntary' action has to be vigorously promoted. The existence of a tight, causal relationship between intention and intelligent action becomes a lynch-pin of the passionately espoused model of conscious-self-as-instigator. As Dennett says in *Elbow Room: The Varieties of Free Will Worth Wanting*:

> If having free will matters, it must be because not having free will would be awful, and there must be some grounds for doubting that we have it. . . . But what exactly are we afraid of?. . . Not having free will would be somewhat like being in prison, or being hyp-notized, or being paralysed, or being a puppet . . . (1984, p. 5).

If the unconscious is admitted, it is only in terms of vague but powerful images — psychological equivalents of mad Mrs Rochester in her unacknowledged attic — that motivate us to protect and prove our imperilled sense of volition: zombies, aliens, Machiavellian manipulators, a sinister 'brains' behind the delicate operation that we take ourselves to be.

The Nature of Intention

One of the most compelling sources of apparent evidence for the folk model of the instigatory self is the apparent coincidence of deliberation, intention and action. I considered; I decided; I intended; and I did. When these events occur across a plausi-ble time scale, and where their contents match, there seem to be good grounds for inferring the identity, and the efficacy, of the 'I' that is the (supposedly) repeated sub-ject of these successive predicates. From the correlation and the sequence we infer the causality, in rather the same way that the possession of supernatural powers is deduced from experiences in which a dream or a premonition is actually followed by the predicted event. 'I was thinking evil thoughts about miserable old Auntie Joan, and sure enough, ten minutes later, Mother rang to say she had been taken into hospi-tal.' 'I had the thought that it was time for me to get up, and, sure enough, seconds later I am struggling into my dressing gown and heading for the bathroom.' The accu-rate anticipation is taken as *prima facie* evidence of the power of thought to control or influence physical events.

Even if such correlations were frequent and reliable, there would remain the famil-iar methodological problems about inferring a causality from a correlation. But are they as robust as we think? Beliefs in the paranormal are famously fuelled by amnesia for all the times when a fleeting thought or fantasy was *not* followed by a correspond-ing reality; and by people's ability to massage their own memories and interpretations (as they do with horoscopes) to enhance the apparent fit. Do we do something similar with the evidence for our own volition? Are intention and intelligent action as tightly coupled as our folk theory of self requires them to be?

It is hardly front-page news that intentions are neither necessary nor sufficient for intelligent actions to occur. What about all the occasions on which such actions occur without any preceding intention: the times I wander round the supermarket absent-mindedly filling my trolley with the produce I want, while totally preoccupied with the presentation I have to make at work on Monday; drive adroitly for miles without even being aware of the traffic; cook whilst chatting; adjust the pace and direction of a seminar discussion without any conscious deliberation, or even without being able, retrospectively, to say what I did or why? The vast majority of my sophisticated volitional virtuosity, in both mundane and professional spheres, plays itself out in the absence of conscious direction from 'mission control'. When asked subsequently how or why we did as we did, we may sometimes produce a plausible rationale, confidently backdated; but equally often we are at a loss, or happily admit that our reasoning represents a *post hoc* inference rather than a prior intent. 'I'm sorry I was so ratty last night, sweetheart; I must have been tired.'

If I observe it closely, even my getting out of bed does not furnish evidence of volition as robust as I might have hoped: what frequently happens is that I think 'I must get up' or 'I'm going to get up', and then my mind drifts onto other things and I continue lying there. What actually happens, often, is that I am in the middle of a completely unrelated train of thought and suddenly 'come to' to find myself already in the process of getting up. The truth is, when I decide to get up, I frequently don't. When I have stopped thinking about getting up, at some point I do. At the very least I have to conclude that the coupling between intention and action is a rather loose one. Failures of 'will power' are as much the rule as the exception, and there is no shortage of paving slabs for the 'road to hell'. If there turns out to be no subsequent manifestation of a publicly declared intention, no follow-through, we may even try to salvage a sense of self-efficacy by sleight-of-hand, claiming that 'I changed my mind' — though who it was that changed what, exactly, remains entirely opaque. Alternatively, we treat such lapses, if we cannot help noticing them, as if they were rare or sporadic aberrations, each of which can be given an *ad hoc* account, and not as cumulative evidence of the inadequacy of the simple 'free will' story. We accept the popular misreading of 'the exception proves the rule' — as substantiating, rather than testing, it — and do not register the fact that such exceptions are, if we look for them, far from rare.

The fact that the phenomenology of decision-making actually has great holes in it has been widely noted in the philosophical literature. For example:

> Are decisions voluntary? Or are they things that happen to us? From some fleeting vantage points they seem to be the pre-eminently voluntary moves in our lives, the instants at which we exercise our agency to the fullest. But those same decisions can also be seen to be strangely out of our control. We have to wait to see how we are going to decide something, and when we do decide, it bubbles up to consciousness from we know not where. We do not witness it being *made*; we witness its *arrival*. This can then lead to the strange idea that Central Headquarters is not where we, as conscious introspectors, are; it is somewhere deeper within us, and inaccessible to us. E.M. Forster famously asked 'How can I tell what I think until I see what I say?' — the words of an outsider, it seems, waiting for a bulletin from the interior (Dennett, 1984, p. 78).

And again, the experience of being the recipient, rather than the architect, of our decisions, cannot be dismissed as a mere glitch or curio of cognition.

> Once we recognize that our conscious access to our own decisions is problematic, we may go on to note how many of the important turning points in our lives were unaccompanied, so far as retrospective memory of conscious experience goes, by *conscious* decisions. 'I have decided to take the job', one says. And very clearly one takes oneself to be reporting on something one has *done* recently, but reminiscence shows only that yesterday one was undecided, and today one is no longer undecided; at some moment in the interval the decision *must have happened*, without fanfare. Where did it happen? At Central

Headquarters, of course. But such a deduction reveals that we are building a psychological theory of 'decision[-making]' by idealizing and extending our actual practice; *by inserting decisions where theory demands them, not where we have any first-hand experience of them.* I must have made a decision, one reasons, since I see that I have definitely 'made up my mind', and hadn't 'made up my mind' yesterday (pp. 80f.; emphases added).

If conscious deliberation and intention are neither necessary nor sufficient for intelligent action, are they at least helpful? Do we do better when we try to think before we act, or think whilst we are acting, than if we do not? Not always, it appears. People who are enjoined to 'think carefully' about important choices (choosing next year's college courses) or aesthetic preferences (an art print to hang at home) are subsequently less happy with their decisions than people who have chosen more 'intuitively' (Wilson and Schooler, 1991). People who are trying to think about their skill whilst they are performing a physical task become clumsy and self-conscious (Masters, 1992), as do beginners trying to speak a foreign language (Krashen, 1987). The appearance of conscious monitoring and intention very often leads to self-consciousness, and a concomitant juddering or even breakdown of performance. Contrariwise, the fluent execution of complex skill under demanding conditions, in the state known as 'flow', is characterized by a complete absence of deliberation, intention or self-consciousness (Csikszentmihalyi, 1990).

As I say, casting philosophical doubt on the naive view of the 'inner person' — sitting in the brightly-lit executive office of consciousness, collecting information, weighing evidence, making decisions and issuing orders — is not new. Gilbert Ryle (1949), for example, asks: 'if voluntary actions are those produced by an agent's 'volitions' [decisions, intentions etc.], are those volitions themselves voluntary? If so, we get an infinite regress; if not, we get voluntary acts as the result of involuntary events'. And the much-maligned B.F. Skinner suggests:

> The function of the inner man is to provide an explanation which will not be explained in turn. Explanation stops with him. He is not [seen as] a mediator between past history and current behaviour; he is a centre from which behaviour emanates. He initiates, originates and creates, and in doing so he remains, as he was for the Greeks, divine. We say that he is autonomous — and as far as a science of behaviour is concerned, that means miraculous (1972, p. 19).

Neuro- and cognitive scientists from Donald Hebb (1949) to Patricia Churchland (1986) have, like Skinner, been at pains to do away with the homunculus which is so often concealed within the folk theory of personhood of which free will is such an integral part. Indeed, one could go on listing sources of evidence, experimental, neurological, philosophical, quotidian and indeed spiritual or transpersonal, that suggest that the folk model of free will is inadequate. However, having adumbrated the problem, it might now be more fruitful to see what an alternative approach to the phenomenology of free will might look like.

The Co-arising of Action and Intention

The fact that conscious intention and voluntary action turn out to be so loosely coupled is a problem for any folk model of free will which posits that the former is the predominant causal determinant of the latter. It is much less so if we adopt the alternative interpretation of a 'correlation': that the statistical co-occurrence (how-ever loose) reflects the operation of underlying processes that are related to both. If A and B covary, and A usually preceded B, that doesn't necessarily mean that A causes B. It could equally be that both A and B are manifestations of a third set of processes, C, the time characteristics of which just happen, every so often, to make A pop up shortly before B. On this picture, the facts that intentions are sometimes followed by the intended action and sometimes not, that voluntary actions sometimes occur with-out concomitant intentions, and that intentions sometimes impede the execution of actions, invite speculation about the relationship between and nature of A, B and C. If we admit that 'C', whatever it is, comprises preconscious processes, then the loose-coupling of A and B no longer has to be construed as aberrant or anathema. Revising the sense of self to include such pre- or unconscious processes would then render the perceptual squint unnecessary.

The idea that conscious intentions and voluntary actions co-arise is substantiated by various neurological findings. Well known are Libet's (1985) data showing that cortical precursors of voluntary movements can be detected about a third of a second before the emergence of the conscious intention to move. More striking still are Grey Walter's (1963) demonstrations that such brain activation can be used to pre-empt people's own conscious decisions. Patients with electrodes implanted in the motor cortex were invited to look at a sequence of slides, advancing from one to the next, at their own speed, by pushing a button. Unbeknownst to them, however, the button was a dummy. What actually advanced the slides was a burst of activity in the motor cor-tex, transmitted directly to the projector via the implanted electrodes. The patients reported the curious feeling that the projector was anticipating their decision, initiat-ing a slide change just as they were 'about to' move on, but before they had 'decided' to press the button. In other studies, Grey Walter found that EEG readiness potentials taken from RAF bombardiers, as they were lining up to drop a simulated bomb, pre-ceded the conscious decision to press the bomb release button. (I regret that I have no reference for this finding, which I vividly remember being illustrated on a rather scratchy film when I was at school.) In cases such as these, physiological measures enable us to infer that 'C', the genuinely causal precursor of both voluntary action and conscious intention, is probably, to put it crudely, the brain.

But we do not need to rely on such indirect inferences. There are occasions when this loosely coupled co-arising of intention and action can be experienced directly — that is, unmediated by the habitual interpretative framework of the conventional self system. Oliver Sacks reports such an experience in his autobiographical book *A Leg to Stand On* (1984, pp. 129–33). Having broken his left leg badly in a fall on a Norwe-gian mountain, Sacks found himself, some weeks later, sharing a hospital bed with an apparently healed leg that felt as if it didn't 'belong' to the rest of his body, and stub-bornly refused to obey orders. 'I gazed at it and felt I don't know you, you're not part of me . . . I was now an amputee. And yet not an ordinary amputee. For the leg, objec-tively, externally, was still there; [but] it had disappeared subjectively, internally.' For three weeks Sacks lay shackled to a lifeless, alien appendage that stubbornly resisted all his most intense efforts to get it to move. And then, one day, when he was *not* trying to move it, the leg suddenly came back, and in a rather unsettling fashion. The feeling of a conscious 'intention' to move returned at the same time as the move-ment, but it did not seem to be the cause of the movement, or in control; rather it was an accompaniment of the movement, one aspect of a whole action that happened 'by itself'. Here is how Sacks describes it.

> When I awoke I had an odd impulse to flex my left leg, and in that self-same moment immediately did so! Here was a movement previously impossible.... And yet, in a trice, I had thought it and done it. There was no cogitation, no preparation, no deliberation, whatever; there was no 'trying'; I had the impulse, flash-like — and flash-like I acted. The idea, the impulse, the action, were all one — I could not say which came first, they all came together. I suddenly 'recollected' how to move the leg, and in the instant of recollection I actually did it. The knowing-what-to-do had no theoretical quality whatever — it was entirely practical, immediate — and compelling. It came to me suddenly and spontaneously — out of the blue.

Gradually these involuntary psychosomatic bundles of impulse-plus-action started to come more frequently, and to involve a re-assertion of ownership: a growing re-incorporation of the errant leg back into Sacks' overall sense of bodily identity.

> The power of moving, the idea of moving, the impulse to move, would suddenly come to me — and as suddenly go. [Yet] these flashes... involuntary, spontaneous, unbidden, as they were, did most certainly, and essentially, and fundamentally, involve *me*: they weren't just 'a muscle jumping' but '*me* remembering', and they involved me, my mind, no less than my body.

Sacks describes this curious phase as the returning of his 'will'.

> Yet there was an extreme limitation, a peculiarity, to this will.... It was always accompanied by an 'impulse' or 'impulsion' — of an oddly intrusive and irrelevant sort.... I welcomed it, enjoyed it, played with it — and finally mastered it. But it was will and action of a most peculiar sort, the resultant being a strange hybrid — half jerk, half act.... I found this experience amusing, fascinating — and somewhat shocking; for it showed very clearly that *one could have a sense or an illusion of free-will, even when the impulse was primarily physiological in nature.*
>
> [First], it seemed to me, I willed — and nothing happened: so that I was forced into a singular doubt, and kept asking myself 'Did I have a will? Have I a will? What has happened to my will?' Now, suddenly, unbidden, out of the blue, I had sudden compulsions, or convulsions, of will.... First I was will-less, unable to command; then I was willed, or commanded, like a puppet; and now, finally, I could take over the reins of command and say 'I will' (or 'I won't') with full truth and conviction [emphasis added].

Sacks' account suggests that the experience of intention as the antecedent cause of action is closely linked to a particular sense of self as owner and instigator. The trauma that led to a disidentification with the shattered limb had two effects: a loss of belonging and a loss of control. And as the leg began spontaneously to move, so the subliminal internal signals that heralded each movement had to be relearned, and as they were, so re-emerged first the ability to predict a movement; then a feeling of control; and finally a rehabilitated sense of ownership.

It does not take a traumatic experience on a Scandinavian mountainside, however, to produce an experiential reappraisal of 'intention'. It happens routinely in certain kinds of meditation. Especially in the *vipassana* traditions of Thai and Burmese Buddhism, meditators are taught to focus their attention on current thoughts, sensations and movements are they come and go. To aid the development of this meticulous awareness, the practitioner is instructed to make a 'mental note' of different kinds of experiences as they arise, change and fade away. For example Mahasi Sayadaw, one of the foremost of contemporary Burmese *vipassana* teachers, advises:

Should an itching sensation be felt in any part of the body, keep the mind on that part and make a mental note *itching*. . . . Should the itching continue and become too strong and you intend to rub the itching part, be sure to make a mental note *intending*. Slowly lift the hand, simultaneously noting the action of *lifting*, and *touching* when the hand touched the part that itches. Rub slowly in complete awareness of *rubbing*. When the itching sensation has disappeared and you intend to discontinue the rubbing, be mindful of making the usual mental note of *intending*. Slowly withdraw the hand, concurrently making a mental note of the action, *withdrawing*. When the hand rests in its usual place touching the leg, *touching* (1971, pp. 5–6).

As practice develops, so the awareness of a rising 'intention' is itself experienced impersonally, as having the same status as an itch or the sound of a cricket. Intentions bubble up into conscious awareness, just as other thoughts and sensations do: they are no longer experienced as having any causal status. 'When an intention and an action match — very good. When they do not match — equally good'. As a result of neurological damage, or of a heightening of attentional acuity, the phenomenology of intention undergoes a radical shift.

The Brains Behind the Operation

As I said in the Introduction, the idea of unconscious intelligence is much more widely accepted within contemporary cognitive science than it is in folk psychology. Evidence comes from a variety of sources, in addition to those, such as the semantic priming and masking studies of Marcel (1983), I alluded to earlier. They include 'hidden observer' effects (Bornstein and Pittman,1992), implicit learning and memory (Berry, 1997; Lewicki *et al.*, 1997), incubation and intuition in decision-making (Schooler *et al.*, 1993), and neurological disorders such as blindsight and neglect (Weiskrantz, 1986). However, these demonstrations have sometimes been construed as a collection of specific curiosities of the mind, rather than, as I have suggested, a cumulative demonstration of both the power and the ubiquity of tacit cognition (Claxton, 1999). In the strongest version of the 'unconscious HQ' model, conscious experiences, even those that seem to show the mind at its most rational, articulate or deliberate, are represented as corollaries of embodied activation states that are themselves neither conscious nor open to direct introspection — ever.

There are any number of ways of modelling the workings of what Dennett referred to as 'central headquarters'. For the present argument, it does not matter whether we use the language of information processing or of 'conceptual nervous systems' (Hebb, 1949) and neural networks — though temperamentally I prefer the latter. In these terms we might visualize the 'intelligent unconscious' as an embodied, distributed 'eco-bio-computer': an interconnected set of modular networks, comprising central and autonomic nervous systems, endocrine and immune systems, as well as a shifting environmental resource bank of materials and tools, both physical and socio-cultural, along the lines recently suggested by authors such as Francisco Varela and others in *The Embodied Mind* (1991) and Andy Clark in *Being There* (1997). But, as I say, all that really is at stake here in the fact that consciousness is not privy to most of the workings of this model.

In any such model, all the operations of perception, anticipation, action selection and assembly, and decision-making are subserved by the sequential transformation of activation patterns over recurrent networks of elements whose 'strengths' are subject to long-term learning and short-term priming effects. 'Consciousness' is associated with or 'produced by' states of the network that possess certain characteristics, and not by those that do not. One of the features that has been most reliably associated with the 'conditions of neuronal adequacy' for consciousness is some kind of rever-beration or prolongation of activity (e.g. Libet, 1985). Thus neural transformations that proceed rapidly and smoothly do not produce any corollary states of conscious anticipation. In familiar domains, where intuitive expertise is high, patterns of neural activation quickly segue into each other without relaxing into any intermediate states of resonance, until they eventuate in patterns that innervate smooth or striate muscle. The processing sequence does not achieve, in the interim, the requisite spatiotempo-ral stability for any anticipatory consciousness to arise, and skilled action is therefore unaccompanied by any sense of intention.

However, when the situational demands are more complex and/or less routine — where the requisite sequence of activation patterns is less clearly prescribed by the connection strengths laid down by previous experience — then the onrush of activa-tion may be slowed or halted from time to time, to allow the evidence to be enriched before action is implemented. As cognition is slowed down, so environmental infor-mation arising through the special senses, and information about multiple, perhaps conflicting inner need-states, can be sampled more fully; lateral connotations and associations within the modular networks can be recruited to flesh out the emerging neural 'picture'; and alternative action scenarios can be activated vicariously to check their possible consequences against currently active goal states. To use Greenfield's (1995) metaphor, 'epicentres' of neural activation can be maintained for longer while their associative ripples spread out and mingle, allowing more information to be recruited and more subtle and creative interweavings of activation to be generated. In such cases, the conditions of neuronal adequacy for anticipatory consciousness are more likely to be met, and what will begin to emerge into conscious awareness are states of the biocomputer that represent the 'options' and information sources which it is currently sampling. More specifically, we might reasonably suppose that, of all the current centres of activation, it will be that energetically interconnected subset which corresponds to the momentary 'front-runner', the current best guess about what is likely to happen, which subserves consciousness.

On this picture, 'intentions' appear to be not forms of control, but of internal pre-diction, and 'free will' is itself reframed as a phenomenon of anticipation rather than of conscious instigation. By drawing on proven (or at least plausible) characteristics of the human biological-ecological system, we are able to provide a psychological model to underpin Ambrose Bierce's prescient definition of 'intention', in his won-derful *Devil's Dictionary* (1958), as: 'the mind's sense of the prevalence of one set of influences over another set: an effect whose cause is the imminence, immediate or remote, of the performance of the act intended by the person incurring the intention'. (Bierce comments on his own definition: 'When figured out and accurately appre-hended, this will be found one of the most penetrating and far-reaching definitions in the whole dictionary', and I suspect he is quite right.)

This approach thus generates natural accounts of the facts that (a) conscious inten-tions are more likely to arise when decisions are complicated and processing is pro-tracted; and (b) they are often wrong. If an intention is really an internal prediction by the biocomputer of its own future state, and if such predictions are based, as they must be, on past regularities, then in complex situations, any processing that occurs after the prediction has been issued is quite likely to turn up unexpected problems or new considerations. These may cause the activation of additional circuitry, or switch activation patterns into unanticipated channels, and thus render the prediction false (or at least disrupt the temporal relationship between prediction and action which might otherwise have supported the interpretation of the former as an intention).

'Free Won't' and Self Control

A variant of this cautious, 'retarded' cognition, evolutionarily advantageous in situations of uncertainty, would allow the assembly and elaboration of the front-runner response to proceed while the corollary checking and resonating is still going on — but to inhibit actual implementation of the prepared action sequence until (at some strategically determined time- or information-limited moment) the check is determined to have been completed, and the 'green light' for the predicted action can be given (or not). Just as a 'racing start' involves revving the engine at the same time as stamping on the brake, so survival would plausibly be enhanced by getting ready to carry out the action that seems, on the basis of a preliminary analysis of the situation, to be the most advantageous, at the same time as one is carrying out such further checks as time allows. If new information or more subtle sources of threat are uncovered by the check, then the prepared action can be aborted at the last minute. Thus it is that Libet and others have come to associate volition more with the vetoing of action than its instigation: Richard Gregory's 'free won't' rather than 'free will'.

Conscious premonitions are attached precisely to actions that look as if they are going to happen — and then, sometimes, don't. Again, what folk psychology construes as 'will power' — with its notorious 'fallibility' — turns out to be a property not of some imperfect agent but of a design feature of the biocomputer. In the case of apparent self control, an earlier prediction (construed as 'Intention 1') is revised, as a result of further processing, and superseded by a second prediction ('Intention 2') which often matches the ensuing action better than the first. The first prediction — that one is about to reach for the cream cake — is 'resisted' as the checking process uncovers and recruits additional goal states and possible consequences that are sufficient to tip the motivational balance. When (as in this example) Intention 2 is judged to be of greater moral worth (as opposed to being merely 'selfish'), or when it seems to instantiate a more long-term goal or interest, or even if it appears a priori less likely than Intention 1, the revision is construed as evidence of 'will power'. The 'will' has apparently triumphed over a baser impulse. On the other hand, if Intention 1 is judged to be the higher, the longer-term or the less likely, and is replaced by a less creditable Intention 2, then the failure of the first prediction is interpreted as a 'failure' of will power. In each case, an updating of prediction is reframed as an inner battle between conflicting intentions — and as further evidence of the existence of the instigatory self.

Interestingly, Oatley and Johnson-Laird's (1987) elegant theory of the function of emotions argues for a similar cognitive economy. The basic 'negative' emotions such as fear, anger, sadness and disgust are, they argue, preparatory survival-based responses of the whole being to different, very general, classes of threat or plan-disruption, as revealed by a preliminary 'diagnosis' of the situation. Core emotions are, functionally, states of readiness of body and mind to correct aversive conditions by fleeing (fear), fighting (anger), withdrawing (sadness) or expelling (disgust), depending on the threat diagnosis that has been given. But these primitive responses can, just as I have suggested here, be modified or inhibited in the light of wider considerations. A person feeling nauseous in a theatre may sit still and fight to control the urge to flee or vomit in order to avoid the alternative threat of social embarrassment, for example. Here again the flow of neural activation towards the construction of a response is bifurcated: one arm continues 'downstream' towards action-readiness; the other is diverted for more detailed analysis.

Expanding the Sense of Self

Why is intention experienced so strongly as a phenomenon of 'self'? Precisely because the self, in contemporary Euro-American cultures, is comprised of an intricate system of (largely conditioned) goals, interests, preferences and threats (Csikszentmihalyi, 1990). Whereas in many so-called traditional societies 'identity' has tended to inhere in a web of social roles, rituals, relationships and responsibilities (Sampson, 1993), the individualized, 'saturated self' (Gergen, 1991) of the West tends to constellate around a personalized set of traits and desire-systems. When this goal structure contains a burgeoning (and potentially conflicting) portfolio of likes and dislikes, identifying with these goal-states, and thus incorporating them within the 'self system', elevates them to the status of 'needs' and 'threats'. Consequently an increasing range of situations, even those that may look, on the surface, straightforward, may have to be read more carefully for motivational pitfalls and opportunities. Instead of the 'retarded' mode of cognition being intermittently useful, it tends to become the default, thus generating the conditions under which a continual array of conscious anticipations will emerge, some of which turn out to be accurate predictions and some of which do not.

Many of the considerations that contribute to this subliminal action-formulation-and-checking process do not themselves, as we have seen, feature in the conscious read-out of the situation. While the overall direction may be 'summed up' in a conscious prediction or 'intention', many of the contributory influences may be too weakly or fleetingly activated to make it directly into consciousness. Thus we may predict or intend, but not know why. We do not have access to the full causal story, especially when some of the factors are themselves faint, or may indeed be actively suppressed (as in the case, for example, of 'perceptual defence'). Dennett again points at this explanatory vacuum.

> The 'firing' of a retinal neuron, for instance, may be 'triggered' by the arrival of a single photon on a retinal receptor. Vast amounts of information arrive on the coattails of negligible amounts of energy, and then, thanks to the amplification powers of systems of switches, the information begins to do some work — evoking other information that was stored long ago, for instance, transmuting it for the present occasion in a million small ways, and leading eventually to an action whose pedigree of efficient (or triggering) causation is so hopelessly inscrutable as to be invisible. We see the dramatic effects leaving; we don't see the causes entering. . . . [Even] from our own first-person 'introspective' vantage point the causal paths are untraceable (1984, p. 77).

Having to answer the question 'Whodunnit?' with the lame — but accurate — response 'I dunno' feels very unsatisfactory, especially to human beings who have been enculturated to believe that conscious comprehension and control are central to their sense of identity. The 'folk' answer — a sleight-of-hand, but a comforting one — is to extend the sense of self to include a kind of dummy instigator who can fill the gap with claims of authorship. And how is the trick worked? By turning predictions into commands. Self-as-instigator is really a simple subroutine, added to the bio-computer, which does not affect the latter's modus operandi at all, but which simply takes the glimmerings of a naturally-arising prediction, and instantly generates a 'command' to bring about what was probably going to happen anyway. 'Faced with our inability to "see", by "introspection", where the centre or source of our free actions is, and loath to abandon our conviction that we really do things (for which we are responsible), we exploit the cognitive vacuum, the gaps in our self-knowledge, by filling it with a rather magical and mysterious entity, the unmoved mover, the active self,' summarizes Dennett.

In this light, Oliver Sacks' leg takes on a different significance. For a little while he was able — privileged, I would venture to say — to break the consensual Cartesian trance, to stand outside it and watch the folk model of self struggling to reassert itself. It is perhaps only in the context of the self's expectation of, and investment in, control, that Sacks' experience seems unusual and disconcerting. What is happening, on the alternative view, is that Sacks is enjoying a less interpreted, less enculturated, reality: one in which both the action *and* the 'intention' are experienced as arising from the unconscious biocomputer. What usually occurs is that intimations of actions, feelings, and thoughts themselves are received by the system of self-related goals, plans and interests, and, *if they fit in with that system*, are then represented in consciousness as if these intimations were the causes, the authors, the instigators of the impending act, rather than merely its accessories. What was happening to Oliver Sacks was that, while his sense of self had washed its hands of the leg (so to speak), the leg's movements, *and the intentions to move*, could not be experienced immediately as belonging to himself, but had to appear as if — as they in fact were — they were coming 'from out of the blue'.

A Concluding Comment: the Value of Relinquishing Control

Like the realization that the earth goes round the sun, and not vice versa, this reframing of 'will' appears less comforting, but is in fact more veridical, and therefore more functional. In both reframings of conventional wisdom, 'we' are displaced from the centre; in the first case, of the universe, in the second, of conscious control. A reappraisal of the human place in the scheme of things is required. In the case of free will, the human psyche must be acknowledged to be intrinsically more mysterious, more ineffable, than we have thought, or desired, it to be. But broadening the sense of identity to embrace the unconscious eco-bio-computer seems to offer concomitant benefits in terms of both creativity and equanimity. As both experimental and anec-dotal evidence show overwhelmingly (Claxton, 1999), creativity and the productive use of intuition rely on the ability to relinquish conscious striving and control, and allow the mind to mull and meander, play and ponder. Earnest deliberation and too much pressure leave no room for insight, and the period of incubation that may precede it (Smith, 1995).

Indeed, the attempt to maintain a facade of consistency and control through conscious effort, sophistry and self-deception is itself debilitating. It is people who struggle most assiduously to maintain conscious control, and to suppress that which is quirky or unwanted, who tend to suffer from various neurotic and even psychotic disorders (Sass, 1994; Wells, 1998). Paradoxically, the acceptance that our minds are more wilful, wayward and whimsical — 'madder' — than we thought can bring an increase in sanity and peace. There are even suggestions from scurrilous seers and disreputable mystics that the eco-bio-computer, if we will let it, can be wiser than 'we' are.

Acknowledgements
I would like to thank Benjamin Libet, Jonathan Schooler and one anonymous referee for comments which have substantially improved the paper.

References

Baars, B.J. (1997), *In the Theater of Consciousness: The Workspace of the Mind* (New York: OUP).
Berry, D. (1997), *How Implicit is Implicit Learning?* (Oxford: Oxford University Press).
Bierce, A. (1958), *The Devil's Dictionary* (Toronto: Dover).
Blakeslee, T. (1996), *Beyond the Conscious Mind: Unlocking the Secrets of the Self* (New York: Plenum).
Bornstein, R.F. and Pittman, T.S. (1992), *Perception without Awareness: Cognitive, Clinical and Social Perspectives* (New York: Guilford Press).
Churchland, P.S. (1986), *Neurophilosophy* (Cambridge, MA: MIT Press).
Clark, A. (1997), *Being There: Putting Brain, Body and World Together Again* (Cambridge, MA: MIT).
Claxton, G.L. (1997/1999), *Hare Brain, Tortoise Mind: Why Intelligence Increases When You Think Less* (London: Fourth Estate; Hopewell, NJ: Ecco Press).
Csikszentmihalyi, M. (1990), *Flow: The Psychology of Optimal Experience* (New York: Harper-Collins).
Dennett, D. (1984), *Elbow Room: The Varieties of Free Will Worth Wanting* (Oxford: Clarendon Press).
Gergen, K.J. (1991), *The Saturated Self* (New York: Basic Books).
Gilovich, T. (1991), *How We Know What Isn't So: The Fallibility of Human Reason in Everyday Life* (New York: The Free Press).
Greenfield, S.A. (1995), *Journey to the Centers of the Mind* (New York: Freeman).
Grey Walter, W. (1963), Presentation to the Osler Society, Oxford University; quoted in *Consciousness Explained*, D. Dennett (Boston, MA: Little, Brown, 1991).
Hebb, D.O. (1949), *The Organization of Behavior* (New York: McGraw-Hill).
Krashen, S.D. (1987), *Principles and Practice in Second Language Acquisition* (New York: Prentice Hall).
Lewicki, P., Czyzewska, C. and Hill, T. (1997), 'Nonconscious information processing and personality', in Berry (1997).
Libet, B. (1985), 'Unconscious cerebral initiative and the role of conscious will in voluntary action', *Behavioral and Brain Sciences*, **8**, pp. 529–66.
Mahasi Sayadaw (1971), *Practical Insight Meditation: Basic and Progressive Stages* (Kandy, Sri Lanka: The Forest Hermitage).
Marcel, A.J. (1983), 'Conscious and unconscious perception: an approach to the relations between phenomenal experience and perceptual processes', *Cognitive Psychology*, **15**, pp. 238–300.
Masters, R.S.W. (1992), 'Knowledge, knerves and know-how: the role of explicit vs implicit knowledge in the breakdown of a complex skill under pressure', *British Journal of Psychology*, **83**, pp. 343–58.
Nisbett, R.E. and Ross, L. (1980), *Human Inference: Strategies and Shortcomings of Social Judgement* (Englewood Cliffs, NJ: Prentice Hall).
Nisbett, R.E. and Wilson, T.D. (1977), 'Telling more than we can know: verbal reports on mental processes', *Psychological Review*, **84**, pp. 231–59.

Oatley, K. and Johnson-Laird, P.N. (1987), 'Towards a cognitive theory of emotions', *Cognition and Emotion*, **1**, pp. 29–50.

Patton, C.J. (1992), 'Fear of abandonment and binge eating: a subliminal psychodynamic activation investigation', *Journal of Nervous and Mental Disorders*, in press; quoted in 'What does it all mean?', by J.M. Masling, in Bornstein and Pittman (1992).

Ryle, G. (1949), *The Concept of Mind* (London: Hutchinson).

Sacks, O. (1984), *A Leg to Stand On* (New York: HarperCollins).

Sampson, E.E. (1993), *Celebrating the Other: A Dialogic Account of Human Nature* (London: Harvester).

Sass, L.A. (1994), *The Paradoxes of Delusion: Wittgenstein, Schreber and the Schizophrenic Mind* (Ithaca, NY: Cornell University Press).

Schooler, J., Ohlsson, S. and Brooks, K. (1993), 'Thought beyond words: when language overshadows insight', *Journal of Experimental Psychology: General*, **122**, pp.166–83.

Skinner, B.F. (1972), *Beyond Freedom and Dignity* (London: Cape).

Smith, S.M. (1995), 'Getting into and out of mental ruts: a theory of fixation, incubation and insight', in *The Nature of Insight*, ed. R.J. Sternberg and J.E. Davidson (Cambridge, MA: Bradford/MIT Press).

Sperry, R. (1985), *Science and Moral Priority: Merging Mind, Brain and Human Values* (NY: Praeger).

Stolzenberg, G. (1984), 'Can an inquiry into the foundation of mathematics tell us anything interesting about mind?', in *The Invented Reality*, ed. P. Watzlawick (New York: W.W. Norton).

Tart, C. (1980), 'The systems approach to states of consciousness', in *Beyond Ego: Transpersonal Dimensions in Psychology*, ed. R.N. Walsh and F. Vaughan (Los Angeles, CA: Tarcher).

Varela, F.J., Thompson, E. and Rosch, E. (1991), *The Embodied Mind: Cognitive Science and Human Experience* (Cambridge, MA: MIT Press).

Velmans, M. (1991), 'Is human information processing conscious?', *Behavioral and Brain Sciences*, **14**, pp. 651–726.

Weiskrantz, L. (1986), *Blindsight: A Case Study and Implications* (Oxford: Oxford University Press).

Wells, A. (1998), 'Cognitive therapy of anxiety', invited presentation to the British Psychological Society Annual Conference, Brighton, March.

Wilson, T.D. and Schooler, J. (1991), 'Thinking too much: introspection can reduce the quality of preferences and decisions', *Journal of Personality and Social Psychology*, **60**, pp. 181–92.

Jeffrey M. Schwartz

A Role for Volition and Attention in the Generation of New Brain Circuitry

Toward A Neurobiology of Mental Force

Obsessive-compulsive disorder (OCD) is a commonly occurring neuropsychiatric condition characterized by bothersome intrusive thoughts and urges that frequently lead to repetitive dysfunctional behaviours such as excessive handwashing. There are well-documented alterations in cerebral function which appear to be closely related to the manifestation of these symptoms. Controlled studies of cognitive-behavioural therapy (CBT) techniques utilizing the active refocusing of attention away from the intrusive phenomena of OCD and onto adaptive alternative activities have demonstrated both significant improvements in clinical symptoms and systematic changes in the pathological brain circuitry associated with them. Careful investigation of the relationships between the experiential and putative neurophysiological processes involved in these changes can offer useful insights into volitional aspects of cerebral function.

Introduction

Advances in the field of neuroscience over the past several decades have greatly enhanced our ability to demonstrate systematic and experimentally verifiable relationships between a wide array of conscious experiences and brain mechanisms which can reasonably be thought to underlie them. A prime example of this kind of work involves recent advances in our understanding of obsessive-compulsive disorder (OCD), a condition affecting approximately 2% of the population (Rasmussen & Eisen, 1998). OCD is characterized by intrusive thoughts and urges that often result in the performance of dysfunctional repetitive behaviours such as excessive handwashing or ritualistic counting and checking. There is now a broad consensus among neuropsychiatrists that brain circuitry contained within the orbital frontal cortex (OFC), anterior cingulate gyrus and the basal ganglia is intimately involved in the expression of the symptoms of OCD (for recent reviews see Schwartz 1997a & b, Rauch & Baxter, 1998).

The manner in which OCD manifests its symptoms renders it a particularly apt subject for the investigation of natural phenomena which occur at the mind–brain interface. People who are affected by this condition are generally quite aware that the bothersome intrusive thoughts and urges with which they are suffering are inappro-

Journal of Consciousness Studies, **6**, No. 8–9, 1999, pp. 115–42

priate and adventitious in the literal sense i.e., the symptoms are experienced as unwanted and extraneous intrusions into consciousness, and have a quality which has classically been described in the clinical literature as 'ego-dystonic' or 'ego-alien' implying 'foreign to one's experience of oneself as a psychological being' (Nemiah & Uhde, 1989). Because of this, people afflicted with OCD can frequently give clear and precise descriptions of how the symptoms are subjectively experienced, which allows investigators to perform studies of how patterns of cerebral activity change with symptom onset. Scott Rauch and the brain imaging group at Harvard University performed studies of just this kind, utilizing both PET and functional MRI to demonstrate changes in cerebral activity after acute symptom exacerbation in patients with OCD. Exposure of patients to stimuli which elicit the intrusive thoughts and urges typical of OCD (e.g., an intense sense of dread and contamination evoked by being visually exposed to a dirty glove) was accompanied by markedly increased activity in the OFC and the anterior cingulate gyrus, brain regions with a well demonstrated capacity to generate alerting 'error-detection' type signals in response to unanticipated alterations in the environment, as well as in the caudate nucleus, a key component of the basal ganglia and the major sub-cortical projection site involved in the functional modulation of the OFC and cingulate (Rauch et al., 1994; Breite et al., 1996).

The ability of OCD patients to clearly describe their symptoms also allows the investigation of how their conscious experiences change with treatment. Since there are now very effective means of alleviating OCD symptoms through the utilization of both pharmacological and psychological interventions (Jenike, 1998; Tallis, 1995; Van Oppen et al., 1995), as well as significant evidence that each of these treatments independently cause similar changes in patterns of cerebral glucose metabolism in patients who respond to them (Baxter et al., 1992; Schwartz et al., 1996), it has become possible to track how post-treatment changes in the cerebral metabolism of functionally well-characterized brain circuits relate to changes in the internal conscious experience of clearly defined neuropsychiatric symptoms.

The use of cognitive-behavioural therapy (CBT) as a means of enabling people suffering from OCD to overcome their repetitive responses to bothersome intrusive conscious phenomena offers a valuable source of data to those interested in the study of the mind-brain interface. Because there is strong evidence that the core experience common to essentially all OCD symptoms — a gnawing, intrusive, inescapable and predominantly passively experienced sense that 'something is wrong' — is generated by faulty brain circuitry (for review see Schwartz, 1997a; 1998a), a close examination of the mental processes used by people learning how to wilfully alter their behavioural responses to OCD can yield significant insights about the processes whereby changes in the meaning or value one places on distressing conscious phenomena can result in active changes in how one responds to those phenomena. The training techniques which are used to accomplish that clinical goal explicitly encourage OCD sufferers to arrive at a new understanding of the relationship between their brain, their conscious experience, and their choice of behavioural responses to that experience (Schwartz, 1996). Since an understanding of the basic brain circuitry involved in OCD forms a key part in the theoretical basis of the cognitive training techniques we utilize at UCLA, and since significant alterations in the metabolic activity of those circuits occurs in response to successful treatment, a brief review of the basic brain mechanisms of OCD seems in order.

OCD: Basic Brain Circuitry

There is, as mentioned above, a broad consensus that brain circuitry contained within the OFC, anterior cingulate gyrus and the basal ganglia is intimately involved in the expression of the symptoms of OCD. The findings of cerebral metabolic rate changes in this circuitry after successful CBT are especially relevant to questions concerning mind-brain relations in light of recent advances in the fields of anatomy and physiology concerning the functional connectivity of these structures. The major findings of this research have been summarized in several elegant review articles (Graybiel *et al.*, 1994; Saint-Cyr *et al.*, 1995; Zald and Kim, 1996a,b). A brief overview of some of this work may help both to elucidate cerebral mechanisms relevant to the pathophysiology of OCD, as well as begin to clarify the relationship between brain function and internal experience in ways that can enhance our understanding of the topology of the mind–brain interface.

A. Micro-anatomy of the caudate nucleus

The basal ganglia, which include the striatum (comprised of the caudate nucleus and putamen), have been implicated in numerous studies of OCD (see Rauch, Whalen *et al.*, 1998 for review). Recent advances in our understanding of the micro-circuitry of the striatum are potentially of great relevance to understanding brain mechanisms of OCD and its treatment.

The entire striatum (fig. 1) contains a profoundly complex system of interacting neuronal micro-circuits or 'modules' comprised of neurochemically specialized zones called striosomes dispersed within a larger compartment called the matrix (see Graybiel *et al.*, 1994 for review). These striosomes, which have a patchy appearance, receive inputs primarily from limbic system structures such as the amygdala and project to the dopamine-containing neurons of the substantia nigra pars compacta (Gerfen, 1992). This pattern of connectivity strongly suggests a role for striosomes in mediating aspects of striatal modulation of emotional arousal (see Graybiel, 1995 for review). Moreover, the prefrontal cortex, which plays a primary role in assessing the behavioural relevance of environmental inputs, also projects into this system. Interestingly, the two prefrontal structures which send the densest projections into the striosomes of the caudate nucleus are the OFC and anterior cingulate gyrus (Eblen and Graybiel, 1995). This seems especially noteworthy given the very substantial data base implicating these two structures in OCD pathology (Rauch and Baxter, 1998) as well as in both pharmacological (Saxena *et al.*, 1998) and psychological treatment response (Schwartz, 1998a).

In contrast to the select striosomal projections of the orbital cortex and cingulate gyrus, projections from the rest of the prefrontal cortex go primarily to the matrix compartment. Projections from areas of the lateral convexity of the cerebral hemispheres, which play a key role in processing information for high order tasks such as anticipation and planning (Stuss and Benson, 1986; Fuster, 1989), seem to be of particular interest, however. These projections form other quite distinct patchy distributions within the matrix, which have been termed matrisomes (Flaherty and Graybiel, 1994). These matrisomes are consistently found in close spatial proximity to striosomes. This sort of micro-anatomical arrangement could be quite conducive to functional interactions between the limbic associated striosomes and matrisomes made up of frontal association cortex projections. This is especially so given the discovery of

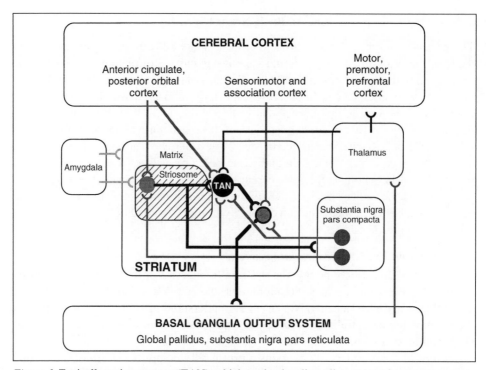

Figure 1. Tonically active neurons (TAN), which tend to localize adjacent to striosomes, appear to integrate information related to limbic system function with other cortical inputs to the striatum. Changes in TAN response patterns during behavioural learning could modify output functions of the basal ganglia. (Localization of matrisomes within the matrix is not shown in this diagram. See text for details.) Adapted from T. Aosaki, M. Kimura and A.M. Graybiel, *J. Neurophysiology*, **73**, 1234–52 (March 1995); schematic revision courtesy of *Science & Medicine*, 1997, **4** (2), p. 20.

cells of a highly specialized nature which seem to localize at striosome-matrix borders, and are in a position to integrate information from both striosomes and matrisomes. These cells, called tonically active neurons or TANs (figure 1), are of great interest insofar as they demonstrate a distinct pattern of firing when cues linked to reward delivery are presented during behavioural conditioning (Aosaki *et al.*, 1995). Modification of TAN activity by behaviourally meaningful stimuli could potentially serve as a gating mechanism for re-directing information flow through the striatum during learning. In this way TANs could potentially help select and generate new patterns of striatal activity in response to the integration of behaviourally significant information. This kind of functional re-gating of neuronal activity patterns could be profoundly important during the acquisition of new behavioural skills in the course of doing CBT which, as we will see, requires the applied use of behavioural planning to modulate one's responses to the powerful emotional feelings mediated by limbic-related areas of the brain.

B. *The caudate's role in gating thoughts and emotions*

A number of researchers who have studied how cortical circuitry is modulated by the caudate during the preparation for and initiation of behavioural activity have used the concept of gating to help explain this process (Baxter, 1995; Swerdlow, 1995). How the flow of information is gated through the complex circuitry of the basal ganglia will help determine whether the signals received by the thalamus result in subsequent excitation or inhibition of behaviourally critical cortical areas. Imbalances in gating the flow of cortical output can thus affect relative levels of cerebral excitation and inhibition in ways which profoundly influence an organism's conscious experience. The study of OCD provides a striking example of this, as demonstrated by the data of the Rauch group at Harvard (see above) in which the essentially contemporaneous onset of intrusive OCD mental phenomena and markedly increased activity in the OFC, cingulate, caudate and thalamus was seen.

Basic research in behavioural neuroscience by the groups of Okihide Hikosaka of Tokyo and Jean Saint-Cyr of Toronto provides further insight into the potential relevance of this circuitry to the symptoms of OCD. In a series of elegant experiments into the mechanisms of saccadic eye movements occurring in response to reward-related visual cues, Hikosaka *et al.* (1989) demonstrated that the caudate can rapidly modulate the activity of neural circuits involved in the preparation for and guidance of environmentally relevant behaviours. Saint-Cyr *et al.* (1995) have proposed that analogous mechanisms involving caudate-prefrontal cortex interactions could enable what he metaphorically calls a 'cognitive grasp reflex' for circuitry used in habitual behaviours. The Saint-Cyr group's research indicates that the caudate is likely to be involved in the development of 'habit patterns' or behavioural responses which can be rapidly mobilized without a large amount of conscious thought or awareness. While these patterns of habitual response are potentially quite adaptive, they could form the basis for symptoms of a disease such as OCD if behaviours of this type were pathologically and repetitively generated by dysfunctional basal ganglia circuits.

Baxter (1995) and Swerdlow (1995) have similarly noted how imbalances in the internal circuitry of the basal ganglia could lead to excessive disinhibition of thalamo-cortical pathways resulting in the self-sustaining activation of a 'worry circuit' involving the OFC and cingulate. The key point on which all of this reasoning is based is that a malfunction in the caudate and associated basal ganglia structures could lead to the dysfunctional gating of cortical circuitry, with resulting intrusions of pathological thoughts and sensations resulting in compulsive behavioural responses.

C. A role for the OFC and cingulate in error detection

The now well established (Rauch & Baxter, 1998) finding of increased metabolic activity in the OFC and anterior cingulate in people suffering from OCD, a disease state characterized by inappropriate repetitive thoughts and behaviours, is quite consistent with the results of prior research on the behavioural physiology of the these two key structures of the limbic cortex. Neurologists have long recognized that patients with damage to these areas of the cortex demonstrate behavioural perseverations, the repetitive performance of behaviours no longer serving a useful function. These patients are now well documented to show deficits in assessing the future consequences of their actions as well as problems associated with socially inappropriate behaviours (Bechara *et al.*, 1994). Studies on the cellular physiology of OFC and cingulate in behaving monkeys provide a firm foundation for interpreting these clinical findings.

In a classic set of studies done in an attempt to clarify the behavioural physiology of the frontal lobe, several groups (Niki and Watanabe, 1979; Rosenkilde *et al.*, 1981; Thorpe *et al.*, 1983) investigated neuronal firing patterns in the OFC and anterior cingulate in monkeys trained to respond to various visual cues in order to receive juice as a reward. These experiments revealed several important aspects of OFC and cingulate function. First, neurons in these structures change their firing pattern in response to visual cues depending on whether these cues are associated with rewarding stimuli. Seeing something associated with a reward triggers neuronal firing in both OFC and anterior cingulate. Thus one aspect of neuronal signalling in these structures is related to informing the organism about the presence of stimuli in the environment which are behaviourally significant. Further, and especially important for understanding behavioural perseveration, responses in both of these areas are very sensitive to the expectations the organism has concerning the stimuli to which it is exposed. For instance, if a monkey comes to expect that a light is associated with receiving juice, but no juice is delivered after the light appears, bursts of neuronal firing will occur in OFC and anterior cingulate. These cellular responses are not elicited after trials in which the expected reward is delivered. These responses, which can be understood as an 'error detection' mechanism, can underlie an internal sense in an organism that 'something is wrong' in the environment. If damage to these structures, with a resulting loss of 'error detection' signals, impairs an organism's capacity to realize that things have changed in the environment and that stimuli previously associated with reward no longer are, it becomes quite understandable why behavioural responses to those stimuli could become repetitive and demonstrate much slower and less effective behavioural adaptation.

In contrast to perseverative behaviours performed as the result of a *failure* of OFC and cingulate to generate appropriate 'error detection' signals, obsessions and compulsions can be understood as behavioural perseverations corresponding to signals of this type being *excessively* generated in a repeated and inappropriate manner due to hyperactivity of these structures. The clinical manifestation of this overactivation, and the associated generation of adventitious 'error detection' signals, would be an internal sense of dread accompanied by an intractable feeling that 'something is wrong.' This kind of an internal feeling state closely approximates how patients describe the experience of OCD symptoms. There is a significant consensus among neurobiologists (see Saxena, Brody et al., 1998; Rauch, Whalen et al., 1998 for review) that an impairment in the modulation of OFC and cingulate activity by the caudate nucleus is a key aspect of the pathophysiology of these symptoms in OCD.

D. Overview

The perspective of the Graybiel group at MIT on the physiology of the cortico-striate system forms an overview which can serve to coherently integrate the large body of neuroscience data presented above (fig. 1). These investigators have generated a body of work which allows us to view the caudate nucleus as an extraordinary mosaic composed of juxtaposed micro-anatomical modules with striosomes, receiving inputs from the OFC, anterior cingulate and other brain structures intimately related to emotional expression, and matrisomes receiving inputs from areas related to behavioural planning. Lying between these two modules are specialized cells which can change their firing patterns in distinctive ways when the organism is presented with stimuli which are perceived to have behavioural significance. This arrangement of anatomical elements could be quite conducive to adaptive changes in the gating of cortical signals related to modifications of behaviour in response to new information.

While much work remains to be done to further elaborate the detailed workings of this system, the relevance of these findings to formulating a possible neuroanatomical foundation for the physiological integration of thought and emotion is a very exciting development in the field of behavioural neuroscience. Further, conceptual models of this sort may well help us to better understand the neural mechanisms which are involved in the acquisition of new behavioural skills by patients with OCD during the course of doing CBT.

The applied use of anticipation and planning to alter behavioural responses to OCD's powerful intrusive thoughts and urges is the key element to success in over-coming the symptoms of this potentially debilitating neuropsychiatric condition. As reviewed above, there are strong reasons to believe that aberrant 'error detection' messages resulting from faulty gating of neuronal information within circuitry involving the OFC, anterior cingulate and the striosome compartment of the caudate nucleus are intimately involved in the generation of the pathological intrusions into consciousness that are the core element of OCD symptoms. In addition, circuits oper-ating within the lateral convexity of the frontal lobe, and projecting into the caudate nucleus at least in part in the form of matrisomes, are very likely involved in the thought processes required for the execution of CBT strategies. These neuronal ele-ments exist in close juxtaposition to highly specialized TAN cells in the caudate which appear to be sensitive to changes in the perceived relevance of sensory inputs and are extremely well positioned to alter the gating of information needed to alter behavioural responses to those inputs. All the necessary neural ingredients seem in place for constructing a meaningful theory of the cerebral mechanism of CBT response in OCD, and the associated and well-documented alterations of cerebral function that accompany it (Schwartz *et al.*, 1996, and below). Yet, to an experienced clinician who actually works with people afflicted with this problem, one huge ele-ment of the theory seems totally unaccounted for — the element of effort which is so critical to driving the treatment forward in a real-life situation. For all our discussion of cognition, information processing, and cerebral processing in turn of the century models of mind-brain relations in neuroscience and philosophy of mind, the critical role of effort as a necessary component for keeping the machinery on track and func-tioning does not seem to adequately enter the picture. But in the case of OCD, a condi-tion involving real people with real and now reasonably well-studied brains, we have an opportunity to take a closer look at the real-life process that occurs during thera-peutic manoeuvers which result in systematic alterations of brain function. And, in so doing, we may uncover an opportunity to gain fresh insights into what promises to be one of the major new fields of investigation in the coming century — the role of voli-tion in brain function.

CBT Interventions for OCD:
An Active Approach at the Mind–Brain Interface

Behavioural approaches to the psychological treatment of OCD are based on the prin-ciple, empirically validated by three decades of research (Marks, 1987), that people suffering from the disorder can learn to perform adaptive behaviours instead of pathological ones in response to the intrusive thoughts and urges which comprise the core symptoms of the condition. To successfully complete therapy patients must effectively tolerate and re-direct their responses to the acutely uncomfortable feeling states that arise as a result of OCD pathophysiology. There is now substantial evidence that the acquisition of specific cognitive skills by patients enables them to perform behavioural therapy techniques more effectively by increasing their ability to maintain their attentional focus on functional activities when confronted by the intensely uncomfortable thoughts and urges that arise during treatment and the profound distractions they understandably cause (Steketee *et al.*, 1998).

At UCLA we have developed a four-step cognitive-behavioural training method (Table 1) which is specifically designed to help patients successfully refocus their attention away from the steady bombardment of intrusive symptoms into their conscious awareness. The educational approach of the method is organized around the working hypothesis that the intrusive thoughts and urges of OCD are caused to a significant degree by a biomedical disease state (Schwartz, 1996; 1997b), and an active attempt should be made to re-interpret the significance of these intrusions so as to better understand how to behaviourally respond to them.

One major goal of this training is to deepen the appreciation of the OCD sufferer to the nature of the relationship that exists between the distressing thoughts and urges intruding into their consciousness and what are basically 'false brain messages' which can safely be ignored. A critical underlying assumption of this process is that an electro-chemical malfunction is causing serious distracting phenomena to intrude into conscious awareness — an assumption which is, of course, now buttressed by a sizable scientific data base, which is presented as part of the educational component of the therapy in ways commensurate with the individual sufferer's cognitive capacity. The goal of treatment is, of course, to learn to respond to these 'false brain messages' in new and much more adaptive ways. This is accomplished through the utilization of techniques of behavioural refocusing, usually applied within a largely self-directed training paradigm in which functional activities are systematically performed in place of habitual OCD responses. These cognitive-behavioural training techniques enable patients to utilize improved self-monitoring capabilities in order to more accurately interpret their conscious experience, resulting in an improved ability to manage their emotional and behavioural responses to the intense anxiety caused by OCD symptoms. This results in an enhanced ability to maintain attentional focus on the performance of consciously chosen adaptive behaviours, rather than capitulating to automaton-like compulsive responses like repetitive washing and checking, when besieged by the fearsome thoughts and urges of OCD.

Table 1: The Four Steps of Cognitive–Behavioural Treatment for OCD	
1. Relable	Recognize the intrusive obsessive thoughts and urges as a *result of OCD*.
2. Reattribute	Realize that the intensity and intrusiveness of the thought or urge is *caused by OCD*; it is probably related to a brain bio-chemical imbalance. Remember: *It's not me, it's the OCD*.
3. Refocus	'Work around' the OCD thoughts by focusing attention on something else at least for a few minutes, i.e., *do another behaviour*.
4. Revalue	Do not take the OCD thought at 'face value'. It is not significant in itself.

(Adapted from Schwartz, 1996)

As the patient's understanding that intrusive OCD symptoms are merely 'false brain messages' is increasingly well integrated into his/her cognitive framework, an extremely important transition begins to take place. The very nature of the conscious experience of the uncomfortable feeling of an OCD symptom begins to change in ways that allow him/her to increasingly create a mental distance or space between the experience of self and the experience of the symptom. While this change in the perception of the nature of the symptom is in some sense an accentuation of the 'ego--dystonic' or 'ego-alien' aspect of it, that is only one small component of the therapeutic process. The essence of this adaptive change in perspective is that the person with OCD becomes increasingly able to experience the intrusive symptom from the point of view of a clear-minded observer, and thus comes to see the symptom as merely the result of a malfunctioning mechanical process in the brain which, while unpleasant, is not of any great personal concern.

It is the ability to observe one's own internal sensations with the calm clarity of an external witness that is the most noteworthy aspect of this experience. Within the terminology of traditional Buddhist philosophy this sort of mental action is called mindfulness or mindful awareness (Silananda, 1990; Schwartz, 1998b). The German monk Nyanaponika Thera, a major figure of twentieth century Buddhist scholarship, coined the term 'Bare Attention' in order to precisely explain to Westerners the type of mental activity required for the attainment of mindful awareness, which by the practice of meditation can be developed into what is called in Pâli *vipassanâ,* or insight. 'Bare Attention is the clear and single-minded awareness of what actually happens *to* us and *in* us, at the successive moments of perception. It is called 'bare,' because it attends just to the bare facts of a perception as presented either through the five physical senses or through the mind. . . without reacting to them.' (Nyanaponika Thera, 1962, p. 30) As a practical matter, shifting one's perspective in this way requires substantial and quite directed effort, especially when it is done in the presence of significant anxiety and fear. It is certainly not a shift that tends to occur spontaneously — it requires significant anticipation and forethought. Yet it is the mental act of adverting attention in this manner which enables sufferers of OCD to develop the insight necessary for consciously choosing new and more adaptive responses to the intrusive and intensely bothersome thoughts and urges which bombard their consciousness.

Mental states of this kind have been described in modern Western philosophy at least since the eighteenth century. Noting the sense in which conscious activity of this kind involves clear observation by, as it were, 'a man within,' the Scottish philosopher Adam Smith (1976) described the associated mental experience as the perspective of 'the impartial spectator.' During CBT utilizing the Four Steps in Table 1, the terms 'mindfulness,' 'mindful awareness,' and 'impartial spectator' are all commonly used to help clarify for patients how to apply their new insight into the biomedical nature of OCD symptoms to help them create a distance between the conscious experience or feel *of* the symptom and their self-concept (Schwartz, 1996 and 1997b). Thus, for example, patients learn to stop making self-statements like, 'I feel like I need to wash my hands again,' and instead make statements of the type, 'That nasty compulsive urge is bothering me again.' This process, which requires profound and painstaking effort, can significantly enable patients to more effectively manage the fears and anxieties associated with OCD symptoms and improve their ability to refocus attention away from the symptoms and onto functional activities. This results in a markedly enhanced ability to prevent the mind from succumbing to the intense distractions that OCD thoughts and urges create, and so increases the capacity to consistently alter behavioural responses in increasingly adaptive ways.

Effects of Cognitive-Behavioural Treatment on Cerebral Function

Systematic changes in cerebral glucose metabolism accompany the clinical improvements achieved using this method of cognitive-behavioural therapy (Schwartz *et al.*, 1996). We investigated cerebral metabolic rate changes in eighteen drug-free subjects studied with PET scans before and after ten weeks of outpatient treatment. Twelve of them demonstrated clinically significant decreases in OCD symptom severity during the treatment period, and six did not. There were two main findings in this study:

(1) Bilateral decreases in caudate nucleus metabolism, divided by ipsilateral hemisphere metabolism (Cd/hem), were seen in responders to treatment compared to non-responders. This finding was more robust on the right (p = .003) than on the left (p = .02). (See fig. 2)

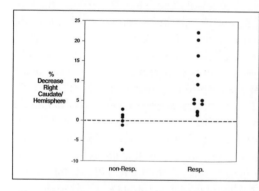

Figure 2. Change in Right Cuadate Glucose Metabolic Rate in Non-responders and Responders to Cognitive-Behavioural Therapy.

Plot of percent change after cognitive-behavioural treatment ((pre-post/pre) x 100) in right head of caudate nucleus metabolic rate divided by ipsilateral hemisphere (caudate/hem) for responders and non-responders to treatment. There is a significant difference between responders and non-responders to treatment (p = .003).

(2) In the right hemisphere, prior to treatment, there were highly significant pathological correlations between the metabolic rate in OFC and the metabolic rates in the caudate nucleus, anterior cingulate, and thalamus. These four brain structures acted as if they were functionally locked together. After effective treatment with CBT, these pathological correlations were significantly reduced. (See Table 2)

Table 2: Extent of Correlation (*r* Values) Between Metabolic Rates in Brain Structures

Left hemisphere	*Before*	*After*	Right hemisphere	*Before*	*After*
Left orbit to left caudate	0.46	–0.01	Right orbit to right caudate	0.74	0.28 *
Left orbit to left cingulate	0.11	0.58	Right orbit to right cingulate	0.87	0.22 *
Left orbit to left thalamus	0.34	0.05	Right orbit to right thalamus	0.81	0.14 *
Left caudate to left thalamus	0.66	0.36	Right caudate to right thalamus	0.69	0.41

Data from 12 patients who successfully responded to drug-free cognitive-behavioural therapy. * = Significant (*p*<.05) difference between before-treatment and after-treatment correlation. Adapted from Schwartz (1997a).

Mindful Awareness, Attentional Refocusing, and Cerebral Change

The reasoning on which the CBT model described above is based derives to a significant degree from developments over the past few decades in the field of behavioural neurobiology (see literature review above). Given the large data base demonstrating that the basal ganglia are involved in the modulation of cortical circuitry involved in the expression of previously learned behaviours, and the growing evidence implicating frontal aspects of that circuitry in the expression of OCD symptoms, it seems reasonable to teach OCD patients a technique intended to enable them to activate more functionally adaptive circuits within the vast array of neuronal connections comprising the cortico-striate system. If OCD symptoms are related to a malfunction in cortical circuit activation, and in particular to an 'error-detection' mechanism in the OFC and cingulate (Schwartz, 1997a and 1998a), then activation of alternative circuitry through the focused performance of adaptive alternative behaviours might, over time, ameliorate the discomfort related to the faulty brain mechanism. On this basis the third step of this cognitive-behavioural method, the Refocus step, gradually evolved. In this step the concept of 'working around' OCD symptoms is stressed. This means learning *not* to wait for the urges to subside before changing behaviour. Instead, patients must learn to change behavioural responses while the uncomfortable intrusive urges are still present in conscious awareness. By shifting to another task as a systematic response to the inner experience of OCD symptoms, new adaptive responses to intrusive OCD thoughts and urges are learned. In conjunction with that process, significant changes are seen in the activity of circuitry which a growing body of research finds related to OCD pathophysiology. The fact that the metabolic activity in this circuitry changes in a manner which is significantly related to alterations in symptom expression (fig. 2 and table 2) underscores the possibility that there is a *causal* relationship between the changes in experience and in brain function.

It is of the utmost importance to appreciate that the changes in behavioural response to the conscious intrusions that characterize OCD are not in any way a passive process, but are, in the most intuitively meaningful sense, active and purposeful choices to respond differently to profoundly distracting aspects of conscious experience. To view this critical therapeutic process, the essence of what the term self-help genuinely refers to, as merely the preordained outcome of an abstract neuronal vector analysis passively occurring in some vast matrix which we generically call the 'nervous system,' reflects a serious misunderstanding about the nature of what actually occurs during the course of a real-life treatment of a case of OCD. In an attempt to clarify this critically important point, it is worth examining in overview some of the clinical data that comprise a typical treatment history.

Let's consider, for purposes of illustration, the therapeutic process in the case of a man with typical OCD. (The clinical aspects of this case will, to save space, be markedly abbreviated. See Schwartz, 1996 for details) At the outset of treatment this man is besieged by very intrusive and persistent thoughts and urges associated with a gnawing gut-level feeling of dread that his hands are contaminated with germs. This almost invariably leads to hand washing of such severity that it causes the skin to become red, raw and chapped. Although he knows that his concerns about germ contamination are excessive to the point of being nonsensical, the gnawing anxiety associated with the obsessive thoughts of possible contamination is so intense he almost invariably succumbs to it with bouts of hand washing. A large body of research data is consistent with the statement that the intrusive gnawing fear that 'something is wrong' with his hands (e.g., they are 'contaminated by germs') is caused by error-detection circuitry which is generating an inappropriate signal. This faulty signal is probably causally linked to excessive neuronal activity in circuitry connecting his caudate nucleus, OFC and anterior cingulate. When we explain this to the man, and give him associated instructional materials, emotional support and time, he comes to readily understand it. This learning process comprises the first two steps, Relabel and Reattribute, of the Four Step Method (see Table 1) which is used as part of the treatment process.

From a clinical perspective, what has the man learned: what is the essence of his new understanding? The practical core of his new knowledge is that the reason his intrusive persistent thoughts and urges are so damnably persistent, the reason they *don't go away,* is due a biochemical imbalance in his brain which results in his consciousness being bombarded with a steady stream of 'false error messages' or (as many patients prefer to call them) 'false alarms.' In other words, he has significantly improved his ability to *correctly interpret* the signals being generated in his conscious awareness by the faulty operation of his brain. One major benefit that accrues to the man on account of this enhancement in the accuracy of his signal interpretations (e.g., from 'My hands feel dirty!! I better go wash them again!!' to 'That bothersome urge to wash caused by my OCD is acting up again.') is that it markedly alters his perspective concerning the *next question* he addresses to himself — the one which will guide the course of his next action, 'Should I wash my hands, or not?' As Stapp points out in detail in his related article in this issue, changing one's perspective with regard to the *next question* posed to nature, i.e., what aspect of nature one *focuses attention on,* has profound implications concerning the quality of the physical processes occurring at the mind-brain interface.

Clearly understanding the mental actions which are performed when our OCD patient applies his training in the first two steps of Relabel and Reattribute will help clarify why this process is so important. By Relabeling we mean making assertive self statements describing accurately the nature of the feeling you're experiencing when suffering from an attack of OCD (e.g.,'my hands don't *really* feel dirty — that's just OCD'). By Reattributing we mean working to remain aware of the fact that the bothersome feeling of OCD symptoms is caused by (and thus properly attributed to) a pathological, but treatable, brain-related imbalance (i.e., *not* my own goal directed mind — thus the popular saying among OCD sufferers 'It's not me, it's the OCD'). Another way of accomplishing these goals is through the systematic use of mental notes, a technique originally described in connection with the performance of vipassanâ mindfulness meditation in the Burmese tradition (Silananda, 1990). In this approach, the practitioner very systematically notes with brief self-statements just where the focus of attention is *in the present moment.* An example of this technique being applied to, say, walking (a common meditation subject in vipassanâ practice) would be, at the moment when lifting the foot, make the quick precise mental note 'lifting,' when moving the foot forward, 'moving,' when placing it down, 'placing' and so on (as one proceeds in meditation practice the noticings and mental notes become *much* more finely grained than in this simple example, especially with respect to the inner experiences associated with movement). When this meditation technique is refined for clinical use in treating OCD it involves patients training themselves to take note of the fact that the bothersome feeling now intruding into their mind is 'OCD', or 'false message', or 'bothersome feeling', etc.

What this accomplishes is a change in perspective *away* from automatic responses (exactly the sort of activity the basal ganglia is wired by many millennia of evolution to perform (Graybiel 1995 and 1997)) and *toward* a more precise, considered, and consciously goal-directed interpretation of the present moment's experience — which is, of course, a much more cortically directed activity. In other words, from a neuroanatomical perspective, what the mind is doing while performing the first two steps of CBT or basic vipassanâ mindfulness meditation on walking is wilfully *shifting* the predominant brain mechanism which is utilized in performing the action going on *right now*. In the case of treating OCD, the mental action is performed to shift out of faulty basal ganglia circuitry and into activities which are more adaptive. In the case of working to sharpen vipassanâ, it is done to shift out of mindless habitual activity and convert to activity which is precisely observed and examined with mindful awareness. In both cases great effort is involved, not least because the brain, which very much has its own agenda, is bombarding consciousness with a series of distractions which must be overcome (i.e., *not* attended to) if success at one's chosen mental training is to be achieved. In the case of CBT the distraction is pathological, threatening and intense ('You're contaminated! Go Wash!'), in meditation it's usually pretty mundane and benign ('This is boring. What's for dinner?'), but in both cases the focus of attention must be shifted away from where the brain 'wants' to take it — and in both cases there are important alterations in the biology (and physics — see Stapp, this issue) of the situation in response to the effort at refocusing attention being actualized *in the present moment* by the practitioner involved.

A key point to grasp when considering the experiential field in which the OCD patient is working is that meaningful changes in the raw sensation of the *actual feelings* of fear and anxiety that constitute OCD symptoms generally do not occur early on in treatment. As our man works to master his responses to the discomforting urges by refocusing his attention on alternative adaptive behaviours, his gut is still churning and the gnawing sense that 'You're contaminated!' is very definitely still present. A very profound and directed *effort* is required for him to refocus his attention in the face of such intense and (neurophysiologically speaking) almost literally gripping distracters. That's almost certainly because the brain mechanisms underlying the inner experience of his symptoms have not changed in any significant way. What *has* begun to change, and the factor that underlies the effort the man is now willing to make to resist those symptoms, is the *value* he now puts on those feelings and sensations. What he is beginning to do is to learn how to control his *emotional reactions* to those thoughts, feelings and sensations, by which I specifically mean the kinds of interpretations and meanings he attributes to them. In the early stages of treatment he basically *feels* the same — but he has begun to change in a critical way how he *understands* those feelings. With that change in understanding he has set the stage for making different choices about how to act on those feelings and sensations — choices which, in the conceptualization of the mind-brain interface formulated by Stapp (this issue), actually change the nature of the *physics* of the situation. Now, by consistently instituting steps three and four of the CBT method outlined in Table 1 — i.e., by Refocusing his behavioural output onto healthful rather than pathological behaviours, while systematically Revaluing his inner experience of OCD symptoms — he can consciously establish new and much more adaptive response patterns to internal experiences which, prior to treatment, were almost always followed by nearly automatic pathological handwashing. And controlled scientific data now exist associating those new consciously chosen response patterns with statistically significant changes in energy use by the very brain circuitry which most probably underlies his painful intrusive thoughts and urges, changes which bring with them a marked amelioration of the intensity and severity of his mental suffering.

The Volitional Modulation of Cerebral Function

As discussed above, the groundbreaking study of Aosaki *et al.* (1995) demonstrated that highly specialized cells called tonically active neurons (TANs) display a distinctive pattern of firing during behavioural conditioning. Specifically, after monkeys were trained to associate the delivery of a juice reward with audible clicks or a light flash, TANs displayed a pause in tonic firing followed by a burst of rebound excitation upon presentation of these stimuli. Since, within the micro-anatomy of the striatum, TANs tend to localize at the interface of limbic and frontal association cortex input, it is hypothesized that these cells could serve a critical role as a gating mechanism for efficiently directing information flow through the striatum in response to behaviourally significant information (or, to use the exact terminology of the investigators, 'conditioned stimuli predictive of reward') (Graybiel *et al.*, 1994). A brain mechanism such as this would also have the potential to provide internally experienced sensations which could function as cues enabling an organism to recognize a sensory stimulus as related to behaviours associated with the delivery of a reward.

Reflecting on how these cutting edge findings in the field of behavioural neuroscience relate to the process of therapeutic change that occurs during the psychological treatment of a person with OCD can shed significant light on the sorts of phenomena that occur at the mind-brain interface. To those committed to the investigation of volitional aspects of brain function, maintaining keen awareness of the critical role of *valuation* in the processing of conscious experience is perhaps the key factor for attaining a clear understanding of the available data. For, while the question of what constitutes a 'reward' (or 'behaviourally significant information') is generally a quite transparent one for non-human animals, for human beings it can raise issues of tremendous complexity. To understand these issues with even a modicum of clarity one must not lose sight of the fact that human consciousness exhibits tremendous latitude and variation with regard to not only the selection of what constitutes a 'reward' at any given moment, but also to the types of responses generated to the phenomena so chosen. This critical process of *valuing* experience has tremendous relevance to a proper understanding of the relationship between the quality of attention (e.g., mindful or non-mindful) directed toward both internal and external stimuli and the role of signal interpretation in the volitional initiation (or inhibition!) of motor responses to experiences generated by activity within the nervous system.

For a monkey, the association of a light flash with juice results in a predictable change in the firing pattern of TANs when the monkey is exposed to the light flash. As a result of its association with a clear-cut reward such as juice, the light flash becomes behaviourally significant information for the monkey. The striatum can then

rapidly and efficiently process input from relevant cortical circuitry in order to prepare and initiate effective behavioural responses (Hikosaka *et al.*, 1989; Graybiel,
1995). For our man with obsessional fears of contamination, a substantial data base
now supports the hypothesis that upon exposure to a cloth soiled with axle grease the
striatum will respond in a pathologic fashion. As reviewed above, work by the Rauch
group indicates that circuitry connecting the OFC, anterior cingulate and striatum
will become metabolically activated in such a situation. As a result the patient could
be bombarded by feelings of impending catastrophe with resulting behavioural
responses consisting of repetitive handwashing — behaviours which, to the symptomatic patient, are linked to a sense of 'reward' insofar as they give him an extremely
brief and evanescent feeling that his contamination is momentarily 'alleviated'.
Unfortunately for the poor OCD sufferer, this momentary relief is quickly terminated
by the intrusion of still more biologically generated sensations of fear and contamination. It is the role of CBT to help the man improve his ability to accurately interpret
the signal conveyed to him by visual exposure to stimuli which tend to induce OCD
symptoms, such as greasy cloths (e.g., 'That's just axle grease. It's anxiety caused by
OCD that's making me feel like washing my hands'). This change in the valuation of
the stimulus, and the resulting change in the nature of the behaviourally significant
information conveyed to the man by the greasy cloth, enables the man to volitionally
inhibit his ingrained pathological rituals and instead actively generate an entirely different set of behavioural responses to such stimuli — behaviours, such as helping his
wife in the garden, which the man, with much effort, comes to systematically link
with a new and much more accurate and sustainable sense of reward. With this
change in the valuation of his sensory experience, the man is performing a mental
action which characterizes the human species — through the hard work of self-
directed volitional training he is activating and bringing to fruition the potential for
sapience that characterizes Homo sapiens at its best. At that moment of making a new
choice he is unique among all of the Animal Kingdom. For his wilful change of his
response to the intrusions of OCD into consciousness yields not only the rewards of
adaptive as opposed to self-destructive behaviours, it also results in an extremely
rewarding sense of true self-esteem — that empowering inner awareness that the
utilization of knowledge has enhanced one's capacity for self-control.

Prior work by Libet (1985; 1998) has demonstrated cerebral activity which appears
to indicate 'the possibility of a role for the conscious function . . . to be one of potentially blocking or vetoing the volitional process so that no actual motor action occurs.
Veto of an urge to act is a common experience for individuals generally (1998,
p. 215).' As we have seen, for a person with OCD to reliably and consistently veto the
urge to perform the motor action involved in a compulsive ritual requires tremendous
effort and considerable training. But it is certainly of interest that a large data base
exists in normal subjects demonstrating brain mechanisms so clearly consistent with
the kinds of volitional modulation of behaviour performed by OCD patients doing
CBT. It also provides an extremely relevant context for understanding the data displayed in Figure 2 and Table 2, which demonstrate that the reductions in the bothersome symptoms that accompany successful CBT are associated with statistically
significant changes in brain function. Changes in the valuation and interpretation of
both inner and outer experience form a critical aspect of how these kinds of systematic changes in both volitional expression and cerebral function take place.

It seems a reasonable working hypothesis that cells such as TANs may play an important role in how this occurs by influencing the probability of the firing of sets of surrounding neurons in the striatum, resulting in more adaptive gating of neuronal information flow as more accurate and insightful interpretations of sensory stimuli lead to the preference of adaptive over maladaptive 'rewards,' and the learning of new responses to replace old OCD behavioural patterns takes place (Graybiel, 1995; 1997). However, from the perspective of understanding the neurobiological dynamics of a process such as this, the key point to focus on is that the modification of TAN activity that would accompany the change in sensory preference would not be likely to occur spontaneously — under the circumstances of a typical treatment it is hypothesized that such a change would occur gradually, step-by-step, over several weeks and require a significant focusing of brain activity generated by the concerted, sustained and highly directed effort exerted by the patient during the peformance of CBT.

Generating New Brain Circuits: The Role of Mindfulness and Mental Force

The finding that CBT alters brain function in circuits now well established to be related to OCD pathophysiology has the potential to help clarify the nature of the relationship that exists between the *experiential* data that OCD patients so vividly relate concerning their very real discomfort and sense of being 'locked in' to maladaptive behavioural patterns and the types of *effort* required to generate the cerebral changes that occur when these patients show clinical improvement. The observation that cognitive training about biomedical aspects of OCD can enhance a patient's ability to alter behavioural responses to intrusive symptoms reflects the fact that improvements in the cognitive processing of internal information can lead to more adaptive behavioural output. However, as stated above, it is of the utmost importance to clearly realize that no element of this process of systematic change occurs without significant effort and work — and that this requirement for work is directly related to the need to generate energy for the purpose of altering powerfully entrained patterns of cerebral activity which are causally linked to the symptomatic experiences which the OCD sufferer is striving to overcome.

Let us return to our man with OCD and reflect on exactly what may be happening in his brain as he struggles to go and assist his wife as opposed to capitulating to his urge to compulsively wash his hands. In scientific terms, it is uncontroversial to assume that newly forming patterns of cerebral activity must be related to the man's growing awareness that 'a faulty brain message' is generating the bothersome urge he's now struggling with. However, while fully granting that quite plausible assumption, it is also clear that in *experiential* terms a task of immense difficulty now confronts our man: for he now must *actualize* his new awareness in behavioural terms by systematically Refocusing his attention on useful adaptive behaviours. This action, if done regularly, will enable him to alter the patterns of neuronal gating in his caudate in scientifically verifiable ways. Given the well-documented scientific basis for believing that changes in TAN firing patterns are related to changes in caudate gating, it may be useful to frame the man's task as one in which he must change the response contingencies of the TANs in his caudate.

In *experiential* terms, how does he go about completing that task? Let us focus for a moment on the newly forming patterns of brain activity which are beginning to emerge in association with the enhanced cognitive processing of sensory input that our man, through his considerable effort, has begun to achieve (e.g., 'If I wash my hands just because I saw some axle grease, in the long run it'll only make these OCD urges even more intense.'). Thought processes such as these, when performed regularly, probably have some effect on the gating of messages through the caudate (Graybiel, 1997) and thus could involve changes in TAN cell response patterns to the axle grease, but the process is still very weak and undependable, since the man is still in the early stages of treatment. What sort of process, what kind of *energy input*, will it take to amplify this process sufficiently to systematically alter the cellular firing patterns, very likely genetically mediated from the start and then further established through decades of repetitive responses, generating the intense intrusive feelings of contamination which so persistently afflict our man — and to do it in an entirely drug-free manner in less than ten weeks?

To put it in the plainest of terms, how does he focus his attention on the 'true message' those new and still frail and inchoate circuits are sending to his consciousness ('Go help your wife in the garden. That's what you need to do to get better.') when he is simultaneously being bombarded by intense, powerful and extremely distracting 'false messages' ('You better go wash! That filthy grease might be on your hands!') which are very much still being 'transmitted' by his hyperactive cortical-basal ganglia circuitry? Where does he find the energy to strengthen the 'good message' signal now forming in his cortex and attempting to forge a new 'gating path' via the fragile and still developing new circuitry beginning to arise in his caudate? And, further, how does he now activate motor circuitry which will take him *away from* rather than *towards* the bathroom sink? The momentous nature of this question becomes especially apparent in light of the fact that for many years now movement *towards* the sink, followed by further damaging handwashing, has been our man's habitual motor response to the OCD urge generated by the 'false brain message.' As a result, that particular set of motor responses will itself have a very well-established brain circuitry with it's own well-developed gating and TAN response patterns, and will thus be generating its own associated drives and urges.

So how does the man with OCD begin to stabilize new striatal gating patterns in response to OCD symptoms? The answer to this question, as every good OCD therapist knows, is that he generates the energy necessary to activate, strengthen, and stabilize his new health-giving and life-affirming circuitry, and the new gating patterns associated with it, through the *exertion of his will*, and the *power of his striving* — a power which can generate a real and palpable force which I propose to term **mental force** (Schwartz, 1999). This force is similar in kind to what Lindahl & Århem (1994) (following Popper *et al.*, 1993) have called 'mind as a force field,' and what Libet (1994; 1996) has termed the 'conscious mental field (CMF).' However, consistent with the basic principles of quantum physics described by Stapp (this issue), I specifically take the strongly felt effort which is clearly experienced as a necessary aspect of the onset of the action of this force to accurately reflect the true nature of its etiology — my working hypothesis is that it is a genuine physical force generated by real mental effort. This mental force, associated in our OCD patient's case with the effort he must exert in order to *mindfully direct and focus* his attention on his new 'true message' and *wilfully actualize* the adaptive behaviour towards which it orients him, will functionally amplify his new brain circuitry and enable it to generate more adaptive patterns of neural gating. This leads to meaningful decreases in the intensity of his intrusive OCD symptoms as well as to improvements in the behavioural and signal interpreting (a.k.a. cognitive) functions with which those newly formed adaptive neural patterns will be associated.

While this newly proposed term, mental force, represents a still largely hypothetical entity, there does seem to be a theoretical need for a force of this kind in nature. The clinical fact that changing one's behaviour in the midst of a barrage of intense and intrusive thoughts and feelings produced by pathological OCD brain circuitry requires a profoundly active process leads naturally to a consideration of the type of mechanism that would be required for such a process to cause the kind of systematic energy use changes those pathological circuits have undergone in the data presented in Fig 2 and Table 2. Forthrightly addressing the question of how that highly targeted effort and those systematic brain changes are related could well lead a reasonable observer to conclude that a mental force, or something very much like it, is necessary if one is to establish a causal relationship between those two quite different sorts of data — and by far the most intuitively clear and satisfying way of viewing how such intense efforts could lead to the kinds of cerebral changes observed is by means of a causal relationship.

Without reference to a naturally occurring mental force, the observed changes in cerebral energy use, which are statistically significant only for those OCD subjects who demonstrate clinically meaningful improvement, would have to be autonomously generated by an entirely *passive* process — but that is plainly inconsistent with a very large amount of clinical data, most especially the verbal reports of patients who have actually undergone these treatments. To precipitously reject such verbal reports as an unimportant or misleading source of data is not only scientifically and methodologically unjustified, it reflects an ad hoc perspective adopted merely to protect a profoundly counter-intuitive way of thinking. The notion of a naturally occurring mental force arises directly as a result of properly attending with an open mind to *all the relevant data* collected in the clinical and basic science studies discussed above. It seems an entirely legitimate means of parsimoniously explaining the data at hand without a need for resorting to reductionist approaches which irrationally prefer materialist as opposed to experiential perspectives.

The Distinction Between Active and Passive Phenomena in Consciousness Research

As was stated at the outset of this paper, the aspect of OCD which renders it a particularly valuable source of information about the mind-brain interface is the so-called 'ego-dystonic' nature of its symptoms — the fact that people who are affected by the condition experience the repetitive intrusive thoughts and urges which comprise the core phenomena of the disorder as unwanted and extraneous intrusions into consciousness. Because of this, OCD symptoms can be viewed as a painfully amplified version of the sorts of desultory and unpredictable mental events that pass through the mental life of essentially all people innumerable times in the course of a day — mental events which are, to a very large degree, passively experienced as essentially arbitrary phenomena not subject to any obvious volitional control. Phenomena which, in effect, pass into and out of consciousness in a quite fleeting and transitory manner.

Of course, in the case of OCD, the very nature of the disease state renders the symptomatic thoughts repetitive and intrusive rather than fleeting and transitory. They also cause significant distress since they are accompanied by a very bothersome sense that 'something is wrong,' a feeling that very much is passively experienced insofar as the person having it is painfully aware that it is false, bothersome, and inappropriate. Not infrequently they experience their behavioural responses to these sensations (e.g., compulsive handwashing) as also having a robotic and disturbingly passive quality. To overcome this disease state, as we have seen, they must take decisive and profoundly active countermeasures, with resulting alterations in their brain's habit generating mechanisms.

This naturally occurring 'amplification effect' on otherwise normal experiences, while pathological and burdensome to those afflicted by it, renders OCD symptoms potentially quite valuable phenomena for modeling several aspects of consciousness in a practical and coherent way. Specifically, the study of OCD can help us address more general questions concerning the crucial difference between passive and active phenomena in conscious experience. The work of the eighteenth century French philosopher Maine de Biran, a seminal figure in the history of modern psychology (Moore, 1970), sheds great light both on these issues and on the kinds of problems which arise in connection with an exclusively 'brain-based' theory of volition. In particular, Biran demonstrates the lack of clarity with which the concept of causation is utilized by philosophers who attempt to reduce volitional phenomena to the realm of material processes.

After three centuries of nearly unchallenged dominance, the position of those philosophers and scientists who uncritically assume that all causal efficacy resides in the material realm has begun to come into question in recent decades, not least due to the advances in the field of quantum physics detailed by Stapp and others in this issue. Some of these recent developments were anticipated by Biran who, in response to Hume's skepticism concerning the nature of causation, observed that our inner experience of a causal relationship between the will to movement and bodily motion is so vivid and direct that it transcends the possibility of reasonable doubt. While honest investigators must acknowledge that Biran's position on the causal efficacy of volition elicits as immediate and intuitive a sense of agreement as any statement concerning causation in the outer world of five sense experience possibly could, it is also an observation whose significance is now further strengthened by the well-documented inadequacy of the classical pre-quantum physics conception of material causation to account for all the data which science must try to explain. Inflexibly clinging to a notion of causation that is both counter-intuitive for conscious phenomena and demonstrably incomplete in the world of material processes can no longer be justified on rational grounds.

The debate on causation between Hume and Biran, and its relevance to current developments in consciousness research, is admirably elucidated in the article on Biran by Philip Hallie in The Encyclopedia of Philosophy:

> According to Maine de Biran, Hume mistakes our *pensées* for our *effort voulu,* confuses disparate outward impressions and their images with intimately related, inwardly simultaneous willing and movement.
>   Hume's . . . objection is that no connection or 'means' connecting the will to the body is present in willed effort. By 'means' Hume chiefly meant physiological means that can

be demonstrated through outward impressions and derived hypotheses concerning the connection between the willed effort and bodily movement. Maine de Biran answered, however, that in the face of the plainly felt experience of inward causation, one need not ask for 'connecting' entities deviously derived from a different sort of experience. Hume, in doing so, simply reasserted his old prejudice in favor of outward impressions and their images. . . .[O]ur certainty in experiencing the *effort voulu* lies in this experience itself, not in any hypothetical structures based on quite different experiences (Hallie, 1967).

For those seeking rigorously data based explanations of conscious phenomena there is much to recommend in Biran's perspective. One can only add that if those committed to the materialist position and its many-fold variants would simply acknowledge that the idea of causal efficacy in the material world is both every bit as hypothetical as any account of causation derived from inner observation and *much less directly experienced* (i.e., much less empirically based), then rigidly asserted modes of reductionist explanation (which recent developments in quantum physics have demonstrated to be radically incomplete) would be more amenable to much needed updating and expansion. That simple acknowledgment would also open up the field of consciousness studies to more precise, pragmatic and experientially based explanations, a development that would both increase the light and decrease the considerable heat which frequently accompanies debates on these issues.

Using the subjective experiences of OCD sufferers as a model for more precisely clarifying our intuitive grasp of the critical distinction between active and passive phenomena in conscious experience can enable us to more clearly delineate the pragmatic grounds for positing a causal role for volition in the process of systematic cerebral change. As described above, the OCD patient in early stages of CBT is faced with a situation in which two systems of brain circuitry are competing for dominance in a present moment of real time. One set of circuitry underlies the passively experienced pathological intrusions into consciousness which characterize the phenomenal *feel* of OCD; the other encodes information which can be utilized to enhance one's cognitive awareness of the true significance of those intrusions. The relative strength of these two neural systems is markedly incommensurate if they are compared with respect to either utilization of metabolic energy or acute effects on conscious experience — the pathological circuitry is clearly dominant with respect to both of these variables. However, from the perspective of the patient doing CBT, the most important difference between them lies in their subjective quality, in the *feel* with which they are associated. For the pathological phenomena are experienced largely as passive and disturbing intrusions which if attended to elicit monotonous, robotic, enslaving types of responses, while the capacity to use knowledge as a basis for resisting the symptoms is very much experienced as potentially active in nature — especially insofar as it provides an informational template for the kinds of responses which can provide, with the painstaking exertion of appropriate effort, adaptive alternatives to life as an 'OCD robot.' *It is the critical difference between these two types of feels that makes genuine volitional choice a real possibility*. And, as the data presented in Table 2 and Figure 2 demonstrate, the conscious choice to exert effort in the service of resisting the false messages and misdirected urges of OCD is accompanied over several weeks by systematic changes in the very neural systems which are implicated in the generation of those symptoms.

In the present context the term *mental force* is defined as a naturally occurring force generated by the volitional effort required to refocus one's attention away from the experiential phenomena of OCD, and associated with the cerebral alterations which are correlated with that attentional refocusing. It is a force which is necessary for the activation of the new patterns of neuronal gating which volitional effort generates, as well as for the stabilization of all the associated adaptive alterations in brain circuitry which occur in concert with the sustained effort required for meaningful behavioural change. Through the regular exertion of directed mental force the reliable operation of what are initially inchoate processes gradually develops, and this accounts for the observed changes in brain function which accompany clinical improvement after the successful application of CBT in OCD sufferers.

A Causal Role for Mindfulness

Because the predominant *feel* of sensory phenomena is essentially passive in nature, the realm of sensory experience (and particularly visual experience) is one in which the analytical power of the scientific method can be imagined to at least potentially provide a genuinely meaningful dissection of so-called 'qualia' of experience into brain-related data points. However, the idea of a similar dissection for the intrinsically *active* feel of volitional phenomena seems lacking in any intuitive basis for what might even be considered face validity. And yet those committed to explanations based in the classical physics of the material world seem unfazed by the profound discrepancies in these two types of data. If nothing else, this provides compelling testimony for the power of 'scientific materialism' to generate a sense of having achieved an adequate explanation in the minds of modern philosophers.

Perhaps the biggest category error committed by philosophers who attempt to advocate a 'scientific' determinism, based on the reduction of volitional phenomena to neuroscience data, is the identification of the conscious elements of our passively experienced thought stream with either the totality of consciousness itself or with its actively experienced volitional component (mistaking 'our *pensées* for our *effort voulu*,' as Biran so insightfully described it). One of the major benefits accruing to philosophers and scientists from the use of the OCD experience as a model is that, through it's 'amplification effect' on normal conscious phenomena, the study of OCD enables us to more clearly discern the difference between the passively experienced thoughts and urges of OCD symptoms and the extremely active nature of the attentional aspect of cognitive-behavioural Relabeling and Refocusing that OCD patients utilize when performing CBT. Cambridge University psychologist John Teasdale, who has independently devised a method for treating depressed patients that has many similarities to the CBT approach described above for OCD (Teasdale *et al.*, 1995), has coined the term 'meta-awareness' to describe the key feature of active attentional processes of this type (Teasdale, 1997). Using a five-point scale to assess the degree of meta-awareness before and after cognitive therapy for depression, his research team rated the extent to which patients report 'a wider perspective on thoughts and feelings as mental events in the field of awareness, rather than as phenomena with which patients identified personally as aspects of themselves.' The subjects who were rated four or above on the scale 'saw their thoughts and feelings in a wider perspective; there was a discrimination of self from thought and feelings.' Depressed patients scored significantly higher on this scale after cognitive therapy compared to a medication only group. As patients' scores on the scale increase they begin to demonstrate 'a different view and relationship to depressive experience in general: "thoughts and feelings as mental events that can be considered and examined", rather than "thoughts as self-evident facts"'.

This conscious perspective of meta-awareness that Teasdale has been investigating and training patients with depression to actively utilize is identical in its main features to the mental state which has been described above as 'mindfulness' or the perspective of 'the impartial spectator.' Discerning clearly the characteristics which distinguish this type of consciousness from its contrasting mental state, which might appropriately be termed 'unmindful' or 'mere' awareness, is greatly enhanced by training within one of the mindfulness-based traditions of meditation which are common to many of the ancient Asian schools of mental development, particularly those based within the Buddhist tradition. The Pâli canon of the Theravâda school of Buddhist tradition places an especially strong emphasis on mental development of this sort, and includes numerous texts which elaborate on distinctions between various sorts of mental attention. Perhaps the most important of these is between what are termed *yoniso* and *ayoniso manasikâra,* which can be loosely translated as wise (or proper, reasoned, methodical) attention (Nyanatiloka, 1980) and unwise attention. Within the Theravâda tradition, and especially with respect to the teachings of the vipassanâ or insight branch of meditation practice, the key distinction stressed between these two types of attention hinges on the presence of mindfulness or Bare Attention in so-called 'wise attention' and absence of it in the 'unwise' variety (Mahâsi Sayadaw, 1983).

A very helpful further clarification of the intimate relationship between mindfulness/Bare Attention and *yoniso manasikâra* has recently been provided to me in a personal communication from Bhikkhu Bodhi, President of the Buddhist Publication Society, Kandy, Sri Lanka, '*Yoniso manasikâra is* not synonymous with mindfulness, though the two work closely together. *Yoniso manasikâra* is close and careful consideration of things taken up for scrutiny. Mindfulness is what makes these available for consideration, but *yoniso manasikâra* goes beyond 'Bare Attention' and actively examines things in a way intended to bring their real characteristics to light. The product of *yoniso manasikâra* is wisdom (*paññâ*). Thus we might consider *yoniso manasikâra* to be the bridge between *sati* (mindfulness) and *paññâ*.'

It is worth noting a key Pâli scriptural text in which Gotama Buddha, through the use of an elegant simile, clarifies the critical implication that the type of attention utilized in the present has for future states of consciousness:

> Just as this body, monks, is supported by food and stands in dependence on it, stands not without it, — even so monks, the five hindrances [to the development of wisdom] are supported by [their own type of] food, and stand in dependence on it, stand not without it...
>
> And what, monks, is food for the arising of ill will not yet arisen, or food for the increase and growth of ill will that has already arisen? There is the aversive feature of things. Unwise attention frequently applied to that, this is food for the arising of ill will not yet arisen, or food for the increase and growth of ill will that has already arisen. (Saṃyutta Nikâya, Pâli Text Society edition, Vol. V, p.64; Translation modified from Woodward, 1930, p. 52.)

(Analogous application of this simile is used in this text for the other four hindrances: sensual lust, sloth & torpor, restlessness & scrupulosity, excessive doubt.)

The key point of this canonical passage is that the *quality of attention* that one places on a sensory or mental object has critical implications for the *types of conscious states* that arise with respect to that object. The particular example I have chosen to quote was selected because of its great relevance to the mental actions performed by a person with OCD when working on the Four Steps of CBT in Table 1. If the man with OCD described in the clinical example above views the aversive feature of the cloth soiled with axle grease with unwise, unmindful, non-methodical attention (i.e., he does not Relabel its dirty appearance as something that elicits his OCD symptoms), the 'ill will' that arises in him with respect to the cloth (e.g., palpable feelings of disgust and a visceral fear that the cloth can contaminate him) will very quickly intensify and become unmanageable, greatly increasing the probability that he will respond with handwashing compulsions. As Rauch's group at Harvard has convincingly demonstrated, this rapid increase in disgust and fear will be accompanied by marked increases in the pathological OCD circuitry contained within the OFC, anterior cingulate, and caudate nucleus.

On the other hand, if our man makes a conscious effort to be mindful and methodically practices the Relabel Step in order to remain aware that the aversive feature of this soiled cloth is nothing but harmless axle grease and that his urge to wash is an OCD symptom that he can Refocus his attention away from, he will in all probability perform an adaptive behaviour instead, such as going to help his wife in the garden. The volitional effort to do so will, through the generation of mental force, amplify and strengthen alternative circuitry developing in his brain which enables him to re-gate his cerebral responses to the aversive sensory stimulus, which will result over time in a growing ease and automaticity in the adaptive behavioural responses he chooses to initiate as an alternative to repetitive handwashing. With several weeks of sustained effort at CBT the man will Revalue the greasy cloth stimulus in a way which will render it non-aversive — i.e., the 'ill will' he harbours towards the cloth will dissipate. There is now significant evidence that alterations of this sort will be followed by measurable changes in his OFC-anterior cingulate-caudate circuitry, and that the application of mindfulness, painstaking volitional effort, and systematic attentional refocusing by the man is necessary for these cerebral changes to take place (see fig. 2).

Conclusion

A reasonable working hypothesis to coherently explain all these data is that the volitional effort and attentional refocusing that occur in conjunction with mindfulness and wise attention at the critical moments of CBT when OCD patients *actively* change their responses to the intensely anxious feelings of obsessive thoughts and compulsive urges generate a *mental force* capable of re-gating entrenched pathological neural circuitry and establishing new and adaptive patterns of neuronal response in their place. The pragmatic clinical conclusion is simply this: with proper training and volitional effort pathological brain circuitry is susceptible to adaptive alteration. To provide that training to real people with real suffering caused by a now reasonably well understood cerebral malfunction requires using a mode of communication which utilizes their entirely natural and empirically validated belief in the efficacy of their own wilful actions — explanations using radically mechanistic terminology derived from theories based on outdated concepts of causation no longer supported by modern physics (see Stapp, this issue) are entirely impractical and totally inappropriate for explaining to actual OCD patients the steps they must follow for the purpose of systematically changing their own brain chemistry. The clinical practice of modern data-driven behavioural medicine absolutely requires the use of the data of inner experience — *very much including the directly perceived reality of the causal efficacy of volition* — in order to operate in an effective manner. This plain fact carries with it the profoundest implications, for it means that the age-old belief that human beings have in their capacity to act as genuinely self-directed agents capable of instituting real self-directed change can now be rationally justified not just on practical, but also on scientific and philosophical grounds.

Acknowledgment

This work was made possible by generous donations from the Charles and Lelah Hilton family.

References

Aosaki, T., Kimura, M. and Graybiel, A.M. (1995), 'Temporal and spatial characteristics of tonically active neurons of the primate striatum', *Journal of Neurophysiology*, **73**, pp. 1234–52.

Baxter, L.R. (1995), 'Neuroimaging studies of human anxiety disorders: cutting paths of knowledge through the field of neurotic phenomena', in *Psychopharmacology: The Fourth Generation of Progress*, ed. F.E. Bloom and D.J. Kupfer (New York: Raven Press).

Baxter, L.R., Schwartz, J.M. *et al.* (1992), 'Caudate glucose metabolic rate changes with both drug and behavior therapy for obsessive-compulsive disorder', *Archives of General Psychiatry*, **49**, pp. 681–9.

Bechara, A., Damasio, A.R. *et al.* (1994), 'Insensitivity to future consequences following damage to human prefrontal cortex', *Cognition*, **50**, pp. 7–15.

Breiter, H.C., Rauch, S.L. *et al.* (1996), 'Functional magnetic resonance imaging of symptom provocation in obsessive-compulsive disorder', *Archives of General Psychiatry*, **53**, pp. 595–606.

Eblen, F. and Graybiel, A.M. (1995), 'Highly restricted origin of prefrontal cortical inputs to striosomes in the macaque monkey', *The Journal of Neuroscience*, **15**, pp. 5999–6013.

Flaherty, A.W. and Graybiel, A.M. (1994), 'Input-output organization of the sensorimotor striatum in the squirrel monkey', *The Journal of Neuroscience*, **14**, pp. 599–610.

Fuster, J.M. (1989), *The Prefrontal Cortex (2nd edn)* (New York: Raven).

Gerfen, C.R. (1992), 'The neostriatal mosaic: multiple levels of compartmental organization in the basal ganglia', *Annual Review of Neuroscience*, **15**, pp. 285–320.

Graybiel, A.M. (1995),'Building action repertoires: memory and learning functions of the basal ganglia', *Current Opinion in Neurobiology*, **5**, pp. 733–41.

Graybiel, A.M. (1997), 'The basal ganglia and cognitive pattern generators', *Schizophrenia Bulletin*, **23**, pp. 459–69.

Graybiel, A.M. *et al.* (1994), 'The basal ganglia and adaptive motor control', *Science*, **26**, pp. 1826–31.

Hallie, P.P. (1967), 'Maine de Biran', in *The Encyclopedia of Philosophy*, ed. P. Edwards (NY: Macmillan).

Hikosaka, O., Sakamoto, M. and Usni, S. (1989), 'Functional properties of monkey caudate neurons. III. Activities related to expectation of target and reward', *Journal of Neurophysiology*, **61**, pp. 814-32.

Jenike, M.A. (1998), 'Drug treatment of obsessive-compulsive disorders', in *Obsessive-Compulsive Disorders: Practical Management (3rd edn)*, ed. M.A Jenike, L. Baer & W.E. Minichiello (St. Louis: Mosby).

Libet, B. (1985), 'Unconscious cerebral initiative and the role of conscious will in voluntary action', *Behavioral and Brain Sciences*, **8**, pp. 529–66.

Libet, B. (1994), 'A testable field theory of mind-brain interaction', *JCS*, **1** (1), pp. 119–26.

Libet, B. (1996), 'Conscious mind as a field', *Journal of Theoretical Biology*, **178**, pp. 223–4.

Libet, B. (1998), 'Do the models offer testable proposals of brain functions for conscious experience?' in *Advances in Neurology,Volume 77, Consciousness: At the Frontiers of Neuroscience*, ed. H.H. Jasper, L. Descarries, V.F. Castellucci, and S.Rossignol (Philadelphia: Lippincott-Raven Publishers).

Lindahl, B.I.B. and Århem, P. (1993), 'Mind as a force field: Comments on a new interactionist hypothesis', *Journal of Theoretical Biology*, **171**, pp. 111–22.

Mahâsi Sayadaw (1983), *Thoughts On The Dhamma* (Kandy, Sri Lanka: Buddhist Publication Society).

Marks, I.M. (1987), *Fears, phobias, and rituals: panic, anxiety, and their disorders* (New York: OUP).

Moore, F.C.T. (1970), *The Psychology of Maine de Biran* (Oxford: Oxford University Press).

Nemiah J.C. and Uhde, T.W. (1989), 'Obsessive-compulsive disorder' in *Comprehensive Textbook of Psychiatry V*, ed. H.I. Kaplan and B.J. Sadock, (Baltimore: Williams & Wilkins).

Niki, H. and Watanabe, M. (1979), 'Prefrontal and cingulate unit activity during timing behavior in the monkey', *Brain Research*, **171**, pp. 213–24.

Nyanaponika Thera (1962), *The Heart of Buddhist Meditation* (York Beach, ME: Samuel Weiser).

Nyanatiloka Mahathera (1980), *Buddhist Dictionary* (Kandy, Sri Lanka: Buddhist Publication Society).

Popper, K.R., Lindahl, B.I.B. *et al.* (1993), 'A discussion of the mind-brain problem,' *Theoretical Medicine*, **14**, pp.167–80.

Rasmussen, S.A. and Eisen, J.L. (1998), 'The epidemiology and clinical features of obsessive-compulsive disorder', in *Obsessive-Compulsive Disorders: Practical Management (3rd edn)*, ed. M.A Jenike, L. Baer and W.E. Minichiello (St. Louis: Mosby).

Rauch, S.L. and Baxter, L.R. (1998), 'Neuroimaging in obsessive-compulsive disorder and related disorders', in *Obsessive-Compulsive Disorders: Practical Management (3rd edn)*, ed. M.A Jenike, L. Baer and W.E. Minichiello (St. Louis: Mosby).

Rauch, S.L., Jenike, M.A. *et al.* (1994), 'Regional cerebral blood flow measured during symptom provocation in obsessive-compulsive disorder using ^{15}O-labeled CO_2 and positron emission tomography', *Archives of General Psychiatry*, **51**, pp. 62–70.

Rauch, S.L., Whalen, P.J. *et al.* (1998), 'Neurobiologic models of obsessive-compulsive disorder', in *Obsessive-Compulsive Disorders: Practical Management (3rd edn)*, ed. M.A Jenike, L. Baer and W.E. Minichiello (St. Louis: Mosby).

Rosenkilde, C.E., Bauer, R.H. and Fuster J.M. (1981), 'Single cell activity in ventral prefrontal cortex of behaving monkeys', *Brain Research,* **209**, pp. 375–94.

Saint-Cyr, J.A., Taylor, A.E. and Nicholson, K. (1995), 'Behavior and the basal ganglia', in *Advances in Neurology, Volume 65, Behavioral Neurology of Movement Disorders*, ed. W.J. Weiner and A.E. Lang (New York: Raven Press).

Saxena, S., Brody, A.L. *et al.* (1998), 'Neuroimaging and frontal-subcortical circuitry in obsessive-compulsive disorder', *Br. J. Psychiatry,* **173** (suppl. 35), pp. 26–37.

Schwartz, J.M. (1996), *Brain Lock: Free Yourself From Obsessive-Compulsive Behavior* (New York: HarperCollins).

Schwartz, J.M. (1997a), 'Obsessive-compulsive disorder', *Science & Medicine*, **4** (2), pp. 14–23.

Schwartz, J.M. (1997b), 'Cognitive-behavioral self-treatment for obsessive-compulsive disorder systematically alters cerebral metabolism: A mind-brain interaction paradigm for psychotherapists', in *Obsessive-Compulsive Disorders: Diagnosis, Etiology, Treatment* ed. E. Hollander & D.J. Stein (New York: Marcel Dekker Inc.).

Schwartz, J.M. (1998a), 'Neuroanatomical aspects of cognitive-behavioral therapy response in obsessive-compulsive disorder: An evolving perspective on brain and behavior', *Br. J. Psychiatry,* **173** (suppl. 35), pp. 38–44.

Schwartz, J.M. (1998b), *A Return to Innocence: Philosophical Guidance in an Age of Cynicism* (New York: Harper Collins).

Schwartz, J.M. (1999), 'First steps toward a theory of mental force: PET imaging of systematic cerebral changes after psychological treatment of obsessive-compulsive disorder', in *Toward a Science of Consciousness III*, ed. S.R. Hameroff, A.W. Kaszniak, D.J. Chalmers (Cambridge, MA: MIT Press).

Schwartz, J.M., Stoessel, P.W. *et al.* (1996), 'Systematic changes in cerebral glucose metabolic rate after successful behavior modification treatment of obsessive-compulsive disorder' *Archives of General Psychiatry,* **53**, pp. 109–13.

Silananda, U. (1990), *The Four Foundations of Mindfulness* (Boston: Wisdom Press).

Smith, A. (1976), *The Theory of Moral Sentiments* (6 ed.), ed. D. Raphael and A. Macfie (Oxford: OUP).

Stapp, H.P. (1999), 'Attention, intention, and will in quantum physics,' *JCS* (this issue).

Steketee, G.S., Frost, R.O. *et al.* (1998), 'Cognitive theory and treatment of obsessive-compulsive disorder', in *Obsessive-Compulsive Disorders: Practical Management (3rd edn)*, ed. M.A. Jenike, L. Baer and W.E. Minichiello (St. Louis: Mosby).

Stuss, D.T. and Benson, D.F. (1986), *The Frontal Lobes* (New York: Raven).

Swerdlow, N.R. (1995), 'Serotonin, obsessive-compulsive disorder and the basal ganglia,' *International Review of Psychiatry,* **7**, pp. 115–29.

Tallis, F. (1995), *Obsessive-Compulsive Disorder: A cognitive and neuropsychological perspective* (New York: John Wiley & Sons).

Teasdale, J.D. (1997), 'The relationship between cognition and emotion: the mind-in-place in mood disorders,' in *Science and Practice of Cognitive Behaviour Therapy*, ed. D.M. Clark and C.G. Fairburn (New York: Oxford University Press).

Teasdale, J.D., Segal, Z.V. *et al.* (1995), 'How does cognitive therapy prevent depressive relapse and why should attentional control (mindfulness) training help?', *Behaviour Research and Therapy,* **33**, pp. 25–39.

Thorpe, S.J., Rolls, E.T. and Maddison, S. (1983), 'The orbitofrontal cortex: neuronal activity in the behaving monkey', *Experimental Brain Research,* **49**, pp. 93–115.

Van Oppen, P., De Haan, E. *et al.* (1995), 'Cognitive therapy and exposure in vivo in the treatment of obsessive-compulsive disorder,' *Behavior Research and Therapy,* **33**, pp. 379–90.

Woodward, F.L. (1930), *The Book of Kindred Sayings, vol. V* (Oxford: Pali Text Society).

Zald, D.H. and Kim, S.W. (1996a), 'Anatomy and function of the orbital frontal cortex, I: anatomy, neurocircuitry, and obsessive-compulsive disorder', *Journal of Neuropsychiatry,* **8**, pp.125–38.

Zald, D.H. and Kim, S.W. (1996b), 'Anatomy and function of the orbital frontal cortex, II: function and relevance to obsessive-compulsive disorder', *Journal of Neuropsychiatry,* **8**, pp. 249–61.

APPENDIX: The Implications of Psychological Treatment Effects on Cerebral Function for the Physics of Mind-Brain Interaction

Henry P. Stapp and Jeffrey M. Schwartz

The data emerging from the clinical and brain studies described above suggest that, in the case of OCD, there are two pertinent brain mechanisms that are distinguishable both in terms of neuro-dynamics and in terms of the conscious experiences that accompany them. These mechanisms can be characterized, on anatomical and perhaps evolutionary grounds, as a lower-level and a higher-level mechanism. The clinical treatment has, when successful, an activating effect on the higher-level mechanism, and a suppressive effect on the lower-level one.

Certain conscious thoughts accompanying the lower-level process are experienced by the subject as intruders into his stream of consciousness: intruders that are not subject to conscious control in a manner commensurate with the rest of his thoughts. On the other hand, the conscious thoughts associated with higher-level process are experienced as integral parts of a stream of consciousness that is able under normal circumstances, with the application of sufficient wilful effort, to exercise control over the course of both bodily and mental actions (e.g., motor responses and attentional focus). Thus these OCD studies exhibit, in sharp relief, two different aspects of the mind-brain connection, one being the effects of the subject's brain upon his thoughts, the other being the effects of his thoughts upon his brain: the OCD studies juxtapose, and relate, exemplars of these two opposite sides of the apparent mind-brain connection.

The key question at issue, in this discussion of volition, is whether the mechanical picture suggested by intrusive OCD symptoms is, in some important sense, the full true picture of the causal structure of the mind-brain connection, or whether, on the other hand, our thoughts and volitions have effects that lie beyond what the brain itself is doing: do our thoughts and volitions themselves really enter into the causal structure in some way that is not fully reducible to mechanical brain processes alone; or is our deep-seated intuition that our thoughts and associated wilful efforts influence our actions an illusion?

This question can be posed at two levels: the pragmatic, and the ontological. At the level of pragmatic clinical practice it appears advantageous to postulate that the causal connection goes both ways: in the clinical treatment the mechanical origin of the intrusive thoughts was emphasized, in order to separate that aspect from the idea of 'self', thereby weakening its power; yet the supra-mechanical power of thoughts and volitions was implicit in the injunctions to resist, by wilful effort, those mechanically generated intrusions.

Certainly, a wholesale abandonment of the notion that our thoughts and volitions have causal efficacy would seriously cripple the sort of communication between subject and therapist that this successful method of treatment depends upon. Yet recognition of the existence of strong mechanical-type effects is also important in pragmatic clinical practice. Thus, within an ideal pragmatic theory of the mind-brain connection, both aspects of the causal connection should be accommodated without contradiction.

If one poses, on the other hand, the ontological question of what really exists then there is again a strong requirement of logical consistency: the entire ontological picture must hang together as a logically coherent whole that must also be compatible with the findings of other branches of science, and in particular with the principles of physics.

Before the OCD studies reported above there already was a major problem at this ontological level. According to the principles of relativistic classical physics, physical reality consists of nothing but a collection of tiny localized realities each causally connected only to its very close neighbours at earlier times. At the ontological level there is, to the extent that relativistic classical physics is valid, no 'emergence' of anything else: one may have good *practical* reasons for wishing to identify various complex structures, or certain approximate properties, and to give them names, but the only realities that are *needed*, dynamically, are the micro-realities defined by the basic physical principles. These microscopic realities and their micro-local connections to close neighbours are all that exist in the fundamental form of modern classical physics: any added elements constitute an epiphenomenal appendage that is causally gratuitous as far as the behaviour of the physical universe is concerned.

A typical moment of conscious experience has a complexity that makes it nonidentical to any one of the basic atomic micro-realities of classical physics: insofar as conscious experience lies within the classical-physics ontology it can *only* be a collection of these ontologically distinct micro-entities; a collection that is in every detail reducible to, and nothing but, this collection, and that has no property that does not follow as a strict logical consequence of the explicitly posited physical properties. Yet the experiential properties of 'greenness' and 'redness' and 'sourness,' for example, are not logically reducible, within the precepts of classical physical theory, to the spatio-temporal properties in terms of which the classical physical principles are formulated. Moreover, the existence of any *physical* reality that can grasp as a whole the macroscopic properties of large collections of the microscopic realities requires an augmentation to the ontology of precisely the kind that classical physics abolished: the very essence of classical physical theory was precisely that it *eliminated* from the physical world all graspings of macroscopic structures as wholes. The basic point of relativistic classical physics was exactly to reduce physical reality to a collection of local properties. Although it is certainly *logically* possible to reinsert now into the ontology some dynamically superfluous macro-entities, that option runs counter both to the core idea of classical physical theory, and also to Occam's razor, which is one of the pillars of good science.

So the question at issue, at the ontological level, is whether, as demanded by the principles of classical physics, all conscious thoughts and volitions are, as regards their connection to brain process, able to do nothing to the physically describable brain that is not done already by that brain and its physical environment alone? Or can a person's conscious thoughts and volitions actually enter into the causal structure in a way concordant with how they seem — subjectively — to act, namely as a force that can focus our thoughts in a way that can oppose and even override, if powered by sufficient volitional effort, the mechanical aspects of brain process?

In the context of this question the main point of this paper is that, whereas it may well be reasonable to postulate that the ego-dystonic elements of an OCD sufferer's experiences — in the form of obsessive thoughts and compulsive urges — have an epiphenomenal character, postulating the existence of 'epiphenomenal effort' is extremely problematic. It may indeed be *logically possible* for the 'feeling of intense effort' that accompanies the subject's successful overcoming of the lower-level process by the higher-level process to be just a *by-product* of the higher-level brain process rallying the resources needed to overcome the power of the lower-level mechanical process, and hence an after-the-fact, or beside-the-fact, superfluity. But it makes no dynamical sense to have this feeling of intense effort be an epiphenomenal by-product of the needed rallying of resources, rather than a *cause* of this rallying. When the effort flags, and is in danger of failing, more support is needed if the higher-level process is to prevail. Some process that actually rallies support for a course of action that has been assigned great value by the high-level conscious processing would be highly advantageous to the human organism. The intense effort *seems* to do just this. It makes no sense for this feeling to exist if it is a mere passive signal that this needed rallying is already occurring, or has already occurred, rather than being what it seems to be, namely part of the process of making what needs to happen actually happen.

A philosopher might object to this demand for 'sensibleness'. Yet surely it is far preferable, all else being equal, to embrace an ontology that makes sense, rather than one that does not. In a sensible picture of nature there would be no 'effort' that seems to be doing something that needs to be done physically, namely rallying needed resources, but that actually does nothing physical at all. Clearly, a vastly more reasonable alternative is one in which this palpable effort actually contributes to the bringing into being of that which is needed. Why should we believe, without good reason, that nature embraces a senseless ontology rather than a sensible one?

If the sensible possibilities were to conflict with the principles of physics then one might be justified in rejecting them in favour of one that makes no sense. But exactly the opposite is true. The basic principles of physics, as they are now understood, are not the deterministic laws of classical physics. They are laws that determine only probabilities for events to occur: other processes are needed to complete the ontological structure, if some definite sequence of physical events is to be actualized. Moreover, the physical reality now appears to be more like evolving information than like evolving matter (Stapp, this issue). And this 'physical reality' is explicitly tied dynamically into our human experiences by the basic precepts of contemporary physics, as these precepts are actually practiced, and as they were enunciated by the founders. Consequently, these contemporary physical laws can accommodate, in a completely natural way, the property that 'psychological effort' can focus the course of physical brain events in just the way that it seems to do. There is no compulsion from the basic principles of physics that requires any rejection of the sensible idea that mental effort can actually do what it seems to do: namely keep in focus a stream of consciousness that would otherwise become quickly defocused as a consequence of the Heisenberg uncertainty principle, and keep it focused in a way that tends to actualize potentialities that are in accord with consciously selected ends (see Stapp, this issue). Mental effort can, within contemporary physical theory, have, via the effects of the wilful focus of attention, large dynamical consequences that are not automatic consequences of physically describable brain mechanisms acting alone.

Henry P. Stapp

Attention, Intention, and Will in Quantum Physics[1]

How is mind related to matter? This ancient question in philosophy is rapidly becoming a core problem in science, perhaps the most important of all because it probes the essential nature of man himself. The origin of the problem is a conflict between the mechanical conception of human beings that arises from the precepts of classical physical theory and the very different idea that arises from our intuition: the former reduces each of us to an automaton, while the latter allows our thoughts to guide our actions. The dominant contemporary approaches to the problem attempt to resolve this conflict by clinging to the classical concepts, and trying to explain away our misleading intuition. But a detailed argument given here shows why, in a scientific approach to this problem, it is necessary to use the more basic principles of quantum physics, which bring the observer into the dynamics, rather than to accept classical precepts that are profoundly incorrect precisely at the crucial point of the role of human consciousness in the dynamics of human brains. Adherence to the quantum principles yields a dynamical theory of the mind/brain/body system that is in close accord with our intuitive idea of what we are. In particular, the need for a self-observing quantum system to pose certain questions creates a causal opening that allows mind/brain dynamics to have three distinguishable but interlocked causal processes, one micro-local, one stochastic, and the third experiential. Passing to the classical limit in which the critical difference between zero and the finite actual value of Planck's constant is ignored not only eliminates the chemical processes that are absolutely crucial to the functioning of actual brains, it simultaneously blinds the resulting theoretical construct to the physical fine structure wherein the effect of mind on matter lies: the use of this limit in this context is totally unjustified from a physics perspective.

Shifting the Paradigm

A controversy is raging today about the power of our minds. Intuitively we know that our conscious thoughts can guide our actions. Yet the chief philosophies of our time proclaim, in the name of science, that we are mechanical systems governed, fundamentally, entirely by impersonal laws that operate at the level of our microscopic constituents.

The question of the nature of the relationship between conscious thoughts and physical actions is called the mind–body problem. Old as philosophy itself, it was brought to its present form by the rise, during the seventeenth century, of what is

[1] This work was supported by the Director, Office of Energy Research, Office of High Energy and Nuclear Physics, Division of High Energy Physics of the U.S. Department of Energy under Contract DE-AC03-76SF00098.

Journal of Consciousness Studies, **6**, No. 8–9, 1999, pp. 143–64

called 'modern science'. The ideas of Galileo Galilei, René Descartes, and Isaac
Newton created a magnificent edifice known as classical physical theory, which was
completed by the work of James Clerk Maxwell and Albert Einstein. The central idea
is that the physical universe is composed of 'material' parts that are localizable in tiny
regions, and that all motion of matter is completely determined by matter alone, via
local universal laws. This *local* character of the laws is crucial. It means that each tiny
localized part responds only to the states of its immediate neighbours: each local part
'feels' or 'knows about' nothing outside its immediate microscopic neighbourhood.
Thus the evolution of the physical universe, and of every system within the physical
universe, is governed by a vast collection of local processes, each of which is
'myopic' in the sense that it 'sees' only its immediate neighbours.

The problem is that if this causal structure indeed holds then there is no need for our
human feelings and knowings. These experiential qualities clearly correspond to
large-scale properties of our brains. But if the entire causal process is already completely determined by the 'myopic' process postulated by classical physical theory,
then there is nothing for any unified graspings of large-scale properties to do. Indeed,
there is nothing that they *can* do that is not already done by the myopic processes. Our
conscious thoughts thus become prisoners of impersonal microscopic processes: we
are, according to this 'scientific' view, mechanical robots, with a mysterious dang-
ling appendage, a stream of conscious thoughts that can grasp large-scale properties
as wholes, but exert, as a consequence of these graspings, nothing not done already by
the microscopic constituents.

The enormous empirical success of classical physical theory during the eighteenth
and nineteenth centuries has led many twentieth-century philosophers to believe that
the problem with consciousness is how to explain it away: how to discredit our misleading intuition by identifying it as a product of human confusion, rather than recognizing the physical effects of consciousness as a physical problem that needs to be
answered in dynamical terms. That strategy of evasion is, to be sure, about the only
course available within the strictures imposed by classical physical theory.

Detailed proposals abound for how to deal with this problem created by adoption of
the classical-physics world view. The influential philosopher Daniel Dennett (1994,
p. 237) claims that our normal intuition about consciousness is 'like a benign user
illusion' or 'a metaphorical by-product of the way our brains do their approximating
work'. Eliminative materialists such as Richard Rorty (1979) hold that mental phenomena, such as conscious experiences, simply do not exist. Proponents of the popular 'Identity Theory of Mind' grant that conscious experiences do exist, but claim
each experience to be *identical* to some brain process. Epiphenomenal dualists hold
that our conscious experiences do exist, and are not identical to material processes,
but have no effect on anything we do: they are epiphenomenal.

Dennett (1994, p. 237) described the recurring idea that pushed him to his counter-
intuitive conclusion: 'a brain was always going to do what it was caused to do by local
mechanical disturbances.' This passage lays bare the underlying presumption behind
his own theorizing, and undoubtedly behind the theorizing of most non-physicists
who ponder this matter, namely the presumptive essential correctness of the idea of
the physical world foisted upon us by the assumptions of classical physical theory.

It has become now widely appreciated that assimilation by the general public of
this 'scientific' view, according to which each human being is basically a mechanical

robot, is likely to have a significant and corrosive impact on the moral fabric of society. Dennett speaks of the Spectre of Creeping Exculpation: recognition of the growing tendency of people to exonerate themselves by arguing that it is not 'I' who is at fault, but some mechanical process within: 'my genes made me do it'; or 'my high blood-sugar content made me do it.' (Recall the infamous 'Twinkie Defense' that got Dan White off with five years for murdering San Francisco Mayor George Moscone and Supervisor Harvey Milk.)

Steven Pinker (1997, p. 55) also defends a classical-type conception of the brain, and, like Dennett, recognizes the important need to reconcile the science-based idea of causation with a rational conception of personal responsibility. His solution is to regard science and ethics as two self-contained systems: 'Science and morality are separate spheres of reasoning. Only by recognizing them as separate can we have them both.' And 'The cloistering of scientific and moral reasoning also lies behind my recurring metaphor of the mind as machine, of people as robots.' But he then decries 'the doctrines of postmodernism, poststructuralism, and deconstructionism, according to which objectivity is impossible, meaning is self-contradictory, and reality is socially constructed.' Yet are not the ideas he decries a product of the contradiction he embraces? Self-contradiction is a bad seed that bears relativism as its evil fruit.

The current welter of conflicting opinion about the mind–brain connection suggests that a paradigm shift is looming. But it will require a major foundational shift. For powerful thinkers have, for three centuries, been attacking this problem from every angle within the bounds defined by the precepts of classical physical theory, and no consensus has emerged.

Two related developments of great potential importance are now occurring. On the experimental side, there is an explosive proliferation of empirical studies of the relations between a subject's brain process — as revealed by instrumental probes of diverse kinds — and the experiences he reports. On the theoretical side, there is a growing group of physicists who believe almost all thinking on this issue during the past few centuries to be logically unsound, because it is based implicitly on the precepts of classical physical theory, which are now known to be fundamentally incorrect. Contemporary physical theory differs profoundly from classical physical theory precisely on the nature of the dynamical linkage between minds and physical states. William James (1890, p. 486), writing at the end of the nineteenth century, said of the scientists who would one day illuminate the mind-body problem:

> the best way in which we can facilitate their advent is to understand how great is the darkness in which we grope, and never forget that the natural-science assumptions with which we started are provisional and revisable things.

How wonderfully prescient!

It is now well known that the precepts of classical physical theory are fundamentally incorrect. Classical physical theory has been superceded by quantum theory, which reproduces all of the empirical successes of classical physical theory, and succeeds also in every known case where the predictions of classical physical theory fail. Yet even though quantum theory yields all the correct predictions of classical physical theory, its representation of the physical aspects of nature is profoundly different from that of classical physical theory. And the most essential difference concerns precisely the connection between physical states and consciousness.

My thesis here is that the difficulty with the traditional attempts to understand the mind-brain system lies primarily with the physics assumptions, and only secondarily with the philosophy: once the physics assumptions are rectified the philosophy will take care of itself. A correct understanding of the mind–matter connection cannot be based on a conception of the physical aspects of nature that is profoundly mistaken precisely at the critical point, namely the role of consciousness in the dynamics of physical systems.

Contemporary science, rationally pursued, provides an essentially new under-standing of the mind–brain system. This revised understanding is in close accord with our intuitive understanding of that system: no idea of a 'benign user illusion' arises, nor any counter-intuitive idea that a conscious thought is identical to a collection of tiny objects moving about in some special kind of way.

Let it be said, immediately, that this solution lies not in the invocation of quantum randomness: a significant dependence of human action on random chance would be far more destructive of any rational notion of personal responsibility than microlocal causation ever was.

The solution hinges not on quantum randomness, but rather on the dynamical effects within quantum theory of the intention and attention of the observer.

But how did physicists ever manage to bring conscious thoughts into the dynamics of physical systems? That is an interesting tale.

The World as Knowings

In his book 'The creation of quantum mechanics and the Bohr–Pauli dialogue', the historian John Hendry (1984) gives a detailed account of the fierce struggles, during the first quarter of this century, by such eminent thinkers as Hilbert, Jordan, Weyl, von Neumann, Born, Einstein, Sommerfeld, Pauli, Heisenberg, Schroedinger, Dirac, Bohr and others, to come up with a rational way of comprehending the data from atomic experiments. Each man had his own bias and intuitions but, in spite of intense effort, no rational comprehension was forthcoming. Finally, at the 1927 Solvay con-ference a group including Bohr, Heisenberg, Pauli, Dirac, and Born come into con-cordance on a solution that came to be called 'The Copenhagen Interpretation'. Hendry says: 'Dirac, in discussion, insisted on the restriction of the theory's applica-tion to our knowledge of a system, and on its lack of ontological content.' Hendry summarized the concordance by saying: 'On this interpretation it was agreed that, as Dirac explained, the wave function represented our knowledge of the system, and the reduced wave packets our more precise knowledge after measurement.'

Let there be no doubt about this key point, namely that the mathematical theory was asserted to be directly about our knowledge itself, not about some imagined-to-exist world of particles and fields.

> Heisenberg (1958a): 'The conception of objective reality of the elementary particles has thus evaporated not into the cloud of some obscure new reality concept but into the trans-parent clarity of a mathematics that represents no longer the behavior of particles but rather our knowledge of this behavior.'

> Heisenberg (1958b): '. . . the act of registration of the result in the mind of the observer. The discontinuous change in the probability function . . . takes place with the act of regis-tration, because it is the discontinuous change in our knowledge in the instant of registra-tion that has its image in the discontinuous change of the probability function.'

Heisenberg (1958b:) 'When the old adage *'Natura non facit saltus'* is used as a basis of a criticism of quantum theory, we can reply that certainly our knowledge can change suddenly, and that this fact justifies the use of the term 'quantum jump'.

Wigner (1961): 'the laws of quantum mechanics cannot be formulated . . . without recourse to the concept of consciousness.'

Bohr (1934): 'In our description of nature the purpose is not to disclose the real essence of phenomena but only to track down as far as possible relations between the multifold aspects of our experience.'

Certainly this profound shift in physicists' conception of the basic nature of their endeavour, and the meanings of their formulas, was not a frivolous move: it was a last resort. The very idea that in order to comprehend atomic phenomena one must abandon ontology, and construe the mathematical formulas to be directly about the knowledge of human observers, rather than about the external real events themselves, is so seemingly preposterous that no group of eminent and renowned scientists would ever embrace it except as an extreme last measure. Consequently, it would be frivolous of us simply to ignore a conclusion so hard won and profound, and of such apparent direct bearing on our effort to understand the connection of our knowings to our physical actions.

This monumental shift in the thinking of scientists was an epic event in the history of human thought. Since the time of the ancient Greeks the central problem in understanding the nature of reality, and our role in it, has been the puzzling separation of nature into two seemingly very different parts, mind and matter. This had led to the divergent approaches of idealism and materialism. According to the precepts of idealism our ideas, thoughts, sensations, feelings, and other experiential realities, are the only realities whose existence is certain, and they should be taken as basic. But then the enduring external structure normally imagined to be carried by matter is difficult to fathom. Materialism, on the other hand, claims that matter is basic. But if one starts with matter then it is difficult to understand how something like your experience of the redness of a red apple can be constructed out of it, or why the experiential aspect of reality should exist at all if, as classical mechanics avers, the material aspect is causally complete by itself. There seems to be no rationally coherent way to comprehend the relationship between our thoughts and the thoughtless atoms that external reality was imagined to consist of.

Einstein never accepted the Copenhagen interpretation. He said:

What does not satisfy me, from the standpoint of principle, is its attitude toward what seems to me to be the programmatic aim of all physics: the complete description of any (individual) real situation (as it supposedly exists irrespective of any act of observation or substantiation). (Einstein, 1951, p. 667)

and

What I dislike in this kind of argumentation is the basic positivistic attitude, which from my view is untenable, and which seems to me to come to the same thing as Berkeley's principle, *esse est percipi*. (Einstein, 1951, p. 669).[Translation: To be is to be perceived]

Einstein struggled until the end of his life to get the observer's knowledge back out of physics. But he did not succeed! Rather he admitted that:

It is my opinion that the contemporary quantum theory . . . constitutes an optimum formulation of the [statistical] connections. (ibid. p. 87).

He referred to:

> the most successful physical theory of our period, viz., the statistical quantum theory
> which, about twenty-five years ago took on a logically consistent form. . . . This is the
> only theory at present which permits a unitary grasp of experiences concerning the quan-
> tum character of micro-mechanical events. (ibid p. 81).

One can adopt the cavalier attitude that these profound difficulties with the classical conception of nature are just some temporary retrograde aberration in the forward
march of science. Or one can imagine that there is simply some strange confusion that
has confounded our best minds for seven decades, and that their absurd findings
should be ignored because they do not fit our intuitions. Or one can try to say that
these problems concern only atoms and molecules, and not things built out of them. In
this connection Einstein said:

> But the 'macroscopic' and 'microscopic' are so inter-related that it appears impractica-
> ble to give up this program [of basing physics on the 'real'] in the 'microscopic' alone
> (*ibid.*, p. 674).

What Is Really Happening?

Orthodox quantum theory is pragmatic: it is a practical tool based on human knowings. It takes our experiences as basic, and judges theories on the basis of how well
they work *for us*, without trying to attribute any reality to the entities of the theory,
beyond the reality *for us* that they acquire from their success in allowing us to find
rational order in the structure of our past experiences, and to form sound expectations
about the consequences of our possible future actions.

But the opinion of many physicists, including Einstein, is that the proper task of
scientists is to try to construct a rational theory of nature that is not based on so small a
part of the natural world as human knowledge. John Bell opined that we physicists
ought to try to do better than that. The question thus arises as to what is 'really
happening'.

Heisenberg (1958) answered this question in the following way:

> Since through the observation our knowledge of the system has changed discontinu-
> ously, its mathematical representation also has undergone the discontinuous change, and
> we speak of a 'quantum jump'.
>   A real difficulty in understanding the interpretation occurs when one asks the famous
> question: But what happens 'really' in an atomic event?
>   If we want to describe what happens in an atomic event, we have to realize that the
> word 'happens' can apply only to the observation, not to the state of affairs between the
> two observations. It [the word 'happens'] applies to the physical, not the psychical act of
> observation, and we may say that the transition from the 'possible' to the 'actual' takes
> place as soon as the interaction of the object with the measuring device, and therefore
> with the rest of the world, has come into play; it is not connected with the act of registra-
> tion of the result in the mind of the observer. The discontinuous change in the probability
> function, however, occurs with the act of registration, because it is the discontinuous
> change in our knowledge in the instant of recognition that has its image in the discontinu-
> ous change in the probability function.

This explanation uses two distinct modes of description. One is a pragmatic
knowledge-based description in terms of the Copenhagen concept of the discontinu-
ous change of the quantum-theoretic probability function at the registration of new
knowledge in the mind of the observer. The other is an ontological description in

terms of 'possible' and 'actual', and 'interaction of object with the measuring device'. The latter description is an informal supplement to the strict Copenhagen interpretation. I say 'informal supplement' because this ontological part is not tied into quantum-theoretical formalism in any precise way. It assuages the physicists' desire for an intuitive understanding of what could be going on behind the scenes, without actually interfering with the workings of the pragmatic set of rules.

Heisenberg's transition from 'the possible' to 'the actual' at the dumb measuring device was shown to be a superfluous and needless complication by von Neumann's analysis of the quantum process of measurement (von Neumann, 1932, Chapter VI). I shall discuss that work later, but note here only the key conclusion. Von Neumann introduced the measuring instruments and the body/brains of the community of human observers into the quantum state, which is quantum theory's only representation of 'physical reality'. He then showed that if an observer experiences the fact that, for example, 'the pointer on a measuring device has swung to the right', then this increment in the observer's knowledge can be associated exclusively with a reduction (i.e., sudden change) of the state of the brain of that observer to the part of that brain state that is compatible with his new knowledge. No change or reduction of the quantum state at the dumb measuring device is needed: no change in 'knowledge' occurs there. This natural association of human 'knowings' with events in human brains allows the 'rules' of the Copenhagen interpretation pertaining to 'our knowledge' to be represented in a natural ontological framework. Indeed, any reduction event at the measuring device itself would, strictly speaking, disrupt in principle the validity of the predictions of quantum theory. Thus the only natural ontological place to put the reduction associated with the increases in knowledge upon which the Copenhagen interpretation is built is in the brain of the person whose knowledge is increased.

My purpose in what follows is to reconcile the insight of the founders of quantum theory, namely that the mathematical formalism of quantum theory is about our knowledge, with the demand of Einstein that basic physical theory be about nature herself. I shall achieve this reconciliation by incorporating human beings, including both their body/brains and their conscious experiences, into the quantum mechanical description of nature.

The underlying commitment here is to the basic quantum principle that information is the currency of reality, not matter: the universe is an informational structure, not a substantive one. This fact is becoming ever more clear in the empirical studies of the validity of the concepts of quantum theory in the context of complex experiments with simple combinations of correlated quantum systems, and in the related development of quantum information processing. Information-based language works beautifully, but substance-based language does not work at all.

Mind–Brain Dynamics: Why Quantum Theory Is Needed

A first question confronting a classically biased mind-brain researcher is this: How can two things so differently described and conceived as substantive matter and conscious thoughts interact in any rationally controlled and scientifically acceptable way? Within the classical framework this is impossible. Thus the usual tack has been to abandon or modify the classical conception of mind while clinging tenaciously to the 'scientifically established' classical idea of matter, even in the face of knowledge that the classical idea of matter is now known by scientists to be profoundly and fundamentally mistaken, and mistaken not only on the microscopic scale, but on the scale of metres and kilometres as well (Tittel, 1998). Experiments show that our experiences of instruments cannot possibly be just the passive witnessing of macroscopic physical realities that exist and behave in the way that the ideas of classical physical theory say that macroscopic physical realities ought to exist and behave.

Scientists and philosophers intent on clinging to familiar classical concepts normally argue at this point that, whereas long-range quantum effects can be exhibited under rigorous conditions of isolation and control, all quantum effects will be wiped out in warm wet brains on a very small scale, and hence classical concepts will be completely adequate to deal with the question of the relationship between our conscious thoughts and the large-scale brain activities with which they are almost certainly associated.

That argument is incorrect. The emergence of classical-type relationships arise from interactions between a system and its environment. These interactions induce correlations between this system and its environment that make certain typical quantum interference effects difficult to observe *in practice*, and that allow certain practical computations to be simplified by substituting a classical system for a quantum one. However, these correlation (decoherence) effects definitely do not entail the true emergence — even approximately — of a single classically describable system (Zurek, 1986, p. 89; Joos, 1986, p. 12). In particular, if the subsystem of interest is a brain, then interactions between its parts produce a gigantic jumble of partially interfering classical-type states: no single approximately classical reality emerges. Yet if no — even approximate — single classical reality emerges at any macroscopic scale, but only a jumble of partially interfering quantum states, then the investigation of an issue as basic as the nature of the mind–brain connection ought *in principle* to be pursued within an exact framework, rather than crippling the investigation from the outset by replacing correct principles by concepts known to be fundamentally and grossly false, just because they allow certain *practical* computations to be simplified.

This general argument is augmented by a more detailed examination of the present case. The usual argument for the approximate *pragmatic* validity of a classical conceptualization of a system is based on assumptions about the nature of the question that is put to nature. The assumption in the usual case is that this question will be about something like the position of a visible object. Then one has a clear separation of the world into its pertinent parts: the unobservable atomic subsystem, the observable features of the instrument, and unobserved features of the environment, including unobserved micro-features of the instrument. The empirical question is about the observable features of the instrument. These features are essentially just the overall position and orientation of a visible object.

But the central issue in the present context is precisely the character of the brain states that are associated with conscious experiences. It is not known, a priori, whether or how a self-observing quantum system separates into these various parts. It is not clear, a priori, that a self-observing brain can be separated into components analogous to observer, observee, and environment. Consequently, one cannot rationally impose prejudicial assumptions — based on pragmatic utility in simple cases in which the quantum system and measuring instrument are two distinct systems, both external to the human observer, and strongly coupled to an unobservable environment — in this vastly different present case, in which the quantum system being measured, the observing instrument, and 'the observer' are aspects of one unified body/brain/mind system observing itself.

In short, the practical utility of classical concepts in certain special situations arises from the very special forms of the empirical questions that are to be asked in those situations. Consequently, one must revert to the basic physical principles in this case where the special conditions of separation fail, and the nature of the questions put to nature can therefore be quite different.

The issue here is not whether distinct objects that we observe via our senses can be treated as classical objects. It is whether, in the description of the complex inner workings of a thinking human brain, it is justifiable to assume — not just for certain simple practical purposes, but as a matter of principle — that this brain is made up of tiny interacting parts of a kind known not to exist.

The only rational scientific way to proceed in this case of a mind/brain observing itself is to start from basic quantum theory, not from a theory that is known to be profoundly incorrect.

The von Neumann/Wigner 'orthodox' quantum formalism that I employ automatically and neatly encompasses all quantum and classical predictions, including the transition domains between them. It automatically incorporates all decoherence effects, and the partial 'classicalization' effects that they engender.

Von Neumann/Wigner Quantum Theory

Wigner used the word 'orthodox' to describe the formulation of quantum theory developed by von Neumann. It can be regarded as a partial ontologicalization of its predecessor, Copenhagen quantum theory.

The central concept of the Copenhagen interpretation of quantum theory, as set forth by the founders at the seminal Solvay conference of 1927, is that the basic mathematical entity of the theory, the quantum state of a system, represents 'our knowledge' of the system, and the reduced state represents our more precise knowledge after measurement.

In the strict Copenhagen view, the quantum state is always the state of a limited system that does not include the instruments that we use to *prepare* that system or later to *measure* it. Our relevant experiences are those that we described as being our observations of the observable features of these instruments.

To use the theory one needs relationships between the mathematical quantities of the theory and linguistic specifications on the observable features of the instruments. These specifications are couched in the language that we use to communicate to our technically trained associates what we have done (how we have constructed our instruments, and put them in place) and what we have learned (which outcomes have appeared to us). Thus pragmatic quantum theory makes sense only when regarded as a part of a larger enveloping language that allows us describe to each other the dispositions of the instruments and ordinary objects that are relevant to the application we make. The connections between these linguistic specifications and the mathematical quantities of the theory are fixed, fundamentally, by the empirical calibrations of our instruments.

These calibration procedures do not, however, fully exploit all that we know about the atomic properties of the instruments.

That Bohr was sensitive to this deficiency is shown by following passage:

> On closer consideration, the present formulation of quantum mechanics, in spite of its great fruitfulness, would yet seem no more than a first step in the necessary generaliza-tion of the classical mode of description, justified only by the possibility of disregarding in its domain of application the atomic structure of the measuring instruments. For a cor-relation of still deeper lying laws of nature . . . this last assumption can no longer be main-tained and we must be prepared for a . . . still more radical renunciation of the usual claims of so-called visualization (Bohr, 1936, pp. 293–4).

Bohr was aware of the work in this direction by John von Neumann (1932), but believed von Neumann to be on a wrong track. Yet the opinion of many other physi-cists is that von Neumann made the right moves: he brought first the measuring instruments, and eventually the entire physical universe, including the human observ-ers themselves, into the physical system represented by the quantum state. The mathematical theory allows one to do this, and it is unnatural and problematic to do otherwise: any other choice would be an artifact, and would create problems associ-ated with an artificial separation of the unified physical system into differently described parts. This von Neumann approach, in contrast to the Copenhagen approach, allows the quantum theory to be applied both to cosmological problems, and to the mind–body problem.

Most efforts to improve upon the original Copenhagen quantum theory are based on von Neumann's formulation. That includes the present work. However, almost every other effort to modify the Copenhagen formulation aims to improve it by *removing* the consciousness of the observer from quantum theory: they seek to bring quantum theory in line with the basic philosophy of the superceded classical theory, in which consciousness is imagined to be a disconnected passive witness.

I see no rationale for this retrograde move. Why should we impose on our under-standing of nature the condition that consciousness not be an integral part of it, or an unrealistic stricture of impotence that is belied by the deepest testimony of human experience, and is justified only by a theory now known to be fundamentally false, when the natural form of the superceding theory makes experience efficacious?

I follow, therefore, the von Neumann/Wigner [vN/W] formulation, in which the entire physical world is represented by a quantum mechanical state, and each thinking human being is recognized as an aspect of the total reality: each thinking human being is a body/brain/mind system, consisting of a sequence of conscious events, called knowings, bound together by the physical structure that is his body/brain.

However, the basic idea, and the basic rules, of Copenhagen quantum theory are strictly maintained: the quantum state continues to represent knowledge, and each experiential increment in knowledge, or knowing, is accompanied by a reduction of the quantum state to a form compatible with that increase in knowledge.

By keeping these connections intact one retains both the close pragmatic link between the theory and empirical knowledge, which is entailed by the quantum rules, and also the dynamical efficacy of conscious experiences, which follows from the action of the 'reduction of the quantum state' that, according to the quantum rules, is the image in the physical world of the conscious event.

In this theory, each conscious event has as its physical image not a reduction of the state of some small physical system that is external to the body/brain of the person to whom the experience belongs, as specified by the Copenhagen approach. Rather, the reduction is in that part of the state of the universe that constitutes the state of the body/brain of the person to whom the experience belongs: the reduction actualizes the pattern of activity that is sometimes called the 'neural correlate' of that conscious experience. The theory thus ties in a practical way into the vast field of mind–brain research: i.e., into studies of the correlations between, on the one hand, brain activities of a subject, as measured by instrumental probes and described in physical terms, and, on the other hand, the subjective experiences, as reported by the subject, and described in the language of 'folk psychology' (i.e., in terms of feelings, beliefs, desires, perceptions, and the other psychological features).

My aim now is to show in more detail how the conscious intentions of a human being can influence the activities of his brain. To do this I must first explain the two important roles of the quantum observer.

The Two Roles of the Quantum Observer

Most readers will have heard of the Schrödinger equation: it is the quantum analogue of Newton's and Maxwell's equations of motion of classical mechanics. The Schrödinger equation, like Newton's and Maxwell's equations, is deterministic: given the motion of the quantum state for all times prior to the present, the motion for all future time is fixed, insofar as the Schrödinger equation is satisfied for all times.

However, the Schrödinger equation fails when an increment of knowledge occurs: then there is a sudden jump to a 'reduced' state, which represents the new state of knowledge. This jump involves the well-known element of quantum randomness.

A superficial understanding of quantum theory might easily lead one to conclude that the entire dynamics is controlled by just the combination of the local--deterministic Schrödinger equation and elements of quantum randomness. If that were true then our conscious experiences would again become epiphenomenal side-shows.

To see beyond this superficial appearance one must look more closely at the two roles of the observer in quantum theory.

Niels Bohr (1951, p. 223), in recounting the important events at the Solvay Conference of 1927, says:

> On that occasion an interesting discussion arose also about how to speak of the appearance of phenomena for which only predictions of a statistical nature can be made. The question was whether, as regards the occurrence of individual events, we should adopt the terminology proposed by Dirac, that we have to do with a choice on the part of 'nature' or, as suggested by Heisenberg, we should say that we have to do with a choice on the part of the 'observer' constructing the measuring instruments and reading their recording.

Bohr stressed this choice on the part of the observer:

> ... our possibility of handling the measuring instruments allow us only to make a choice between the different complementary types of phenomena we want to study.

The observer in quantum theory does more than just read the recordings. He also chooses which question will be put to Nature: which aspect of nature his inquiry will probe. I call this important function of the observer 'The Heisenberg Choice', to contrast it with the 'Dirac Choice', which is the random choice on the part of Nature that Dirac emphasized.

According to quantum theory, the Dirac Choice is a choice between alternatives that are specified by the Heisenberg Choice: the observer must first specify what aspect of the system he intends to measure or probe, and then put in place an instrument that will probe that aspect.

In quantum theory it is the observer who both poses the question, and recognizes the answer. Without some way of specifying what the question is, the quantum rules will not work: the quantum process grinds to a halt.

Nature does not answer, willy-nilly, all questions: it answers only properly posed questions. A question put to Nature must be one with a Yes-or-No answer, or a sequence of such questions. The question is never of the form 'Where will object O turn out to be?', where the possibilities range in a smooth way over a continuum of values. The question is rather of a form such as: 'Will the centre of object O — perhaps the pointer on some instrument — be found by the observer to lie in the interval between 6 and 7 on some specified 'dial'?'

The human observer poses such a question, which must be such that the answer Yes is experientially recognizable. Nature then delivers the answer, Yes or No. Nature's answers are asserted by quantum theory to conform to certain statistical conditions, which are determined jointly by the question posed and the form of the prior state (of the body/brain of the observer.) The observer can examine the answers that Nature gives, in a long sequence of trials with similar initial conditions, and check the statistical prediction of the theory.

This all works well at the pragmatic Copenhagen level, where the observer stands outside the quantum system, and is simply accepted for what he empirically is and does. But what happens when we pass to the vN/W ontology? The observer then no longer stands outside the quantum system: he becomes a dynamical body/brain/mind system that is an integral dynamical part of the quantum universe.

The basic problem that originally forced the founders of quantum theory to bring the human observers into the theory was that the evolution of the state via the Schrödinger equation does not fix or specify where and when the question is posed, or what the question actually is. This problem was resolved by placing this issue in the hands and mind of the external human observer.

Putting the observer inside the system does not, by itself, resolve this basic problem: the Schrödinger evolution alone remains unable to specify what the question is. Indeed, this bringing of the human observer into the quantum system intensifies the problem, because there is no longer the option of shifting the problem away, to some outside agent. Rather, the problem is brought to a head, because the human agent is precisely the quantum system that is under investigation.

In the Copenhagen formulation, the Heisenberg choice was made by the mind of the external human observer. I call this process of choosing the question the Heisenberg process. In the vN/W formulation, this choice is not made by the local deterministic Schrödinger process and the global stochastic Dirac process. So there is still an essential need for a third process, the Heisenberg process. Thus the agent's mind can continue to play its key role. But the mind of the human agent is now an integral part of the dynamical body/brain/mind. We therefore have, now, an intrinsically more complex dynamical situation, one in which a person's conscious thoughts can — and evidently must, if no new element is brought in, — play a role that is not reducible to the combination of the Schrödinger and Dirac processes. In an evolving human brain governed by ionic concentrations and electric-magnetic field gradients, and other continuous field-like properties, rather than sharply defined properties, or discrete well-defined 'branches' of the wave function, the problem of specifying, within this amorphous and diffusive context, the well-defined question that is put to nature is quite nontrivial.

Having thus identified this logical opening for efficacious human mental action, I now proceed to fill in the details of how it might work.

How Conscious Thoughts Could Influence Brain Process

Information is the currency of reality. That is the basic message of quantum theory.

The basic unit of information is the 'bit': the answer 'Yes' or 'No' to some specific question. In quantum theory the answer 'Yes' to a posed question is associated with an operator P that depends on the question. The defining property of a projection operator is that P squared equals P: asking the very same question twice is the same as asking it once. The operator associated with the answer 'No' to this same question is $1-P$. Note that $(1-P)$ is also a projection operator: $(1-P)^2 = 1 - 2P + P^2 = 1 - 2P + P = (1-P)$.

To understand the meaning of these operators P and $(1-P)$, it is helpful to imagine a trivial classical example. Suppose a motionless classical heavy point-like particle is known to be in a box that is otherwise empty. Suppose a certain probability function F represents all that you know about the location of this particle. Suppose you then send some light through the left half of the box that will detect the particle if it is in the left half of the box, but not tell you anything about where in the left half of the box the particle lies. Suppose, moreover, that the position of the particle is undisturbed by this observation. Then let P be the operator that, acting on any function f, sets that function to zero in the right half of the box, but leaves it unchanged in the left half of the box. Note that two applications of P has exactly the same effect as one application, $P^2 = P$. The question put to nature by your probing experiment is: 'Do you now know that particle is in the left half of the box?' Then the function PF represents, apart from an overall normalization factor, your new state of knowledge if the answer to the posed question was YES. Likewise, the function $(1-P)F$ represents, apart from overall normalization, the new probability function, if the answer was NO.

The quantum counterpart of F is the operator S. Operators are like functions that do not commute: the order in which you apply them matters. The analog of $PF = PFP$ is PSP, and the analog of $(1-P)F = (1-P)F(1-P)$ is $(1-P)S(1-P)$.

This is how the quantum state represents information and knowledge, and how increments in knowledge affect the quantum state.

I have described in my book (Stapp, 1993, Ch. 6) my conception of how the quantum mind–brain works. It rests on some ideas/findings of William James.

William James (1910, p. 1062) says that:

> a discrete composition is what actually obtains in our perceptual experience. We either perceive nothing, or something that is there in sensible amount. This fact is what in psychology is known as the law of the 'threshold'. Either your experience is of no content, of no change, or it is of a perceptual amount of content or change. Your acquaintance with reality grows literally by buds or drops of perception. Intellectually and on reflection you can divide these into components, but as immediately given they come totally or not at all.

This wholeness of each perceptual experience is a main conclusion, and theme, of Jamesian psychology. It fits neatly with the quantum ontology.

Given a well-posed question about the world to which one's attention is directed, quantum theory says that nature either gives the affirmative answer, in which case there occurs an experience describable as 'Yes, I perceive it!' or, alternatively, no experience occurs in connection with that question.

In vN/W theory the 'Yes' answer is represented by a projection operator P that acts on the degrees of freedom of the brain of the observer, and reduces the state of this brain — and also the state S of the universe — to one compatible with that answer 'Yes': S is reduced to PSP. If the answer is 'No', then the projection operator $(1-P)$ is applied to the state S: S is reduced to $(1-P)S(1-P)$. [See Stapp (1998b) for technical details.]

James (1890, p. 257) asserts that each conscious experience, though it comes to us whole, has a sequence of temporal components ordered in accordance with the ordering in which they have entered into one's stream of conscious experiences. These components are like the columns in a marching band: at each viewing only a subset of the columns is in front of the viewing stand. At a later viewing a new column has appeared on one end, and one has disappeared at the other (cf. Stapp, 1993, p. 158). It is this possibility of having a sequence of different components present in a single thought that allows conscious analysis and comparisons to be made.

Infants soon grasp the concept of their bodies in interaction with a world of persisting objects about them. This suggests that the brain of an alert person normally contains a 'neural' representation of the current state of his body and the world about him. I assume that such a representation exists, and call it the body-world schema (Stapp, 1993, Ch. 6).

Consciously directed action is achieved, according to this theory, by means of a 'projected' (into the future) temporal component of the thought, and of the body-world schema actualized by the thought: the intended action is represented in this projected component as a mental image of the intended action, and as a corresponding representation in the brain, (i.e., in a body-world schema) of that intended action. The neural activities that automatically flow from the associated body-world schema tend to bring the intended bodily action into being.

The coherence and directedness of a person's stream of consciousness is maintained, according to this theory, because the instructions effectively issued to the unconscious processes of the brain by the natural dynamical unfolding that issues from the actualized body-world schema include not only the instructions for the initiation or continuation of motor actions but also instructions for the initiation or continuation of mental processing. This means that the actualization associated with one thought leads physically to the emergence of the propensities for the occurrence of the next thought, or of later thoughts. (Stapp, 1993, Ch. 6)

The idea here is that the action — on the state S — of the projection operator P that is associated with a thought T will actualize a pattern of brain activity that will dynamically evolve in such a way as to tend to create a subsequent state that is likely to achieve the intention of the thought T. The natural cause of this positive correlation between the experiential intention of the thought T and the matching confirmatory experience of a succeeding thought T is presumably set in place during the formation of brain structure, in the course of the person's interaction with his environment, by the reinforcement of brain structures that result in empirically successful pairings between experienced intentions and subsequently experienced perceptions. These can be physically compared because both are expressed physically by similar body-world schemas.

As noted previously, the patterns of brain activity that are actualized by an event unfold not only into instructions to the motor cortex to institute intended motor actions. They unfold also into instructions for the creation of the conditions for the next experiential event. But the Heisenberg uncertainties in, for example, the locations of the atomic and ionic constituents of the nerve terminals, and more generally of the entire brain, necessarily engender a quantum diffusion in the evolving state of the brain. Thus the dynamically generated state that is the pre-condition for the next event will not correspond exactly to a well-defined unique question: some 'scatter' will invariably creep in. However, a specific question must be posed in order for the next quantum event to occur!

This problem of how to specify 'the next question' is the central problem in most attempts to 'improve' the Copenhagen interpretation by excluding 'the observer'. If one eliminates the observer, then something else must be brought in to fix the next question: i.e., to make the Heisenberg choice.

The main idea here is to continue to allow the question to be posed by the 'observer', who is now an integral part of the quantum system: the observer is a body/brain/mind subsystem. The Heisenberg Choice, which is the choice of an operator P that acts macroscopically, as a unit, on the observing system, is not fixed by the Schrödinger equation, or by the Dirac Choice, so it is most naturally fixed by the experiential part of that system, which seems to pertain to macroscopic aspects of brain activity taken as units.

Each experience is asserted to have an intentional aspect, which is its experiential goal or aim, and an attentional aspect, which is an experiential focussing on an updating of the current status of the person's idea of his body, mind, and environment.

When an action is initiated by some thought, part of the instruction is normally to monitor, by attention, the ensuing action, in order to check it against the intended action.

In order for the appropriate experiential check to occur, *the appropriate question must be asked*. The intended action is formulated in experiential terms, and the appropriate monitoring question is whether this intended experience matches the subsequently occurring experience. *This connection has the form of the transference of an experience defined by the intentional aspect of an earlier experience into the experiential question attended to — i.e., posed — by a later experience.*

This way of closing the causal gap associated with the Heisenberg Choice introduces two parallel lines of causal connection in the body/brain/mind system. On the one hand, there is the physical line that unfolds — under the control of the local deterministic Schrödinger equation — from a prior event, and that generates the physical *potentialities* for succeeding possible events. Acting in parallel to this physical line of causation, there is a mental line of causation that transfers the experiential intention of an earlier event into an experiential attention of a later event. These two causal strands, one physical and one mental, join to form the physical and mental poles of a succeeding quantum event.

In this model there are three intertwined factors in the causal structure: (1), the local causal structure generated by the Schrödinger equation; (2), the Heisenberg

Choice, which is based on the experiential aspects of the body/brain/mind subsystem that constitutes a person; and (3), the Dirac Choice on the part of nature.

The point of all this is that there is within the vN/W ontology a logical necessity, in order for the quantum process to proceed, for *some process* to fix the Heisenberg Choice of the operator P, which acts over an extended portion of the body/brain of the person. Neither the Schrödinger evolution nor the Dirac stochastic choice can do the job. The only other known aspect of the system is our conscious experience. It is possible, and natural, to use this mind part of body/brain/mind system to produce the needed choice.

The mere logical possibility of a mind-matter interaction such as this, within the vN/W formulation, indicates that quantum theory has the potential of permitting the experiential aspects of reality to enter into the causal structure of body/brain/mind dynamics, and to enter in a way that is not fully reducible to a combination of local mechanical causation specified by the Schrödinger equation and the random quantum choices. The requirements of quantum dynamics *demand* some further process, and an experience-based process that fits both our ideas about our psychological make up and also the quantum rules that connect our experiences to the informational structure carried by the evolving physical state of the brain seems to be the perfect candidate.

What has been achieved here is, of course, just a working out in more detail of Wigner's idea that quantum theory, in the von Neumann form, allows for mind — pure conscious experience — to *interact* with the 'physical' aspect of nature, as that aspect is represented in quantum theory. What permits this interaction is the fact that the physical aspect of nature, as it is represented in quantum theory, is informational in character, and hence links naturally to increments in knowledge. Because each increment in knowledge acts directly upon the quantum state, and reduces it to the informational structure compatible with the new knowledge, there is, right from the outset, an action of mind on the physical world. I have just worked out a possible scenario in more detail, and in particular have emphasized how the causal gap associated with the Heisenberg Choice allows mind to enter into the dynamics in a way that is quite in line with our intuition about the efficacy of our thoughts. It is therefore simply wrong to proclaim that the findings of science entail that our intuitions about the nature of our thoughts are necessarily illusory or false. Rather, it is completely in line with contemporary science to hold our thoughts to be causally efficacious, and reducible neither to the local deterministic Schrödinger process, nor to that process combined with stochastic Dirac choices on the part of nature.

Idealism, Materialism, and Quantum Informationism

I have stressed just now the idea-like character of the physical state of the universe, within vN/W quantum theory. This suggests that the theory may conform to the tenets of idealism. This is partially true. The quantum state undergoes, when a fact becomes fixed in a local region, a sudden jump that extends over vast reaches of space. This gives the physical state the character of a representation of knowledge rather than a representation of substantive matter. When not jumping, the state represents potentialities or probabilities for actual events to occur. Potentialities and probabilities are normally conceived to be idea-like qualities, not material realities. So, as regards the intuitive conception of the intrinsic nature of *what is represented* within the theory by the physical state, it certainly is correct to say that it is idea-like.

On the other hand, the physical state has a mathematical structure, and a behaviour that is governed by the mathematical properties. It evolves much of the time in accordance with local deterministic laws that are direct quantum counterparts of the local deterministic laws of classical mechanics. Thus, as regards various structural and causal properties, the physical state certainly has aspects that we normally associate with matter.

So this vN/W quantum conception of nature ends up having both idea-like and matter-like qualities. The causal law involves two complementary modes of evolution that, at least at the present level of theoretical development, are quite distinct. One of these modes involves a gradual change that is governed by local deterministic laws, and hence is matter-like in character. The other mode is abrupt, and is idea-like in *two* respects.

This hybrid ontology can be called an information-based reality. Each answer, Yes or No, to a quantum question is one bit of information that is generated by a mental-type event. This event is registered as a reduction of the quantum state of the universe to a new form. This information is stored in this state, which evolves deterministically in accordance with the Schrödinger equation. Thus, according to the quantum conception, the physical universe — represented by the quantum state — is a repository of evolving information that has the dispositional power to create more information.

Quantum Zeno Effect and The Efficacy of Mind

In the model described above, the specifically mental effects are expressed solely through the choice and the timings of the questions posed. The question then arises as to whether just the choices about which questions are asked, with no control over which answers are returned, can influence the dynamical evolution of a system.

The answer is 'Yes': the evolution of a quantum state can be greatly influenced by the choices and timings of the questions put to nature.

The most striking example of this is the Quantum Zeno Effect. (Chui *et al.*, 1977, and Itano, *et al.* 1990). In quantum theory, if one poses repeatedly, in very rapid succession, the same Yes-or-No question, and the answer to the first of these posings is Yes, then, in the limit of very rapid-fire posings, the evolution will be confined to the subspace in which the answer is Yes: the effective Hamiltonian will change from H to PHP, where P is the projection operator onto the Yes states. This means that evolution of the system is effectively 'boxed in' in the subspace where the answer continues to be Yes, if the question is posed sufficiently rapidly, even if it would otherwise run away from that region.

This fact that the Hamiltonian is effectively changed in this macroscopic way shows that the choices and timings of which questions are asked can affect observable properties.

Free Will and Causation

Personal responsibility is not reconciled with the quantum understanding of causation by making our thoughts *free*, in the sense of being completely unconstrained by anything at all. It is solved, rather, by making our thoughts *part* of the causal structure of the body/brain/mind system, but a part that is not under the complete dominion of myopic (*i.e., microlocal*) causation and random chance. Our thoughts then become aspects of the causal structure that are *entwined* with the micro-physical and random elements, yet are not completely reducible to them, or replaceable by them.

Pragmatic Theory of the Mind–Brain

This vN/W theory gives a conceivable ontology. However, for practical purposes it can be viewed as a pragmatic theory of the human psycho-physical structure. It is deeper and more realistic than the Copenhagen version because it links our thoughts not directly to objects (instruments) in the external world, but rather to patterns of brain activity. It provides a theoretical structure based explicitly on the two kinds of data at our disposal, namely the experiences of the subject, as he describes these experiences to himself and his colleagues, and the experiences of the observers of that subject, as they describe their experiences to themselves and their colleagues. These two kinds of descriptions are linked together by a theoretical structure that neatly, precisely, and automatically accounts, in a single uniform and practical way, for all known quantum and classical effects. But, in contrast to the classical-physics based model, it has a ready-made place for an efficacious mind, and provides a rational understanding of how such a mind could be causally enmeshed with brain processes.

If one adopts this pragmatic view then one need never consider the question of non-human minds: the theory then covers, by definition, the science that we human beings create to account for the structure of our human experiences.

This pragmatic theory should provide a satisfactory basis for a rational science of the human mind–brain. It gives a structure that coherently combines the psychological and physical aspect of human behaviour. However, it cannot be expected to be exactly true, for it would entail the existence of collapse events associated with increments in human knowledge, but no analogous events associated with non-humans.

One cannot expect our species to play such a special role in nature. So this human-based pragmatic version must be understood, from the ontological standpoint, as merely the first stage in the development of a better ontological theory: one that accommodates the evolutionary precursors to the human knowings that the pragmatic theory is based upon.

So far there is no known empirical evidence for the existence of any reduction events not associated with human knowings. This impedes, naturally, the development of a science that encompasses such other events.

Future Developments: Representation and Replication

The primary purpose of this paper has been to describe the general features of a pragmatic theory of the human mind/brain that allows our thoughts to be causally efficacious yet not controlled by local-mechanistic laws combined with random chance. Eventually, however, one would like to expand this pragmatic version into a satisfactory ontology theory.

Human experiences are closely connected to human brains. Hence events similar to human experiences would presumably not exist either in primitive life forms, or before life began. Hence a more general theory that could deal with the *evolution of consciousness* would presumably have to be based on something other than the 'experiential increments in knowledge' that were the basis of the pragmatic version described above.

Dennett (1994, p. 236) identified intentionality (aboutness) as a phenomenon more fundamental than consciousness, upon which he would build his theory of consciousness. 'Aboutness' pertains to representation: the representation of one thing in another.

The body-world schema is the brain's representation of the body and its environment. Thus it constitutes, in the theory of consciousness described above, an element of 'aboutness' that could be seized upon as the basis of a more general theory.

However, there lies at the base of the quantum model described above an even more rudimentary element: self-replication. The basic process in the model is the creation of events that create likenesses of themselves. This tendency of thoughts to create likenesses of themselves helps to keep a train of thought on track.

Abstracting from our specific model of human consciousness, one sees the skeleton of a general process of self-replication.

Fundamentally, the theory described above is a theory of events, where each event has an *attentional* aspect and an *intentional* aspect. The attentional aspect of an event specifies an item of information that fixes the operator P associated with that event. The intentional aspect of the event specifies the functional property injected into the dynamics by the action of P on S. This functional property is a tendency of the Schrödinger-directed dynamics to produce a future event whose attentional aspect is the same as that of the event that is producing this tendency. The effect of these interlocking processes is to inject into the dynamics a directional tendency, based on approximate self-replication, that acts against the chaotic diffusive tendency generated by the Schrödinger equation. Such a process could occur before the advent of our species, and of life itself, and it could contribute to their emergence.

Conflation and Identity

A person's thoughts and ideas appear — to that person himself — to be able to do things: a person's mental states seem to be able cause his body to move about in intended ways. Thus thoughts seem to have functional power. Indeed, the idea of *functionalism* is that what makes thoughts and other mental states what they are is precisely their functional power: e.g., my pain is a pain by virtue of its functional or causal relationship to other aspects of the body/brain/mind system. Of course, this would be merely a formal definition of the term 'mental state' if it did not correspond to the occurrence of an associated element in a person's stream of consciousness: in the context of the present study — of the connection between our brains and our inner experiential lives — the occurrence of a mental state in a person's mind is supposed to mean the occurrence of a corresponding element in his stream of consciousness.

The identity theory of mind claims that each mental state is *identical* to some process in a brain. But combining this idea with the classical-physics conception of the physical universe leads to problems. They stem from the fact that the precepts of classical physical theory entail that the entire causal structure of any complex physical system is completely determined by its microscopic physical structure alone. Alternative high-level descriptions of certain complex physical systems might be far more useful to us in practice, but they are in principle redundant and unnecessary if the principles of classical physics hold. Thus it is accurate to say that the heat of the flame caused the paper to ignite, or that the tornado ripped the roofs off of the houses and left a path of destruction. But according to the precepts of classical physical theory the high-level causes are mere mathematical reorganizations of microscopic causes that are completely explainable micro-locally within classical physical theory. Nothing is needed beyond mathematical reorganization and — in order for us to be able to apply the theory — the assumption that we can empirically know, through observations via our senses, the approximate relative locations and shapes of sufficiently large macroscopically localized assemblies of the microscopic physical elements that the theory posits.

In the examples just described, our experiences themselves are not the causes of the ignition or destruction: our experiences merely help us to identify the causes. In fact, the idea behind classical physical theory is that the local physical variables of the theory represent a collection of ontologically distinct physical realities, each of whose ontological status is (1), intrinsically microlocal, (2), ontologically independent of our experiences, and (3), dynamically non-dependent upon experiences. That is why quantum theory was such a radical break with tradition: in quantum theory the physical description became enmeshed with our experiential knowledge, and the physical state became causally dependent upon our mental states.

Quantum theory is, in this respect, somewhat similar to the identity theory of mind: both entangle mind and physical process already at the ontological level. But the idea of the classical identity theory of the mind is to hang on to the classical conception of physical reality, and aver that a correct understanding of the true nature of a conscious thought would reveal it to be none other than a classically describable physical process that brings about what the thought intends, given the appropriate alignment of the relevant physical mechanisms.

That idea is, in fact, what would naturally emerge from quantum theory in the classical limit where the difference between Planck's constant and zero can be ignored, and the positions of particles and their conjugate momentum can both be regarded as well defined, relative to any question that is posed. In that limit there is no effective quantum dispersion caused by the Heisenberg uncertainty principle, and hence no indeterminism, and the only Heisenberg Choices of questions about a future state that can get an answer 'Yes' are those that are in accord with the functional properties of the present state. So there would be, in that classical approximation to the quantum process described above, a collapse of the two lines of causation, the physical and the mental, into a single one that is fixed by the local classical deterministic rules. Thus in the classical approximation the mental process would indeed be doing nothing beyond what the classical physical process is already doing, and the two processes might seem to be the same process. But Planck's constant is not zero, and the difference from zero introduces quantum effects that separate the two lines of causation, and allow their different causal roles to be distinguished.

The identity theory of mind raises puzzles. Why, in a world composed primarily of ontologically independent micro-realities, each able to access or know only things in its immediate microscopic environment, and each completely determined by micro-causal connections from its past, should there be ontological realities such as conscious thoughts that can grasp or know, as wholes, aspects of huge macroscopic collections of these micro-realities, and that can have intentions pertaining to the future development of these macroscopic aspects, when that future development is already completely fixed, micro-locally, by micro-realities in the past?

The quantum treatment discloses that these puzzles arise from the conflation in the classical limit of two very different but interlocked causal processes, one micro-causal, bound by the past, and blind to the future, the other macro-causal, probing the present, and projecting to the future.

Postscript: Mental Force and the Volitional Brain

The psychiatrist Jeffrey Schwartz (1999) has described a clinically successful technique for treating patients with obsessive compulsive disorder (OCD). The treatment is based on a programme that trains the patient to believe that his own *willful redirection* of his attention away from intense urges of a kind associated with pathological activity within circuitry of the basal ganglia, and toward adaptive functional behaviours, can, with sufficient persistent effort, systematically change both the intrusive, maladaptive, obsessive-compulsive symptoms, as well as the pathological brain activity associated with them. This treatment is in line with the quantum mechanical understanding of mind–brain dynamics developed above, in which the mental/experiential component of the causal structure enters brain dynamics via intentions that govern attentions that influence brain activity.

According to classical physical theory 'a brain was always going to do what it was caused to do by local mechanical disturbances,' and the idea that one's 'will' is actually able to cause anything at all is 'a benign user illusion'. Thus Schwartz's treatment amounts, according to this classical conceptualization, to deluding the patient into believing a lie: according to that classical view Schwartz's intense therapy causes directly, in the patients behaviour, a mechanical shift that the patient delusionally believes is the result of his own *intense effort* to redirect his activities, for the purpose of effecting an eventual cure, but which (felt effort) is actually only a mysterious illusionary by-product of his altered behaviour.

The presumption about the mind–brain that is the basis of Schwartz's successful clinical treatment, and the training of his patients, is that willful redirection of attention is efficacious. His success does not prove that 'will' is efficacious, but it does constitute prima facie evidence that it is. In fact, the belief that our thoughts can influence our actions is so basic to our entire idea of ourselves and our place in nature, and is so essential to our actual functioning in this world, that any suggestion that this idea is false would become plausible only under extremely coercive conditions, such as its incompatibility with basic physics. But no such coercion exists. Contemporary physical theory does allow our experiences, *per se*, to be truly efficacious and non-reducible: our experiences are elements of the causal structure that do necessary things that nothing else in the theory can do. Thus science, if pursued with sufficient care, demands no cloistering of disciplines, or interpretation as user illusions of the apparent causal effects of our conscious thoughts upon our physical actions.

References

Bohr, Niels (1934), *Atomic Theory and the Description of Nature* (Cambridge: CUP).

Bohr, Niels (1936), 'Causality and complementarity', *Philos. of Science*, **4** (Address to Second International Congress for the Unity of Science, June, 1936).

Bohr, Niels (1951), 'Discussion with Einstein on epistemological problems in atomic physics', in Einstein (1951).

Bohr, Niels (1958), *Atomic Physics and Human Knowledge* (New York: Wiley).

Chiu, C.B., Sudarshan, E.C/G. and Misra, B. (1977), 'Time evolution of unstable quantum states and a resolution of Zeno's paradox', *Phys. Rev. D*, **16**, p. 520.

Dennett, Daniel (1994), in *A Companion to the Philosophy of Mind*, ed. Samuel Guttenplan (Oxford: Blackwell).

Einstein, A. (1951), *Albert Einstein: Philosopher-Physicist*, ed, P.A. Schilpp (New York: Tudor).

Heisenberg, W. (1958a), 'The representation of nature in contemporary physics', *Daedalus*, **87**, pp. 95–108.

Heisenberg, W. (1958b), *Physics and Philosophy* (New York: Harper and Row).

Itano, W., Heinzen, D., Bollinger, J. and Wineland, D. (1990), 'Quantum Zeno effect', *Phys. Rev.*, **41A**, pp. 2295–300.

James, William (1910), 'Some problems in philosophy, Ch X; in *William James/ Writings 1902–1910* (New York: The Library of America, 1987).

James, William (1890), *The Principles of Psychology, Vol I* (New York: Dover).

Joos, E. (1986), 'Quantum theory and the appearance of a classical world', *Annals NY Acad. Sci. Vol 480*, pp. 6–13.

Pinker, Steven (1997), *How the Mind Works* (New York: Norton).

Rorty, Richard (1979), *Philosophy and the Mirror of Nature* (Princeton, NJ: Princeton University Press).

Schwartz, Jeffery M. (1999), 'A role for volition and attention in the generation of new brain circuitry: Toward a neurobiology of mental force', *Journal of Consciousness Studies*, **6** (8–9), pp. 115–42.

Stapp, Henry P. (1972), 'The Copenhagen Interpretation', *Amer. J. Phys.*, **40**, pp. 2098–1116. Reprinted in Stapp (1993).

Stapp, Henry P. (1993), *Mind, Matter, and Quantum Mechanics* (New York, etc.: Springer-Verlag).

Stapp, Henry P. (1998a), 'Pragmatic approach to consciousness', in *Brain and Values: Is a Biological Science of Values Possible?*, ed. Karl H. Pribram (Mahwah, NJ: Lawrence Erlbaum); or at www-physics.lbl.gov/\~stapp/stappfiles.html\\

Stapp, Henry P. (1998b), at www-physics.lbl.gov/\~stapp/stappfiles.html\\ (See 'Basics' for mathematical details about the vN/W formalism.)

Tittel, W., Brendel, J., Zbinden, H. and Gisin, N. (1998), 'Violation of Bell inequalities by photons more than 10 km apart', *Physical Review Letters*, **81**, pp. 3563–6.

von Neumann, J. (1932), *The Mathematical Principles of Quantum Mechanics* (Princeton, NJ: Princeton University Press, 1955).

Wigner, E. (1961), 'The probability of the existence of a self-reproducing unit', in *The Logic of Personal Knowledge*, ed. M. Polyani (London: Routledge & Kegan Paul).

Zurek, W. (1986), 'Reduction of the wave packet and environment-induced superselection', *Annals, NY Acad. Sci. Vol 480*, pp. 89–97.

Ulrich Mohrhoff

The Physics of Interactionism

Physics has been invoked both to refute and to support psycho-physical interactionism, the view that mind and matter are two mutually irreducible, interacting domains. Thus it has been held against interactionism that it implies violations of the laws of physics, notably the law of energy conservation. I examine the meaning of conservation laws in physics and show that in fact no valid argument against the interactionist theory can be drawn from them. In defence of interactionism it has been argued that mind can act on matter through an apparent loophole in physical determinism, without violating physical laws. I show that this argument is equally falla-cious. This leads to the conclusion that the indeterminism of quantum mechanics cannot be the physical correlate of free will; if there is a causally efficacious non-material mind, then the behaviour of matter cannot be fully governed by physical laws. I show that the best (if not the only) way of formulating departures from the 'normal', physically determined behaviour of mat-ter is in terms of modifications of the electromagnetic interactions between particles. I also show that mental states and events are non-spatial, and that departures from the 'normal' behaviour of matter, when caused by mental events, are not amenable to mathematical description.

I: Introduction

There is another hard problem, in addition to the problem of how anything material can have the subjective, first-person phenomenology of consciousness (Chalmers, 1995). It is the problem of how anything material can have freedom. By 'freedom' I mean a person's ability to behave in a purposive, non-random fashion that is not determined by neurophysiological structure and physical law. I do not mean the absence of other determining factors, as this would render freedom synonymous with randomness.[1]

I decide to raise my right arm and up it goes. This decision — a mental event — appears to me to be both the cause of the ensuing physical event and a causal primary. (A causal primary is an event the occurrence of which is not necessitated by antece-dent causes.) I can think of various reasons for raising my arm (I may want to catch a ball), and these may involve antecedent causes (e.g., the ball was thrown in my direc-tion); but if there is anything that made it inevitable that I should raise my arm, I know nothing of it.

---

[1] I have no quarrel with compatibilism, the view that free will is compatible with determinism. My freedom may well consist in being governed by what I intrinsically am (what the Indian contemporaries of Plato and Aristotle would have called my 'self-nature' or 'self-law', *svabhava*, *svadharma*) rather than by universal laws or a combination of universal laws and randomness.

Journal of Consciousness Studies, **6**, No. 8–9, 1999, pp. 165–84

To be sure, ignorance of an antecedent cause does not prove its nonexistence. But what does? We can aspire to establish that events of type C are regularly followed by events of type E. If we succeed, we are free (are we?) to imagine a hidden string between individual events such that each event of type C is the cause of an event of type E. Failure to establish the existence of a type of event C the instances of which are regularly followed by events of type E, on the other hand, is not a proof that events of type E lack antecedent causes. It doesn't prove anything beyond our ignorance of the antecedent causes of events of type E. Proving an event a causal primary is an impossible task. But from this it does not follow that there are no such events. What does follow is that empirical science cannot aspire to know that an event is a causal primary. That is why scientists may ignore causal primaries. But this is no reason for philosophers to dismiss their possible existence.

The absence of causal primaries is often called 'the causal closure of the physical world', where 'physical' means 'non-mental' rather than 'governed by the laws of physics'. This causal closure is a trivial consequence of the lack of scientific interest which results from being unable to identify causal primaries. What is causally closed is the scientifically known world, not the world as such. Yet there are many philosophers who look upon causal closure as an ontological truth and go on to invoke it as an argument against interactionism, the doctrine that mind and matter are two mutually irreducible, interacting spheres. Interactionists as I understand them are motivated primarily by a desire to make room for free will, the denial of which is both counter-intuitive and at odds with notions (moral and otherwise) that are central to the fabric of our active lives. While repudiating the causal closure of the physical world, interactionists nevertheless shrink from contesting the validity of the laws of physics, not realizing that this is contingent on the presumption of causal closure.

That is how we come to witness futile fights between philosophers of mind who reject interactionism on the ground that it is incompatible with the laws of physics and, in particular, the law of the conservation of energy, and interactionists who meekly defend their position, claiming that, by exploiting the loophole of quantum-mechanical indeterminism, non-material mind is capable of influencing matter without violating conservation laws. Both the charge and the defence are misconceived. The law of energy conservation is either true by virtue of the meaning of 'energy', and therefore is not threatened by interactionism, or it is contingent upon the causal closure of the physical world, and therefore is no threat to interactionism. The loophole hypothesis, on the other hand, violates basic physical laws other than the law of energy conservation.

This should not come as a surprise. To be causally efficacious, mental events that are causal primaries must make a difference to the behaviour of matter and thus to the behaviour of its constituent particles. The effects of such events on the behaviour of particles have to be expressed in the language of physics, for this is the only language suitable for describing the behaviour of particles. But the laws of physics presuppose causal closure and describe the behaviour of matter in the absence of causal primaries. Hence it follows that the behaviour of matter in the presence of a causally efficacious non-material mind cannot be fully governed by those laws.

The hard problem of consciousness and the hard problem of freedom appear at first sight to be logically independent. To embrace the irreducibility of consciousness, one need not deny the causal closure of the physical world, and one need not attribute to consciousness a causal role, as has been stressed by Chalmers (1997). On the other hand, it is possible to have physical events interspersed with non-physical causal primaries that lack subjective properties. Take Eccles' (1994) theory in which 'psychons' in the mind affect physical processes in the brain. As Chalmers (1997) has pointed out, the question of whether psychons have any experiential qualities is irrelevant to the causal story.

But this apparent independence of causality and subjectivity is called into question every time someone utters the word 'consciousness'. To see this, suppose that consciousness is irrelevant to the causal story. Then it is explanatorily irrelevant to our claims about consciousness: the physical act of making a judgement about experience is not sensitive to the experience itself (Kirk, 1996). In other words, there are two mutually irrelevant kinds of experience, the experience^E that we actually have and the experience^L about which we make statements. Zombie philosophers make judgements about experience^L, but it would be self-contradictory for them to conceive of the distinction between experience^E and experience^L. These conclusions seem to constitute a *reductio ad absurdum* of the supposition that consciousness is irrelevant to the causal story. Hollywood, it seems, has got it right: zombies are shuffling affect-less brutes, not smart philosophers of mind (DeLancey, 1996). Taking the hard problem of consciousness seriously thus appears to make it necessary to take the hard problem of freedom as seriously.

And so we have more than sufficient reason to address the latter problem as vigorously as the former has been addressed in recent issues of this journal and elsewhere. In the present article I will apply myself to the preliminary task of 'deconstructing' physics-based arguments purporting to prove the nonexistence of freedom. Section II reviews the argument from energy conservation — the claim that it is inconsistent with the interactionist doctrine — and the counter-argument that purports to show that interactionism and free will are consistent with the unbroken reign of physical law.

Section III refutes the arguments against interactionism that invoke conservation laws. It begins with an examination of what physicists mean by 'energy' and 'momentum'. The respective conservation laws are shown to be consequences of these meanings. They are necessarily true whenever 'energy' and 'momentum' are well-defined concepts. For these concepts to be well defined, it is however not necessary that the quantities they denote are conserved everywhere and under all circumstances. If they fail to be conserved, it can be for either of two reasons. It may be that energy and momentum are indeed meaningless; the curved space–time of Einstein's general theory of relativity provides an instructive example of this possibility. Or it may be that they are conserved somewhere but not everywhere. Then they are meaningful even where they are not conserved, as for example where matter is causally open to a non-material mind.

Section IV refutes the argument purporting to show that quantum mechanics offers a way of reconciling interactionism with the unbroken reign of physical law. According to this argument, an intention to act can be causally efficacious by merely modifying the probabilities associated with individual quantum events. I show that, on the contrary, an intention to act cannot be causally efficacious without modifying the statistics of ensembles of such events. And this is the same as saying that it cannot be causally efficacious without modifying some physical laws.

Section V shows how the departures from the laws of physics due to non-material mind can (and must) be formulated in the language of physics. The appropriate mathematical entity is the electromagnetic four-vector potential (or, simply, the electromagnetic field). As a summary representation of possible effects on moving particles that makes no reference whatever to causes, the electromagnetic field necessarily represents the effects of both material and non-material causes. Section VI shows that a causally efficacious non-material mind is not something that exists in space, and that its action on matter is not amenable to mathematical description.

A more technical discussion of the physics is available (Mohrhoff, 1997).

II: Energy Conservation and the Interactionist Hypothesis

Attempts to address the mind–body problem along interactionist lines have traditionally been faulted for taking liberties with physical conservation laws, notably the principle of the conservation of energy (also known as the first law of thermodynamics). M. Bunge (1980, p. 17) and D.C. Dennett (1991, p. 35) speak for the prosecution.

> If immaterial mind could move matter, then it would create energy; and if matter were to act on immaterial mind, then energy would disappear. In either case energy . . . would fail to be conserved. And so physics, chemistry, biology, and economics would collapse.

> Let us concentrate on the returned signals, the directives from mind to brain. These, *ex hypothesi*, are not physical; they are not light waves or sound waves or cosmic rays or streams of subatomic particles. No physical energy or mass is associated with them. How, then, do they get to make a difference to what happens in the brain cells they must affect, if the mind is to have any influence on the body? A fundamental principle of physics is that any change in the trajectory of any physical entity is an acceleration requiring the expenditure of energy, and where is this energy to come from? It is this principle of the conservation of energy that accounts for the physical impossibility of 'perpetual motion machines', and the same principle is apparently violated by dualism. This confrontation between quite standard physics and dualism has been endlessly discussed since Descartes' own day, and is widely regarded as the inescapable and fatal flaw of dualism.

Dualists have taken these strictures to heart. Even Karl Popper, by proclaiming himself not to be 'in the least impressed by the danger of falling foul of the first law of thermodynamics' (Popper and Eccles, 1983, p. 564), implicitly acknowledges the danger. From the early days of quantum mechanics, the strategy of the defence has consisted in claiming that quantum-mechanical indeterminism allows non-material mental events to act on matter (specifically the brain) without violating conservation laws. Eddington (1935) was probably the first to speculate publicly that the mind may influence the body by affecting quantum events within the brain through a causal influence on the probability of their occurrence.

More recently H. Margenau (1984) has suggested that the mind may be 'regarded as a field in the accepted physical sense of the term', yet not be 'required to contain energy in order to account for all known phenomena in which mind interacts with brain' (p. 97): 'In very complicated physical systems such as the brain, the neurons and the sense organs, whose constituents are small enough to be governed by probabilistic quantum laws, the physical organ is always poised for a multitude of possible changes, each with a definite probability' (p. 96).

Standard axiomatizations of quantum mechanics recognize two kinds of change: the probabilistic collapse of a quantum-mechanical superposition which occurs during a measurement, and the deterministic evolution of the quantum state which takes place between measurements (von Neumann, 1955). Margenau proposes that the causal efficacy of mind rests on the following sequence of steps: (i) The relevant physical system develops, in accordance with the deterministic evolution of states, into a superposition of alternative states, each associated with a probability. (ii) Mind alters the physically determined probabilities, possibly by superimposing its own probability field on the physically determined probability field. (iii) The resulting superposition collapses to one of its elements in accordance with the probabilistic change of states. In this way, Margenau argues, mind can act on the brain without disturbing the balance of energy. D. Hodgson (1996) likewise invokes the mind's ability to load the quantum dice.

Seizing on Margenau's proposal, J.C. Eccles, in collaboration with F. Beck (Beck and Eccles, 1992; Eccles, 1994), has put forward one of the most elaborate and specific hypotheses of mind–brain interaction to date. It capitalizes on the basic unitary activity of the cerebral cortex, exocytosis. Exocytosis is the emission of chemical transmitters into the synaptic cleft by a vesicle of the presynaptic vesicular grid, a paracrystalline structure situated inside the terminal expansion (bouton) of a nerve fibre. It is an all-or-nothing event, which has been found to occur with a probability of about one fourth to one third when a bouton is activated by a nerve impulse. Eccles and Beck assume this probability to be of quantum-mechanical origin. They cite increasing evidence for a trigger mechanism that may involve quantum transitions between metastable molecular states, and propose a model for the trigger mechanism based on the tunnelling of a quasi-particle through a potential barrier.[2] According to their model, during a period of the order of femtoseconds the quasi-particle is distributed over both sides of the barrier. One side corresponds to the activated state of the trigger, the other side to the non-activated state. At the end of this period exocytosis has been triggered with the aforesaid probability. Eccles and Beck propose that mental intentions act through a quantum probability field altering the probability of exocytosis during this brief period.

While the postsynaptic effect due to the change in probability of exocytosis by a single vesicle is many orders of magnitude too small for modifying the patterns of neuronal activity even in small areas of the brain, there are many thousands of vesicles per bouton and many thousands of similar boutons on a pyramidal cell (the principal type of neuron of the cerebral cortex), and there are about 200 neurons in the region of a dendron, the basic anatomical unit of the cerebral cortex (Eccles, 1994, p. 98). The hypothesis of mind–brain interaction according to Eccles and Beck is that mental intention becomes neurally effective by momentarily increasing the probabilities for exocytosis in the hundreds of thousands of boutons in a whole dendron.

> In summary it can be stated that it is sufficient for the dualist-interactionist hypothesis to be able to account for the ability of a non-material mental event to effect a changed probability of the vesicular emission from a single bouton on a cortical pyramidal cell. If that

---

[2] The microtubule hypothesis adopted by Penrose (1994) is a membrane-physiological proposal for this trigger mechanism, as F. Beck (1994) has pointed out. It realizes the motion of the quasi-particle as the motion of one, or a few, hydrogen atoms in the membrane.

can occur for one, it could occur for a multitude of the boutons on that neuron, and all else follows in accord with the neuroscience of motor control (Eccles, 1994, p. 78).

It is reassuring that all of the richness and enjoyment of our experiences can now be accepted without any qualms of conscience that we may be infringing conservation laws! (Eccles, 1994, p. 170).

III: Conservation of Energy and Momentum: A Closer Look

Originally, momentum was defined as 'mass-times-velocity'. It soon became apparent that (within Newtonian physics) this was a conserved quantity. Then the special theory of relativity superseded Newtonian physics, and mass-times-velocity was no longer conserved. By this time, however, the property of being conserved was accorded much greater importance than the original definition in terms of mass and velocity. Momentum accordingly was redefined so as to match its original definition in the low-speed limit, where the two theories make identical predictions, as well as to retain its status of a conserved quantity.

But a redefinition that consists in the substitution of one theory-dependent *definiens* for another, can only be a halfway stop. It must be possible to define the *definiendum* at a more basic level, independently of the specific principles of either theory and hence in a way that is valid for both. It indeed soon transpired that the different mathematical embodiments of momentum in the respective theories of Newton and Einstein were specific instances of a quantity that could be invariantly defined for a large class of theories. In 1918 E. Noether discovered a deep connection between symmetries[3] and conservation laws. This exists in all theories that can be derived from a mathematical expression known to physicists as the Lagrangian. In all such theories (and these include not just all experimentally well-confirmed theories to date but all theories esteemed worthy of consideration by contemporary physicists), a continuous symmetry[4] implies the existence of a locally conserved quantity.[5] And one of these locally conserved quantities implied by the continuous symmetries of the Lagrangian is called 'momentum'. Thereafter it was possible to claim that this has always been the true definition, even when the concept was insufficiently differentiated from its then sole instantiation, mass-times-velocity.

The same holds true of energy. Both energy and momentum are defined as conserved quantities. They are conserved by definition. Either they make sense and are conserved, or they don't make sense. They don't make sense whenever the mathematically described world (or, equivalently, the Lagrangian) does not possess the symmetries that imply their respective conservation laws; in other words, whenever the corresponding symmetry transformations, applied to a mathematical description of a physical situation, yields not just a different description but a different physical situation.

---

[3] In physics a symmetry is both a consequence and an expression of the fact that the mathematical description of the world is underdetermined by observational data. Just as a symmetrical figure can be transformed into itself (for instance, by a rotation), so a mathematical description of the world can be transformed into a different mathematical description of the same world (for instance, by a rotation of the coordinate system).

[4] 'Continuous' here means that the corresponding transformation, like a rotation of the coordinate axes, can be carried out continuously rather than in discrete steps only.

[5] Saying that a physical quantity is locally conserved is the same as saying that the amount of it inside any bounded region of space can change (from B_1 to B_2, say) only if the difference $B_2 - B_1$ passes through the boundary of the region.

The symmetry that gives meaning to 'momentum' is known as the homogeneity of space; it consists in the mechanical equivalence of all locations in space, or in the fact that every closed mechanical system behaves in the same way anywhere. The symmetry that gives meaning to 'energy' is known as the homogeneity of time; this consists in the mechanical equivalence of all moments of time, or in the fact that every such system behaves in the same way anytime. Translate the coordinate origin in space and/or time, and what you get is a different description of the same physical situation. This has the nature of a postulate: differences in the outcomes of identical experiments performed at distinct locations and/or times are to be ascribed to the different physical conditions (known or unknown) prevailing at these distinct locations and/or times, not to these locations and/or times *per se*. An instance of the synthetic *a priori* judgement that everything that happens has a cause, this postulate has more to do with what we (investigating humans) make of our experiences than with any particular experience of ours. If we did not assume the existence of a cause, we would not look for one; and if we did not assume the existence of physical causes to explain the spatial or temporal inhomogeneities we observe, we would not look for such causes but rest content with attributing those inhomogeneities to space or time *per se*.

And so it would seem that the homogeneity of space and the homogeneity of time are *a priori* certain; that momentum and energy are therefore always well defined; and that they are always conserved. However, there are riders to this series of conclusions. Whatever is *a priori* certain is so only with regard to our mental constructs. Whether or not these can be thought of as descriptions of objective reality is another matter. Also, before anything can be derived from the said homogeneities, they must be given formal expression within the framework of a physical theory. And there is no *a priori* guarantee that this is possible. In fact, there are reasons to surmize the opposite, as will become apparent in what follows.

There is nothing controversial about the way in which space and time are rendered manifestly homogeneous (that is, the way in which their homogeneities find mathematical expression in a physical theory). Either one introduces a privileged class of coordinate systems (called 'inertial systems') or one lets a mathematical entity known as the metric tensor (or simply, the metric) do the privileging (by taking a particularly simple form in the privileged systems). However, what is capable of manifesting homogeneity also lends itself to the manifestation of inhomogeneities. The metric needed to manifest the flatness[6] of space or space–time could instead serve to manifest the curvature of a Riemannian space or space–time. This is the same as saying that the metric texture of space or space–time offers a handle for the formulation of an interaction law. Matter could act on matter via the intermediate representation of the metric in much the same way as electric charges act on electric charges via the intermediate representation of the electromagnetic field. The curvature at any space–time point p, determining partly if not fully the motion of matter at p, could depend on the distribution and motion of matter elsewhere and at earlier times. It could thus represent a causal influence on the motion of matter at p due to the earlier distribution and motion of matter elsewhere.

This *a priori* possibility is an actual feature of the objective world. The interaction in question is gravity; the theory just outlined is the general theory of relativity. Now,

---

[6] It will become evident below that the 'flatness' of space(–time) is actually the same as the mechanical equivalence of locations heretofore called the 'homogeneity' of space(–time).

gravity appears to be quite indispensable to the creation of what Squires (1981) has called an 'interesting world'. Without gravity there would exist no stars, no planets, nor (for all we can imagine) any sites hospitable to something as interesting as life. In view of this it might be asserted that curvature is implied by our own existence, or that since we are here, space–time cannot be flat.

At any rate, the metric connection lends itself to the manifestation either of spatio–temporal homogeneity or of gravity. As far as the description of objective reality is concerned, the choice is not ours but Nature's. And Nature has opted for gravity. The metric which could have offered a handle for the incorporation, in our mental picture of reality, of a homogeneous space and a homogeneous time, is already used up. From this and what has been said earlier one might draw the conclusion that in situations in which gravity plays a significant role, energy and momentum are undefined. But such a conclusion would ignore that even curved space–time is locally flat,[7] and that, as a consequence, the energy and the momentum of all non-gravitational fields are locally (as opposed to globally) conserved. This is sufficient for them to be well-defined. What is ill-defined in any generic space–time is the gravitational energy/momentum, and hence the total energy/momentum. The energy/momentum associated with a curved region of space–time is, strictly speaking, definable only in model space–times that are flat 'at the edges'.[8]

At certain junctures in the history of physics the law of energy conservation has been called in question. Bohr at one time felt that he had to renounce it, and not a few particle physicists despaired of it before the neutrino was proposed and, in due course, discovered. It should not be supposed that these physicists were unaware of the deep connection between the conservation laws for energy and momentum and the homogeneity of time and of space. Rather they were driven to consider the possibility that these homogeneities were not, after all, respected by Nature. Bohr thought that the problems facing atomic theory were 'of such a nature that they hardly allow us to hope that we shall be able, within the world of the atom, to carry through a description in space and time that corresponds to our ordinary sensory perceptions' (in Honner, 1982). If the feasibility of such a description cannot be taken for granted, the homogeneity of space and of time cannot be taken for granted either.

More recently, in connection with the so-called measurement problem in quantum mechanics, the stochastic generation (and hence non-conservation) of energy has emerged as a theoretical possibility (Ghirardi et al., 1986; Pearle, 1989). This amounts to introducing stochastic inhomogeneities in the 'flow' of time, and to redefining energy as the quantity whose conservation would be implied if those inhomogeneities were absent. If such a definition is adopted, the view that the conservation of energy is part of the meaning of 'energy', can no longer be entertained.

The situation, then, is this: If the energy conservation law is part of the meaning of 'energy', the interactionist hypothesis cannot imply a violation of this law. And if physicists can invoke inhomogeneities in the 'flow' of time and define energy in such a way that it is conserved only when and where those inhomogeneities are absent,

---

[7] Reduced to two dimensions this means that any sufficiently small (infinitesimal) patch of a smoothly curved surface is approximately (exactly) flat.

[8] This does not mean that gravitational energy/momentum cannot be approximately defined whenever and wherever space–time can be considered as approximately flat. If it can, the departures from flatness can be treated as a gravitational field in flat space–time.

interactionists can do the same. The causal efficacy of non-material mind could be based on its generating similar (but not stochastic) inhomogeneities. As long as there exists an experimental realm in which mind-generated inhomogeneities are absent or negligible (and from a physicist's point of view, given present experimental limitations, they may well be negligible everywhere), energy remains well-defined even where matter is causally open to non-material mind. If no such realm existed, attributing energy to matter would be gratuitous, since in this case any mathematical expression would do. None could be tested, because the proof that one has the right expression lies in the experimental corroboration of its conservation. But if the formula for the energy associated with matter is testable somewhere, nothing prevents one from using the same formula everywhere, including where matter is open to the action of non-material mind and energy is not necessarily conserved.

IV: Interactionism Violates Physical Laws

While the argument from energy conservation does not succeed, the notion that mental events can influence physical events through the loophole of quantum-mechanical indeterminism, without in any manner whatsoever infringing on the deterministic regime of physical laws, is chimerical, as is shown presently.

Consider a causally efficacious mental event (say, the intention to flex the right index finger). If this occurs in the mind associated with any healthy body, the intended action takes place. If the same intention occurs in the minds associated with an ensemble of healthy bodies, all of those bodies flex their right index fingers as a result. There is no randomness in the causal concatenation between intention and intended action. Throughout the ensemble, the same mental event brings about the same physical event.

Consequently, if the causal efficacy of a mental intention is postulated to involve modifications of quantum-mechanical probabilities associated with 'collapsible' wave functions, these modifications are statistically significant. In the simplest case in which the modifications amount to the selection of one out of two possible outcomes in a single collapse, the same outcome is selected every time the intention occurs. In the Eccles–Beck model, in which the intended action is the effect of many weak modifications, accumulated over a large number of collapses, the fact that the same action is produced every time entails that the individual modifications likewise exhibit statistically significant trends.

A clear distinction must be maintained between sets of active sites in the same brain and the statistical ensembles of active sites relevant to the present discussion. The latter involve different brains or, more precisely, different instances of identical brains. Consider an ensemble of such brains. Then consider an ensemble of vesicles such that each vesicle is from a different brain and all vesicles occupy identical positions in their respective brains. There are as many such vesicle ensembles as there are vesicles in each brain. Let us compare two cases. In the first case all brains are influenced by a certain mental intention; in the second case none of the brains is influenced by it, other things being equal. What needs to be compared in particular is the behaviour of each vesicle ensemble in the two cases. If none of the vesicle ensembles shows any difference in the percentage of 'firing' vesicles, the intention cannot be causally efficacious. If it is causally efficacious, the intended effect takes place whenever the intention is present in the minds associated with those brains, and only then. In this case there must be some vesicle ensembles for which the percentages of 'firing' vesicles differ in the two cases.

In a word, if single-case probabilities get modified, there are statistical ensembles whose behaviours get modified. What gets modified is not merely individual quantum events but the statistics of entire ensembles of such events. And these statistics, unlike the individual events, are fully determined by physical laws. Changing them means changing the physical laws.[9] Altering the single-case probabilities associated with individual measurement-like events without changing the laws of physics is possible only if the relative frequencies associated with every ensemble of identical such events remain unaltered. But this is possible only if the individual modifications of probability are themselves probabilistic. Suppose that some of the single-case probabilities are increased and some are decreased such that the overall probability remains unchanged. Then the laws of physics remain unchanged, but there can be no talk about causation, mental or otherwise. Whatever 'causes' such statistically insignificant modifications of probability cannot be causally efficacious. To be causally efficacious, an event must make a difference every time it occurs. It must make a difference to the behaviour of some ensemble, that is, it must be statistically significant. The basic tenet of the interactionist position — causal openness of the material to the non-material mental — thus entails a violation (that is, an occurrence of modifications) of physical laws.[10] Probability distributions, determined jointly by initial conditions and some quantum-mechanical equation of motion such as the Schrödinger equation, are altered. One might leave it at that. But one might also wonder if any such alteration could not be formulated just as well in terms of the well-known physical quantities that determine probability distributions during the deterministic phase of their evolution. This is the case, as I proceed to show.

V: Interactionism without Quantum Collapses

As an illustration of how the altered probability distributions entailed by the interactionist hypothesis could arise within the formalism that physicists use to calculate probability distributions, rather than as *ad hoc* modifications of the results of the calculations, we will now consider an open one-particle system. A system consisting of just one particle obviously cannot accommodate the creation or annihilation of particle pairs, but it seems reasonable to assume that minds do not cause either type of event. (The energy needed for pair creation is available in cosmic rays and high-energy physics laboratories, not in brains. The antiparticles needed for annihilation events are not normally present in brains.) We further assume that mental

---

[9] Measurements on ensembles of identical quantum-mechanical systems evolving under identical initial and boundary conditions yield identical distributions of results. Modified statistical distributions observed on ensembles of identically prepared systems indicate modified boundary conditions. Modified boundary conditions can arise from modifications either of the spatial distribution of environmental matter or of the fields generated by this matter. Modified boundary conditions given identical such distributions (that is, modified fields) imply a modification of the physical laws according to which the fields are generated.

[10] The same violation is entailed when the non-material self is replaced by a 'superintelligence' who, as F. Hoyle (1983) surmises, guides the evolution of the cosmos by altering the probabilities associated with quantum processes.

events do not induce particles to change type. This is tantamount to ruling out the so-called strong and weak forces as vehicles of mental causation, for it is these that cause type conversions. (The weak force can for instance convert electrons into neutrinos.)

The strong and weak forces are unlikely vehicles of mental causation because both of them are short-range forces. The strong force is confined to the interior of certain subatomic particles, the mesons and the baryons. A residue of this force, the so-called nuclear force, is confined (in brains if not in neutron stars) to the interior of the atomic nucleus, as is the weak force. None of these forces is effective at the scale of chemical processes; none therefore is relevant to the chemistry of the brain. The goings-on inside atomic nuclei have no influence on when neurons fire, or how likely they are to fire, which is how the causal efficacy of the mind must make itself felt.

And since the most general formulation of effects on the motion of a spinless particle already includes the possible effects on a particle with spin, we can confine our discussion to that type of particle which is represented by a single wave function (rather than one of those multicomponent wave functions known as spinors). Such a particle is known as a scalar particle.

The entire physics of a quantum-mechanical system is formally contained in a mathematical expression known as the probability amplitude. This amplitude allows physicists to calculate (at least in principle) the likelihood with which the system transits from any initial state to any final state in any given interval of time. The entire physics of a scalar particle is in fact known if one knows the amplitude associated with how likely the particle is to travel from point x to point y in any given time span.

It is a remarkable fact about quantum mechanics that this amplitude (let's represent it by the symbol $<y|x>$) can be calculated by 'summing over' (that is, adding up contributions from) all space–time curves that connect x at the starting time with y at the time of the particle's arrival — as if the particle went from x to y by travelling along every possible path (Feynman and Hibbs, 1965). Each curve simply contributes a complex number of unit magnitude. Such a number is fully specified by what is called its phase. The phase of a curve is the sum of the phases associated with its segments, and this fact makes it possible to think of the phase of a curve as its length. For an uncharged particle this mechanical length of a curve in space–time is simply proportional to the geometric length of the same curve, and the proportionality factor is simply the particle's mass.[11]

Clearly, the only way of influencing the motion of a scalar particle (charged or uncharged) is to modify the mechanical lengths of curves in space–time.[12] This can be done in one of two ways: in the manner of gravity, by changing the geometric lengths of curves and thereby warping space–time itself, or by changing the mechanical lengths without changing the geometric lengths.[13] When it is weak

---

[11] As is customary among theoretical physicists, we pretend that some universal constants are equal to 1.

[12] This is the reason why homogeneity (or the mechanical equivalence of locations in space–time) is tantamount to the flatness of space–time.

[13] Admittedly it is difficult for non-mathematicians to see how the same curve can have different lengths, a geometric and a mechanical one, and how it can even have different mechanical lengths for different types of particle. As a useful analogy, consider all the routes from Zurich to Copenhagen, say. There are (at least) three ways of measuring their 'lengths': in kilometers, in hours, and in litres of petrol. One route may be the shortest in the ordinary sense, another route may be the shortest as measured in hours,

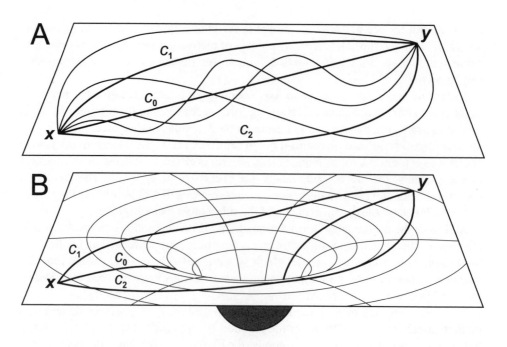

Figure 1.

The upper diagram (A) shows a few of the curves contributing to $\langle y|x \rangle$, the amplitude associated with the probability that a particle initially located at x is later found at y. By Euclidean standards, the shortest curve is the straight line c_0. The possible effects on the motion of a particle are mathematically represented by a non-Euclidean way of measuring lengths. In terms of *mechanical* lengths, the shortest curve connecting x and y may be c_1, or it may be c_2, or it may be c_1 for particles of a certain type and c_2 for particles of a different type.

Diagram B: Because gravity affects all particles alike, its effect on the mechanical lengths of curves can be thought of as a warping of space-time itself. The surface with the dip represents space-time. The extra dimension into which it is warped is not physical; its sole purpose is to make it possible to visualise the warping of space–time. The dip could be due to a massive object at its centre. Because of the dip, c_0 is no longer the shortest curve connecting x and y. A classical particle travelling from x to y will take the shortest curve on either side of the dip, and this makes it seem as if a force, gravity, were pulling the particle towards the centre of the dip as it travels around it.

enough to permit a human brain to function normally, gravity plays no significant role in a region of space the size of a brain, which is why we only need to consider the latter option.[14]

As an illustration of the kind of effect caused by changes in the mechanical lengths of space–time curves, imagine a plane (see fig. 1A). In it imagine two points x and y and a bundle of curves beginning at x and ending at y. One of these curves (call it c_1)

---

and yet another may be the shortest in terms of petrol consumption. It is even more difficult to see how a particle can behave as if it travelled simultaneously along all possible curves connecting two locations. It should however be born in mind: (i) that this is a rather straightforward description of one of the most successful mathematical formalisms used in physics; (ii) that there is no reason whatever to expect visualisable models drawn from everyday experience to be appropriate for dealing with the extreme limits of human experience; and (iii) that a consistent realistic interpretation of the formalism is yet to be found, if one can be found at all.

[14] Further reasons for dismissing gravity as a possible vehicle of mental causation are given below.

will have a shorter mechanical length than every other curve. By no means does this have to be the straight line c_0. Next suppose that the mechanical lengths of all curves are increased in such a way that those of curves entirely to the left of c_1 increase more than those of curves entirely to the right of c_1. As a result, the mechanically shortest curve will no longer be c_1 but a different curve c_2 to the right of c_1. One of the effects of altering the mechanical lengths of space–time curves is thus equivalent to bending the curve of minimum mechanical length between any two space–time points. (Usually there is just one such curve, but see fig. 1B for a situation in which the shortest curve connecting x and y is not unique.)

In the so-called classical limit, in which quantum mechanics degenerates into classical mechanics, the only contributions to $<y|x>$ that 'survive' come from the curve (or curves) of minimum mechanical length. (More precisely, from curves that are shorter than their nearest neighbours.) This explains why a classical particle travels from x to y (in the specified time span) along the mechanically shortest curve (or one of the mechanically shortest curves) between x and y. What gets bent are the space–time trajectories of classical particles. But bending the space–time trajectory of a classical particle is the same as accelerating the particle, and this is the reason why in classical physics one talks about acceleration-causing forces instead of modifications of mechanical lengths.

How does one mathematically represent modifications of the mechanical lengths of curves that leave the geometric lengths unchanged? The answer is straightforward: by means of some field.[15] This field (let's call it A) associates with every infinitesimal curve segment (depending on both the location and the direction of the segment) the extra bit of mechanical length that the segment has for a charged particle. (For an uncharged particle, recall, the mechanical length of the segment is simply its geometric length times the particle's mass. Uncharged particles do not 'experience' the non-gravitational modifications of mechanical lengths.)

The field A is known to physicists as the electromagnetic vector (or four-vector) potential. It contains exactly the same information as the electric and magnetic fields together.[16] The electric field is what bends the projections of classical trajectories on space–time planes that include a time axis (that is, it accelerates charges in a fixed direction), while the magnetic field is what bends the projections of classical trajectories on spatial planes (that is, it accelerates charges in directions perpendicular to their directions of motion).

The vector potential (equivalent to the electromagnetic field) is thus the summary representation of all possible non-gravitational effects on the motion of a scalar particle, including all effects caused by mental events. Physicists habitually associate the vector potential not only with the way in which it influences the motion of charged particles but also with a particular way (given by Maxwell's laws) in which it is generated by the motion and distribution of charges. They don't question (and as physi-

---

[15] Reminder: mathematical details can be found in a companion article to this paper (Mohrhoff, 1997).

[16] A pedant would mention that the experimental phenomenology is in one-to-one correspondence with the electric and magnetic fields (different fields giving rise to different observable effects) but not with the vector potential. The latter has extra degrees of freedom due to that symmetry of the Lagrangian that implies the conservation of electric charge. The origin of those extra degrees of freedom is readily seen: if the mechanical lengths of all curves from x to y are changed by the same amount, the curve of minimum mechanical length — and with it the physics — remains unchanged.

cists, concerned solely with the behaviour of inanimate matter, need not question) the assumption that this is also the only way of generating it. But, in fact, anything — be it physical, mental or whatever — that has a (non-gravitational) effect on the motion of a particle, necessarily contributes to the electromagnetic vector potential.[17] If a mental event is to influence the behaviour of the quasi-particle in Eccles' model of a trigger mechanism for exocytosis, it must modify the barrier — a potential barrier — penetrated by the quasi-particle.

When the electromagnetic field was introduced by Maxwell, it was thought of as the property of a mechanical substrate pervading space. When Einstein discarded this substrate, the erstwhile property became a physical entity in its own right. The symbol took on a life of its own; the mathematical description took the place of the thing described. Today many physicists believe that reality is mathematical. While the present investigation ought not to be biased in favour of any such metaphysical claim, it is safe to say that the empirical reality investigated by science is, first of all, a complex of mental constructs. (I am not saying that it is 'nothing but' mental constructs.) What these constructs have in common, and what distinguishes them from mere fantasies, is that they are objectifiable, that is, they are capable of being thought of as features of an objective world. The vector potential is such a construct (after quantization, at any rate), and from the role it plays in our account of particle motion it is clear that it cannot be partial to any particular type of causal agent. It serves to represent the effects of mental causes just as well as those of physical causes.

Now that we know that the second manner of modifying the mechanical lengths of space–time curves is, in actual fact, the way of the electromagnetic force, we have another reason for dismissing gravity (the first manner) as irrelevant to mental causation. Considering that exocytosis is controlled by the influx of Ca^{2+} ions into a synaptic vesicle (Eccles, 1994, pp. 149–53), mental causation is likely to be effected through a modification of the physically determined forces exerted on ions (that is, on charges), particularly those involved in the propagation of nerve impulses. But the electromagnetic interaction between, say, two protons is about 10^{36} times stronger than their gravitational interaction. Hence if the mentally generated modification of the force exerted on a charged particle were of gravitational nature, the mental self would have to generate an implausibly strong gravitational field (about that many times stronger than the physically generated one), while it would only need to generate an electromagnetic field that is weak in comparison with the physically generated one.

Yet another reason why the electromagnetic interaction is the more likely vehicle of mental causation is the selectivity of the electromagnetic force. While this acts on charges only, gravity affects everything. If one wants to make an ion move through a neutral medium, one had better not also accelerate the medium, as this would simply cause a congestion; if one tries to move both the ion and the medium, nothing will move.

---

[17] D. Papineau (1996) writes: 'The central problem facing any contemporary dualist is that twentieth-century science denies any causal powers to unreduced phenomenal properties. Phenomenal properties differ in this respect from electromagnetic forces.' As a matter of fact, they don't. The effects of irreducible phenomenal properties on scalar particles are included in the electromagnetic field.

However, all said, nothing fundamental stands in the way of the notion that the mind contributes to any or all of the four fundamental forces, inasmuch as the weak and strong forces no less than the metric tensor and the electromagnetic vector potential are simply ways of formulating possible effects on the behaviour of particles, whether their origin be physical, mental or whatnot. For reasons indicated above I believe however that the electromagnetic field is the single most effective vehicle of mental causation, and that therefore the other possibilities are not worth considering.

If non-physical causes do indeed contribute to the vector potential, the well-known dynamical laws of the vector potential (that is, Maxwell's laws or their quantum-mechanical counterparts) are violated, in the sense that they describe some but not all contributions to the vector potential. It is worth emphasising that there are neither theoretical nor experimental reasons to rule out such a violation. While empirical evidence of non-physical contributions to the vector potential may as yet be lacking, absence of evidence is not the same as evidence of absence. Evidence of absence is not available because systems in which such contributions might occur are notoriously complex, difficult to analyse, and no less difficult to experiment with. It could be argued, moreover, that if the non-physical contributions to A amounted to a substantial modification of the physically determined component of A, mind would be able to actuate matter through a less complex physiology. While the complexity of the body is no argument against interactionism, it certainly suggests that a non-material mind cannot cause more than minute modifications of the physically determined component of A.

As for theoretical derivations of the dynamical law for A, they tell us no more than what was initially assumed. Because A can be considered as a quantum-mechanical system in its own right, its dynamics is known if one knows how to calculate the amplitude for the transition from any initial field configuration to any final field configuration in any given time span. As there are contributions to the amplitude $<y|x>$ from all curves connecting x and y, so there are contributions to this transition amplitude from all 'histories' of the field A (that is, from all curves in the infinite-dimensional space of field configurations). And as before, each contribution only depends on the mechanical length of the corresponding history/curve.

A crucial difference however arises when it comes to finding the correct mathematical expression for the mechanical lengths of field histories. The formula for the mechanical lengths of space–time curves 'experienced' by a scalar particle contains the representation of all possible effects on the motion of a scalar particle. We can be sure that none have been left out. On the other hand, we can be sure that we have the right formula for the mechanical lengths of field histories only if all sources contributing to the field are represented in it, and only if the effects represented by the field are linked to their causes according to universal mathematical laws. In order to be able to derive Maxwell's equations (along with their quantum-mechanical counterparts) we must therefore assume (i) that the motion of a particle cannot be affected by anything except the motion and distribution of particles, and (ii) that the action of particles on particles is amenable to mathematical description. Hence the argument that mind cannot affect the behaviour of charged particles because this is governed by Maxwell's laws, obviously begs the question.

VI: Mind, Space and Mathematical Description

The aim of this section is to show (i) that mind is non-spatial and (ii) that the action of a non-material mind on matter is not amenable to mathematical description. The latter conclusion in fact is a consequence of the former.

On the interactionist view, mind is non-spatial and, as causal agent, independent. ('Independent' here means that its acts of will are not fully determined by physiological microstructure and physical law. 'Non-spatial' means that the mental cause of an effect on the motion of particles in the brain does not consist in the spatial distribution and/or the state of motion of objects in space.) From this it follows that the condition that the effects represented by the electromagnetic field must be linked to their causes via universal mathematical laws, cannot be satisfied for the direct effects of volitions. For one thing, if this condition is to be satisfied, the causes must be, at the very least, amenable to mathematical description. Since this is essentially synonymous with spatio–temporal description, they must have positions in space. For another thing, if the link between a causal primary in the mind and its physical effect were amenable to mathematical description, one could write down a Lagrangian for the mind as causal agent. But if that were possible, this causal agent would be just another kind of matter subject to just another kind of physical law — something whose existence neither dualists nor materialists are likely to endorse. For the dualists, it would be too materialistic; for the materialists, too dualistic.

It is in fact unnecessary to assume the non-spatiality of the mental, as is shown presently. If the self were an object in space, it would have to make sense to talk about the position of the self relative to other objects in space. Let us see why it does make sense to talk about the relative positions of particles. Like the non-material self, a fundamental particle can't be seen. Its position relative to other material objects can nevertheless be inferred from its observable effects, for instance from a trail of droplets in a cloud chamber. But this inference is possible only because there exists a physical law that relates the position of the particle to the positions of its effects. Applying our knowledge of this law to observational data (the positions of the droplets), we can infer the (approximate) position of the particle. And how did we come to know this law? It is an extrapolation from regularities observed in the relative positions of larger charged objects that can be seen.

By the same token, attributing to the self a position appears to make sense only if there exists a law relating the position of the self to the positions of observable effects caused by the self. If we knew such a law, we could infer the self's position from its effects. But how could we discover such a law? By observing regularities in the positions, relative to observable material objects, of larger selves that can be seen? There may be psychophysical laws (Chalmers, 1995) relating mental states to physical configurations in the brain, but so far nobody has suggested that these laws involve the positions of mental states. I suppose that this is because there simply is no way of making sense of the position of a mental state. Only the physical effects that the self, *ex hypothesi*, is capable of producing, are localizable in space.

Not all theorists of consciousness would agree. M. Lockwood (1989, p. 101), for one, takes special relativity to imply that mental states must be in space given that they are in time. This conclusion, however, appears to rest on a too naive identification of two distinct concepts of time. What 'time' means in the context of psychological experience is not the same as what it means in the context of special relativity. Without an in-depth study of their relation (not offered by Lockwood), only the physical effects of mental states can be said to necessarily exist in space–time. See Clarke (1995) for a refutation of Lockwood's arguments in support of the spatio–temporal localization of mental events.[18]

A priori, the modifications of the electromagnetic field 'experienced' by certain constituents of the body could be effected in two ways: the non-material self could contribute to the electromagnetic field as a separate source, or it could modify the way in which the field is built up by material sources. However, to act as a separate source, the self would have to exist in space, and this notion has just been rejected. Hence it follows that material particles are the only sources of the electromagnetic field, and that the non-material self can only influence the summary effect — represented by the electromagnetic field — of the action of particles on particles.

The causal efficacy of the self thus rests on the causal efficacy of the particles, or on the ability of the particles to modify their individual contributions to the electromagnetic field. The causal behaviour of particles (meaning, the way particles influence each other's motion, as distinct from the way particles move) accordingly comes in two modes: a physical mode which obeys the laws of physics, and a non-physical mode through which modifications of the physical mode are effected. But this means that the only causal agents in existence are the fundamental particles, and that the non-material self cannot be as non-material as dualists would have it. Interactionism thus cannot be the last word. The implications of this, as well as the possible relationship between the self and the body's constituent particles, will be explored in another article (Mohrhoff, submitted).

VII: Summary and Outlook

The following results have been obtained:

(1) The conservation of energy and momentum is a consequence of the homogeneity of time and of space. This is warranted for systems that are causally closed. As to material systems that are open to causal influences from non-material mind, either energy/momentum is/are ill-defined or there is no reason why it/they should be conserved.

(2) Assuming that part but not all of matter is causally open to non-material mind, it makes sense to attribute (non-conserved) energy and momentum even to physical systems that interact with non-material mind.

---

[18] If one thinks of mental representations as non-physical properties of conscious organisms, one may posit a separate non-physical substance as the substrate for those properties. But there is no need to distinguish between a physical and a non-physical substance; the same substance can have both physical and non-physical determinations. It can also have both spatial and non-spatial determinations, for it is only the spatial determinations that are necessarily in space, not their intrinsically indeterminate substrate. Nor (since not even the substrate for physical determinations necessarily exists in space) would a separate substrate for non-physical determinations necessarily exist in space. (Even the fundamental constituents of matter do not necessarily exist in space; there is nothing in the theories or the phenomenology of physics that would contradict the view that space contains the relative positions of fundamental particles rather than the particles themselves.)

(3) The causal efficacy of non-material mind implies departures from the statistical laws of quantum physics. These departures are capable of being formulated in terms of modifications, by the conscious self, of the electromagnetic interactions between particles; and they are more consistently formulated in this manner.

(4) Because the electromagnetic field is a summary representation of effects on the motion of particles, the effects caused by mental events are necessarily among the effects represented by it. It is not that one cannot formulate the effects of the self in terms of a separate probability field, to use Margenau's (1984) term. The point is that this field would be indistinguishable from a contribution to the electromagnetic field, which makes it obvious that departures from the laws of physics are involved. Thinking of the effects of the self as contributions to the electromagnetic field is preferable for two reasons. First, it eschews the contentious notion that measurement-like events take placein the unobserved brain. Second, it leads to a more unified treatment of causality. There is no reason whatever for having probabilities determined twice over, once during their deterministic evolution by the physically determined vector potential, and once at the end through a superimposed probability field generated by the self.

(5) Quantum-mechanical indeterminism cannot be the physical correlate of free will. Free will implies departures from the laws of physics.

(6) Mind is non-spatial. There is no point in attributing positions to mental states and events.

(7) The departures from the physical laws caused by non-physical mental events are not amenable to mathematical description. It is worth emphasizing that they are not therefore random. They could be necessitated by something of a primarily qualitative nature, something that manifests itself in quantitative, spatio–temporal terms but is not reducible to these terms.

Although there are no compelling theoretical or experimental reasons why mental events should not be capable of causing departures from physical laws, it may remain difficult for interactionists and proponents of free will, at least for some time to come, to disabuse the contemporary physicist, biologist, or philosopher of science of the doctrine of physicalism, which has been a reigning orthodoxy for well over a century. So much was this doctrine taken for granted, that until recently it was considered as almost indecorous to waste much thought over the dismissal of its antithesis. Thus, after stating that 'very few people any longer suppose that living things violate any laws of physics (as some thinkers supposed as late as the nineteenth century)',[19] Hilary Putnam (1992, p. 83) makes known why this should be so: 'Physics can, in principle, predict the probability with which a human body will follow any given trajectory.' Are we to suppose that the mountaineer who fell to his death would have been able to choose a less ruinous trajectory if only Eccles' hypothesis of mind–brain interaction had been true?

---

[19] Among those 'very few people' are the biologists A. Szent-Györgi (1961), W. Elsasser (1966), M. Delbrück (1986), and Mae-Wan Ho (1993). Their work supports the view that the behaviour of particles in living systems differs from the behaviour of the same particles in inanimate objects.

What interactionists and proponents of free will claim, in effect, is that the non-material self becomes materially effective by modifying the electromagnetic interactions between constituents of the body. Not only is this consistent with the assumption that the trajectory of the body's centre of mass is fully determined by physical laws, but also it agrees with our sense of free will which interactionists wish to take seriously. I decide to raise my hand and it goes up; but nothing in my experience leads me to expect that I could alter my trajectory once I have jumped off a cliff.[20]

Yet there is cause for optimism. If the hard problem of consciousness is taken as seriously as it now is, the hard problem of freedom is bound to follow suit. Many researchers in cognitive studies now admit the irreducibility of consciousness. And most of the philosophers who speculate about the shape of a fundamental theory of consciousness invoke some form of panpsychism.[21] Yet, with few exceptions, these philosophers still find it necessary to reduce conscious events to 'causal danglers': they affirm that pain is not reducible to its physical correlate yet deny that it causes us to pull our hands out of fires. Such a position is inherently unstable, as Lowe (1995) has pointed out. It is under intense pressure either to lapse back into materialism (which restores the causal efficacy of conscious feelings by identifying them with their physical correlates) or to take the further step of admitting the causal efficacy of consciousness. The present article has shown that, from the point of view of physics, nothing stands in the way of taking this long overdue step.

Acknowledgement

I wish to thank Jean Burns for many helpful suggestions.

References

Beck, F. (1994), 'Quantum mechanics and consciousness', *Journal of Consciousness Studies*, **1** (2), pp. 253–5.

Beck, F. and Eccles, J.C. (1992), 'Quantum aspects of brain activity and the role of consciousness', *Proc. Natl. Acad. Sci. U.S.A.*, **89**, p. 11357.

Bunge, M. (1980), *The Mind-Body Problem* (Oxford: Pergamon Press).

Chalmers, D.J. (1995), 'Facing up to the problem of consciousness', *Journal of Consciousness Studies*, **2** (3), pp. 200–19.

Chalmers, D.J. (1997), 'Moving forward on the problem of consciousness', *Journal of Consciousness Studies*, **4** (1), pp. 3–46.

Clarke, C.J.S. (1995), 'The nonlocality of mind', *Journal of Consciousness Studies*, **2** (3), pp. 231–40.

DeLancey, C. (1996), 'Emotion and the function of consciousness', *Journal of Consciousness Studies*, **3** (5-6), pp. 492–9.

Delbrück, M. (1986), *Mind from Matter? An Essay on Evolutionary Epistemology* (Palo Alto, CA: Blackwell Scientific).

Dennett, D.C. (1991), *Consciousness Explained* (London: Allen Lane / Penguin).

Eccles, J.C. (1994), *How the Self Controls Its Brain* (Berlin: Springer).

Eddington, A. (1935), *The Nature of the Physical World* (London: Dent).

Elsasser, W. (1966), *Atoms and Organism* (Princeton: Princeton University Press).

[20] My self has something to do with the particles constituting my body, not with particles in other material aggregates. There is thus a clear case for (i) the distinction between interactions that take place between the particles in my body and interactions that involve particles outside my body, and (ii) the supposition that my self is capable of modifying only the former.

[21] For explicit panpsychist proposals see, e.g., Hut and Shepard (1996), Rosenberg (1996) and Seager (1995).

Feynman, R.P. and Hibbs, A.R. (1965), *Quantum Mechanics and Path Integrals* (New York: McGraw-Hill).

Ghirardi, G.C., Rimini, A. & Weber, T. (1986), 'Unified dynamics for microscopic and macroscopic systems', *Physical Review D*, **34**, pp. 470–91.

Ho, Mae-Wan (1993), *The Rainbow and the Worm: the Physics of Organisms* (Singapore: World Scientific).

Hodgson, D. (1996), 'The easy problems ain't so easy', *Journal of Consciousness Studies*, **3** (1), pp. 69–75.

Honner, J. (1982), 'The transcendental philosophy of Niels Bohr', *Stud. Hist. Phil. Sci.*, **13** (1), pp. 1–29 (Letter to Høffding, 22.9.1923, Bohr Scientific Correspondence, microfilm No. 3, p. 5).

Hoyle, F. (1983), *The Intelligent Universe* (London: Michael Joseph).

Hut, P. and Shepard, R. (1996), 'Turning the hard problem upside down and sideways', *Journal of Consciousness Studies*, **3** (4), pp. 313–29.

Kirk, R. (1996), 'Review of Chalmers: *The Conscious Mind: In Search of a Fundamental Theory*', *Journal of Consciousness Studies*, **3** (5–6), pp. 522–3.

Lockwood, M. (1989), *Mind, Brain and the Quantum* (Oxford: Basil Blackwell).

Lowe, E.J. (1995), 'There are no easy problems of consciousness', *Journal of Consciousness Studies*, **2** (3), pp. 266–71.

Margenau, H. (1984), *The Miracle of Existence* (Woodbridge, CT: Ox Bow).

Mohrhoff, U. (1997), 'Interactionism, energy conservation, and the violation of physical laws', *Physics Essays*, **10** (4), pp. 651–65.

Mohrhoff, U. (Submitted), 'Consciousness and particles: A Vedantic synthesis'.

von Neumann, J. (1955), *Mathematical Foundations of Quantum Mechanics* (Princeton: Princeton University Press).

Papineau, D. (1996), 'A universe of zombies?,' *Times Literary Supplement*, **4864** (June 21, 1996), pp. 3–4.

Pearle, P. (1989), *Physical Review A*, **39**, p. 2277.

Penrose, R. (1994), 'Mechanisms, microtubules and the mind', *Journal of Consciousness Studies*, **1** (2), pp. 241–9.

Popper, K.R. and Eccles, J.C. (1983), *The Self and Its Brain* (London: Routledge and Kegan Paul).

Putnam, H. (1992), *Renewing Philosophy* (Cambridge, MA / London: Harvard University Press).

Rosenberg, G.H. (1996), 'Rethinking nature: a hard problem within the hard problem', *Journal of Consciousness Studies*, **3** (1), pp. 76–88.

Seager, W. (1995), 'Consciousness, information and panpsychism', *Journal of Consciousness Studies*, **2** (3), pp. 272–88.

Squires, E.J. (1981), 'Do we live in the simplest possible interesting world?', *Eur. J. Phys.*, **2**, pp. 55–7.

Szent-Györgi, A. (1961) in *Light and Life*, ed. W.D. McElroy and B. Glass (Baltimore: John Hopkins Press).

David L. Wilson

Mind–Brain Interaction and Violation of Physical Laws

If mind is not a part of the physical universe but is able to influence brain events, then violations of physical laws should occur at points of such mental influence. Using current knowledge of how the nervous system functions, the minimal necessary magnitude of such violations is examined. A variety of influences that could produce action potentials is considered, including the direct opening of sodium channels in membranes, the triggering of release of neurotransmitter at synapses, the opening of postsynaptic, ligand-gated channels, and the control of neuromodulation. It is shown that the magnitude of the disturbance required is significantly greater than allowed for under quantum-mechanical uncertainty. It is concluded that violations of fundamental physical laws, such as energy conservation, would occur were a non-physical mind able to influence brain and behaviour.

I: Introduction

There are hypotheses of the relationship between mind and brain which do not accept a physical or material explanation for processes such as consciousness and volition. Such hypotheses include various forms of dualism and some more extreme emergence hypotheses (Broad, 1951). It has been argued that any hypothesis proposing that non-physical minds exist, and that such minds play an active role in influencing physical events, requires violation of physical laws (Wilson, 1976; 1995). Nevertheless, some scientists retain such views, as do a great number of non-scientists. In this paper I explore the issue of violation of physical law by asking how minimal such a violation can be. That is, how little can a non-physical mind interfere with physical events while still influencing brain events adequately to allow for volition, willing, etc.?

One could argue that any violation of a physical law is a concern, so why should this issue of the minimum necessary magnitude of such violations be considered important? One reason relates to whether such violations would be detectable. Could such violations occur at a level that is not detectable, or is it at least possible, in principle, that a test for the violations could be devised?

Journal of Consciousness Studies, **6**, No. 8–9, 1999, pp. 185–200

Another reason for asking how minimal such violations can be is that the magnitude and type of violation necessary might influence the acceptability of the notion by some individuals. For instance, some might be more concerned about a violation of conservation of energy than a disturbance below the level of quantum-mechanical uncertainty.

There are several laws and theories of physics that will be considered in this paper. One is the first law of thermodynamics, or energy conservation, which states that energy can neither be created nor destroyed. The second law of thermodynamics states that entropy, a measure of disorder, cannot decrease in a closed system—things get more disordered with time. The principle of conservation of momentum, for our purposes, can be stated as: a particle's mass times its velocity is a constant in the absence of applied forces. Finally, a fundamental principle of quantum mechanics is that events related to collapse of a wave function, or events occurring under quantum mechanical uncertainty, occur randomly. An example of the last principle is the random decay of radioactive atoms: non-random decay would be a violation of physical law.

I will begin by asking what minimal level of energy is required to cause nerve cells in the brain to fire action potentials. Most simply, volitional acts by a non-physical mind would supply such energy. However, I will also briefly consider whether a non-physical mind might harness, rather than supply, such energy during volitional acts, and will ask whether other physical laws would necessarily be violated by such acts of a non-physical mind. I will also examine earlier models that claimed that non-physical control of brain processes could occur without violation of any of the conservation laws of physics.

II: How the Brain Works

I will assume that today's neuroscience gives us a reasonable view of how the nervous system works. In particular, conscious mental functions such as volition would somehow have to produce action potentials (nerve impulses) in neurons. Such action potentials are signals that transmit information along axons and, in most neurons, initiate the process of synaptic transmission of a chemical signal to follower (postsynaptic) cells. Action potentials are necessary to bring about muscle contractions, which produce all behaviour, from simple movements to coordinated actions and speech.

Action potentials are produced by opening sodium channels in neuronal membranes, which allow the movement of sodium ions across the membrane. Action potentials also involve potassium channels, but we can ignore that complexity for the purpose of this analysis. The flux of sodium ions through the sodium channels produces a voltage change across the membrane. The resulting action potential self-propagates along the axon. The sodium channels are voltage-gated in that they can be opened by changes in the voltage across the membrane. Other channels, such as those at the synaptic connections between neurons, can indirectly induce an action potential by allowing ions to move across the membrane, which alters the voltage, and thereby induces the opening of the voltage-gated sodium channels that produce the action potential.

III: Mind–Brain Interaction Mechanisms

I will first consider what minimally would be required of a non-physical mind to trigger a single action potential in a single neuron. There are a number of points in the process that must be considered. Then I will go on to ask how many such events would be needed to generate volitional acts such as speaking or moving hands and fingers.

a. Opening sodium channels

Perhaps the simplest way of causing an action potential would be by opening enough voltage-sensitive sodium channels to trigger an action potential directly. The opening of sodium channels involves a conformational change in the membrane protein that allows sodium ions to pass across the membrane. The conformational change is normally triggered by a reduction in the magnitude of the resting potential across the membrane of the neuron (a depolarization).

The opening of sodium channels through direct conformational change requires energy. That requirement for energy, if met by a non-physical mind, would violate the first law of thermodynamics (energy would be created). Such a violation might go undetected if the energy required, coupled with the time during which it would need to be available, were low enough that it could be "hidden" under quantum-mechanical (Heisenberg) uncertainty. That possibility is considered in Appendix A, below, and is determined not to be the case. That is, the opening of even one channel for an adequate period of time requires an energy input that is orders-of-magnitude greater than possible under quantum-mechanical uncertainty. In addition, causing an action potential would usually require the opening of a number of such channels.

Can the requirement for energy be met by a non-physical mind harnessing existing energy? That is a question that I will discuss later in this paper.

b. Altering voltage gradients

A second way to open sodium channels would be by altering the voltage across the membrane. This voltage change would trigger the voltage-gated sodium channels to open. A voltage gradient is a potential-energy gradient, and thus, in the simplest case, would require the expenditure of energy to modify. Such modification might occur, for instance, by moving charges. Enough positive charges on the inside of the membrane could be moved towards the membrane, and/or enough negative charges away from the membrane, to depolarize to threshold.

A nerve cell typically generates an action potential when its axon hillock region has a membrane potential that reaches threshold, an area that would contain a number of voltage-gated sodium channels. In Appendix A I show that just modifying the voltage gradient over a single channel, a much smaller area than an axon hillock, requires too much energy to be 'hidden' under the uncertainty principle. The maximum possible time period for such an energy increase, as allowed by the uncertainty principle, would be too brief to allow for any ion flow.

Given our knowledge of neurophysiology, actions at the level of quantum mechanical uncertainty do not appear to be adequate to generate action potentials by the above mechanisms. It would thus appear that a non-physical mind, which generated action potentials by supplying the energy necessary either to directly open sodium channels or to indirectly open such channels by altering voltage gradients, would violate the first law of thermodynamics. However, there are other ways of generating action potentials and other ways for non-physical mind to influence brain which still must be considered.

c. Synaptic transmission

1. The presynaptic neuron

Synaptic transmission involves the release of a chemical transmitter from the presynaptic terminal. The chemical transmitter is stored in membrane-bound packages, called vesicles, in the presynaptic terminal. Synaptic transmission involves the linkage and fusion of one or more synaptic vesicles with the presynaptic membrane, releasing the chemical transmitter from the presynaptic cell. Once released, the transmitter interacts with receptors on the postsynaptic cell to cause changes in membrane potential of that cell. Those changes, if great enough, can result in an action potential in the postsynaptic neuron. The fusion process that releases the transmitter is complex and appears to involve the action of several proteins and the hydrolysis of ATP (Rothman and Sollner, 1997).

An influx in calcium ions through the presynaptic membrane triggers the release of synaptic transmitter. The entry of calcium ions into the cell results from the opening of voltage-gated calcium channels in the presynaptic membrane. The opening of such calcium channels is normally brought about by the change in membrane potential caused by an action potential in the presynaptic neuron. Considering all of the events involved in synaptic transmission, the opening of the calcium channel would appear to represent the point of minimum energy requirement. An alternative view of Beck and Eccles (1992), that the release process itself represents such a point of minimal energy requirement, will be considered in section c3, below. The opening of a single calcium channel involves a change in conformation of the protein that forms the channel, allowing a net flow of calcium ions into the cell. However, this is the same kind of event that was considered in Appendix A for the direct opening of sodium channels, and the calculation would be the same. In fact, genetic evidence suggests that voltage-gated sodium and calcium channels share a common mechanism of gating (Koester, 1991).

Thus, again, a necessary violation of energy conservation, well outside of the limit of quantum mechanical uncertainty, would result from non-physical mind opening even one such channel. In addition, the opening of a single calcium channel would not usually be adequate to allow enough calcium into the presynaptic terminal to assure release of synaptic transmitter. At a typical synapse, a considerable number of the channels open at about the same time, causing a thousand-fold rise in local calcium concentration in less than a millisecond.

There is yet a further complication for any non-physical mind. The transmitter is stored in synaptic vesicles. The release of synaptic transmitter from a vesicle is an all-or-nothing event. The typical number of vesicles whose contents are released at a synapse depends on the type of synapse. Several hundred can be released at a nerve-muscle synapse to trigger a single muscle contraction. In the brain, some synapses might release only one synaptic vesicle in response to an action potential, but the release of one vesicle alone would not usually be enough to cause an action potential in the postsynaptic neuron, as discussed below.

How many synapses need to be activated to assure that the postsynaptic neuron generates an action potential? That would depend upon the state of the neuron. If, at the moment of interaction by a non-physical mind, the neuron were poised just below threshold, then a single vesicle released at a single synapse might do it. But a typical neuron has a membrane potential that is varying with time, as it receives input from a variety of presynaptic neurons forming, typically, thousands of synapses on the receiving neuron. That neuron can be firing action potentials many times per second. Most presynaptic neurons form a number of synapses on each of their follower cells. Single synapses can be unreliable. The release of synaptic transmitter from a few vesicles from a single presynaptic neuron produces a postsynaptic potential of only a few hundred microvolts (Hille, 1992). Many millivolts of potential change are required to raise the membrane potential from resting to threshold for production of an action potential. Thus, to assure that the intervention by a non-physical conscious-ness is effective, transmitter release from a considerable number of excitatory syn-apses would appear be required, and, in some instances, would need to be coupled to the suppression of the action of inhibitory synapses on the same neuron.

Eccles (1970) has proposed that neurons that are sensitive to input from a non-physical mind could be poised with a membrane potential so close to threshold that stimulation from synaptic transmitter released from a single synaptic vesicle would be adequate to cause an action potential. There are several problems with this view. First, such a neuron would be very unstable, firing randomly due to small fluctuations in normal input. Second, there are no known neurons that maintain a constant mem-brane potential, within tens of microvolts, just below threshold for production of an action potential. Thus, the ability of mind to influence brain would be limited to those times when appropriate neurons were near to threshold, but not close enough to "fire" without additional (non-physical) input. Third, there is no known mechanism whereby a neuron could maintain its potential just below threshold and within such precise limits. Most brain neurons appear to have rapidly changing membrane poten-tials due to changes in synaptic inputs, metabolic alterations of ion channels, and to changes in the activity of electrogenic pumps, such as the sodium-potassium ATPase.

2. The post-synaptic neuron

If we examine the postsynaptic membrane as another possible site for intervention by a non-physical mind, we find similar limitations. The trigger points for production of change in the membrane potential in the postsynaptic cell are the ligand-gated ion channels that are activated by binding synaptic transmitter molecules. While the details of the conformational changes that are involved in opening such ligand-gated channels have not been determined, this kind of channel has been identified as con-sisting of proteins in several different cases (Hille, 1992). Thus, the general mechan-ism is similar enough to the voltage-gated channels that the considerations in the first part of Appendix A hold. Furthermore, the opening of a single ligand-gated channel would not usually be adequate to trigger an action potential. A considerable number of such channels located at more than one synapse would usually be required (Hille, 1992).

3. The Beck and Eccles Models

Two specific models have previously been proposed to explain how a non-physical mind might generate volitional acts without violation of the conservation laws of physics. The earlier model of Eccles (1970) proposed that synaptic vesicles had a great enough uncertainty of location under the uncertainty principle that they would be able to move to the presynaptic membrane for exocytosis. Eccles (1970) had calculated an uncertainty of distance of 5 nanometers over a millisecond of time. It was pointed out that there was an error in the calculation (Wilson, 1976) since the equation that Eccles used was based on the assumption that the vesicle was in a vacuum, not in the viscous medium of a presynaptic terminal. Just given the viscosity of water, the actual uncertainty in location of a synaptic vesicle is on the order of one picometer (Wilson, 1993), which is four orders-of-magnitude smaller than the Eccles (1970) estimate, and is a very small distance, about one percent of the width of an atom.

The second, more recent model was developed by Beck and Eccles (1992; see also Eccles, 1994). They propose that volitional acts of a non-physical mind momentarily increase the probability of exocytosis of synaptic vesicles in presynaptic terminals. They further propose that this can occur without the violation of conservation laws of physics because of the nature of the mechanism of synaptic transmission. They propose that synaptic vesicles are packaged in a presynaptic vesicular grid (PVG) that is paracrystalline. Further, they propose that the trigger mechanism (by which a synaptic vesicle fuses with the presynaptic membrane and releases its content of synaptic transmitter) involves bringing the PVG into a metastable state from which exocytosis can occur. They argue that the transition to the metastable state is by a quantum transition. With these assumptions, they conclude that vesicle exocytosis is a quantum mechanical event, and propose that a non-physical mind can influence the quantal selection process. Were such a model accurate, the actions of mind would at least violate the requirement for randomness in such quantum mechanical processes.

In addition, the model of synaptic vesicle release presumed by Beck and Eccles (1992) is not a likely or reasonable model given our current knowledge of the mechanism of synaptic transmission (Sollner and Rothman, 1994; Jahn and Sudhof, 1994; Matthews, 1996). While that knowledge is still being developed, and details are not firmly established, the evidence does not support a model of transmitter release that involves the transition of a PVG to a metastable state. Instead, specific active zones at the presynaptic membrane have been recognized as the sites of release of synaptic transmitters (Kandel, 1991). Synaptic vesicles do cluster adjacent to such active sites, and the synaptic vesicles appear to be connected by cytoskeletal components, such as actin filaments. However, rather than being a PVG in a metastable state, the vesicles must actually be released from the cluster before docking and fusing at the plasma membrane. Influx of calcium into the presynaptic terminal is the triggering event for transmitter release, and the calcium appears to be involved in several different events related to synaptic transmission (Burgoyne and Morgan, 1995). One is the release of the individual vesicles from cytoskeletally linked pool, and another is the fusion of the vesicles with the plasma membrane at the active zone. Both of these events appear to involve the binding of calcium to proteins, followed by conformational changes in the proteins. The first event is a calcium-calmodulin activated process that disrupts the linkage of the vesicles by actin filaments, releasing one or more vesicles from the cluster of vesicles. Calcium is thought to play a further role in the actual docking of the vesicle to the plasma membrane, triggering release of the transmitter. Many of the proteins involved in these processes have been identified, and detailed models, with some experimental support, have been developed (Sollner and Rothman, 1994; Littleton and Bellen, 1995; Jahn and Sudhof, 1994; Matthews, 1996; Martin, 1997). It is thought that phosphorylation of a synpasin (one of the proteins), triggered by calcium, frees the vesicle to move into the active zone. Other proteins mediate recognition of vesicle and release site (Sollner and Rothman, 1994). In brief, current evidence and data indicate that the events involved in synaptic transmitter release require, at least, the same kind of conformational changes in proteins described earlier in this article. The modification of such events by a non-physical influence would require violation of conservation laws of physics, either energy conservation, as discussed above, or other conservation laws, as discussed below in the section on harnessing energy. There is no evidence favouring the Beck and Eccles model that synaptic transmission is the result of quantum mechanical selection events among states occurring in paracrystalline arrays of synaptic vesicles. Without that model being correct, their hypothesis concerning how a non-physical mind might act collapses.

Summing-up this section, non-physical mind acting through synaptic transmission appears to require energy, at well above a quantum-mechanical level, and confronts other complexities if the likely need to activate a number of such synapses is taken into account. Finally, there are more than ten trillion synapses in a single human brain. We have not considered how a non-physical mind could identify exactly which ones to activate, and whether such identifications might require further violations of physical laws.

d. Neuronal modulation

In addition to opening ion channels directly, some neurotransmitters, including norepinephrine, serotonin, dopamine, and some neuropeptides, act as modulators of nerve activity. These modulators produce biochemical changes in postsynaptic cells, which alter the longer-term sensitivity of the neurons to other synaptic input. Such biochemical events offer another point for mental influence, as many of these neuromodulatory processes act through a cascade (a series of biochemical reactions), altering enzymatic activity, and allowing for a considerable amplification of the signal within the neuron. Such amplifying cascades are similar to the ones operating with hormones. In neurons, the end products can include modified ion channels, whose sensitivity to future synaptic inputs can be altered.

Were a non-physical mental influence able to alter an early event in the cascade, greater change would be generated than similar actions later in the cascade. In Appendix B I explore the magnitude of energy that would be required to initiate a cascade, and find that it appears to be significant, and certainly not allowable under the uncertainty principle. A violation of energy conservation would again be necessary.

There are other limitations of modulation of neuronal activity which make it unsuitable as a point for volitional influences from a non-physical mind. Modulation serves more as an amplifier than an initiator of action. It may be important in setting one's mood or arousal, but modulation alone does not cause neurons to fire action potentials—it merely adjusts the response level of neurons to other inputs. Thus, it cannot take part in the specifics of decision making or volitional action. The probability of firing action potentials in certain situations could change, but the initiation of action that volition would seem to entail is more like a signal than the amplification of the signal.

Furthermore, the above would require that the neurons capable of initiating volitional acts possess the necessary receptors and biochemical machinery of neuromodulation.

Finally, the time course of such modulatory actions would appear to be too slow. Modulatory influence has a time course that is considerably slower than voltage-gated or ligand-gated actions, typically having an initiation time that is measured in seconds (Hille, 1992). Volitional acts, such as the pressing of a button in response to a flash of light, can be complete in tenths of a second. In brief, for several reasons, the control only of these neuromodulatory synapses would be inadequate for volitional control of particular actions.

e. Self-generation of action potentials by neurons

Some neurons have special channels, typically potassium and calcium channels, that allow for the self-generation of action potentials. Many of these neurons are pacemaker cells, similar to the kind of pacemaker cells that are found in the heart. They have an oscillating membrane potential that periodically depolarizes the cell to threshold, resulting in an action potential, or a burst of several action potentials.

We need to consider the possibility that non-physical mind might act through the modulation of such channels. However, the mechanism for such self-generation of action potentials appears to be similar to the modulation mechanism described above (Hille, 1992). Thus, the analysis in Appendix B serves to show that the level of disturbance required directly to influence this mechanism by a non-physical mind would similarly require violation of energy conservation. In addition, the number of neurons exhibiting pacemaking activity appears to be even smaller than those containing the machinery for neuromodulation. Finally, as with modulation, the time course would be slow and unable to account for rapid mental influences.

IV: Harnessing Energy

In all of the above considerations, the level of energy required for a non-physical mind to trigger volitional acts was estimated. One might ask whether a non-physical mind might avoid violation of the law of conservation of energy by harnessing existing energy to bring about the required changes in protein conformation or voltage gradients.

For instance, a non-physical mind might cause changes in the direction of motion of enough ions in the vicinity of a sodium channel to generate the voltage change needed to cause the voltage-gated sodium channel to open. In this case it would appear that a much larger number of individual events would have to be influenced (as thousands of ions and molecules individually have their directions altered), but the individual influences might not have to violate energy conservation if each molecule retains its kinetic energy unchanged during its alteration of direction of motion, and if the resulting change in the potential energy of the local voltage gradient is offset by a change in heat energy, or other form of energy.

However, in this and all such cases that I can imagine, such harnessing of existing energy sources would require the violation of other physical laws. In the particular case above, consider the selective, directional movement of ions with specific charges on them—positively charged in one direction, negatively charged in the opposite direction—over a brief period of time, generating a significant shift in membrane potential. A variant of a Maxwell's demon, or a number of such demons, would appear to be necessary for such alterations of motion. Such demons were originally given the ability merely to open a trap door, allowing faster moving gas molecules to pass in a given direction. The general idea of a Maxwell's demon has been well studied (Leff and Rex, 1990), and it is recognized that the actions of such demons violate the second law of thermodynamics. In addition, in our case, the volitional demons could not just use trap doors because the demons would have to change the direction of movement of ions (or the direction of movement of other molecules that might collide, or not, with the ions) in a liquid. Minimally, such changes in the direction of motion of ions or molecules would violate conservation of momentum. Thus, with this one example, both the second law of thermodynamics and the principle of conservation of momentum would appear to be violated. Furthermore, the need for a non-physical mind to act, individually, on many ions or molecules would add to the complexity of the volitional interaction. Thousands of select, individual interactions would appear to be required just to initiate the opening of a single membrane channel.

A demonstration that laws of physics other than energy conservation would always be violated by a non-physical mind "borrowing" energy from existing sources to generate an action potential is beyond the scope of the present paper. However, the view that such violations would always occur does not appear to be unreasonable given the ability of physical laws to account for the movements of ions and molecules. Thus, indirectly producing the conformational changes needed to produce action potentials, by events that result in harnessing the required energy, appears only to shift the problem of violation of physical laws to those earlier events that volitional acts would influence, and to compound the number of possible events that would have to be individually controlled.

V: How Many Action Potentials for a Volitional Act?

Up to this point we have been considering what is needed to trigger a single action potential in a single neuron. For a volitional act to be carried out, how many action potentials are needed in a given neuron, and how many different neurons must initiate action potentials?

In order to cause muscles to contract, the brain must generate action potentials in spinal cord motor neurons. Each action potential in a spinal cord motor neuron will, in turn, directly trigger a twitch (brief) contraction in, typically, a few muscle fibres in a muscle. The input to such spinal cord motor neurons is complex, and comes from a number of sources. One of these sources is the primary motor cortex of the brain. Volitional acts are not instigated directly at the primary motor cortex of the brain, but during volitional acts, action potentials in other brain neurons are thought to lead to action potentials in the output neurons of the motor cortex (Penfield, 1958).

Minimally, it would appear that at least one brain neuron would have to be activated for a volitional act. What is not clear today is whether a single action potential in a single neuron would be adequate or whether a very large number might be needed. There are several reasons for the uncertainty.

It is known that voluntary movements involve the activity of neurons in various brain regions (Georgopoulos, 1991; Hanes and Schall, 1996; Snyder, et al., 1997). However, it is possible that one or a few so-called command neurons might exist and have the ability to govern volitional acts. It is known that, in some invertebrates, there are single command neurons that can trigger complex, co-ordinated behavioural responses (Stein, 1978).

Might such command neurons exist in humans, one for each of the possible volitional acts we perform, so that only one neuron would need to be triggered for each such act? If one considers the complexity and uniqueness of the motor responses related to higher-level conscious activity, and the way that we learn complex behavioural actions, the idea of a single command neuron initiating each volitional act appears inadequate, as indicated below.

The command neuron in invertebrates works well for repetitive, sequenced behaviours, such as certain forms of movement. In contrast, what often characterizes conscious volitional behaviour is new combinations of muscle contractions. Consider language. The strength of language is its ability to generate a near-infinite variety of meanings from unique combinations of words. Volitional acts can involve original, creative speech. Such new combinations of words require unique sequencing of muscle contractions. At most, one could imagine something like command neurons that could trigger output of individual words or phrases, but the unique sequencing of such words or phrases into sentences would appear to require individual disturbances of brain function by a non-physical mind for each word or phrase. At least for more complex volitional acts, the firing of a number of neurons would appear, minimally, to be required.

Another complexity in determining the number of action potentials required for volitional acts comes from studies of voluntary acts in individuals. Libet *et al.* (1983) have shown that brain activation leading to a simple voluntary act has a temporal component (readiness potential) that can be measured from the scalp, and that lasts at least one-quarter to one-half second before action. These researchers indicate that the readiness potential begins several hundred milliseconds before subjects indicate that a conscious decision to act has been made. Libet (1985) has proposed that the function of conscious will is not to initiate specific voluntary acts, but to exercise conscious veto control over the cerebral processes that precede the act. It might be argued that such control could be exercised with the activation of fewer neurons, perhaps through strategically activated inhibitory interneurons. However, the readiness potential, a measurable potential on the scalp, involves activity in a very large number of neurons. A suppression of that activity might equally well involve the firing of many neurons.

Again, we are left with considerable uncertainty about the minimal number of neurons that would need to be independently activated to generate (or veto) a volitional act. For more complex acts it would appear to be more than one, as indicated above, but we do not yet know if the minimum number for a typical act is a few or very many.

VI: Input: From Brain To Non-physical Mind

In addition, there would be a need for any non-physical mind to monitor the activity in numerous brain neurons to gain and maintain input about brain states, perceptions, feedback concerning movements, etc. Thus, any non-physical mind would have to have some means of detecting the state of firing of neurons. In this paper we have gained some sense of the minimal level of disturbance that would be required of a non-physical entity to take action in the physical world, but we have no way of knowing how much disturbance of the physical world would be required by a non-physical entity to detect the state of brain neurons. However, the difficulty that such an entity would face should be obvious. For instance, if perceptions are something occurring in a non-physical mind, and result from "input" to the mind from the brain, then the mind would need to be able continually to monitor millions of neurons whose locations are spread through large regions of the cortex (Crick, 1994).

VII: Discussion

Mind-brain interaction is not the only instance for which some scientists have proposed hypotheses that require violation of currently accepted physical laws. The steady-state hypothesis of the universe (Bondi, 1952), which offered an alternative to the big-bang hypothesis, required the ongoing production of matter throughout the universe, a violation of conservation of energy. That hypothesis has been largely discarded, and a similar fate may await dualistic, interactionist hypotheses of the relationship between mind and brain. However, for those who support monistic views, it will be necessary to produce a physical explanation for consciousness and volition, a challenge much discussed but not yet met.

The above considerations outline what, minimally, would be necessary for a non-physical control of brain function sufficient for conscious acts and volition. There appears to be no way that a non-physical mind could act without violating physical laws. Furthermore, there appears to be no obvious way, consistent with our knowledge of neurophysiology and neurochemistry, for such a non-physical mind to bring about volitional acts by altering brain events only at a level within quantum-mechanical uncertainty. In each case examined, any effective actions by a non-physical entity would produce violations of one or more of the principles or laws of physics. Even were a minimal interference, under the uncertainty principle, shown to be possible, it would not allow a non-physical mind to influence brain without the violation of physical laws because any events occurring within quantum-mechanical uncertainty are required to be random. The patterned firing of action potentials in neurons that appear to be required by volitional actions would be highly non-random.

What the analysis reported here makes obvious is that the uncertainty principle leaves one very little to work with at the level of an individual neuron, and even at the level of individual membrane channels or enzymes within neurons. The design of experiments to detect violations of physical laws caused by non-physical, mental influences would obviously be quite difficult. Nevertheless, were a non-physical mind to influence events in brains, I conclude that it would not be able to 'hide' under quantum-mechanical uncertainty.

In summary, our current understanding of brain function has reached a stage such that violations of physical laws appear to be necessary if a non-physical mind is to influence brain. Beyond the seemingly necessary violation of physical laws, any such non-physical entity would require some means of selectively influencing the appropriate channels or synapses among the many trillions existing in the brain — no mean task.

For those who believe that free will must be totally independent and free of physical causes, the idea that physical laws must be violated should not be taken as a negative but almost as an expectation, especially to the extent that physical laws appear to specify a universe that is either determined or randomly probabalistic. If a non-physical mind exists, the research project for the next century should be to explore the impact of such non-physical influences—where in the brain does such influence occur and what laws are broken?

Of course, there are other hypotheses of the relationship between mind and brain. The postscript in Crick (1994) gives a description of what the feeling of free will might entail under a monistic view. Under such monistic views, volitional acts are brain acts and do not require initiation by a non-physical entity. Some argue that such views leave volition a mere illusion. In this paper I have attempted to base my arguments on our current understanding of physical laws and knowledge of neurobiology. It is exciting to consider the possibility that a solution to the problem of consciousness might give us better insight into the nature of matter (Cairns-Smith, 1996) as well as free will. Our scientific world-view remains incomplete without that solution.

Appendix A: Opening Gates On Membrane Channels

a. Directly opening gates

Each sodium channel can be viewed as having a gate which opens the channel in response to a depolarization of the voltage across the membrane. When the channel is open, sodium can flow through the channel. The voltage-gated sodium channel is a membrane protein. Proteins are chains of linked amino acids. In the simplest model, the gate can be viewed as an arm of the protein, a part of the chain. One recent model of how the sodium channel works (Catterall, 1988) is considerably more complex, and involves the rotation of regions of the protein that form alpha-helices. Each alpha helix is proposed to be linked to a series of positive charges, and breaks, rotates about sixty degrees, and then remakes shifted linkage points. The rotation of a set of these coils changes the shape of the protein so as to produce an open channel. There are other models of how the voltage-gating opens a channel in the membrane (Hille, 1992), but independent of the particular model, the measured magnitude of gating currents supports considerable movement of a significant piece of the protein (Papazian and Bezanilla, 1997). It is also thought that all three of the major kinds of voltage-gated channels; sodium, calcium, and potassium, use the same general mechanism, based on similarities in their amino acid sequence (Koester, 1991). For our purposes, the movement of one short arm on an amino acid chain will be used as a model. Is the energy required to move such an arm significantly greater than what would be available through quantum-mechanical uncertainty?

From the standpoint of quantum mechanics, how far can this arm or gate move without being detectable by the uncertainty principle? The uncertainty principle states that:

$$(\Delta E)(\Delta t) \quad \frac{h}{2}$$

where: ΔE is uncertainty in energy

Δt is uncertainty in time

and h is Planck's constant

is the approximate maximum uncertainty. So, for a non-physical influence to be undetectable, the uncertainty in the product of energy and time involved in the process of moving the gate must be less than this, or,

$$(\Delta E)(\Delta t) \quad \frac{h}{2}$$

Several different kinds of forces or bonds are involved in determining the conformation of a protein, including hydrogen bonds, ionic bonds, and covalent disulphide bonds. A fourth kind of force that can be involved consists of hydrophobic interactions, but these actually relate to the formation, or lack of formation, of hydrogen bonds by water molecules surrounding the protein. Such hydrophobic interactions are involved, for instance, in determining the membrane-buried part of channel proteins. For our purposes, such hydrophobic interactions can be viewed as related to hydrogen bonding.

One or more of the above four bonds or forces will be involved in maintaining a particular arm of a protein in a particular position, but if there is to be stability in the shape of the protein, enough force must be involved that the arm does not 'flap' open and closed due to random thermal motions. The weakest of the above forces is the hydrogen bond, which is ten to twenty times weaker than a typical ionic or covalent bond. Although surely an underestimate of the forces involved, given the need to maintain a stable conformation, let's consider the case where one hydrogen bond (the weakest of the above) is all that is involved in holding the channel in a closed configuration. Under the uncertainty principle, how long can the channel be open (hydrogen bond be broken) and go undetected under the uncertainty principle? The energy involved in breaking hydrogen bonds is about 20 kJoules/mole. For a single hydrogen bond this amounts to

$$20 \text{ kJ}/6.02 \times 10^{23} = 3.3 \cdot 10^{-20} \text{ Joules.}$$

Inserting this value as ΔE in the above formula from the uncertainty principle and solving for   t gives

$$\Delta t < 3.2 \times 10^{-15} \text{ sec.}$$

This is such a very brief period of time for the channel to remain open that no ions would have time to pass through the channel. The time required just to open a membrane channel appears to range from tens of microseconds to fractions of a millisecond (Hille, 1992).

Since the uncertainty principle involves the product of energy change and time, one could increase the time available by reducing the energy required. Thus, to allow the channel to open for a millisecond under the uncertainty principle would entail reducing the energy involved by a factor of about one trillion! It should be clear that

the direct opening of a single channel by a non-physical mind could not escape undetected under the uncertainty principle.

b. Changing voltage across the membrane

There is a second way to view the problem, namely, to look at the magnitude of the
energy involved in the change of potential across the membrane. Consider just a single channel in the membrane. A rough estimate of the minimal size of the patch of
membrane whose potential must change is a square area, 100 angstroms on a side,
centred on the channel (this area is not so much larger than an individual channel plus
immediate surrounding area that most greatly influences electrical potential). An estimate of the amount of energy required to bring that small patch from resting potential
to a potential that will trigger the opening of the channel is given below.

Typical capacitance for a neuronal membrane is 1 microfarad per square centimetre.
The difference in potential between resting and threshold is about 25 millivolts. The
energy involved in generating a change of about 25 millivolts in potential, per square
centimetre is given by:

$$\frac{1}{2}C(\Delta V)^2$$

where C is capacitance
and ΔV is 25 millivolts.

Multiplying by the estimate of the minimum area required at a single channel,
$(100 \text{ Å})^2$, gives:

$$\text{Energy} = 3.1 \times 10^{-22} \text{ joules.}$$

Inserting this as   E in the Heisenberg uncertainty equation, gives

$$\Delta t < 3.3 \times 10^{-13} \text{ seconds}$$

which is too brief, by many orders of magnitude, to allow for any significant change
in the conformation of the channel protein and initiation of flux of sodium, which
requires fractions of a millisecond, not fractions of a picosecond (Hille, 1992). Thus,
there is insufficient time under the uncertainty principle for the flux of sodium ions
through the channel, given the energy change required to open the channel. Once
again, there is a failure to 'hide' under the uncertainty principle by many orders-of-
magnitude.

Appendix B: The Biochemical Approach

How much energy is required for the initiation of the cascade that results in neuromodulation? The influence, to be most effective with the least energy expenditure,
should occur at or near the beginning of the cascade. We will consider only a single
triggering of the cascade, although this probably would be quite inadequate to bring
about the desired level of modulation.

What energy is required for the single triggering of a cascade? To answer this question we need to examine the details of how such cascades are initiated (Schwartz and
Kandel, 1991). In all cases, the binding of a neuromodulator to receptors on the membrane causes a conformational change in a protein receptor. This change is like that
considered above for ligand-gated ion channels. The next step in all known cases of

neuromodulation consists of the activation of a G protein by the altered receptor. The G protein has its conformation altered by this interaction, and as a result, binds a molecule of GTP in place of GDP. Later steps in modulation differ, but all appear to involve, at the least, conformational changes in proteins, and for the cascade amplification to be significant, often involve the phosphorylation of proteins, which requires even more energy than a simple conformational change. Thus, the influence of a non-physical mind on the early stages of neuromodulation would involve the same kind of conformational adjustment considered in the first part of Appendix A, above, with the same conclusion applying. Once again, the conclusion is that, by any reasonable mechanism, the energy requirement would be significantly greater than allowed for under the uncertainty principle, and the first law of thermodynamics would be violated by action of a non-physical mind.

References

Beck, F. & Eccles, J.C. (1992), 'Quantum aspects of brain activity and the role of consciousness', *Proceedings of the National Academy of Science USA*, **89**, pp. 11357–61.

Bondi, H. (1952), *Cosmology* (Cambridge: Cambridge University Press).

Broad, C.D. (1951), *The Mind and Its Place in Nature* (London: Routledge and Kegan Paul).

Cairns-Smith, A.G. (1996), *Evolving the Mind: On the Nature of Matter and the Origin of Consciousness* (Cambridge: Cambridge University Press).

Catterall, W.A. (1988), 'Structure and function of voltage-sensitive ion channels', *Science*, **242**, pp. 50–61.

Crick, F.H.C. (1994), *The Astonishing Hypothesis* (New York: Charles Scribner's Sons).

Eccles, J.C. (1970) *Facing Reality* (New York: Springer-Verlag).

Eccles, J.C. (1994), *How the Self Controls Its Brain* (Berlin: Springer-Verlag).

Georgopoulos, A.P. (1991) 'Higher order motor control', *Annual Rev. Neuroscience*, **14**, pp. 361–77.

Hanes, D.P. & Schall, J.D. (1996) 'Neural control of voluntary movement initiation', *Science*, **274**, pp. 427–9.

Hille, B. (1992), *Ionic Channels of Excitable Membranes* (Sunderland, Mass.: Sinauer Associates).

Jahn, R. & Sudhof, T.C. (1994) 'Synaptic vesicles and exocytosis', *Annual Rev. Neuroscience*, **17**, pp. 219–46.

Kandel, E. (1991), 'Transmitter release', in *Principles of Neural Science*, ed. E.R. Kandel, J.H. Schwartz, & T.M. Jessel (Norwalk, Conn.: Appleton & Lange).

Koester, J. (1991), 'Voltage-gated ion channels and the generation of the action potential', in *Principles of Neural Science*, ed. E.R. Kandel, J.H. Schwartz, & T.M. Jessel (Norwalk, Conn.: Appleton & Lange).

Leff, H.S. & Rex, A.F. (1990), *Maxwell's Demon: Entropy, Information, Computing* (Princeton: Princeton Univ. Press).

Libet, B. (1985), 'Unconscious cerebral initiative and the role of conscious will in voluntary action', *Behavioral and Brain Sciences*, **8**, pp. 529–66.

Libet, B., Gleason, C.A., Wright, E.W., Jr., & Pearl, D.K. (1983), 'Time of conscious intention to act in relation to onset of cerebral activities (readiness-potential); the unconscious initiation of a freely voluntary act', *Brain*, **106**, pp. 623–42.

Littleton, J.T. & Bellen, H.J. (1995) 'Synaptotagmin controls and modulates synaptic-vesicle fusion in a Ca-dependent manner', *Trends in Neuroscience*, **18**, pp. 177–83.

Martin, T.F.J. (1997) 'Stages of regulated exocytosis', *Trends in Cell Biology*, **7**, pp. 271–76.

Matthews, G. (1996) 'Neurotransmitter release', *Annu. Rev. Neuroscience*, **19**, pp. 219–33.

Papazian, D.M., & Bezanilla, F. (1997), 'How does an ion channel sense voltage?', *News in Physiological Sciences*, **12**, pp. 203–10.

Penfield, W. (1958) *The Excitable Cortex in Conscious Man*, (Springfield, Ill.: Charles C. Thomas Publisher).

Rothman, J.E. & Sollner, T.H. (1997), 'Throttles and dampers: controlling the engine of membrane fusion', *Science*, **276**, pp. 1212–3.

Schwartz, J.H. & Kandel, E.R. (1991), 'Synaptic transmission mediated by second messengers', in *Principles of Neural Science*, ed. E.R. Kandel, J.H. Schwartz, & T.M. Jessel (Norwalk, Conn.: Appleton & Lange).

Snyder, L.H., Batista, A.P., & Andersen, R.A. (1997) 'Coding of intention in the posterior parietal cortex', *Nature*, **386**, pp. 167–70.

Sollner, T. & Rothman, J.E. (1994) 'Neurotransmission: harnessing fusion machinery at the synapse', *Trends in Neuroscience*, **17**, pp.344–48.

Stein, P.S.G. (1978) 'Motor systems, with specific reference to the control of locomotion', *Annu. Rev. Neuroscience*, **1**, pp. 61–81.

Wilson, D.L. (1976), 'On the nature of consciousness and physical reality', *Perspectives in Biology and Medicine*, **19**, pp. 568–81.

Wilson, D.L. (1993), 'Quantum theory and consciousness', *Behavioral and Brain Sciences*, **16**, pp. 615–16.

Wilson, D.L. (1995), 'Seeking the neural correlate of consciousness', *American Scientist*, **83**, pp. 269–70.

David Hodgson

Hume's Mistake

Hume claimed that anything that happens must either be causally determined or a matter of chance, and that a person is responsible only for choices caused by the person's character; so that if any sense is to made of free will and responsibility, it must be on the basis that they are compatible with determinism. In this paper I argue that Hume's claim depends on a covert assumption that whatever happens to any system in the world must be either the only development of the system which is consistent with causal laws, or else a development which is random. I argue that it is a serious mistake to make such an assumption covertly; and that without this assumption, good sense can be made of a concept of free will and responsibility as being indeterministic, thereby providing a viable alternative to compatibilist views

It is philosophical and scientific orthodoxy that anything that happens in the world must either be causally determined or random. And many philosophers and scientists draw from this that, if any sense is to be made of human free will and responsibility, it must be on the basis that human choices and actions are cases of *deterministic* causation — because, it is said, random or chance occurrences cannot reasonably be regarded as exercises of free will for which a person may be responsible.

A contrary view, which I have supported in my book *The Mind Matters* (1991) and other writings, is that the causation we observe in the physical world, apparently progressing conformably with some combination of deterministic laws and randomness, is just one kind or mode or aspect of causation; and that there is in addition another kind or mode or aspect of causation operating in the conscious decisions and actions of human beings, and perhaps also of non-human animals. I call the former 'physical causation', the latter 'volitional causation' or 'choice'.[1] Then, a concept of free will as something neither deterministic nor random can be developed on the basis of the notion of volitional causation or choice.

The orthodox position on this kind of approach is that any causation involved in our conscious decisions and voluntary actions is nothing other than a type of, or a working out of, the ordinary physical causation of rules and randomness; or to put it another way, that the exercise of choice is just one of a number of levels of operation of physical causation.

---

[1] I have previously used the term 'agent causation'; but because of certain connotations of that expression, I now think it best to use a different term.

Journal of Consciousness Studies, **6**, No. 8–9, 1999, pp. 201–24

And many philosophers and scientists go further, and say that a notion of volitional causation or choice as being distinct from ordinary physical causation is inconceivable, or at least logically impossible; and that in any event such a notion could have no bearing on questions of free will and responsibility. There are two strands to the argument in support of this view, both of them exemplified in the writings of David Hume: (1) whatever happens must either be causally determined by its antecedents or else be a matter of chance; and (2) for a person to be responsible for an action which that person chooses, the choice must be caused by the person's character.

In this paper, I set out to show that this view is a serious mistake. Because of its close association with David Hume, I call it Hume's mistake.

I: Hume's Argument

Hume's argument (which I take from *An Enquiry Concerning Human Understanding* [1748], Section VIII) begins with the observation, based on Newton's physics, that when physical forces are applied to matter, the outcome is necessary in the sense that no other outcome is possible. However, he says, we *know* this only because of repeated observations of such occurrences, not because of any *logically* necessary connection between cause and effect.

In the same way, we repeatedly observe human beings behaving in similar ways in similar circumstances: pursuing happiness, avoiding pain, and so on. In so far as people behave differently in similar circumstances, this is because they have different characters; and so this is by no means inconsistent with regular conjunction of like causes and effects. Even when particular actions seem 'out of character', this does not mean that they are not the outcome of ordinary regular causation: rather, our difficulty in explaining them must be because of the 'minuteness and remoteness' of the causes, or 'the secret operation of contrary causes' — and Hume gives the analogy of a tiny piece of dust interfering with the proper functioning of a watch.

To Hume, there was no question of human reason interfering with the regular operation of causes in our motivation. Hume distinguished sharply between beliefs and desires, and argued that only desires could motivate us: reason could not prevent us acting in accordance with our desires, except by giving rise to a contrary desire; and we always act in accordance with the preponderance of our desires.

Our failure to acknowledge that our actions are determined in the same way as the processes of physical matter, Hume argued, is due to two factors.

(1) We tend to think there is a necessary connection between cause and effect in the physical world, and we see our own actions as *not* having any necessary connection with its antecedents in our character and circumstances. However, Hume claimed, there is no logically necessary connection between cause and effect in the physical world, just the regular conjunction of causes and effects — and the same is true of our actions.

(2) We sometimes seem to have a 'liberty of indifference' between alternative courses of action open to us, and still to be able to select between them. However, this feeling is unreliable and misleading; and when we reflect on what we and others have done, we can see that it was in fact the causal product of character and circumstances.

None of this, Hume argued, is inconsistent with personal liberty (by which Hume meant what we would call free will), because liberty means our power of acting according to the determinations of our will, that is, as we choose — even though our choice is in fact determined by causes. It is constraint, not determination by causes, which can deprive us of this liberty. If our actions were not determined by causes, then they could only be a matter of *chance*, so that they could not be an exercise of personal liberty. (Hume in fact asserted that chance has no existence; but even if, consistently with orthodox quantum mechanics, one accepts that there is objective chance in the world, in the sense of random events, one may agree that chance in that sense would not be conducive to what we ordinarily regard as choice.)

Hume went on to argue that his version of determinism was not inimical to our common-sense ideas of responsibility, but on the contrary was necessary to make sense of responsibility. This, he said, was for two main reasons.

(1) A person is not responsible for actions unless they proceed from a cause in the character or disposition of the person. The more premeditated an action is, the more we regard it as caused by the person's character and the more responsible we consider the person to be. On the other hand, we consider people less responsible for actions performed hastily.

(2) The imposition of rewards and punishments for actions for which we suppose people are responsible makes sense only if we believe that rewards and punishments have consistent and regular effects on their behaviour; that is, if we believe that the prospect of rewards for certain behaviour and the prospect of punishment for other behaviour will consistently influence people to engage in the former and to refrain from the latter.

II: More Recent Statements

Hume's approach has remained fashionable right up to the present, despite some persuasive opposition (e.g. Anscombe, 1971; Nozick, 1981; Flew and Vesey 1987). I will give some examples of more recent restatements by philosophers of essentially the same line of argument.

The most colourful of these is R.E. Hobart's 1934 article 'Free will as involving determinism and inconceivable without it'. Hobart writes:

> Indeterminism maintains that we need not be impelled to action by our wishes, that our active will need not be determined by them. Motives 'incline without necessitating'. We choose amongst the ideas of action before us, but need not choose solely according to the attraction of desire, in however wide a sense that word is used. Our inmost self may rise up in its autonomy and moral dignity, independently of motives and register its sovereign decree.
>
> Now, *in so far* as this 'interposition of the self' is undetermined, the act is not *its* act, it does not issue from any concrete continuing self; it is born at the moment, of nothing, hence it expresses no quality; it bursts into being from no source. The self does not register *its* decree, for the decree is not the product of just that 'it'. The self does not rise up in *its* moral dignity, for dignity is the quality of an enduring being influencing its actions, and therefore expressed by them, and that would be determination. *In proportion* as an act of volition starts of itself without cause it is exactly, so far as the freedom of the individual is concerned, as if it had been thrown into his mind from without — 'suggested' to him — by a freakish demon. . . . *In proportion* as it is undetermined, it is just as if his legs should suddenly spring up and carry him off where he did not prefer to go. Far from constituting freedom, that would mean, in the exact measure in which it took place, the loss of freedom. It would be an interference, and an utterly uncontrollable interference, with

his power of acting as he prefers. In fine, then, *just so far* as the volition is undetermined, the self can neither be praised nor blamed for it, since it is not the act of the self.

More prosaically, in 1956 Alfred Ayer wrote:

> But now we must ask how it is that I come to make my choice. Either it is an accident that I choose to act as I do or it is not. If it is an accident, then it is merely a matter of chance that I did not choose otherwise; and if it is merely a matter of chance that I did not choose otherwise, it is surely irrational to hold me morally responsible for choosing as I did. But if it is not an accident that I choose to do one thing rather than another, then presumably there is some causal explanation of my choice: and in that case we are led back to determinism.

And in 1961, J.J.C. Smart advanced a similar thesis in his article 'Free will, praise and blame'. He argued that every event is either causally determined or, if not, it is due to chance: there is no third possibility other than 'this event happened as a result of unbroken causal continuity', and 'this event happened by pure chance' (p. 296). That is, he contended, there is no logical room between determinism and chance.

Galen Strawson's 1986 book *Freedom and Belief* contains very full discussions of the first strand of Hume's argument. At pages 52–4 he expressly considers a 'Leibnizian' view that 'reasons for action affect agents' decisions, but in so doing only incline them towards, and do not necessitate them in, particular decisions to perform particular actions'. He asks: 'upon what, exactly, are the agent's decisions about actions now supposed to be based, other than upon its reasons?', and goes on:

> The trouble with the picture is familiar. If the agent is to be truly self-determining in action this cannot be because it has any *further* desires or principles of choice governing the decisions about how to act that it makes in the light of its *initial* desires or principles of choice. For it could not be truly self-determining with respect to these further desires or principles of choice either, any more than it could be self- determining with respect to its initial desires or principles of choice. But if it does not have any such further desires or principles of choice, then the claim that it exercises some special power of decision or choice becomes useless in the attempt to establish its freedom. For if it has no such desires or principles of choice governing what decisions it makes in the light of its initial reasons for action, then the decisions it makes are rationally speaking random: they are made by an agent-self that is, in its role as decision-maker, entirely non-rational in the present vital sense of 'rational' — it is reasonless, lacking any principles of choice or decision. The agent-self with its putative, freedom-creating power of *partially* reason-independent decision becomes a some entirely non-rational (reasons-independent) flip-flop of the soul.

Finally, as we will see, there are reflections of this same argument in recent criticisms of suggestions made by me and others that the indeterminism of quantum mechanics is relevant to freedom of the will.

III: Hume's Mistake

The fundamental mistake underlying Hume's position and that of his twentieth-century followers is that they assume without discussion or disclosure (indeed sometimes assume as if it were a logical necessity) something very close to what they claim to prove: they assume that whatever happens to any system must be either (1) the only development of the system which is consistent with universal and impersonal causal laws, or (2) a development which is random, albeit perhaps complying with probability parameters established by such laws. It is hardly surprising that, if you accept *that*, then choice, as something other than the physical causation of rules and randomness, will be excluded; but the most significant step in the argument is made covertly by an assumption which is given no justification.

The history of science since the time of Newton provides some explanation of why many philosophers have made this assumption, and why they apparently have not even realized it was an assumption that needed justification. In a word, this assumption seems to arise from (1) the progressive success of science in explaining the processes of the physical world in terms of laws of nature and randomness; (2) the fact that our brains are part of the physical world; and (3) the apparent dependence of our choices on processes in our brains of which we are unaware. Now these three factors provide arguments supporting the assumption underlying Hume's position, but they are far from conclusive — and there are contrary arguments which could be stronger. So the assumption should not have been made covertly: rather, it should have been presented as a hypothesis to be confirmed or refuted.

Associated with this fundamental mistake are a number of other mistakes apparent in Hume's discussion, and at least implicit in the work of his followers.

First, there is the assimilation of motives for action to physical forces in Newtonian physics. Forces in Newtonian physics are measurable, commensurable, and conclusive: any piece of matter will necessarily be accelerated precisely as required by the vector sum of all forces acting on it. Hume claimed that we are motivated only by desires; and he assumed that desires like forces are commensurable, and that we always act in accordance with the preponderance of our desires. Both of these assumptions are questionable, indeed I would say false; and it is a serious mistake not to recognize the need to justify them. Alternative views, namely that our motives are diverse and incommensurable, that motives are characteristically inconclusive, and that a preponderance of motivation is established only by a choice, are ignored by Hume and his followers, or at most given lip service only.

Second, there is the associated assumption that, if reasons alone do not determine a choice in this quasi-Newtonian way, then reasons plus something else must determine it in this way; and that otherwise the outcome has to be random. This ignores the possibility that outcomes may be selected by agents on the basis of non-conclusive reasons — the selection requiring a qualitative judgement, rather than either a quantitative computation or a mere factual preponderance of some quantity of 'desire'.

The hold that this assumption has on philosophers today is illustrated by the lengths to which even philosophers who are sympathetic to the idea of free will have gone, in their efforts to explain how choice could work. In order to account for a choice to do one thing rather than another, which gives effect to some reasons and not others, these writers have felt it necessary to invoke *something else*, other than the reasons and the choice — a *clincher*, as it were — to explain why one set of non-conclusive reasons prevailed over another set of non-conclusive reasons.

For example, Harry Frankfurt (1971) and Charles Taylor (1976) suggest that there is a higher-level evaluation of our conflicting reasons; although this of course gives rise to the question of what determines the result of *this* higher-level evaluation. Thomas Nagel (1986, pp. 116–17) suggests that the only way to complete an explanation of why an agent acted for certain reasons, rather than refraining from acting for other reasons, is to trace the cause or explanation into the formative causes of the agent's character (cf. Hodgson, 1991, pp. 391–2). And Robert Kane (1985, p. 85) seems to suggest that the choice must be clinched by something akin to coin-tossing or dice-rolling; although in a more recent book (1996), Kane has moved to a position closer to my own: I will specifically consider this book shortly (in Section V).

A recent example of this quest for a clincher is McCall (1994, p. 277), where we find the following:

> As we saw above, an indeterministic chess-playing machine could employ a randomiser to create options, but if so the selection of one of these options to be acted upon was by sheer chance. This is not good enough. The brain not only needs to create options, using something like the indeterministic intermediate-level mechanism just described, but it also needs to evaluate its options and arrive at an order of preference. It then selects its best option and acts on it. Now the process of evaluation and the selection of the best option need not be indeterministic. One would hope in fact that they were not: that the establishment of a ranked list of options was in accordance with set aims and goals, and that the brain could use a rational procedure like the hedonistic or utilitarian calculus, or the principle of universalizability and the categorical imperative, or for that matter a rigid and complete set of rules which in casuistic fashion covered every conceivable alternative, to determine its best course of action. The upshot would be that the initial indeterminism that created the choice-set was subordinated to a higher selection process which could be entirely deterministic.

To me, it seems clear that, if the supposedly open alternatives are set up only for a selection to take place by a deterministic process, then there is no reason why the alternatives cannot be set up by a pseudo-random (deterministic) process, as suggested by Dennett (1984) — and we are no closer to anything like genuine choice.

Third, there is the contention that responsibility requires that actions be caused (along with the operation of desires in this quasi-Newtonian way) by *character*, and that the only alternative is *chance*. This is at the heart of Hobart's contentions, as well as Hume's. What it ignores is that an action could perhaps be caused by a person's character in the sense that it is chosen by the person from alternatives *limited by* the person's character, on the basis of non-conclusive reasons which appear as they do and carry the persuasive force that they do *because of* the person's character. The choice could then be not predetermined yet not random; and the person's character could be important to the choice because it limits the available alternatives and affects how they are presented and thus inter alia how *easy* or how *hard* it is for the person to make one choice rather than another.

Fourth, there is the suggestion that without determinism, there could not be the broad predictability of human behaviour, both in general and in relation to a particular person, or the susceptibility of persons to encouragement by reward or deterrence by punishment. This ignores the obvious fact that, even if motives never necessitate actions by normal persons, they can *very strongly* incline them to act in certain ways; so that it may be very hard for them to act otherwise, and very unlikely that they will do so.

Mistakes of this kind are made even in Galen Strawson's careful discussion. He assumes (1986, p. 54) that a decision, on the basis of reasons which do not necessitate the decision, must either be governed by 'further desires or principles of choice', or else be random as 'lacking any principles of choice or decision'. This is a false dichotomy, because it assumes what may not be the case, namely that the only possible connection between reasons and decision is one of *determination* (in which reasons determine decisions) rather than *choice* (in which decisions are made by an agent on the basis of non-conclusive reasons). That is, like Hobart, Ayer and Smart, Strawson ignores the possibility that choice is a mode of causation in which an agent resolves non-conclusive reasons; not for any *other* reason, but by means of a capacity, which all normal human beings have — and can't help having — to make such choices.[2] And in suggesting that any undetermined part of a choice would have to be non-rational, Strawson ignores the possibility that human rationality itself may not be fully captured by rules and may thus be partly indeterministic — a possibility that I have strongly supported in Chapter 5 of *The Mind Matters* and in Hodgson (1995).

IV: How It Could Be?

Given that our brains are physical systems which, like other physical systems, appear to change over time in accordance with universal and impersonal laws, how *could* choice be anything other than the working out of such laws?

1. The general picture

It would seem that choice must either be (1) inconsistent, or (2) consistent, with the physical causation of rules and randomness; and if consistent must either (a) select the *only* result consistent with physical causation or else (b) select between two or more results all consistent with physical causation. Alternative (1) seems unlikely: although our understanding of the brain is far from complete, I think we can be fairly confident that no actual violations of physical laws are involved in volitional causation or choice. Alternative (2a) is in effect Hume's position, and that of mainstream science and philosophy today. Alternative (2b) is the alternative I wish to explore.

The general picture that I suggest is as follows. What I propose is that, while the human brain-and-mind is a single system, the way this system changes over time in normal persons is best understood in terms of two overlapping causal histories, each of which is intellectually respectable and valid; but which are complementary, and are mutually irreducible in the sense that neither can be fully explained in terms of the other. One is the *objective* history of the brain, to which the concept of physical causation is applicable; while the other is the *subjective* history of the mind, to which the concept of volitional causation or choice is applicable. I suggest that each of these two histories is incomplete on its own, yet not inconsistent with the other. On the one hand, while the objective features of the brain which correlate with conscious experiences and actions will undoubtedly come to be specified with increasing accuracy, a person's conscious actions may not be uniquely determined by the development over time of those 'neural correlates' in accordance with universal laws; and on the other hand, while a person's conscious actions are uniquely determined by the person's choice, made for reasons, those reasons may not capture all the unconscious or non-conscious factors which contribute to the actions.

2. An example

To put this in more concrete terms. Suppose that I am trying to decide what to do with $500 which I have. It occurs to me that I could spend it on a new amplifier for my sound system, or send it for famine relief; or buy a cheaper amplifier for $250 and

---

[2] Since writing this, I have come across two somewhat similar arguments against Strawson (see Abelson, 1988, pp. 182–4; O'Connor ,1995, pp. 188–9).

send \$250 for famine relief; or save it for later. Suppose that, in addition to thinking about such things as the unsatisfactory performance of my present amplifier and how much better music would sound from a new one, and the needs of the people affected by the famine and how I should help satisfy them, I also think such things as 'famine relief will be provided whether I contribute or not', 'very little of what I contribute would get to where it is needed', and 'aid is counter-productive because it leads to a vicious circle of dependency'. Let's say I decide to spend the \$500 on an amplifier.

3. Resolving inconclusive reasons

The first point to make is that however fully and honestly I try to express my reasons, no verbal expression of my reasons will ever be conclusive of one result or another. So far as my subjective motivation can be expressed, before decision there are only inconclusive reasons, and it is my decision which makes some of them prevail over others. Yet, assuming I have expressed my reasons fully, there are no other reasons for my decision. My decision was a choice which resolved the issue, not a matter of chance: apparently, what was conclusive was not a further reason which arbitrated between the inconclusive conflicting reasons, nor was it a chance occurrence — rather, it was a choice based on these very reasons and no others, notwithstanding that they were, prior to the choice, inconclusive. Seemingly, *that is the nature of reasons* and *that is the nature of choice*: there is no clincher, other than the choice itself.

It might be argued that, although I cannot *express* my subjective reasons in a way that makes them conclusive, they must in fact come with 'weights' which, although I am unable to measure them, do in fact determine the issue. Certainly, my reasons do *feel* to me to be more or less persuasive, to press strongly or not so strongly. Even if the respective strengths or weights of reasons cannot be measured by me and are not commensurable to me, it can be argued that my reasons must have neural correlates with properties which, like any physical properties, are quantitative and sufficiently commensurable to be subject to the quantitative laws that govern all physical systems: this is in substance the mainstream view, and I cannot say it is not a possible view.

What I do say however is that another view is also possible — and in fact I have argued in *The Mind Matters* and elsewhere that this other view is the more reasonable and probable. In short, if a choice is in fact just the working out of quantitative physical laws acting on physical systems with quantitative physical properties, why are there any subjective feelings at all?

4. Character and choice

It might also be argued that my account leaves out the role of my character in the process of choice: the reasons affect me as they do because of my character, and my character in turn is embodied in the physical system which is my brain. It is my character which makes the outcome of decisions like this reasonably predictable: if I am a selfish person, the amplifier will win hands down; while if I am altruistic, the famine relief will win.

I accept that my brain is the immediate physical manifestation of my character, and that my brain has physical properties relevant to my choice which are expressive of my character. These physical properties will limit the alternatives open to me: it is because I am as I am that the alternatives which occur to me are to spend the money on an amplifier or on famine relief. These properties will affect the way I see the alternatives, and the appeal which the conflicting reasons have: the more selfish I am, the stronger and more persuasive will seem the reasons favouring the amplifier; the more altruistic I am, the stronger and more persuasive will seem the reasons favouring famine relief. This will mean in turn that the likelihood of one or the other outcome is affected by my character — but it does not mean that any outcome must be inevitable or predetermined.

Rather, a choice is made by me, a person having a certain character and also a capacity to choose — and since I have this capacity to choose, it is I, and not just my character, that makes the choice. I suggest that people are no different from each other in respect of their capacity to choose, except in so far as there are differences in their characters, manifested in their physical brains and thus in the alternatives available to them and the way these alternatives appear. And if this is the case, then there is no unfairness in attributing responsibility for choices to persons, considered as having both character and capacity to choose — with *degrees* of responsibility affected by those advantages and disadvantages of character which are beyond the person's control. I say a little more about this in Section IV. 8.

Furthermore, there is a possible and plausible physical correlate to this picture. If orthodox quantum mechanics is broadly correct, it is conceivable that, immediately prior to my decision, my brain is in a superposition of states (cf. Nozick, 1981, pp. 298–9): if the decision is ultimately between just the two alternatives of spending the whole of the $500 on the amplifier or giving it all to famine relief, the superposition could be of just two states, one for each alternative. If I am a selfish person, the quantum mechanical probabilities of the two states might be 0.95 for the amplifier and 0.05 for famine relief; if I am altruistic, they could be the other way round. When one result occurs, according to quantum mechanics this will be a random event within those probability parameters; but from the subjective point of view, it could be my choice, with the actual choice having been made likely (but not inevitable) or unlikely (but not impossible) by the felt strength or persuasiveness of the reasons. On this approach, the objective probabilities determined by the physical aspect of the causal process could be broadly reflected in the felt strength of the reasons operative in the mental-volitional aspect of the causal process — although of course, whereas objective probabilities are commensurable, I am proposing that the felt strengths of different reasons are not commensurable, and that the result requires a choice by me.

5. Rationalization

Next, it could be argued that this account presupposes that I have a clear understanding of my reasons or motives, whereas in fact there will be reasons or motives operating of which I am unaware, or not fully or accurately aware. For example, the three reasons given above in quotes, although seen by me as genuine reasons, may more fairly be considered rationalizations produced unconsciously to justify a selfish decision. If I am a selfish person, given to rationalization and self-justification, then this may be a more accurate account of how I made the choice than one which presents the choice as a wholly conscious resolution of genuine well-understood reasons.

I see this as a matter of degree. Undoubtedly, we are not altogether clear-sighted about our true motivation, but this does not mean that our choices are not genuine choices based on the reasons as we see them to be. In my example, if I do have sufficient insight into my own character and motivation, I may question my reliance on the quoted reasons, and ask whether I am not just rationalizing a selfish choice. To under-take this questioning would itself be a choice between alternatives thrown up by my character, made on the basis of further non-conclusive reasons; and the pursuit and outcome of this questioning may involve further such choices. In general, the better my understanding of myself and my motivation, the more complete is my authorship of and my responsibility for my choice: this is the place I see for the higher level of evaluation of conflicting reasons, considered in Frankfurt (1971) and Taylor (1976). However, I would argue that all normal adult human beings have sufficient insight into their motivation to be regarded as responsible for their voluntary choices and actions.

More broadly, I believe that there is choice wherever there is consciousness: the very function of consciousness is to allow for choice from available alternatives on the basis of consciously-felt reasons. Thus, if as I believe at least some non-human animals are conscious, it would follow that these animals make choices. But I suggest that their rationality and their insight into their own motivation is insufficient for them to be considered as having free will or responsibility for their actions; whereas the rationality and insight of normal adult human beings, even though far from com-plete or perfect, is generally sufficient for them to be considered as having free will and responsibility.

6. *Longer-term choice processes*

I noted a moment ago that in the course of choosing what to do with my $500, I might pursue subsidiary questions which themselves involve choices. I suggest that this in fact exemplifies a very usual feature of our decision-making. In any extended process of making a choice, it would be surprising if the alternatives which were possible at the beginning of the process, and which then had certain objective probabilities, all remained available with the same probabilities at the instant before the final decision; and if only at the final decision was there suddenly just one elimination of all but the chosen alternative. A far more plausible scenario would be that throughout the process, volitional causation was adjusting the probabilities of alternatives, eliminat-ing some and introducing or varying the probabilities of others; so that immediately before the choice, physical causation could give a very high objective probability for an alternative which had a much lower probability at the outset of the process, and the ultimate selection of this alternative could then follow almost as of course.

Indeed, in my example it could be that I have over many years been thinking about the conflicting claims of self-interest and altruism; and my decision about the $500 could be an outcome of many long processes of volitional causation during which very many intermediate choices have been made. It could also be that, if objective probabilities for my decision about the $500 could have been calculated at the outset of these processes, they would have favoured one result (say, famine relief), whereas immediately before the decision, because of the intermediate choices, they very strongly favoured the other result (the amplifier). Then, my choice of the amplifier could fairly be regarded as a free choice for which I am responsible, even though by the time it came it was almost inevitable.

This can be applied to an example discussed elsewhere in this context (see Dennett, 1984, p. 133). Martin Luther's decision to defy the Church of Rome can be consid-ered a free choice, for which he was responsible, even if at the time of his final decision he spoke substantially the truth when he said 'Here I stand. I can do no other' — because it was the outcome of a long process of choice-making in the course of which many intermediate choices had been made, and it was these intermediate choices which made the ultimate choice virtually inevitable (cf. Kane, 1996, pp. 38–40).

And this line allows a further response to Hume's point about responsibility and character. I have argued that character could be important as both limiting alternatives for choice and affecting how they are presented, rather than by simply pre-determining what is done or chosen, leaving the person (not just his or her character) responsible to a greater or lesser degree for the action or choice; and this means in turn that, in so far as the person's character has been affected by prior choices of this kind, the person has some responsibility for character as well. A similar point made by Aristotle is dismissed by philosopher Bernard Williams (1995, p. 27) as 'hopeless', on the grounds that it 'shifts the question back' and 'offers very rough justice'. However, rough justice is better than no justice; and so long as there is some responsibility for all choices, the justice is in fact not all that rough. So I think Aristotle was on the right track, and that Williams is led astray by Hume's mistake.

7. Kinds of motives

My $500 example was one where there were two main motives operating, one being a non-moral motive and the other being a moral or altruistic motive; and indeed I formulated the example as one where there were two conflicting motives plainly of different types, so that their incommensurability was obvious. However, I want to make it clear that I am not saying (as have some philosophers, such as C.A. Campbell, 1951) that there are just two types of motives, namely non-moral motives or 'desires', and moral motives or 'duties': rather I say that there is no sharp distinction between non-moral and moral motives, that there are many different kinds of motives, and that it is a very general characteristic of motives that they are incommensurable and inconclusive.

To give some examples. A runner in a marathon is in pain after 38 kilometres and wants to stop running so the pain will stop, but is determined to finish: there are two conflicting motives here, both basically selfish, but not commensurable. I am at a restaurant deciding between the fish and the beef, I generally prefer beef but I had beef yesterday, and I choose the fish: again, I do not believe the conflicting motives are commensurable. Nor do I believe that the choice in either case is random, although the opposing reasons are inconclusive and there are no other reasons. Of course, sometimes we do something akin to mentally tossing a coin because it is more important that a decision be made than that it go one way or the other — as it was for Buridan's ass, which supposedly died of hunger and thirst because it could not choose between two sources of food and water located at points equally distant from it — but I do say that is not the way we generally resolve conflicting inconclusive reasons.

We also sometimes have a choice as to what to *believe*, as well as what to *do*; and in these cases the conflicting reasons may have little to do with either self-interest or altruism, but may still be inconclusive and incommensurable. This is particularly clear in the case of a judge deciding the facts in a court case: she has to reach a belief, at least on the balance of probabilities, as to whether the facts are such as to entitle the plaintiff to a court order of the kind that the plaintiff is seeking. The conflicting evidence and arguments are generally inconclusive: the clincher is not some further reason nor the tossing of a coin, but the conscious decision based on these very reasons. This matter is considered in Chapter 5 of *The Mind Matters* and Hodgson (1995):[3] the discussion there strongly supports the view that rationality is not fully captured by rules, and so undermines Strawson's assumption that indeterminism implies nonrationality.

My examples do not show that the orthodox view is wrong: what they do show, I contend, is that it is wrong to suggest that no other view is even possible, on the basis that anything that happens must as a matter of logic be predetermined or random. It is that suggestion, exemplified in Hume's writing, which is a fundamental mistake that infects and distorts much current thinking about the mind in general, and about freedom and responsibility in particular.

8. Responsibility

An important feature of this account is that it has an answer to the basic dilemma about responsibility, which is strongly expressed by Galen Strawson (1986, esp. at pp. 311–12):

> (1) There is a clear and fundamental sense in which no being can be truly self-determining in respect of its character and motivation in such a way as to be truly responsible for how it is in respect of character and motivation.
>
> (2) When we act, at a given time, the way we act is, in some quite straightforward sense, a function of the way we then are, in respect of character and motivation. We act as we act *because of* how we then are, in respect of character and motivation.
>
> (3) It follows that there is a fundamental sense in which we cannot possibly be truly responsible for our actions. For we cannot be truly responsible for the way we are, and we act as we act because of the way we are.

My account accepts that nothing an agent does or can do *at the time of any choice or action* can make the agent responsible for what alternatives are then available to the agent, for the way those alternatives then appeal, or indeed for having the capacity to choose between them — but claims that, leaving aside any question of responsibility for *these* matters, the agent can still be responsible for *the way the agent exercises the capacity to choose.* The way the agent is, in respect of character and motivation, does not determine what the agent does: it only determines what the alternatives are and how they appeal. The agent is not responsible for having the capacity to choose between these alternatives, but is not constrained in how that capacity is exercised, *even by the way the agent then is in respect of character and motivation*; and so the agent (and no-one and nothing else) is responsible for the way that capacity is exercised. That responsibility may be greater or less, by reason of the nature of the choice posed by the way agent now is — the harder it is, by reason of the agent's inclinations, for the agent to make the 'right' choice, the less blameworthy will be the 'wrong' choice — but on this view, normal adult human beings always have some responsibility for their choices and voluntary actions (see Hodgson, 1996/1998).

---

[3] In this article, I argue in some detail that judicial fact-finding cannot be explained in terms of application of rules, such as Bayes' theorem.

And this means in turn that the agent may have some responsibility *through prior choices* for the way the agent now is in respect of character and motivation, and thus for presently-operating reasons and the way they appeal — thereby vindicating Aristotle against Williams.

V: Robert Kane

In Section III, in discussing the search for a clincher, I suggested that Kane (1985) proposed that conflicts between competing inconclusive reasons were resolved at random. In his 1996 book *The Significance of Free Will*, Robert Kane has substantially developed and modified his views on free will, and has dealt carefully and at length with suggestions like this one of mine. In this Section, I will make a brief comparison of Kane's approach with my own, which may be of interest to readers familiar with Kane's book: others may prefer to go straight on to Section VI.

There is in fact little if anything I disagree with in Kane's development of his account of free will in Chapters 8–10 of his book: indeed, that part of the book endorses four of the key contentions that I argued for in earlier writings — as well as in this paper.

(1) The contention that, prior to a choice being made, an agent's reasons are characteristically inconclusive, inter alia because they are incommensurable; and that it is the agent's choice or decision which resolves the issue (Hodgson, 1991, pp. 133–5; Hodgson, 1994). Kane endorses the idea of incommensurability at p. 167; and at p. 133, he postulates that in situations where an agent has to choose between alternative courses of action and has reasons or motives supporting each alternative, the agent *makes* one set of reasons or motives prevail over the others by *deciding*.

(2) The contention that what the physical perspective can only treat as a chance occurrence may correctly be seen from the mental or experiential perspective as an agent's choice (Hodgson, 1991, pp. 389–93, 444–7; Hodgson 1994). Kane says, at p. 147, that from the physical perspective, *free will looks like chance* — that from a physical perspective, there is just an indeterministic chaotic process with probabilistic outcomes; but experientially considered, the process is the agent's effort of will and the single outcome is the agent's choice.

(3) The contention that the problem of free will is closely interlinked with the problems of consciousness and of the indeterminism disclosed by quantum mechanics (Hodgson, 1991, *passim* and esp. pp. 393–4; Hodgson, 1994). Kane asks, at p. 148, 'How can a physical process of the brain be at the same time a consciously experienced effort of will?'; and suggests that this is just part of the mystery of 'how neural firings in the brain could be conscious mental events'. And on pp. 150–1, he suggests it is also implicated with the general problem of indeterminacy-in-nature introduced by quantum physics.

(4) The contention that the objective probabilities for various outcomes are to some extent reflected in the subjectively-felt strength of reasons; and that rational decisions may nevertheless be made in favour of actions with lower antecedent probabilities (Hodgson, 1991, pp. 392–3). At p. 177, Kane points out that antecedent probabilities of available alternatives do not necessarily indicate which of them are more or less rational for the agent to choose.

However, Kane's position might seem at variance with mine in that, whereas he apparently eschews special forms of agency or causation, I treat the distinction between physical causation and volitional causation as central to my argument in this paper. But I believe that a closer consideration shows that his rejection of special forms of agency or causation is qualified in a way which makes it less than clear; and that the latter part of his book, where he comes close to my position, does involve an implicit introduction of a special form of agency or causation.

In order to develop this point, it is necessary first to say a word about terminology. Although Kane argues that free will, in the usual sense of involving available alternatives and substantial responsibility (or 'ultimate responsibility', as Kane puts it) is incompatible with determinism, he nevertheless acknowledges that there are legitimate senses of what he calls '*free agency*', not involving ultimate responsibility, that are compatible with determinism.

At p. 115, Kane notes that, in order to account for how an agent can choose rationally, voluntarily, and with voluntary control, advocates of free will have conjectured that there must be some explanatory factor *over and above* past circumstances and laws of nature; and that they have looked for this factor in special forms of agency or causation. At p. 116, Kane eschews any appeal to any special forms of agency or causation *that are not also needed by deterministic accounts of free agency*. But determinists who accept reductionism can simply claim that free agency just *is* a particular kind of working out of past circumstances, laws of nature, and chance, expressed in a different language; whereas, as noted above, Kane argues that agents *make* one set of reasons prevail over another, and that although this looks like chance from a physical perspective it is, experientially considered, the agent's choice. So surely he is saying, as I do, that in the exercise of free will *something more* is happening over and above the working out of past circumstances, laws of nature, and chance — this 'something more' involving the conscious activity of the agent.

Now Kane may accept this and still claim that it does not involve a special form of agency or causation not also needed by deterministic accounts of free agency; but if so, he needs to explain how the causation involved in *making something happen* relates to the rules-and-randomness causation presupposed by the physical sciences. Perhaps Kane assumes, as I do, that there is a single ongoing causal process involved in the exercise of free will, and perhaps he is looking for a unitary concept for, and a unitary account of, this physical-and-mental causation. But I think it is preferable to recognise that we do not at present have an adequate language for such a unitary account, and to make the best use we can of the concepts which we actually do have. Kane accepts, as I do, that agents *cause* things by *doing* them, in a way not apparent to the physical viewpoint — and I say that what is involved here is best classified and developed with reference to the distinction I have drawn between physical causation and volitional causation.

One other significant difference between Kane's position and mine is that he appears to distinguish sharply between theoretical reasoning or deciding what to believe, and practical reasoning or deciding what to do (pp. 22–3), and he considers free will only in relation to the practical reasoning; whereas I closely link free will with consciousness and plausible reasoning generally, and I suggest that volitional causation can be exercised in deciding what to believe, as well as what to do. This brings out what I see as the important link between volitional causation and rationality; and it makes possible an account of volitional causation and free will that makes them a natural and vital part of human activity, and understandable as a product of evolution.

VI: Quantum Mechanical Randomness and Choice

An echo of Hume's mistake can be found in recent attacks on suggestions that quantum mechanics may be relevant to free will and responsibility. The idea that the indeterminism of quantum mechanics leaves room for the operation of free will was put forward as long ago as 1927 by Arthur Eddington (1929, Ch14); and more recently it has been supported by people such as John Eccles (1994) and myself (Hodgson, 1991; 1994). One standard response to this suggestion has been that the exercise of choice is actually incompatible with the randomness which is the only indeterminism postulated by quantum mechanics.

In *The Mind Matters*, I argued that what, to the mental viewpoint, was a choice made between available alternatives for non-conclusive reasons, might appear to the physical viewpoint as the outcome of a combination of deterministic and random processes. I suggested (Hodgson, 1991, p. 392) that 'the quantum physical probabilities of the alternatives [for choice] may be related to the consciously-felt weight of competing reasons for the different actions':

> Where the alternative which occurs is an action which was objectively highly probable, one might have a case of an action with small 'mental input', an action done virtually by habit or as of course. Where the alternative which occurs is an action which was objectively improbable, perhaps one could have a case of concentration, effort, exercise of 'will-power'. Where a decision has to be made between alternatives of objectively similar probability, perhaps the weighing, judgemental aspect of decision-making is especially exercised.

I noted the standard response of incompatibility (pp. 392–3):

> In similar vein, there is a reference in Gomes (1978: 450) to an argument by Schrödinger to the effect that quantum physics is in fact inconsistent with free choices being made between superposed alternatives of quantum states, because those free choices could violate the statistical predictions of quantum physics. Even if this were correct, it would not be conclusive: it could simply mean that, when choices are made, the 'known' as represented in the relevant state function is not all there is to know, because these is a mental element involved which cannot be so represented. In any event, the argument seems to overlook that every choice is a unique event: each person is unique, and a matter for choice cannot be precisely one which has previously faced the person (that would itself be a difference!). Accordingly, the quantum physical superposition of alternatives corresponding to each choice must itself be a single unique highly complicated quantum state; so that there could never be a series of like state reductions in which statistical effects could be disclosed.

In his review of my book, Oxford philosopher Michael Lockwood (1991) took up this objection:

> [T]he widespread occurrence of 'improbable' outcomes, even with respect to individually unrepeatable situations, would still, in aggregate, violate the quantum mechanical statistical algorithm. Thus, if the quantum statistics are to be preserved, exercisers of Hodgson's brand of free will would have to be subject to some sort of non-local mutual

constraint — rather like contestants in a race, each of whom may in some sense have the ability to win, even though none can do so save to the exclusion of the others. (Perhaps we have here the basis of a novel approach to the problem of evil!).

The incompatibility argument is also raised in the review of my book by Jeffrey Barrett (1994).

John Eccles (1994) proposed that exocytosis (the discharge of neurotransmitters across synapses) could be influenced by quantum-scale events. In his review of this book, biologist David Wilson (1995) again raised the incompatibility argument:

> It is doubtful that the trigger mechanism for exocytosis requires so little in the way of physical movement, but there is an even greater difficulty with this model. There is no way it can avoid violating the requirement of randomness in such quantum mechanical events. Human intentions are quite nonrandom, and even a single intentional movement, say of an arm and hand to lift an object, would require the firing of a number of cortical neurons in a strictly nonrandom way. It would be like a nonrandom radioactive decay of atoms, a clear violation of physical law. It appears that the Eccles model includes the difficulty that all interactionist dualist models seem to share — violation of physical law where the nonphysical mind is supposed to influence the physical world.

The argument is also found in Chalmers (1996, Ch. 4).

I do not think that any of these writers has answered my points that (1) the felt strength of reasons, and thus the free choices based on them, could tend to follow quantum mechanical probabilities, (2) the choice of an open but improbable outcome could be due to some mental property which the quantum state vector can take no account of, and (3) the unrepeatability of situations of choice would preclude measurable departure from the quantum mechanical algorithm.

Only Lockwood really addresses these points; and even he deals only with the third of them, arguing that, because my suggestion could involve many unique events which were improbable, there could in aggregate be a measurable departure from the quantum mechanical algorithm.

On that point, I do accept that quantum mechanics gives probabilities for individual events, and that the quantum mechanical statistical algorithm could be violated by the combined (im)probabilities of many individual events of different kinds. But we are not considering just *any* individual events: we are considering *unique* events of *extreme complexity*; and I question whether quantum mechanics, with its holistic approach, even permits the assignment of definitive probabilities to such events. While in reductionist Newtonian physics there can always be a calculation to take account of any feature of a situation that has never occurred before, quantum mechanics says that the properties of parts of a system depend on the properties of the whole as well as vice versa; so there must surely be extreme difficulty, if not impossibility, in assigning definitive probabilities to unique events of the complexity involved in human choices.

And of course there are in addition my two other points. I need not elaborate here the first point — that significant conflict with quantum mechanics is unlikely if, as seems plausible, the felt strength of reasons in a general way tends to reflect quantum mechanical probabilities — except to say that these probabilities would, consistently with what I have just said, be quantum mechanical probabilities determined *leaving out of account* any unique unprecedented features of the whole situation of each individual choice.

However, there is more I should say about the second point — that there could be a contribution from a mental property — which relates this point to the other two points. It has been suggested by philosopher David Griffin (1997, p. 255) that the randomness of quantum mechanics may be a manifestation of a *spontaneity* which is a very general feature of the universe. Thus, spontaneity may be manifested as randomness in systems that are relatively simple, like individual particles of matter or radiation, or aggregates of such particles in which randomness is either preserved or cancelled out. However, in systems which are complex and organised appropriately, this spontaneity could plausibly be manifested as a kind of indeterministic self-organisation; and in systems with the complexity and organisation of certain living organisms, spontaneity could be manifested as volitional causation of the kind I am postulating. On this approach, quantum mechanics could not deal fully with spontaneity in systems having this much complexity and organisation, at least without being modified or supplemented; yet would not be violated in relation to any of the systems to which it has successfully been applied to date.

I believe the incompatibility argument assumes an interpretation of quantum mechanics which has the consequence that the question of choice and free will is begged. In considering the problem of free will, a central question is whether or not there might be such a thing as a choice between genuinely open alternatives, made for non-conclusive reasons. If it is assumed that quantum mechanics means that everything *must* always change over time randomly within rule-governed probability parameters (i.e. that quantum mechanics *compels* randomness), then this assumption immediately excludes genuine choice and free will: this is Hume's mistake again. I suggest that, particularly where the interpretation of quantum mechanics is controversial, a more scientific approach would be to hypothesise the existence of choice and free will, and to see if a conflict with any reasonable interpretation of quantum mechanics could be demonstrated by experiment.

Now the standard interpretation of quantum mechanics postulates that events occur at random within the probability parameters given by the rules of quantum mechanics. Those rules may give such a high probability for some result (say, the decay of between one quarter and three quarters of one billion atoms of a radioactive substance during the half life of the substance in question) that any different result would be considered so improbable as to conflict decisively with the rules of quantum mechanics (even though, on the many-worlds interpretation of quantum mechanics favoured by many physicists and cosmologists — and Michael Lockwood — there must be numerous infinities of minds or points of view which are actually observing such things all the time!). Even if the rules of quantum mechanics indicate an equal probability of two outcomes of a particular experiment, so that no result of an individual experiment could conceivably conflict with the rules of quantum mechanics, conflict with quantum mechanics could emerge from many repetitions of this experiment. Thus, suppose one hundred such experiments are conducted, and the numbers of each result noted, and that this is repeated ten thousand times: quantum mechanics would predict that the results would be grouped in a bell-shaped curve centred on the 50/50 result. A result very different from this would be possible, but the probability of such a result could be so small that it would be considered as conflicting decisively with quantum mechanics.

Could the hypothesis of free will be shown thus to conflict with the rules of quantum mechanics? Having regard to my three points, the possibility of a demonstrated conflict between free will and quantum mechanics seems remote indeed. It should also be kept in mind that a quite improbable event may be the result of a number of probable events; so that if, for example, an outcome required a combination of four events, each having an independent probability of 0.7, then the probability of the outcome would be only about 0.24. So if a free choice of a particular result required a combination of possible events, then a quite improbable choice could result from a combination of quite probable events, a combination which was itself no less probable than any other single combination of such events and/or their alternatives.

Or, to take another approach, suppose that psychological experiments gave results which suggested consistent statistics concerning 'choices' made by persons in particular circumstances, but randomness within those statistics. This could not be taken as suggesting that each individual case was not a genuine choice of the person concerned. Although the psychological testing could do no more than give statistics, it could well be that in each case the person chose between genuinely open alternatives, with the choice resolving the non-conclusive reasons supporting each alternative — and that the choice in each case could, consistently with all applicable universal laws of nature, have been different.

A complaint could be made that I have dodged the issue of whether (1) the quantum mechanical probabilities are correct and in the long run a series of choices will always fit the probabilities perfectly, or (2) in some cases the quantum mechanical probabilities are overridden by choices and thus made incorrect. I have indeed not answered this question, because I think it is at this stage the wrong question, for reasons I have given. These reasons show that the real question at present is whether there can be a plausible account of the operation of choice and free will which is compatible with the broad picture of physical causation suggested by quantum mechanics; and the task of doing this is far less daunting than that of reconciling free will with the determinism of classical physics. It is certainly not ruled out by the argument that quantum mechanical randomness is inconsistent with choice.

VII: Chess, Life and Superlife

The general shape of an account of choice which is compatible with physical causation as suggested by quantum mechanics can be approached by considering analogies provided by games.

1. Chess

One early use of that kind of analogy was by Gilbert Ryle in *The Concept of Mind*: he suggested (Ryle, 1949, p. 77) that we should not be concerned about what he called 'the bogy of mechanism'; and he likened the laws of nature to the rules of the game of chess, pointing out the scope which is left in that game for the exercise of intelligence and choice. However, contrary to the main thesis of Ryle's book, that analogy in fact suggests a kind of *dualism*. If one took the constituents of the physical world to be like a chessboard and chess pieces, the laws of nature to be like the rules of chess, and the development over time of the world to be like the progress of a game of chess, then one would have to postulate something over and above the physical world and the laws of nature — something making choices between alternatives left open by the laws of nature — if one were to explain what goes on in this world; just as one has to postulate players making choices to explain what goes on in a game of chess.

Suppose that some human scientists, to whom the game of chess was unknown, somehow gained access to a universe, distinct from their own, which so far as they could ascertain consisted entirely of what we would understand be myriad games of chess played competently (with reasonable skill, and no illegal moves) to a finish (no resignations or agreed draws). The space of that universe would be vast numbers of chessboards, the fundamental particles would be various kinds of chess pieces (in two colours); there would be successive discrete time-like steps, and also discrete whole processes corresponding to whole chess games.

The scientists would work out rules governing the movement of the various particles, and rules determining when each process came to an end (and the board in question returned to what they would recognise as an initial configuration). They would work out (1) what moves were possible for particles that we know as pawns, bishops, knights, etc.; (2) that, from the beginning to the end of a process, one particle moves in each time step, and different coloured particles move in successive time steps; (3) how particles can be caused to disappear (can be 'captured'); (4) that the particle we know as a king (of either colour), alone of all particles, cannot move to any position where it could be captured by a particle of the other colour; and (5) that a process ends when a king can be captured in the next move by a particle of the other colour and cannot itself move ('checkmate'), or where none of the particles of the colour whose turn it is to move can move ('stalemate'), or where the same configuration of particles occurs three times ('draw by repetition').

They would also detect some further regularities. For example, where it was possible to end a process by 'checkmate' in one time step, this would happen in almost all cases; and where it was possible for this to happen in three time steps, irrespective of what happens in the second of those time steps, it would happen in a great but lesser majority of cases. Where it was possible for a process to end in stalemate by one move of a particle of a certain colour, this would happen more often when there were fewer particles of that colour than when there were more. And so on. The scientists could work out quite extensive and elaborate statistics on such matters.

It may be that the scientists would come up with the hypothesis that there were two purposive systems operating in each process, one associated with each colour of the particles; with each system moving its particles with the purpose that the process end in 'checkmate' of the king of the other colour, or at worst, in 'stalemate' or 'draw by repetition'. That hypothesis would have the disadvantage that there would need to be much more to the universe in question than the space, the particles, the time-like steps, the mandatory rules, and the statistics: it would require that there also be whatever was necessary to constitute systems having purposes, and having the capabilities necessary to pursue those purposes with some effectiveness. However, the hypothesis would not be excluded by the fact that all observations were substantially in accordance with the statistics which the scientists had worked out; and it would have the advantage that it would make sense of the statistics, which would otherwise be brute facts with no rhyme or reason. If the scientists happened to become aware of the game of chess in their own universe, I think it is likely that they would prefer this 'dualistic' hypothesis. (Of course, it could turn out that the purposive systems in fact operated wholly in accordance with deterministic rules other than those of the rules of chess, as do chess-playing computers in our world; but that is another matter — in a chess universe, such systems would still involve a dualism.)

2. *Life*

Now suppose that these scientists gain access to a second universe, which so far as they could ascertain consists entirely of what we would understand to be the Game of Life, played on a vast scale. This game was devised in about 1970 by John Conway, a Cambridge mathematician. Its rules can be stated shortly:

> Life occurs on a virtual [and potentially infinite] checkerboard. The squares are called cells. They are in one of two states: alive or dead. Each cell has eight possible neighbours, the cells of which touch its sides or corners.

> If a cell on the checkerboard is alive, it will survive in the next time step (or generation) if there are either two or three neighbours also alive. It will die of overcrowding if there are more than three live neighbours, and it will die of exposure if there are fewer than two.

> If a cell on the checkerboard is dead, it will remain dead unless exactly three of its eight neighbours are alive. In that case, the cell will be 'born' in the next generation (Levy 1993, p. 52).

It is clear that, once an initial configuration of live cells is set up, everything that happens thereafter in this game is entirely determined by these rules. However, given an initial state with sufficient potential, the game unfolds in ways which have some similarities to life in our world. In particular: (1) large-scale events occur, which in many cases unfold in accordance with large-scale rules; (2) minute differences in initial configurations can produce huge differences in outcomes; and (3) accordingly, there is substantial unpredictability as to what will happen when previously unknown large-scale configurations arise.

The space of the Life universe to which our scientists gain access would be a limitless checkerboard, the fundamental particles would be the two possible states of each square or cell ('alive' and 'dead'), and there would be successive discrete time-like steps. The scientists would no doubt work out Conway's two rules: if a cell is alive in one time-step, it will be alive in the next time-step if and only if 2 or 3 of the 8 adjoining cells are alive; and if a cell is dead in one time-step, it will be alive in the next time-step if and only if 3 of the 8 adjoining cells are alive. They would hypothesize that everything that happens in this universe is determined by those two rules; and that hypothesis would not be falsified. They would observe interesting larger-scale patterns, and no doubt would work out rules relating to the development of these patterns; but these rules could only indicate the same developments as the two basic rules indicate. The scientists would be unlikely to hypothesise that any purposive systems were operating in this universe.

What about our own universe? Is it more like the chess universe, or the Life universe?

It seems to me fair to say that, after Descartes, a common view among educated Westerners would have been that the physical universe is like the Game of Life everywhere except in parts of the human brain, where (perhaps in the vicinity of the pineal gland) it is like chess. By the end of the nineteenth century, advances in the physical sciences, coupled with Darwin's theory of evolution, had given rise to a strongly competing view among educated Westerners that there is nothing about the human brain to suggest that different rules apply there; and that our universe is like the Game of Life everywhere.

Twentieth-century science has told us a lot more about the details of the laws of nature governing the development of our universe. Obviously, the laws are vastly more complicated than the rules of the Game of Life; but that in itself does not suggest any efficacious purposive systems. In addition, however, it appears that the laws of nature are partly indeterministic — so that they allow for genuine alternatives in the way our universe develops over time. These alternatives, however, seem to occur randomly within statistical parameters; and they generally tend to cancel out at scales much above that of atoms and molecules, so that at those larger scales, we generally seem to have rules which are as deterministic as those of the Game of Life.

One way of putting the issues which I see as dividing the approach to human purpose of people like myself, who contemplate a substantive role for purposive choice and free will, from that of the majority of scientists, who don't, is this: could the indeterminism, which appears to exist at the atomic level, (1) give rise to genuinely open alternatives at the level of human choice and action (like the alternatives open to a chess player); and (2) involve the actual exercise of choice and purpose in selection between those alternatives?

3. Superlife

Let us now suppose our scientists gain access to a third universe. In this universe, there appears to be a vast and complex game — let us call it Superlife — with regularities which suggest some deterministic and some statistical rules. There also appear in this universe to be many broadly integrated and continuous systems of vast numbers of the particles of this universe, which the scientists call 'agents'. Each of the states of these systems is unique, being different from all its own earlier states and from all states of all other systems; but contains traces of its own earlier states, which the scientists call 'memories'. These systems appear to develop over time generally in accordance with the rules of the universe (deterministic and statistical). But unlike the Life universe, the rules of this universe cannot be shown to exclude genuine alternatives in the development of these systems, at a macroscopic scale which the scientists can readily observe; and developments which actually occur tend to suggest that each of the agents is a purposive system, just as was suggested in the case of the systems associated with the different colours in each process in the chess universe.

The scientists come up with two rival hypotheses about this third universe. One is that the development over time of this universe is entirely governed by deterministic and/or statistical rules (and is purely random within the probability parameters indicated by the statistical rules): insofar as purpose appears to be displayed by the systems they call agents, this does not involve genuine choices between available alternatives, and is explained entirely by the history of how these systems were produced, over aeons of time, through countless generations of earlier systems which emerged and dissipated ('evolution'). The other hypothesis is that, while the development over time of the universe does conform to rules, there are leeways left by these rules, and within those leeways the systems called agents really do pursue purposes and really do make choices, between alternatives which the rules really do leave open to them: each choice between such alternatives is a unique efficacious occurrence, determined not by any rules but *by the system itself in its then unique unprecedented state*, with only the alternatives and tendencies being determined by the rules.

The former hypothesis has the advantage of simplicity: there is no need to postulate anything beyond the particles, space, time, and the rules (deterministic and statistical). The latter does require the additional postulate of purpose or choice; but in this universe, unlike the chess universe, there is no necessity to postulate that there is anything more to this universe than the game. Conceivably, it could just be a fact about Superlife that these systems, by virtue of their own properties coupled with the rules and the existence of alternatives, can detect the existence of alternatives and non-conclusive reasons supporting these alternatives, and can make a choice between the alternatives on the basis of those reasons.

Assuming that the scientists can experiment with this Superlife universe, they could try to refute one or other of these hypotheses — but it could be difficult. On the one hand, the scientists could try to show that what appear to be genuine macroscopic alternatives are not really open, or are not relevant to the apparent purposes of the systems. On the other hand, they could try to show that the systems appear to have and give effect to purposes in ways that can't be fully explained by rules and randomness and evolution.

But suppose now that, in the absence of any conclusive or near-conclusive experiment, the scientists notice that the Superlife universe is indistinguishable from their own universe, that the apparently purposive systems are indistinguishable from human beings in their own universe, and that these systems in fact report having experiences and purposes which seem to the scientists to be similar to those which the scientists themselves have. To me, that would make it reasonable for the scientists to treat very seriously indeed the hypothesis that there are real choices and purposes in the Superlife universe — *as indeed in their own*.

4. Summary

So: I have discussed three types of universe — a chess universe, a Life universe, and a Superlife universe. The chess universe involves outright *dualism*, with purpose provided entirely from outside the particles and rules of the physical universe. The Life universe is a *monistic physicalist* universe, in which everything that happens is just a working out of the behaviour of the particles as required by the rules of the universe. The Superlife universe, our own, appears to have within it both rules and purpose: the mainstream scientific view at present would have it that it is just a more elaborate version of a Life-type universe, with the apparent purposeful conduct being simply the working out of the rules, with or without randomness; whereas I would argue that a very plausible alternative is a strong *dual aspect* view, according to which genuine choice coexists with statistics within a unitary universe, and within certain unitary systems of that universe — with the statistics being apparent to an objective, third-person, physical viewpoint; and choice being apparent to a subjective, first-person, mental viewpoint, and involving real selection between alternatives which the physical viewpoint can only treat as statistical probabilities. In such a universe, there could be compatibility between (apparent) randomness and choice.

VIII: Conclusion

The widely-held view that determinism is compatible with free will, maybe even necessary for it, has been appealing just because the influence of Hume's mistake has hindered the articulation of a viable alternative. I believe this paper shows there is a viable alternative to compatibilism, one that makes perfectly good sense of a notion of free will and responsibility which is incompatible with determinism.

And although it goes beyond the scope of this paper to argue at length for the *probability*, as distinct from the *possibility*, of free will of that kind, I suggest that it fits in very well not only with common-sense ideas of responsibility, but also with a theory of plausible reasoning as involving, not just algorithms, but also the ability of conscious subjects to make holistic judgements that (fallibly) resolve non-conclusive reasons. It is that ability which I say is not available to zombies, or to computers as presently understood. And this in turn can explain the advantage of consciousness, which has promoted its development in evolution and the mechanisms that ensure we use it in dealing with novel situations. These points are elaborated in *The Mind Matters* and other writings, and particularly in my forthcoming book *The Nature of Choice*, on one chapter of which this paper is based.

In a recent article, Galen Strawson (1998) suggested that everything to be said about the metaphysics of free will had been said before, and that there could not possibly be any answer to his dilemma of responsibility. Well, the contents of this paper are not entirely new: some of the ideas have their origin in Nozick (1981), and others are just an elaboration and systematisation of common-sense ideas. But the totality is I believe original and new; it does answer Strawson's dilemma; and certainly it is not taken into account in Strawson's writing.

References

Abelson, R. (1988), *Lawless Minds* (Philadelphia: Temple University Press).

Anscombe, G. (1971), 'Causality and determinism', in (1981) *Metaphysics and the Philosophy of Mind* (Oxford: Oxford University Press).

Ayer, A.J. (1956), 'Freedom and necessity', in *Philosophical Essays* (London: Macmillan).

Barrett, J.A. (1994), review of Hodgson (1991), *Philosophical Review*, **103**, pp. 350–2.

Buser, P.A. and Rougel-Buser, A. (ed. 1978), *Cerebral Correlates of Conscious Experience* (Amsterdam: North-Holland).

Campbell, C.A. (1951), 'Is "freewill" a pseudo problem?', *Mind*, **60**, pp. 441–65.

Chalmers, D. (1996), *The Conscious Mind: Toward a Theory of Consciousness* (New York: Oxford University Press).

Dennett, D. (1984), *Elbow Room* (Oxford: Oxford University Press).

Eccles, J.C. (1994), *How the Self Controls its Brain* (Berlin: Springer).

Eddington, A. (1929), *The Nature of the Physical World* (London: Dent).

Flew, A. and Vesey, G. (1987), *Agency and Necessity* (Oxford: Blackwell).

Frankfurt, H. (1971), 'Freedom of the will and the concept of a person', *Journal of Philosophy*, **68**, pp. 5–20.

Gomes, A.O. (1978), 'The brain-consciousness problem in contemporary scientific research', in Buser and Rougel-Buser (1978).

Griffin, D. (1997), 'Panexperientialist physicalism and the mind-body problem', *Journal of Consciousness Studies*, **4** (3), pp. 248–68.

Hameroff, S., Scott, A. and Kaszniak, A. (ed. 1998), *Toward a Science of Consciousness II* (Cambridge, MA: MIT Press).

Hobart, R.E. (1934), 'Free will as involving determinism and inconceivable without it', *Mind*, **43**, pp. 1–27.

Hodgson, D. (1991), *The Mind Matters* (Oxford: Oxford University Press).
Hodgson, D. (1994), 'Neuroscience and folk-psychology — an overview', *Journal of Consciousness Studies*, **1** (2), pp. 205–16.
Hodgson, D. (1995), 'Probability: the logic of the law — a response', *Oxford Journal of Legal Studies*, **14**, pp. 51–68.
Hodgson, D. (1996/1998), 'Folk psychology, science, and the criminal law', paper delivered April 1996 at Science and Consciousness Conference, Tucson, Arizona; in Hameroff *et al.* (1998).
Hume, D. (1748), *A Enquiry Concerning Human Understanding*.
Kane, R. (1985), *Free Will and Values* (New York: SUNY).
Kane, R. (1996), *The Significance of Free Will* (New York: Oxford University Press).
Levy, S. (1993), *Artificial Life* (Harmondsworth: Penguin).
Lockwood, M. (1991), Review of Hodgson (1991), *Times Literary Supplement*, 15 November, p. 31.
McCall, S. (1994), *A Model of the Universe* (Oxford: Oxford University Press).
Nagel, T. (1986), *The View From Nowhere* (New York: Oxford University Press).
Nozick, R. (1981), *Philosophical Explanations* (Oxford: Oxford University Press).
O'Connor, T. (1995), 'Agent causation', in *Agents, Causes, and Events*, ed. T. O'Connor (New York: Oxford University Press).
Ryle, G. (1949), *The Concept of Mind* (London: Hutchinson).
Smart, J.J.C. (1961), 'Free-will, praise and blame', *Mind*, **70**, pp. 483–94.
Strawson, G. (1986), *Freedom and Belief* (Oxford: Oxford University Press).
Strawson, G. (1998), 'Luck swallows everything', *Times Literary Supplement*, 26 June, pp. 8–10.
Taylor, C. (1976), 'Responsibility for self', in *The Identities of Persons*, ed. A. Rorty (University of California Press).
Williams, B. (1995), *Making Sense of Humanity* (Cambridge: Cambridge University Press).
Wilson, D.L. (1995), Review of Eccles (1994), *American Scientist*, **83**, May/June, p. 269.

E.J. Lowe

Self, Agency and Mental Causation

A self or person does not appear to be identifiable with his or her organic body, nor with any part of it, such as the brain; and yet selves seem to be agents, capable of bringing about physical events (such as bodily movements) as causal consequences of certain of their conscious mental states. How is this possible in a universe in which, it appears, every physical event has a sufficient cause which is wholly physical? The answer is that this is possible if a certain kind of naturalistic dualism is true, according to which the conscious mental states of selves, although not identifiable with physical states of their brains, are emergent effects of prior physical causes. Moreover, mental causation on this model promises to explain certain aspects of physical behaviour which may appear arbitrary and coincidental from a purely physical point of view.

I: Introduction

The following claims all seem fairly compelling, upon reflection, and yet they appear not to form a consistent set:

(1) The self, although physically embodied, is not to be identified with any physical body nor with any part of such a body.

(2) The self is by its very nature an agent, something that is naturally capable of performing intentional actions, some of them with physical results.

(3) Every physical event has a set of wholly physical causes which are collectively causally sufficient for the occurrence of that event (and rarely if ever is a physical event causally overdetermined).

The apparent inconsistency of this set of claims has led many philosophers to reject one or more of them. Some reject (1), either denying that there is any such thing as the self, or else identifying it with something bodily, such as an animal organism or brain. Some reject (2), holding that our experience of volitional control over our bodies is merely illusory. And some reject (3), maintaining that the self's intentional states are non-physical causes of certain physical events which lack sufficient wholly physical causes. (This appears to have been Descartes' view.) Instead, I shall argue that claims (1), (2) and (3) are in fact perfectly consistent. Whether all of those claims are *true* is

Journal of Consciousness Studies, **6**, No. 8–9, 1999, pp. 225–39

another matter — though, clearly, if they are all not only fairly compelling but also consistent, something is to be said in favour of their all being true. I should add, though, that elsewhere I have argued in defence of claims (1) and (2) (see Lowe, 1996). Consequently — in view of the widespread acceptance of claim (3) — I have a vested interest in establishing the consistency of the three claims.[1] So, before proceeding, let me briefly explain why I think that claims (1) and (2) are true.

II: The Self Is Not Its Body

I believe, first of all, that selves exist, not least because I believe that *I* exist and consider myself to be a 'self'. I use the term 'self' interchangeably with the term 'person'. I take it, however, that the term 'self' is a particularly appropriate synonym for 'person' because it reflects the fact that a necessary condition of personhood is a capacity for *self-reference* — a capacity which is manifested linguistically by use of the first-person pronoun, 'I'. A person or self, in short, is a being which can have thoughts *about itself*, of the sort that are appropriately expressed (in English) by sentences containing the first-person pronoun, 'I', as their grammatical subject — sentences such as 'I feel hot' and 'I am six feet tall'. But I also believe that a person or self, even though physically embodied, is never to be *identified* with its physical body nor with any part of it, such as that body's brain. This is claim (1) above.

Our ordinary self-conception seems to involve a commitment to claim (1). For example, when I have a conscious first-person thought — such as the thought that I feel hot — I regard *myself* as being the subject of this thought, both in the sense of being the thing having the thought and in the sense of being the thing that the thought is about. But I am not at all inclined to regard *my body* or *my brain* as being its subject, in either sense. Since I am the subject of the thought but neither my body nor any part of it is, it follows that I am not identical with my body or any part of it. Of course, with the benefit of a little scientific knowledge, I may well be prepared to concede that, but for the existence and normal functioning of my brain, I could not so much as have this or any other thought: but that doesn't (or shouldn't) persuade me to believe that *my brain* is, after all, the subject of my thoughts. That would be like inferring that my feet run from the fact that I could not run without having feet. Anyway, quite apart from anything else, it seems clear that, even granted that I need *a* brain in order to be able to think, I don't need to have the particular brain that I do have. I find nothing inconceivable in the thought that I might wake up one morning to be told (truly) that, overnight, I had undergone an operation in which my old organic brain was somehow replaced by a new inorganic one.

Here it may be objected that, if I am not to be identified with my physical body nor any part of it, then it only remains for me to be identified with something altogether *non*-physical, such as a spirit or soul or 'Cartesian ego' — and this, it will be said, is a view wholly at odds with a naturalistically acceptable conception of persons. However, it is a simple mistake to suppose that if I am not to be identified with my physical body or any part of it, I must therefore be identified with something non-physical, that is, with something possessing no physical characteristics whatever. And, indeed, identifying oneself with something non-physical is quite as counterintuitive as identi-

---

[1] For a recent example of a philosopher who endorses claim (3) — and espouses a thoroughgoing physicalism as a consequence — see David Papineau (1993), p. 22.

fying oneself with one's physical body or brain. It seems to me no less literally true that *I* have a certain height than it seems literally false that *my brain* has certain thoughts.

The self can be a 'physical' thing — possess physical characteristics such as height — even though it has different identity-conditions from those of the body or brain. Somewhat analogously, a statue can be a physical thing — possess physical characteristics such as shape — even though it has different identity-conditions from those of the piece of matter which composes it. The analogy isn't perfect, however, for I don't want to say that the relation of embodiment is simply one of composition: I am not composed by my body, in the way that the statue is composed by bits of matter. Indeed, I don't believe that the self is a composite entity at all: I don't believe that it is literally *made up of* distinct and separable parts. The self, I want to say, possesses a strong kind of unity which is incompatible with its being a composite thing. I don't have space to argue for this view here (but see further Lowe, 1996, Ch. 2). All I want to stress at present is that claim (1) above is not only plausible, but is perfectly consistent with the equally plausible claim that the self is a physical thing, in the sense of being a thing which possesses physical characteristics or states.

III: Mental States Are Not Physical States

However, it doesn't follow from this that *mental* states of the self can intelligibly be thought of as being *physical* states of it, akin to such physical states as height and weight. Indeed, I very much want to *deny* that mental states are physical states, even though they are states of something physical — the self. This is because I can make no clearer sense of the idea that a conscious mental state might just *be* a physical state than I can of the idea that a physical object might just *be* a natural number (cf. Geach, 1979, p. 134). Consider a typical mental state, such as this one: consciously thinking of Paris. I know what it means to be in such a state, at least as clearly as I know what it means to be in the physical state of sitting in a chair. But I cannot at all understand what it would mean to say that the state of consciously thinking of Paris just *is* a 'physical' state. This is because — as I understand it — a physical state is, by its very nature, one whose possession by a thing makes some real difference to at least part of the space which that thing occupies. Thus, my sitting qualifies as a physical state of me because, in virtue of possessing it, I fill out a part of space in a certain way, rendering that part of space relatively impenetrable by my presence. But my consciously thinking of Paris has no spatial connotations of this sort whatsoever, so far as I can see (cf. McGinn, 1995). In fact, the identity-conditions of mental states would appear to be thoroughly unlike those of physical states — as unlike them as the identity-conditions of physical objects are unlike those of the natural numbers (see further Lowe, 1989, pp. 131–3 and Lowe, 1996, pp. 25–30). And consequently the thesis that mental states 'just are' (identical with) physical states is simply unintelligible.

A whole generation of philosophers has, alas, mistaken this unintelligible thesis for something much more exciting, namely, a profound truth which has only now begun to be revealed to us through the advance of science. (I don't expect to be able to shake their faith, however, any more than one could hope to shake the faith of a dedicated Pythagorean.) Truths of identity simply *cannot* be exciting in the way such metaphysicians fondly imagine, because it can only be intelligible to identify items *of the same kind* (that is, kinds importing the same identity-criteria for their instances), and the 'exciting' identifications — of physical objects with mathematical objects, or of mental states with physical states — all violate this principle by trying to identify items of quite *different* kinds.

IV: Selfhood Requires Agency

A word or two is now needed in defence of claim (2) — that the self is by its very nature an agent, something that is naturally capable of performing intentional actions, some of them with physical results. Since I have already characterized the self as something necessarily capable of self-reference, I have already implicitly character-ised it as something necessarily possessing agency, since self-reference is a species of intentional action. To refer to oneself as 'I', whether in speech or merely in thought, is to perform a kind of intentional act. If done merely in thought, this act may perhaps have no physical results, though if done in speech it clearly must. However, the idea that there might be a self which, throughout its life, was *only* capable of engaging in intentional actions of a purely mental kind — never, thus, in actions having physical results — is one that is hard to credit.[2] Such a self would be constitutionally incapable of communicating with other selves. It is strongly arguable, however, that the development of self-awareness is necessarily linked to the development of other-awareness and that both are necessarily linked to the development of powers of com-munication, whether through language or merely through various kinds of non-verbal behaviour. If that is so, then there couldn't be a self which was constitutionally inca-pable of communicating with other selves throughout its life — though there might, conceivably, be a self which *lost* this capability having once developed it, as is sug-gested by cases of so-called 'locked-in syndrome' (people who seem to remain self-aware even though they have lost all control over their bodies through complete paralysis of the non-autonomic nervous system).

Another reason for thinking that a self must be capable — at least at some stage during its existence — of performing intentional actions which have physical results is that it is strongly arguable that only a being capable of such actions can develop a concept of *causation* and that possessing such a concept is a necessary condition of self-reference and thus of selfhood itself. (It is a necessary condition of self-reference because to self-refer is to perform an intentional action, to perform an intentional action is to act in a certain way *knowing* that one is so acting, the concept of inten-tional action is a causal concept, and knowledge is possible only for one who pos-sesses the requisite concepts.) The thought here, then, is that a being that was condemned from birth to complete physical passivity, even though endowed with powers of sensation and perception, would be incapable of distinguishing between causal and non-causal sequences of events, because an ability to make this distinction depends upon an ability to *intervene actively* in the course of nature, with a view to discovering by means of experimental manipulation which events do or do not depend upon which other events (cf. von Wright, 1971, pp. 69–74). One's own inner mental life does not present a sufficiently independent arena in which this capacity could be developed, it seems: one needs to be able, as it were, to get to grips with

---

[2]   Thus I find Galen Strawson's imaginary example of the 'Weather Watchers' highly implausible (see Strawson, 1994, Ch. 9).

things *outside* oneself in order to get any purchase on the thought that some events stand in causal relations of dependence to one another whereas others are only accidentally conjoined.[3] This line of reasoning is, I confess, only very sketchily presented here, but that is because its full articulation would require much more space than I have available.

V: Are the Three Claims Inconsistent?

Why should the three claims stated at the beginning of the paper be *thought* to be inconsistent? For the following reasons, I imagine. First of all, claim (2) seems to imply — indeed, I agree that it *does* imply — that intentional states of the self can be causes of physical events. This is because the concept of an intentional action is a causal one: when an agent acts intentionally, an intentional state of that agent plays a causal role in the production of some event — an event which, in the case of an intentional action which has a physical result, will obviously be a physical one.

Next, claim (1) seems to imply that intentional states of the self are states of something non-physical and are therefore themselves non-physical states. Now, of course, we have just seen that claim (1) does *not*, in fact, imply that the self is something non-physical. But we have also seen that there is, all the same, good reason to think that even though the self is physical, inasmuch as it possesses physical states, *mental* states of the self — including its intentional states — are *not* physical states of it and so are indeed non-physical states. So, although claim (1) does not strictly have the implication it might seem to have — that intentional states of the self are non-physical states — I think that any adherent of claim (1) ought nonetheless to *accept* the thesis that intentional states of the self are non-physical states.

Finally, claim (3) seems to imply that no physical event can have a non-physical state amongst its causes. (We shall examine this alleged implication in a moment.) Together, then, claims (1), (2) and (3) — or, more accurately, claims (2) and (3) together with the thesis, consistent with claim (1), that intentional states of the self are non-physical states — seem to imply that non-physical states *both are and are not* causes of physical events: a contradiction. However, even if we grant the alleged implications of claims (1) and (2), this reasoning is incorrect, because it ignores the *transitivity of causation*, as we shall now see. (The key point to appreciate here is the very simple one that if x is causally sufficient for y and y is causally sufficient for z, then, by transitivity, x is causally sufficient for z, but that this doesn't imply that z is *causally overdetermined* by both x and y.)

VI: Naturalistic Dualism Is Possible

It is possible for claim (3) to be true — that every physical event has a set of wholly physical causes which are collectively causally sufficient for the occurrence of that

---

[3] Against me here it might be urged that a capacity to discriminate perceptually between (at least some) causal and non-causal sequences of events could be *innate*, even in a completely passive creature, and indeed that there is some empirical evidence for such an innate capacity in human infants. However, it could still be argued that such a capacity would inevitably be destined to lie dormant or atrophy in any creature incapable of engaging in active exploration of its perceptual environment (including here as 'active exploration' a creature's voluntary direction of its sense organs, such as its eyes, towards stimuli selected by it for attention).

event — and yet for it also to be true that some physical event, *P*, has a non-physical event or state, *M*, amongst its causes (without envisaging this as involving the causal overdetermination of *P*). This is because *M* itself may have a set of wholly physical causes which are collectively causally sufficient for *its* occurrence. If *M* is a cause of *P*, then, by the transitivity of causation, all of those physical causes of *M* are also causes of *P* — and, clearly, they may form a subset of a set of wholly physical causes which are collectively causally sufficient for the occurrence of *P*. Hence, claims (1) and (2) are not inconsistent with claim (3), but only with something much stronger, namely

(4) No physical event has a non-physical cause.

Obviously, however, no one can pretend that claim (4) is strongly confirmed by empirical evidence, however much it may be an article of faith with some philosophers. Even claim (3), although significantly weaker than claim (4), is not exactly strongly confirmed empirically. A presumption in its favour, however, is that modern science encourages us to believe that the universe is a causally closed system whose origins were wholly physical. At the time of the 'big bang', we suppose, all events were wholly physical — and all subsequent physical events have been and will continue to be long-term effects of those initial events. (Here I am assuming a thoroughgoing causal determinism, but not much is affected by assuming instead that a good deal of causation is irreducibly probabilistic.) But this presumption in no way rules out the possibility that, at some stage during the evolution of the universe, *non-*physical events or states have come into existence, along with subjects of those events or states (that is, selves, conceived of in accordance with claim (1)). There is no reason to disparage this idea as 'spooky', since it need involve no element of supernaturalism — taking 'supernaturalism' to be the view that some events are brought about by agents (such as a divine being) which do not exist within the space–time universe. (Such an agent would, of course, be a non-physical thing, quite unlike human selves as I conceive of them.)

   Even if it is conceded that this is a genuine possibility and that claims (1), (2) and (3) are not logically inconsistent, it may nonetheless be thought that the suggestion that this is how things *actually are* is an extravagant one which somehow violates canons of parsimony or simplicity in matters metaphysical. On the contrary, I shall now attempt to show how the invocation of mental states, conceived of as non-physical causes of physical events, has the potential to strengthen our causal explanations of certain physical events. This is because such non-physical causes can be represented as rendering *non-coincidental* certain physical events which, from the perspective of purely physical causation, may appear to occur merely by coincidence.

VII: On Coincidental Events

An event *occurs by coincidence*, or *coincidentally*, in the sense I now have in mind, when two or more events co-occur and jointly cause that event, but those causes are themselves causally independent, in the sense of having no common cause amongst their various causes. (Some philosophers describe the *co-occurrence* of two or more events which have no common cause as being a 'coincidence', and I have no quarrel with this usage: but my concern now is with the notion of a *single* event which occurs *by* coincidence, in the sense just explained. I am not concerned, then, with the question, which exercises some of those philosophers, of whether 'coincidences', in their sense, have causal explanations. See e.g. Owens, 1992, ch. 1, and Sorabji, 1980, ch. 1.)

Here is a familiar example. A man walks past a house just as a gust of wind dislodges a slate from the roof, causing it to fall, with the result that he is hit by it and killed. The man's walking there and the slate's falling there co-occur and jointly cause his death, but, we assume, there was no common cause of the man's walking there and the slate's falling there. Consequently, his death occurred by coincidence. But if, say, the man's approaching the house had set off a trip-wire attached to the slate, causing it to fall just as he passed underneath it, then his walking there and its falling there *would* have had a common cause and so his death would not have been coincidental.

An event which occurs by coincidence is not an *uncaused* event: it has causes, which themselves have causes, which likewise have causes, and so on — what makes it coincidental is the fact that its immediate causes have independent causal histories. An event which does not occur by coincidence is one whose immediate causes share a common cause, rendering the causal histories of its immediate causes non-independent. At least, this will do, to a first approximation, as an account of the distinction between an event which occurs by coincidence and one which does not. (We might need to refine this account in order to avoid having to describe as 'non-coincidental' certain events whose immediate causes do share some common cause, but only a relatively insignificant one lying in the remote past of their respective causal histories. After all, we have already conceded that all current physical events are ultimately effects of events which occurred at the time of the 'big bang', but we don't want *this* to count as a reason for denying that certain current physical events are 'coincidental'.)

In our foregoing illustration of the distinction between coincidental and non-coincidental events, it is clear that the two different cases in which the man is killed by the falling slate differ, not only in respect of some of the physical events which occur and are causally responsible for the man's death in each case, but also in respect of some of the relations of physical causation which obtain between various physical events which occur in both cases. Thus, in the non-coincidental case, but not in the coincidental case, the physical event of the man's setting off the trip-wire occurs and is one of the causes of his death. And in the non-coincidental case, but not in the coincidental case, the physical event of the man's approaching the house is related by physical causation — via the movement of the trip-wire — to the physical event of the slate's falling. This is because the common cause which makes the difference between the coincidental and non-coincidental cases in our illustration is not only a physical event itself, but also one which links the causal histories of the immediate causes of the man's death by means of a chain of purely *physical* causation. But matters may be otherwise if what links the causal histories of the immediate physical causes of some non-coincidental physical event is a causal chain involving *non-*physical events, as I shall now demonstrate.

VIII: A Comparison Between Two Possible Worlds

Suppose that two independent causal chains of physical events, P_{11}, P_{12}, P_{13} and P_{21}, P_{22}, P_{23} jointly give rise to a physical event P as the immediate effect of P_{13} and P_{23}. Here the occurrence of P is coincidental. But, I submit, it is metaphysically possible for P to have (in a sense explained below) exactly the same *physical* causal history and yet *not* to occur by coincidence, because it is metaphysically possible for the immediate physical causes of P — namely P_{13} and P_{23} — to share a common cause which links them by a *non*-physical causal chain, thereby rendering their causal histories non-independent. It might be the case, for instance, that in this alternative scenario P_{11} is a cause of a mental event M which is in turn a cause of P_{22}: see the diagram below.

A note on how to read this diagram: each node, marked by a letter, represents a particular event and a line drawn between two nodes — whether or not it passes through other nodes — signifies that the event represented by the upper of those two nodes *is a cause of* the event represented by the lower of those two nodes. I should perhaps emphasise that to say that one event *is a cause of* another event is by no means to rule out the possibility that a third event, also, *is a cause of* that second event: that is to say, in the sense of 'cause' now in play, an event may have many different causes, without thereby being causally overdetermined. I am taking it that to say that one event *is a cause of* another event is — barring the possibility of causal overdetermination — at least to imply that if that first event had not occurred, then that second event would not have occurred either.

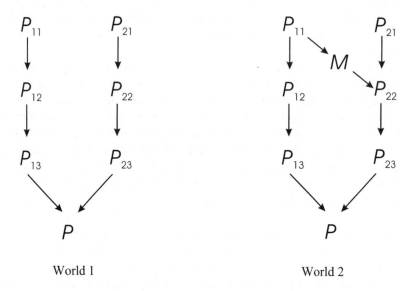

World 1   World 2

World 1 and world 2 are the same in the following respects: (i) the same physical events occur in both (in the space–time region with which we are concerned) and (ii) those events bear the same relations of purely physical causation to one another. By (ii) I mean that wherever two physical events in one of the worlds are linked by a certain chain of purely physical causation (causation not involving any non-physical event), they are linked in the same way in the other world. That is to say, wherever, in one of the worlds, a certain physical event *is a cause of* another physical event, either directly or via certain other intervening physical events, those events stand in that same relation in the other world as well: in the other world, too, the first physical event *is a cause of* the second physical event, again either directly or via the same intervening physical events.[4] Of course — assuming that causation is law-governed — the two worlds are *not* the same in respect of the causal laws which obtain in them, because in world 2 certain psychophysical laws obtain which do not obtain in world 1. I shall return to this point in a moment. But what is of special interest to us now is that in world 1 the occurrence of P is *coincidental* whereas in world 2 it is *not* coincidental.

So we see that two worlds could contain the same physical events standing in the same relations of purely physical causation to one another and yet it be the case that in one of the worlds a certain physical event was coincidental whereas in the other it was not, because in the second world a certain non-physical (mental) event rendered the causal histories of that physical event's immediate physical causes non-independent. Incidentally, the existence of this possibility does much, in my view, to undermine the popular — though rather obscure — thesis that mental events 'supervene' upon physical events: if the thesis is taken to be that worlds which are the same in respect of what physical events occur in them and what relations of purely physical causation obtain between those events are worlds which are the same in respect of what mental events occur in them and what causal relations those events stand in, then we see, first, that this could at best be true of a restricted range of worlds and, second, that there is no positive reason to suppose that our world is one of those worlds. Of course, not all true counterfactual conditionals concerning physical events in one of our two depicted worlds could also be truths in the other of those worlds. For instance, in world 2 of our diagram — where P_{11} is depicted as being a cause of P_{22}, albeit only via the mental event M and not, thus, via any chain of purely physical causation — it is true that if P_{11} had not occurred, then P_{22} would not have occurred (barring causal overdetermination, which is not at issue here), whereas in world 1 it is *not* true that if P_{11} had not occurred, then P_{22} would not have occurred. But that just reflects the fact that different causal laws are operative in our two worlds and that different events (though not different *physical* events) occur in them. I should perhaps stress here, if it isn't sufficiently obvious already, that I am by no means suggesting that the situations depicted in the two worlds of our diagram are *compossible*: thus, the *actual* world could not simultaneously be *both* as depicted in world 1 *and* as depicted in world 2. However, it *is* implicit in what I have said that if one were to know, concerning the physical events depicted in our diagram, *only* which events they were and what relations of *purely physical* causation they bore to one another, one would not be in a position to decide on that basis whether the actual world was world 1 or world 2, for the simple reason that world 1 and world 2 do not differ in these respects. The significance of this fact will emerge in a moment.

---

[4] Since, manifestly, some events do not have exactly the same causes and effects in the two worlds as I have represented them, I am assuming that it is not an implication of any acceptable principle of transworld identity for events that an event has the same causes and effects in any world in which it occurs. But I take it that this is uncontroversial, since to say that it is metaphysically impossible for an event to have had causes and effects other than those which it actually has is to violate Hume's principle that there is no metaphysically necessary connection between cause and effect.

Another important point to observe concerning our worlds 1 and 2 is that *both* of them — not just world 1 — can be worlds in which claim (3) is true, that is, in which every physical event has a set of wholly physical causes which are collectively causally sufficient for the occurrence of that event. (Note here that the diagrams representing worlds 1 and 2 are not meant to be *complete* representations of those worlds, so that, for instance, it is not implied that P_{11} and P_{21} *lack* causes in those worlds.) For, as was pointed out earlier, it is perfectly possible that the non-physical event M of world 2 should itself have a set of wholly physical causes which are collectively causally sufficient for its occurrence. This can be so even if, as is plausible, M also has some other *non*-physical events amongst its causes (provided that each of these likewise has a set of wholly physical causes which are collectively causally sufficient for its occurrence).[5]

IX: The Significance of these Findings

What is the significance of these findings? Just this: they show that even if one has identified all the physical causes of a certain physical event within a certain space–time region — for instance, even if one has identified all the neural events causally responsible for a certain bodily movement — this doesn't preclude the possibility that the existence of a *non-physical* (mental) event or state, such as a person's belief or desire or intention, might serve to explain why that movement is *non-coincidental*, in a way in which the purely physical causal history of that movement does not. One might, thus, have truly discovered all the *physical* causes of the movement and this discovery might be consistent with the possibility that these were indeed *all* the causes of the movement — in which case the movement would be coincidental — and yet the discovery would also be consistent with the possibility that there were, in addition to these physical causes, certain *non*-physical causes which served to render the movement non-coincidental. So, merely to have satisfied ourselves that we have discovered all the physical causes of such a movement and to have satisfied ourselves that such causes *could* provide a complete causal explanation for the occurrence of the movement, is not yet to have ruled out the possibility that they *don't* in fact provide a complete causal explanation — because the question may still be left open as to whether or not the movement occurred by coincidence.

Positing certain non-physical (mental) causes of a physical event, in addition to the physical causes which have already been discovered, may serve an explanatory purpose which cannot be served by appeal to the physical causes alone. The non-physical part of the explanation need not deny anything which has been discovered about the identity of the physical causes and their purely physical causal relations and is in this sense perfectly compatible with the purely physical part of the explanation — though,

---

[5] Incidentally, it is important to distinguish both world 1 and world 2 from yet another possible world — call it world 3 — which is just like world 1 save that in it there is an additional relation of *purely physical* causation between event P_{11} and event P_{22}. In world 3, as in world 2, event P is not coincidental. But, of course, worlds 1 and 3 are *not* the same in *both* of the respects (i) and (ii) stated above — unlike worlds 1 and 2 — since worlds 1 and 3 differ from each other in respect (ii): the physical events in them do not bear exactly the same relations of purely physical causation to one another. In consequence, P does not have exactly the same *physical* causal history in worlds 1 and 3, whereas it does in worlds 1 and 2. Naturally, I have no wish to deny that non-coincidental events may *sometimes* have a purely physical causal explanation, as in world 3: I am only concerned to show that, and how, they may sometimes have a causal explanation which is at least partly *non*-physical and which is nonetheless consistent with the truth of claim (3).

as has been noted, accepting the non-physical part of the explanation *as well as* the physical part, rather than just accepting the physical part alone, will require adopting a different view as to what causal laws and what counterfactual conditional truths obtain.

Of course, if it should turn out, in a particular case, that a *physical* event can be discovered which renders a bodily movement (say) non-coincidental, then appeal to a non-physical event will be otiose in that particular case: the case will be like that of the non-coincidental death caused by the falling slate, where the triggering of a trip-wire rendered the death non-coincidental. But what if it were to be discovered that this can be done in *all* cases in which we now see reason to invoke items such as beliefs in our causal explanations? That, I suppose, might be taken by some to be a reason for holding that beliefs and so forth just *are* physical items (neural states or events, perhaps). However, my own view, on the contrary, is that it would instead be (at best) a reason for holding either that beliefs and so forth do not really exist at all (eliminativism) or else that they are causally inefficacious (epiphenomenalism). I take this view of the matter because, as I explained earlier, I do not consider that the thesis that mental states 'just *are*' physical states is even an intelligible one (though, to be fair, I don't regard either eliminativism or epiphenomenalism as being in much better shape, conceptually, so that I am pretty much committed to denying that we *could*, even in principle, make the discovery that has just been contemplated).

What I am chiefly concerned to point out for the moment, however, is that it is perfectly conceivable that we *should* discover, in the case of some bodily movement, that all of the physical (say, neural) events which we can implicate in its occurrence are such that, as far as their purely physical causal relations to one another are concerned, they do nothing to show that that movement is anything other than coincidental. And in such a case, my claim is, we could quite consistently and plausibly invoke a *non*-physical (mental) event as rendering that movement *non*-coincidental, without denying anything that had hitherto been claimed about the identities of that movement's physical causes and their purely physical causal relationships to one another and to the movement in question.

X: Intentionality and Mental Causation

So far I have said nothing about *how* mental events and states might cause physical events and states. For that matter, of course, neither have I said how *physical* events and states might cause physical events and states. But there is good reason to suppose that mental causation has some distinctive features which relate to the intrinsic natures of mental causes. We have been taking mental causes to be items such as beliefs, desires and intentions — in short, *intentional* states of the self. (The *onsets* of such states are events, but beliefs, desires and intentions are states rather than events — not that very much turns on the distinction between events and states in what follows.) Of course, some mental states — such as 'pure' sensations (if such there be) — are not intentional states, since they lack any intentional content (they are not 'about' anything, in the way that beliefs and desires are always 'about' something). But I am not really concerned with such non-intentional mental states at present. One distinctive feature of mental causation by intentional states is that *what* is caused by such states is intimately related to the intentional content of those states. In the case of normal voluntary action, movements of the agent's body have amongst their causes intentional states of that agent which are 'about' just such movements. For instance, when I try to raise my arm and succeed in doing so, my arm goes up — and amongst the causes of its going up are such items as a desire of mine *that my arm should go up*. The intentional causes of physical events are always 'directed' upon the occurrence of just such events, at least where normal voluntary action is concerned (see further Lowe, 1996, Ch. 5). Nothing like this seems to be the case when physical events or states cause other physical events or states: such purely physical causation always appears to be 'undirected' or 'blind'.

Notice, however, that although, in normal voluntary action, an intentional state of the agent is 'directed' upon an event of the kind which it causes, it is not 'directed' upon the *particular* event which it causes. When I try to raise my arm and succeed in doing so, my desire that my arm should go up is amongst the causes of the event of my arm's going up: but my desire is not that *that particular event of arm-rising* should occur, but merely that *an* event of arm-rising of the appropriate kind should occur at a certain time, or during a certain interval of time. This has to be so because, even if I know that my attempt to raise my arm will succeed, I cannot know in advance *which* particular event of arm-rising will occur as a result of my success, since this will depend on factors outside my knowledge and control, such as the speed with which my nervous system reacts at the time of the attempt. Consequently, when my arm goes up as a result of my successfully trying to raise it, what is causally explained by my desire that my arm should go up is not merely the occurrence of this particular event of arm-rising, but the obtaining of the *general* state of affairs of an event of that kind's occurring during a certain interval of time — a state of affairs which happens to be 'realized' on this occasion by this particular event of arm-rising, but which could equally well have been 'realized' by a different particular event of arm-rising, provided it had been one of a suitable kind and had occurred at the right time.[6]

There is, I believe, a connection between this feature of intentional causal explanation and the already proposed role of mental causes in rendering certain of their physical effects non-coincidental. As we have seen, what qualifies an event as being 'non-coincidental' is a fact about the causal history of that event: the fact that its immediate causes have a common cause, that is, the fact that its immediate causes do not have independent causal histories. And I have suggested that when a mental state causes some physical event, its causal role may be one of rendering that event non-coincidental, which it can do by rendering non-independent the causal histories of that event's immediate physical causes. My further suggestion, now, is that this feature of the causal role of mental states is intimately related to the way in which they serve to provide causal explanations of certain *general* physical states of affairs and not merely of particular physical events. By causally connecting what would otherwise be independent chains of physical causation, I suggest, a mental cause can render the common effect of those chains non-coincidental and in so doing explain why an event *of that kind* occurred, not merely why *that particular event* occurred. For it seems that the way in which a mental cause interconnects chains of physical causation is such as to ensure that the common effect of such chains is, in the following

---

[6] Not all philosophers like to include 'states of affairs' in their ontology — but see Armstrong (1997) — and those who do are not necessarily in favour of including *general* states of affairs. But that is a debate for another occasion.

sense, *robust*: in all relatively 'close' possible worlds in which some of the physical events in those chains are different from those of the actual world but the interconnecting mental cause is still present, their common effect is nonetheless still *of the same kind* as that of the actual world — namely, the kind specified by the intentional content of that mental cause. This suggestion can perhaps best be elucidated by means of an example.

XI: An Illustrative Example

An assumption behind the following example will be that 'fusions' of events are, in general, themselves events: for instance, that if five battles occur over a certain period of time, then there is an event which occurs over that period of time and contains those five battles as parts (we might call this event a 'campaign', perhaps).[7] Most of the macroscopic events we normally talk about are event-fusions in this way. For example, even so 'simple' an event as the rising of a person's arm consists of many sub-events, such as the flexing of certain muscles and the movements of various parts of the arm.

Suppose that, over a period of several minutes, the following series of purely physical events is observed to occur: one after another, all of the coloured balls remaining on a snooker table are struck by the cue ball and as a result fall into pockets. The fusion of all these events of a snooker ball falling into a pocket is itself an event, call it event E. Suppose, now, we ask why event E occurred. Clearly, in one sense, E occurred because each of the sub-events of which E is the fusion occurred — but this is not a *causal* explanation of E. However, each of the sub-events — each event of a snooker ball falling into a pocket — has a causal explanation and one might suppose that the causal explanation of E is simply the conjunction of all those causal explanations (though we shall see in a moment that there could be good reason to challenge this supposition). Moreover, one might suppose that each event of a snooker ball falling into a pocket has a *wholly physical* causal explanation, adverting solely to prior physical events, such as movements of the snooker cue, movements of the player's hand (we are assuming here that there is just one player involved), neuronal events in the player's efferent nerves and motor cortex, and so forth. However, I suggest, if that *is* all there is to the explanation of event E, then we shall have to regard event E as having happened merely 'by coincidence'. Moreover, this explanation will not serve to explain, in any interesting sense, why an event *of this kind* occurred: we shall only be able to say that an event of this kind occurred 'because' this particular event occurred and was an event of this kind (and such a 'because' is not causal in force).

Now, of course, most of us would be extremely surprised if this were all there were to the explanation of event E. Most of us would surmise that E occurred because the snooker player had *formed and acted upon a desire* to pot all the coloured balls remaining on the table (and possessed the skill needed to achieve this). That desire would not be a desire specifically for event E to occur, but only a desire for the occurrence of an event of a certain kind, namely, an event consisting in the potting of all the remaining balls. We would surmise that, even if some of the balls had moved somewhat differently from the ways in which they actually moved — or, indeed, even if there had been more or fewer balls remaining on the table — the player would have adjusted his action so as to ensure the same *kind* of result, even though event E itself

---

[7] On the notion of an 'event-fusion', see Thomson (1977), pp. 78–9.

would not have occurred in those circumstances. Citing the player's desire as an explanation of event *E*, then, explains not merely why *E* occurred, but, more interestingly, why an event of *that kind* occurred. And, it seems, no purely physical explanation of all of the sub-events of which *E* is the fusion can provide an interesting explanation of this sort. Such a purely physical explanation makes *E* appear to be a merely coincidental event and a 'fluke', in the sense that it provides us with no rational expectation that an event of *this kind* would still have occurred even if many of the individual movements of the balls had been rather different. Such a rational expectation can only be provided, it seems, by an explanation in terms of the player's *intentional state*. And such an explanation requires us to assign a *causal* role to that intentional state, a role which no purely physical state seems apt to occupy.

But what I have just said about the explanation of event *E* very often applies equally to the explanation of other event-fusions, such as the sort of event-fusion which constitutes an arm-rising. The advantage of focusing on event *E*, for our purposes, is simply that it is very much less likely, in its case, than it is in the case of an arm-rising, that such an event *could* be provided with a wholly physical causal explanation other than one which made it appear to be a mere 'fluke' which happened purely by coincidence.

XII: An Objection and a Reply

At this point I anticipate the following sort of objection. Surely, it may be said, someone could design a snooker-playing robot which could be pretty well relied upon to pot all of the snooker balls on a table — and when it did this there would occur an event of the same kind as *E*, which would be neither a 'fluke' nor 'coincidental': and yet, clearly, this event *would* have a purely physical causal explanation, since the robot would be a purely physical device possessing no mental states whatever, let alone a 'desire' to pot all of the snooker balls. So how can we be at all confident in denying that a wholly physical causal explanation of event *E* is available in the case of the *human* snooker-player?

My response is as follows. I agree that such a snooker-playing robot could, in principle, be designed and constructed. But note, first of all, that this is not to abandon appeal to *intentional causation* in our explanation of its feats, since we are quite explicitly appealing to the intentional states of the robot's designer and maker. It is not remotely plausible to suppose that a device like this could come into being *completely without* any causal contribution from the intentional states of any thinking being. Secondly, note that, in describing the workings of the robot, we have conceded that *it* possesses no intentional states whatever, such as a desire to pot all of the snooker balls on a table. Indeed, the force of the objection that has been raised — that the robot provides an example of how an event of the same kind as event *E* could have a purely physical causal explanation — rests upon the presumption that the robot does *not* have any intentional states. But then it follows that if we are to see the example of the robot as providing an alternative paradigm for the explanation of event *E* in the case of the *human* snooker-player, we have to regard that paradigm as an *eliminativist* one, in which appeal to the player's 'desire' to pot all of the balls has no genuine explanatory force.

Now, I concede that it is *possible* for every physical action which is performed by a human being to be caused in a wholly 'robotic' way, without any causal contribution from intentional states. But the point is that this possibility is an *extremely remote* one: we have no good reason whatever to suppose that it has been realized in this, the *actual* world. On the contrary, we have every reason to think that people's beliefs and desires *do* contribute causally to their physical behaviour and help to explain it. What we *cannot* do, however, is try to combine this conviction with the thought that, somehow, human behaviour does, in principle, have a purely physical causal explanation along the lines of robotic behaviour, in the hope of reconciling intentional causation with a thoroughgoing physicalism. We can either take intentional causation seriously, in which case we must abandon physicalism, or else we can cleave to physicalism, in which case we must be eliminativists (or, perhaps, epiphenomenalists) about the mental. There is no middle ground which allows us to have it both ways. However, as I have tried to show, we *can* espouse a version of 'dualism' (for want of a better word) which preserves one central tenet of physicalism, namely, claim (3): that *every physical event has a set of wholly physical causes which are collectively causally sufficient for the occurrence of that event.* If it is only a concern that this claim is denied by dualism which persuades some philosophers to reject dualism in favour of physicalism, then I hope I have shown them why that concern is quite misplaced. If, on the other hand, their physicalism is motivated by a faith in claim (4) — that *no physical event has a non-physical cause* — then I can only say that it seems to me that their doctrine is an unwarranted dogma which commits them, whether they like it or not, to eliminativism or epiphenomenalism regarding the mental. The kind of 'dualism' that I am defending is fully deserving of the title 'naturalistic' — provided that the term 'naturalism' is not hijacked as a mere synonym for 'physicalism', but is accorded its proper meaning as denoting a repudiation of the *super*natural.

Acknowledgements
Many thanks to John Heil for making me think about many of these matters, though we disagree about a lot of them. Thanks to him also, to Jim Edwards, and to members of audiences at the Universities of Durham and Stirling for their comments on an earlier draft of the paper. I am also grateful to an anonymous referee.

References

Armstrong, D.M. (1997), *A World of States of Affairs* (Cambridge: Cambridge University Press).
Geach, P.T. (1979), *Truth, Love and Immortality: An Introduction to McTaggart's Philosophy* (London: Hutchinson).
Lowe, E.J. (1989), *Kinds of Being: A Study of Individuation, Identity and the Logic of Sortal Terms* (Oxford: Blackwell).
Lowe, E.J. (1996), *Subjects of Experience* (Cambridge: Cambridge University Press).
McGinn, C. (1995), 'Consciousness and space', *Journal of Consciousness Studies*, **2** (3), pp. 220–30.
Owens, D. (1992), *Causes and Coincidences* (Cambridge: Cambridge University Press).
Papineau, D. (1993), *Philosophical Naturalism* (Oxford: Blackwell).
Sorabji, R. (1980), *Necessity, Cause and Blame: Perspectives on Aristotle's Theory* (London: Duckworth).
Strawson, G. (1994), *Mental Reality* (Cambridge, MA: MIT Press).
Thomson, J.J. (1977), *Acts and Other Events* (Ithaca, NY: Cornell University Press).
Von Wright, G.H. (1971), *Explanation and Understanding* (London: Routledge and Kegan Paul).

John McCrone

A Bifold Model of Freewill

The folk psychology view of the faculty of freewill is that it is innate, unitary, structureless and, of course, free. A bifold[1] approach to the mind, as taken by Vygotsky, Mead, Luria and others, argues that, like all the other higher mental abilities of humans, freewill is in fact largely a socially-constructed and language-enabled habit of thought. There is a neurology for this habit to latch on to — after all, the 'raw' animal brain is built for acting rather than contemplating. But it is the social superstructure — the habit of monitoring and even directing our planning behaviour — which creates much of the traditional mystery. Indeed, ironically, it is actually central to the socially-constructed Western 'script' of freewill that we deny the social origins of this ability to take charge of our own brains.

---

[1]   The term bifold (McCrone, 1993) is used to denote the general idea that the human mind is the product of two kinds of evolutionary process — the biological and the cultural. But it is also used to indicate a specific subset of such theories — ones like those of Vygotsky, Luria and Dennett in particular that share certain key features. So, for instance, unlike some recent memetic theories of consciousness (Blackmore, 1999), the internalization of language rather than some general brain faculty of 'imitation' is seen as the mechanism by which cultural patterns of thought come to have a hold on our minds. The memes encouraged by a culture are also expected to have a reasonably clear social utility and not to be just ones that flourish simply because they are good at flourishing.

Other key bifold themes that are perhaps not so well developed in much of the recent Vygotskian-flavoured literature (Dewart, 1989; Donald, 1991; Deacon, 1997) include the argument that the animal mind is different because it is locked into the present, that the developmental plasticity of the brain means that language and culture can literally reshape the brain's circuits, that the relationship between thought and language is one of a scaffolding device (Clark, 1998) or cognitive crutch (Dennett, 1998) with words being used to probe for meaning, and that thought and inner speech eventually become largely fused within the adult mind so that just the 'inkling' of a speech act can do the thought-driving work of a fully-expressed speech act (McCrone, 1999).

The claim that speech and speech-enabled habits of thought are things that 'grow into the brain' during development also places the bifold view apart from a currently popular vein of theorizing within evolutionary psychology which sees language as being central to the special mental abilities of humans, but treat it and even many of the associated abilities (like Theory of Mind) as genetically-evolved brain modules (Carruthers, 1996; Mithen, 1996; Bickerton, 1995).

Equally, the bifold model — stressing as it does an interaction between culturally-evolved thought habits and the natural thinking and reasoning powers of the animal brain — is distinct from theories in which the pendulum swings too far to the cultural side, so, for example, denying thought to infants or animals (Wittgenstein, 1922; Davidson, 1984), or claiming that learnt grammatical structures have a radical effect on even perception (Whorf, 1956).

Journal of Consciousness Studies, **6**, No. 8–9, 1999, pp. 241–59

Introduction

Freewill seems a straight-forward enough business. I feel the mental effort of making a choice and anyone who tells me my choices are predetermined can quickly be proved wrong — I will simply do the opposite of what's expected. Of course there are a few mysteries. When I crook a finger or raise a hand, it is hard to be sure how I really make these simple actions happen. Alternatively, when I want to get out of a cosy bed on a cold winter's morning, willing the equally simple act of throwing back the covers becomes curiously problematic (James, 1981). So there are some complexities to the story. But the ancient tripartite division of the mind into thought, feeling and will seems indisputable (Ryle, 1949). Nestled somewhere in the humid folds of our brains must be a moving soul-stuff or at least some clever neural machinery of volition.

Such is the folk psychology (Morton, 1980) view of volition and already many of the standard suppositions about the nature of freewill are apparent. It is seen as a unitary faculty — any differences are of degree rather than kind. It is innate — all humans are born with the power, although its shoots may need nurturing to grow healthy. It is dimensionless — the willing of an act is a point-like event, clearly separate from deliberations that may have preceded it. And free means free — don't you dare call it an illusion.

As will be seen, this prickly response to the threat of deterministic-sounding explanations of freewill is in fact a big clue to its true nature. But first, how should science tackle the problem?

Many would favour the normal reductionist route. Focus on the smaller components out of which the complex apparatus must be built. Thus we see research which looks for the brain bump that becomes particularly active when a person shifts a joystick in one of four possible directions (Spence *et al.*, 1997) and attempts to track the emergence of a 'spontaneous' impulse into bright awareness (Libet, 1985).

But an alternative is instead to look to the big picture and work back from a more general model of the human mind and its various 'mental faculties'. The argument made here is that the human mind is bifold[1] with socially-constructed habits of thought being the software that exploits resources to be found in the biological 'hardware' of brains. And so, therefore, far from being innate and unitary, the faculty of freewill turns out to be as much a social idea as a neurological process.

Of course, going for the big picture is to risk seeming sketchy on the details. Particularly when talking about the convoluted history of the Western concept of psychological faculties (Danziger, 1997) or the vexed question of how language may interact with the brain to produce thought (Carruthers & Boucher, 1998), the account given here will seem over generalized. But the intent is really to demonstrate how different an old problem might look once placed in a new, more broadly-based, setting.

The General Argument for a Bifold Strategy

It is a commonplace that the human mind is shaped by culture (Jahoda, 1992). But the normal assumption is that the effect is merely 'horticultural' (Vygotsky and Luria, 1994; McCrone, 1993). The mental faculties of humans are believed to be innate, being genetically-formed and so present in seed form at birth. They need only a modicum of watering and perhaps some later judicious pruning to achieve their glorious flower. Therefore the impact of cultural factors on some essential ability like freewill would be superficial.

But a more radical line has been taken by a series of authors (Müller, 1888; Vygotsky, 1978; 1986; Luria, 1976; 1982; Mead, 1934) and has found modern expression within psychology and sociology in such camps of thought as the socio-cultural school of cognitive development (Zivin, 1979; Wertsch, 1991; Diaz and Berk, 1992), the social constructionist movement (Coulter, 1979; Berger and Luckmann, 1979; Gergen and Davis, 1985; Burr, 1995), and, most recently, in the philosophy of language and thought (Dennett, 1991). Their argument is that we are born with naked animal brains, then, through the learning of language, we are able to internalize an apparatus of socially-formed thought habits. These language-enabled skills give us all our distinctively human abilities such as self-awareness, recollective memory, socialized emotions and structured thought. We become loaded with a mental software that can drive our brains to places they would not normally go.

In this view, the 'raw' animal brain has consciousness, but it is a consciousness locked into the present tense (Walker, 1983; McCrone, 1999). Even a casual acquaintance with animals tells that they do not lack for intelligence or awareness. They can associate, anticipate, recognise, choose, inhibit, show emotion — the full range of mental responses. But these responses are to the events of the moment.

Few people would claim that a cat lazing on the lawn is likely to be reminiscing about the mice it used to catch in its youth or making plans for the evening about how to get its own back on the tom down the road. A cat lives in the moment and something has to happen — the rustle of a mouse or an upswelling pang of hunger — for its mind to be stirred into a response. The philosopher Ludwig Wittgenstein summed up the situation neatly when he asked: 'We say a dog is afraid his master will beat him, but not that he is afraid his master will beat him tomorrow. Why not?' (1976, para. 650).

Admittedly, this argument is much easier to sustain for a creature like a cat than a more active animal like a chimpanzee. But, while the complex social lifestyle of chimps demands a more constant level of mental alertness and response (de Waal, 1982), there is still no behavioural evidence that they can rifle freely through their memory banks to recall childhood events or pursue contextually-displaced lines of thought, such as worry about who will care for them in their old age (Walker, 1983). Language, when it evolved in humans, made a difference because it could be used to lead the brain out of the current moment and turn its responding powers onto displaced or even entirely imaginary contexts.

Words obviously have the power to summon knowledge from a suitably-trained brain. Hearing a word like rhinoceros or oil-well instantly begins to evoke images and unlock associations in the mind. And combinations of words can be used to rouse highly specific contexts — compare saying simply rhinoceros to 'a rhinoceros dancing in a pink tutu' or 'that rhinoceros image which sprang to your mind just a moment ago'. And because words are just puffs of air — vocal acts of standard dimensions — it is as easy to use a word to open a door into thoughts about something vague or abstract, like love, life, or the Universe, as something concrete, like rhinos or oilwells (de Saussure, 1959; Aitchison, 1994).

The other part of the machinery of language is grammar — the ability to take a complex situation and break it down into a sequential tale of cause and effect. The common feature of all human grammars is that they demand that people talk in sentences — speech units which are only complete if they contain a subject, a verb and an object (Chomsky, 1965). The order of these components may differ across cultures (Greenberg, 1963) and sometimes a component may be implied rather than uttered (Bloom, 1970). But the aim remains to tell an agent-based tale of who did what to whom — to take the analogue complexity of real life and express it in a serial, digital, stream of words.

The importance of grammar is that it acts as an engine to thought, giving it an in-built momentum. We do not simply murmur rhinoceros and leave it at that. We feel obliged to extract a sentence from the situation — such as 'my, that's an angry look-ing rhino' or 'hasn't he got a dusty skin?'. We pull out new words — like angry and dusty — that can then become the stimulus for further sentence forming (Jackendoff, 1996). Rousing the idea of dustiness might bring with it associated images of animals rolling in dust-bowls or knowledge about skin parasites. As we comment on this unlocked knowledge in turn, our minds will be moved even further away from the events of the current moment along some independent train of thought (McCrone, 1993; 1999).

It should be noted that in this view, there is not the traditional difficulty about which comes first, the word or the thought (MacNamara, 1977), as the argument is that words provoke ideas and ideas provoke more words in a self-fuelling cycle of mental activity. Language only leads in the sense that without its formal structure, it would be impossible to scaffold the brain's natural thinking abilities and direct them away from a response to the current moment to a response to imagined or remem-bered moments (Clark, 1998; Dennett, 1998).

The question of when language evolved and how much of its structure is genetically-determined are obviously contentious issues. Suffice it to say that there is reasonable evidence that only Homo sapiens had the necessary vocal equipment for articulate, grammatically-complex, speech (Lieberman, 1991). And the genetic component probably has more to do with the fact that the human brain is generally good at sequenced motor acts (Kimura, 1979) and that the infant brain finds it almost impos-sible to avoid extracting grammatical rules from the most rudimentary speech input (Elman et al., 1996; Saffran et al. 1996), rather than because grammar is, in some Chomskian sense, wired in.[2]

But what really matters here is the use to which language ability is put in driving minds. And it is crucial to note that the effect of language can be both overt and cov-ert. It is overt when we speak to rouse specific contexts in the minds of others or use self-addressed sub-vocal speech to rouse new contexts in our own. But the words we learn, and the networks of meaning which become attached to them, also texture our

---

[2] It is plain that the Chomskian view of grammar as an innate faculty is still the dominant view within much of science — witness the continuing approbation of Chomskian-minded thinkers like Pinker (1994). And certainly there is no intent to deny that the human brain and vocal tract show at least some genetic adaptations for articulate speech (McCrone, 1990; 1999). But the rise of connectionist models of computation (Elman et al., 1996; Clark and Thornton, 1997) have made it easier to see how brains can 'extract' much of the structure of grammar from apparently impoverished input, while more care-ful thought about what the Chomskian view requires in terms of genetic coding (Mueller, 1996) have undermined the innateness hypothesis at an even more fundamental level — simply put, the genome does not have room to code for the precise placement of brain circuitry in the way a Chomskian approach would seem to demand.

brain circuitry. In simple terms, they carve out memory paths that would not otherwise be present in our heads.

One of the great surprises of recent neuro-imaging has been the discovery that the human brain responds to words with highly distributed patterns of activity — words are not decoded within a single module such as Wernicke's area but rouse activity in far-flung corners of the cortex. So, for example, when subjects are shown a black and white drawing of an object like a pencil and asked to associate either an action or a colour with it, saying *yellow* stirs the colour processing areas of the visual pathways while saying *write* stirs motion perception areas (Martin *et al.*, 1995).

The precise way the brain represents different classes of words is still in some doubt (see Damasio *et al.*, 1996; Pulvermüller, 1999). But the general message is that the structure of words and grammar penetrates deep into the organisation of the brain. Categories and schemas that might have evolved culturally can become part of the brain's apparent biology. And indeed, some have argued that the greatly delayed maturation of the human brain (Lenneberg, 1967) — which makes human infants so dangerously helpless for the first few years of their lives — may be a positive adaptation to allow each individual brain to become imprinted with the language rhythms and thought habits of the culture into which it finds itself born.

Thus while the bifold model claims that the origins of mental behaviour has two sources — one genetic, the other cultural — in practice the boundary becomes blurred as the software comes to texture the hardware. Ways of organising knowledge that may have evolved within society can come to form associative networks in our brains and then do hidden work in driving our thoughts in particular directions or to leap to certain memories. So, even if notions to do with selfhood and willing might have a social, word-encoded, origin, they too could come physically to mould the brain's neural landscape in ways that conceivably would show up in suitably deft neuro-imaging experiments.[3]

Unravelling the Faculties

What does this then say about the mental faculties of humans? The bifold model claims that behind every apparently unitary and innate faculty there will be a set of raw hardware powers — the abilities every animal brain can bring to bear on the processing of a moment — and then the language-based habits that humans create to extend these powers in desired directions.

Taking memory as an example, the argument would be that the brain has evolved to recognise and associate — to apply memory in finding meaning in the moment. But to recollect — to reconstruct earlier moments of awareness or recall knowledge

---

[3] Luria (1973) was able to mount a subtle argument about the way the regulatory structure of language grows into the human brain — particularly the prefrontal cortex — based largely just on EEG and lesion data, so there is nothing especially modern about the idea. It should also be noted that while Dennett (1991) has recently argued a similar case, he undoubtedly goes too far in claiming that language and culture act to install a serial machine in what is essentially parallel hardware, so creating the illusion of a virtual user dwelling amidst the multiple drafts of possible experience. While it is said here that culture does indeed install a strong sense of self and a habit of self-monitoring in our heads, it is an important feature of the 'raw' brain that it forms an attention-based angle into each passing moment — it views life from a series of perspectives, forming each new mental 'frame' at roughly the rate of about one every half second — and so is already both a serial and a parallel machine (McCrone, 1999).

independently of context — we must prod our memory banks (or neural landscapes to use a more appropriate metaphor) with the organized use of words (Whitten and Leonard, 1981). Quite simply, to remember what we ate for breakfast, we must ask ourselves the question and wait to see if the words jog a set of impressions to life. Through association, the word breakfast should rouse typical breakfast-like experiences like toast or cornflakes. As such possibilities are roused, the brain can then recognize the correct choice. It may even generate a 'snapshot' memory of ourselves raising a slice of marmalade-smeared toast to our mouths. Or, to be more accurate, the brain may generate a vivid anticipatory image (Neisser, 1976) of what it would be like to be back in that moment — an image that would be more a best-guess reconstruction than a faithful mental replay of prior events (Bartlett, 1932; Neisser, 1967; Conway, 1990).

So we humans can roam our internal memory landscapes 'at will' because we have words to rouse contexts — to make guesses and suggestions — and brains that then will respond to those contexts with a click of recognition and a flow of associations or anticipatory images. Voluntary remembering feels like an effort because we have to pay attention to the process and keep prodding our brains until they give up the desired information. But we also have involuntary remembering when it is our current environment that triggers the association. We might meet an old schoolfriend one day and a host of long forgotten memories about schoolday escapades will come flooding back.

All the mental faculties can be broken down in this fashion — and, in so doing, come to be seen as different ways of looking at the same basic bifold interaction (McCrone, 1993;1999). Imagination divides into a natural brain ability — the ability to anticipate or stir up a state of quasi-perceptual priming (Rao and Ballard, 1999) — and the use of words to provoke the brain into generating such anticipatory states independent of any current context. Reason divides into the natural brain ability to associate and anticipate, and the use of words to direct such powers in the pursuit of goals not dictated by the immediate environment. Even consciousness itself breaks down into raw awareness — the subjective experience of responding to the demands of the moment — and the learnt ability of humans to introspect — to step back from the flow of each moment and use the power of words over thought and memory to contemplate the fact of having subjective experiences (Mead, 1934).

It has to be admitted that, despite the best efforts of psychologists like Vygotsky and Luria, the evidence for such an understanding of the human mind remains more circumstantial than direct. While there may be some 'natural' experiments to consider (Singh and Zingg, 1941; Lane, 1976; Luria and Yudovich, 1956; for review see McCrone, 1993), it is plainly impossible to carry out the required controlled test in which a sample of children are deprived of exposure to language and culture in order to discover the effect on their mentality. However, the study of the development of self-regulation in children (Diaz and Berk, 1992), across cultures (Luria, 1976), and particularly in the field of memory (Vygotsky, 1978), coupled with a careful consideration of the mentality of animals (Walker, 1983) and the implausibility that the genome could code for the level of mental structure claimed for humans (Mueller, 1996), does allow a strong case to be made. As the philosopher Andy Clark put it:

Language [is] the ultimate upgrade: so ubiquitous it is almost invisible; so intimate, it is not clear whether it is a kind of tool or an added dimension of the user. But whatever the boundaries, we confront a complex coalition in which the basic biological brain is fantastically empowered by some of its strangest and most recent creations: words in the air, symbols on the printed page (1998, p. 182).

The Social Construction of Mental Habits

The bifold approach goes beyond saying that the higher mental abilities of humans are merely language-enabled. It says the kinds of concepts and mental habits we are taught are socially constructed — they evolve socially and exist primarily for the furtherance of society. The software is loaded into the brains of each new generation not for the benefit of the individual but because minds primed to think in certain ways have proved to be successful for a particular social group, in a particular habitat, in the classical Darwinian struggle of life.

The Social Constructionist school in psychology and anthropology (Burr, 1995) gives a way of studying this fact by focusing on the vocabulary used by a society — particularly words to do with emotions and personal qualities — and showing how these words encode socially-useful ways of thinking that can then be transmitted efficiently across generations.

This role of vocabulary is easiest to appreciate when the language of another culture or time is being considered. For instance, Japanese culture has many words that have a surprisingly alien ring to Western ears. There is the emotion of *amae* — the sweet feeling of being helplessly dependent (Morsbach and Tyler, 1986). Amae exists naturally between son and mother, but is also valued between worker and manager or pupil and teacher. For those reared in the emotional economy of Western culture, with its emphasis on individualism and self-reliance, the idea of helpless dependence sounds far from sweet. And the behaviour implied by 'feeling' amae towards a social superior — the putting on of a show of fawning babyish ineptitude so as to bring out a motherly response — sounds positively distasteful.

The Japanese have many such terms for describing fine nuances of emotion which relate to situations that are socially-valued in their culture. There is *ijirashi* — the feeling that comes from witnessing a worthy person overcoming a difficult obstacle. Or *on* — the sense of debt that every individual gladly feels towards family and ancestors. By contrast, Western words that describe passive, dependent, social relationships (like to fawn or to presume) tend mostly to carry negative overtones — they spell out ways not to behave. In their stead, Western culture is rich in words that glorify the feelings of being an individual (with an individual will) such as independent, strong-minded, extrovert, leader, dominant.

By the same token, with the Westernisation of Japanese youth has come the adoption of Western terminology. So, for example, the importation of the Western idea of love as a magnetic attraction between two free spirits has necessitated the importation of Western words as well. Japanese couples now talk about being *happee* with their partners and living in the cosy glow of a *romanchiku moodo* (Buruma, 1984).

The effect of such role-describing words on the new minds being born into a particular society is subtle yet strong. As the sociologist Charles Cooley wrote (1912, p. 69): 'Such words for instance as good, right, truth, love, home, justice, beauty, freedom, are powerful makers of what they stand for. "This way," says the word, "is an

interesting thought: come and find it." And so we are led on to rediscover old knowledge.' The social constructionist argument is that a child learns the words and
through the words gets a handle on the social role and kinds of behaviour the words
imply.

The General Value of Having 'Willed' Individuals

Already suspicions should have been raised about the nature of freewill — about the
reality that lies behind the deceptive simplicity of a single emotionally-charged word.
But to make sense of the cultural side of the bifold story, we need to dig a little deeper
and ask what is the evolutionary value in creating 'willed' individuals? Why foster an
apparent power for choice, and so deviance, when it might seem that blind social obedience would have a greater pay-off?

Paleoanthropologists have often noted that the great apes seemed to be heading
down an evolutionary blind alley. The big brains of apes might seem a good thing, but
the metabolic cost of feeding such a hungry organ (Kety and Schmidt, 1946), and the
years needed to train it, means that species like gorillas and chimpanzees produce
very few offspring. A chimp mother normally manages one infant every three to five
years or barely half a dozen in a lifetime (Sluckin and Herbert, 1986). Such a low
replacement rate puts the apes on a knife-edge of survival. And early Hominid species, despite bipedal walking, opposable thumb, and their other physical adaptations,
would presumably have suffered from the same reproductive mathematics.

The way out of this bind would have been the emergence of some level of self-
control. Comparing ape and human lifestyles, it has been argued (Johanson and Edey,
1982; McCrone, 1990) that the key to early hominid success was the development of
a new social style — one based on food-sharing, a division of labour, reasonably
monogamous pair bonding, and co-operative child care. If the modern-day hunter-
gatherer society stands as a good model (Service, 1962), then the solution to the
Hominid problem of raising large numbers of helpless and hungry-brained infants
was to mix high-risk hunting with a low-risk foraging strategy, then ensure the systematic sharing of the proceeds.

Sharing obviously implies self-control. There is some evidence of group hunting in
chimpanzees with a sharing of the spoils (Boesch, 1990). But quite another level of
forbearance is required for a human hunter to travel a day alone in search of game or
honey then return with a heavy load to base camp to feed the greater group. Or,
indeed, for those who stayed foraging close to home to save some food for a luckless
and hungry hunter.

Food sharing is the most immediately convincing example. But the same principle
applies to any other activity in which individual forbearance or willingness to tolerate
risk is necessary to produce a pay-off in terms of group survival. Despite their considerable intelligence, chimpanzees cannot help but be largely selfish animals, seeking
always to satisfy their current wants. And to the extent that they show deliberately
co-operative behaviour, such as hunting or grooming, it is as a response to the
demands and possibilities of the moment. However humans, once they had the language to pin down abstract concepts such as fairness and duty, could internalize the
needs of their societies. They could make the individual mind a supervised place. As
Mead (1934) argued, the 'self' that runs the show is really a social idea — the

generalized other. We build up a picture of what is thought to be standard behaviour and standard goals within our culture then attempt to filter our actions through that internalized schema.

In this view, somewhat ironically, we are born without the habit of introspection and then become sharply aware of ourselves as individual consciousnesses because society places a duty of care in our heads. Using the structure of self-addressed speech to organize our thinking — to turn our attention on ourselves — we begin to reflect and deliberate, passing a social rule over our every impulse towards action (or inaction). And the more complex the social schemas — the more complex the inner negotiations we must mediate and outer mask we must present (Goffman, 1969) — the more conscious of being an agent with individual responsibilities and possibilities we become.

The reason why this active sense of self would be better than a simple programmed obedience is that a culture could not code for what would be the right course of action in every situation. So, by setting broad goals and leaving individuals to negotiate the detailed answers, society would be ensuring the most creative solutions. The kind of freedom a society would be aiming to give its members would be the freedom to work as hard as they could to do general good for the society — to be good team players, in other words.

The Ifaluk View of Self-Regulation

The idea that self-awareness (or the habit of introspecting and thus the forging of a sense of personal identity) is a social construct designed to make us creatively self-policing may be hard to stomach. But the social origins of 'innate' character traits such as forbearance, conscience or honesty is again perhaps easier to appreciate in cultures other than our own.

One culture whose self-regulation has been studied in depth by anthropologists (Lutz, 1986; 1988) is the Ifaluk, a group of four hundred Polynesians on a half-mile square, hurricane-lashed, coral atoll in the Western Pacific. In good times, the Ifaluk can grow more than enough taro, breadfruit and coconut to survive. But hurricanes can bring unpredictable years of hardship. To cope, the Ifaluk have a tight-knit social code that promotes the sharing of food, the sharing of labour in the fields and even the sharing of children — the Ifaluk have an unusual policy of adoption where nearly half their children are fostered out to relations.

The general success of this social style can be judged by the fact that murder is unknown on the island — the most aggressive act witnessed by Lutz during her year there was when one islander seized the shoulder of another (an act for which he was immediately fined). And when she awoke one night to find a male intruder in her hut, her terrified screams had the islanders laughing for days afterwards. The man had simply lost his way in the dark while attempting to rendezvous with a lover. That Lutz might have any cause for alarm seemed quite outlandish (Lutz, 1988).

But it was the reason why the Ifaluk felt they were well-behaved that was signifi-cant. Lutz reported that when asked to explain emotion words — words that signified mental causation — the islanders always talked in terms of external situations and actions rather than internal feelings.

For example, one islander explaining four different types of unhappiness, said (Lutz, 1986, p. 271): 'If someone goes away on a trip, you feel *livemam* (longing) and *lalom-weiu* (loneliness/sadness), and if you had nothing to give them [as a going away gift] you feel *tang* (frustration/grief) and *filengaw* (incapable/uncomfortable).' As Lutz noted (1986, p. 283): 'While [Westerners] define emotions primarily as internal feeling states, the Ifaluk see the emotions as evoked in, and inseparable from, social activity.'

The Ifaluk were equally straight-forward about the reason for their good behaviour. The same word *metagu* (anxiety/fear), was used for the fear of physical threats like storms and sharks and for the fear of knowingly committing social transgressions. Rather than appealing to inner qualities, the language of the Ifaluk acknowledged that they acted out of a sense of social pressure — and the thought of being socially-controlled carried no negative connotations within their culture.

A flip-side to the feeling of *metagu* was the feeling of *song* — a sense of justified anger when witnessing another doing wrong. If an Ifaluk male were to walk past a seated group of elders without bending respectfully, there would be shocked comments aimed at the individual (Lutz, 1988). Or, if a woman's cousin failed to help in the fields as custom demanded, then the woman would denounce her cousin bitterly in front of the rest of the village. In modern Western society, the belief that goodness must come from within means that attempts to exert peer pressure are rarely so direct. To be scolded in public is to be treated like a child who does not know any better — an affront to our innate reason. But in tribal societies, public mocking and shaming are seen as entirely natural, not a fall-back mechanism to be employed when some individual's inner instincts have gone awry.

The Western Model of Freewill

By now we should be alert to the fact that the Western idea of volition or freewill might be a highly particular one.[4] And if there are philosophical confusions about the concept of freewill, they may be confusions actually written into the script provided by our culture. So what is the history of that script?

The Western folk psychology model of the mind begins with Greek philosophy, particularly the tripartite model of Plato (Dodds, 1963; Simon, 1978), and the similar, though not identical, views of Aristotle (Danziger, 1997). Plato introduced the idea of a particular psychic structure. The lowest part of the mind (*epithumetikon*) consisted of base appetites such as lust and hunger which inhabited the lower body. The nobler passions (*thumoeides*) beat in the breast while the highest part of the mind, reason (*logistikon*), occupied the head.

Although the Greeks divided the mind into these still familiar partitions, their view on the source of right-thinking action was perhaps rather different (Sorabji, 1993). For Aristotle, satisfying desire was basically good unless carried to excess. And the way to counteract any wrongful tendencies was simply clear thinking. Inspired by their success with mathematics, the Greeks believed the universe to be a lawful place

---

[4] There is also an 'Eastern' mythology of the will, of course — one that with Asian culture's emphasis on the social rather than the individual puts the situation almost exactly the other way round. The Eastern goal, as made explicit in religious practices such as Zen meditation, becomes not to express the individual will but to become utterly passive, to release all sense of willed action and allow the self to dissolve back into the universal consciousness.

and that the exercise of reason put humans in touch with these natural laws. The Greeks had no need for the concept of motivating willpower because it was clear or confused thought that automatically led them to their actions (Danziger, 1997).

Plato's tripartite model was eventually welded into place in Western culture with its adoption by the Catholic Church (Haren, 1985). The Christian faith, in contrast to others such as Judaism and Islam (Harré, 1983), had always been distinctive in stressing the idea of an inner battle between spirituality and animality. For other faiths, as with the Ifaluk islanders, it was enough to observe social mores. But Christianity saw evil as something personal, something to be rooted out of the individual soul.

The reasons for this view are complex. One of the core beliefs of Christianity was that the soul departed the body at death, leaving behind the body's sensuous appetites and passions (whereas in many other mythologies, bodily form went with the deceased to ensure they could still have a good time on the other side!). So, as scholars such as Plotinus, St Augustine and Aquinas reworked the Platonic model into a full-blown theology, the idea of a contest between good and bad — a battle of higher self over base impulse — became the abiding moral issue. The call was for a separation of spirit and flesh in life as well as in death. Salvation depended on an inner victory — achieving true purity of mind — rather than merely making an outward, or social, show of piety. So what for the Greeks had been a rather undemanding quest for a reasonable balance in behaviour (which found its expression in a literature of 'self-care' — Foucault, 1990), became the Catholic Church's tortured inner quest for sanctity of thought and deed, scaffolded by a social framework of confessionals, penances, parables and threats of eternal damnation.

However, this very particular model of mind fostered by Christianity may have been more than just a fluke of a belief system. Taking the memetic view of religion as a self-propagating thought virus (Dawkins, 1993), an obvious key to the success of early Christianity was its portability across different cultures. By casting moral issues as a choice — do you continue to follow the pagan ways of your local culture, which are so obviously just fleetingly-held social constructions, or do you tap into the true order through the private exercise of your reason? — Christian theology acted to detach individuals from their existing social contexts and convince them to forge an allegiance to a new abstract moral context.[5] So the rapid spread of Christianity even in Roman times would have had much to do with the efficiency of a conversion mechanism based on the idea of a personal relationship with God and therefore personal responsibility for all acts — with the mirror image demand that individuals resist the coercive forces that might exist within their own now alien local culture. Out of this potent mix emerged a clear theme of individualism and inner contest, even if the Christian Church itself came to embrace many variants of the basic proselytizing creed.

The general Greek view of the mind became the general Christian one. Then, with the scientific revolution of the Enlightenment and the Romantic reaction it largely inspired, Plato's tripartite model became subtly recast yet again.

The birth of science, with the deterministic physics of Galileo and Newton and the new clockwork contrivances of the day, led Enlightenment philosophers like Hobbes (1951), Locke (1975), and Condillac (1930), to see the mind as little more than a

---

[5] Much could probably be made of the fact that the embodiment of Christianity in the single figure of Christ, together with the insistence on a single God, itself presents the paradigmatic model of the 'willed individual', above any social setting and so faced with the 'problem' of moral choice.

complex machine. Humans, they argued, were essentially civilized animals. It was language and education that turned them into rational, well-behaved members of society. So being good was a matter of sober reason and social pressure rather than a mystical inner force. This realisation led reformers like Hutcheson and Bentham to seek better designed social structures that would produce better behaved people (Hampson, 1968). And the need for an evolutionary balance — a trade-off between individuals and their societies — was explicitly recognized in slogans such as creating the greatest happiness for the greatest number.

A particularly influential philosopher in the development of the modern idea of freewill was Hume. The Greek distinction had been essentially between clear and unclear thinking with no particular need for a concept of motivation — people did harm when their passions ran over and good when they saw the reason inherent in the Universe. But by making reason a matter of ordinary education rather than contact with the divine mind, the Enlightenment turned it into something dry and disputable. So, looking for what might drive the mind instead, Hume (1967) popularized the idea of emotion — a mental motion or agitation. For Hume, there were both calm dispositions and violent feelings. But his crucial step was to strip away the social and rational context for human action and credit fundamental motive power to a set of internal, bodily mechanisms.

Of course, Hume was not wrong in suggesting that human biology comes with a basic repertoire of appetites and instinctual needs. But he was arguing that the whole 'package' of a socially constructed emotion such as love, honour, guilt or valour — complex feelings which describe both a socially-defined way of behaving and the kinds of sensations that normally accompany the playing of that role (Harré, 1986), — was something innate. More importantly, Hume helped to popularize the necessary jargon that eventually led to a highly distilled notion of the will as a pure and contextless motive force.

In many ways, Hume was ahead of his time. Generally speaking, the Enlightenment encouraged a more pragmatic view of the mind in which the shaping hand of culture remained apparent. So, for example, there was Locke's story on self-awareness as being a learnt construct — the perceiving of being a perceiver (Locke, 1975). But while the idea of rational behaviour brought about by the civilizing influence of society carried the day in politics, economics and education, it did not triumph in popular culture. Instead, the Enlightenment generated its own backlash — the Romantic Movement — which eventually produced an even more charged notion of will.

One of the ironies of the Enlightenment was that it shocked people into realizing that the rules of their society were man-made, not God-given, and so could be changed to make life fairer for all. But instead of embracing this fact, almost immediately writers such as Rousseau began to treat society's rules as if they were a straitjacket on the soul (Mason, 1979). Petty reason was now something to be rejected. The real self lay in giving expression to what was natural — or increasingly, what seemed irrational.

Writers, poets, painters and musicians led the way, but soon philosophers like Nietzsche (1961) were joining in this rebellion against reasoned behaviour. In their writings, the Platonic tripartite model shifted ground yet again. Reason remained but was now demoted to lowly rank. The different types of feeling — base appetite and noble passion — became fused as Humean varieties of emotion. And the new, now dominant, component of the tripartite model became the will — a pure psychic force.

Ironically, this final reification of the will had much to do with contemporary scientific discoveries about magnetism, hydraulic pressure and other forms of 'invisible' force (Danziger, 1997). Science seemed to be saying that all systems were made of mechanically organized components which were then driven by some hidden source of energy. Many believed that life itself had a motive force — the *élan vital*. Likewise, an animating energy seemed necessary to fire up the brain, explaining how its machinery could be moved to act in often unpredictable ways. The connection became all the stronger with late eighteenth century discoveries about the electrical properties of nerves. Physiologists like Bain (1977) spoke about nervous energy accumulating as the result of the digestion of food and this stored energy needing to find some discharge in action.

This glorification of pure will power — the essence of the individual mind — continued into the twentieth century. In science proper, the will actually began to turn back into something much tamer. Psychologists preferred to talk in terms of instincts and then, later, drives or motives. With the rise of cognitive science, even motivation became a matter of deterministic computation — another dry information process — while the affective aspects — what emotions feel like or what cognitive structures they might underpin (McCrone, 1993) — became a matter almost entirely undiscussed.

But while science headed towards one extreme, popular culture was heading towards the other. Freud served up a highly successful version of the Romantic myth in which the id — the monstrous energy of the unconscious — was forever threatening to break through the defences of the rational but socially-repressed ego. French Existentialist philosophers like Sartre offered up another vision of the human condition with their calls for authenticity and the smashing of the iron band of bourgeois restrictions placed around the human heart.

And plainly, modern culture has become obsessed with images of the individual will *in excelsis*. From broken-down gun slingers to cartoon-like Rambo figures, the story is about being true to the self within despite the toughest social pressures to conform. Even clothing and manner have become a formal assertion of the possession of freewill. From teddy boy quiffs to modern day body piercings, the look is about social rebellion — if not actual, then at least potential.

Yet the point is not that modern society is sick or doomed. To a surprising extent, given the boldness of the imagery, people still remain embedded in a web of social ties and are well able to exercise self-restraint. Even those famous for their anti-social stance, such as New Yorkers or Hell's Angels, still rub along, living a life of daily small kindnesses and co-operation.[6] Also, it could be argued that the falsely heightened sense of individual will in Western society does have its own evolutionary payback. Many see the socially constructed emphasis on individuality as the driving force behind the great expansion of Western culture over the past thousand years.[7]

---

[6] Even accounts of Hell's Angels that play up their outlaw status (Thompson, 1966) cannot help but also emphasize how tightly controlled they are by the social construction of what it is to be a Hell's Angel. Or indeed, how ordinary is their emotional role-play when they are not being called upon to live up to some of the more specialized demands of their well-defined cultural code.

[7] In effect, this would be a continuation of the same trick that worked for Christianity — the detaching of individuals from a local social context so as to control their behaviour through an allegiance to a set of

However, it does emphasize how the roots of our impulse-filtering and decision-making behaviour have come to be disguised. It is central to the script of modern Western society that moral agency lies within and that this self is essentially free. Even our legal, political and educational systems depend on the assumption that it is fair to treat individuals as point-like moral agents, fully in charge of what comes out of their own minds. Of course, in practice, allowances are made for sanity, maturity and other extenuating circumstances. But the clear goal is to keep pushing individuals until they can live up to a model of autonomous behaviour set by Western culture.

In thousands of tiny lessons — from the mother who crossly tells her son not to fuss when he falls off his bike and grazes a knee to the manager raising the weekly sales target for his staff — the message is to take charge of yourself and your feelings so society can then judge you hard for the quality of your self-regulation and decision-making.

So What Is Freewill?

Simply put, freewill is a socially-potent word to which we attempt to live up. The general need for willed — or at least self-policing — individuals has always been there in human history. Through much philosophical agonizing, that need has taken on condensed form in a single word. Problems then arise when we become entangled in the mythology — when we go looking for the pure motivating essence that is implied but is not actually there.

The greatest difficulty with freewill is that we seem to need a loophole that will allow a deterministic biological system — the human brain — to act in undetermined ways. Attempts to counter the bogy of Newtonian determinism (Ryle, 1949) can be seen in recent appeals to quantum mechanical effects (Zohar, 1990), or even the new mathematics of chaos (Trefil, 1997).[8] But this is to fall for the myth of freewill as an entirely biological production, and not a bifold exercise that involves a heavy dash of culture.

In its strange way, human choice is indeed determined — it is socially determined because the cognitive and even emotional framework within which we make our choices is culturally evolved and inserted into us via social learning (Harré and Gillett, 1994). And yet this social script demands that we feel autonomous and so have some capacity to rebel. Indeed, because knowing what is the socially approved course of action always implies its opposite — knowing what we should not be doing — the greater the socialization of the individual mind, the more heightened becomes our sense of making active choices. Children will rush noisily about in public places or

---

more abstract, and so portable, social principles. In tribal societies, there is little possibility of escaping the watchful eye of a peer group and so less need to internalize a set of moral principles. But the price of this would be that there was also less room for social innovation. The Enlightenment and the rise of a mercantile economy brought about its own detachment from an existing moral framework — one based on theology and feudal rule — so setting individuals free (relatively speaking of course) within a new framework based on a tolerance for social experimentation and economic entrepreneurship. In this sense, the rationalists and the romantics were pulling in the same direction. The more individuals were made to assume the responsibility for writing their own script in life, the more effectively they exported the expansionist memes of Western culture — and, of course, the more acutely aware those individuals became of their status as 'free agents'.

[8] To be fair to Trefil and other chaos theorists, their appeal to chaos as an 'out' for freewill is typically made in only a weak sense. Whereas for quantum mysterians, the need for an out for freewill is often the central plank in their arguments.

fail to say their pleases and thank-yous quite unself-consciously. But for most adults, even tiny social transgressions are something they cannot help but think about. Even an apparent omission of self-control — like dropping an empty sweet wrapper on the ground — often must follow a moment of inner deliberation.

Finally, in a broader sense, culture does actually free us from the 'locked into the moment' minds of an animal. The social world into which we are born provides us with a highly polished machinery of language and the thought habits that words and grammatical structure enable. We become equipped to take a step back from the pressing flow of the moment and pursue the private traffic of images and plans that make us thinking, self-aware, individuals. And while it may be a fact that we use our mental independence from the moment mostly to apply a social filter to our actions, we are still undetermined — free to consider options — in a way that animals are not.

Not Forgetting the Neurology of Freewill

Of course, none of what has been said so far is to deny that there is not a neurology of will which needs to be accounted for. The bifold model of mind only says that culture exploits certain capabilities to be found in the biology of the brain.

Plainly the body has its appetites and these serve as a spur for action. The feeling, or rather noticing (Wall, 1999), of these bodily pangs is a complex business, involving both low level brain areas such as the hypothalamus and high level cortex regions such as the anterior insula, ventromedial prefrontal and anterior cingulate cortex (Damasio, 1994). And as well as relatively coarse-grained emotions like hunger, thirst, lust, anxiety, and pain, the body makes a constant series of fine-grain adjustments to match its arousal state to the events of each passing moment. Automatic changes in blood pressure, noradrenaline release, sweating, and many other homeostatic adaptations precisely calibrate the body and brain to the expected level of action (Sokolov, 1963; Lynn, 1966). So the brain cannot help but generate urges, impulses, and even generalized states of arousal or relaxation. The bifold part of the story is that we then wrap a framework of social thinking around this biology in an attempt to negotiate the expression of any urges.

The raw animal brain also has an obvious capacity for making plans and controlling the execution of those plans. In fact, the most convincing current models of brain processing are those which stress that the brain exists for generating action rather than the passive contemplation of sensory data (James, 1981; Luria, 1973; Baars, 1988). The story is that whatever falls within the eye of attention automatically begins to unlock ideas about potential responses. If we notice a door handle, we cannot help but begin to feel the urge to grasp and turn it. Much recent work has shown how the frontal lobes, in conjunction with sub-cortical areas such as the basal ganglia and cerebellum, are organized to decompose the current focus of attention into a fully expressed response (Passingham, 1993). And an important part of this machinery is the ability to hold a plan in mind — to keep an intention flying in working memory — before deciding the moment for its release (Williams and Goldman-Rakic, 1995).

Neuroscience also has much to say about why many of our actions seem unwilled — that is, not the result of focal planning but released automatically or spontaneously. The rousing of a global intention creates a dominant context (Baars, 1988) in which any habitual actions compatible with that context will simply be released. So, for example, if our explicit intention is to enter a room, then this implicitly permits the many component acts needed to get us into that room, such as taking steps down a corridor and reaching for a door knob. The way the basal ganglia learn to slot in such component skills has recently been described in some detail (Graybiel, 1998).

A renewed interest in reafference messages (Wolpert *et al.*, 1995) — the communication of an intention to act to the sensory cortex so that it can correct sensory impressions for self-generated movements — is also helping to explain how we know what we are about to do, as when we suddenly become conscious of a 'spontaneous' urge to flex a finger (Libet, 1985). In the now famous Libet experiment, verbal instructions to the subjects set up the initial dominant context (a clear mental image of the kind of act they should perform, along with the requirement that the act should happen with no pause for sub-vocal deliberation). Thus primed, the brain could simply permit the highly-habitualised act of flexing a finger to take place (and even the ability to generate a convincingly pseudo-random timing of the action presumably depended on prior learning — at least, children do not seem so good at such a trick). The mystery of what constituted the 'becoming conscious' of the actual urge is neatly explained by the broadcasting of the reafference image necessary to stop the subjects from feeling that the finger flexing was being imposed by some outside agency (Spence *et al.*, 1997). It is noteworthy that James (1981, p. 1111), with his usual clarity, talked about consciousness of an intention being the combination of an awareness of a fiat (a permissive context), and then of the anticipatory image of the sensorial consequences.

A further important point is that the idea of a brain centre that does our 'willing', or even a 'willing' circuit, is highly misleading. A good argument can be made that the brain has a general circuit for focusing its output plans — for taking a mass of possible responses to the central aspect of a moment and turning it into a single, explicitly represented intention (Passingham, 1993; McCrone, 1999). And that this 'endogenous' circuit is also sensitive to 'exogenous' interruptions (Posner and Rothbart, 1994). That is, we can plan to reach for a cup of coffee but be interrupted, our hand frozen in mid-air by a 'plan flattening' dopamine flush in the nucleus accumbens (Gray *et al.*, 1991), if a car happens to backfire unexpectedly in the street outside.

But while the brain does have areas that seem to play a key role in the planning and control of action, attempts to draw up circuit diagrams of this output apparatus end up having to include most of the brain anyway (Gray, 1995). And when it is considered that the entire frontal cortex sheet should be considered as a three-legged hierarchy (Passingham, 1993), for decomposing the focus of each moment into a concrete output plan (with separate streams of decomposition to provide an appropriate motor, attentional and verbal response), and that the intention to respond is then broadcast as a warning anticipatory image to all relevant corners of the sensory cortex, it can be seen that indeed the whole brain becomes drawn into service in organizing an act of willing. So volition, even in animals, is not the responsibility of some tacked-on brain module but a consequence of the fact that the entire brain is shaped by the need to come up with an optimal behavioural response to each moment. Simply put, volition, not contemplation, is what brains evolved to do.

Conclusion

There is no shortage of neuroscience to explain the brain's rich ability to find the appropriate focus of attention within each moment and mobilize its stored knowledge to deal with this focus. But the difference between animals and humans is that we can make our brains react to imaginary contexts — we can do things like think about what it would be like to go into a room and find a handbag left on a chair. And we also habitually bring a socially-expanded sense of context to bear on each moment — our social training will make us imagine what people would say if they saw us rifling through that handbag, even if we just happened to be sneaking a peak out of curiosity.

In the end, it is the individual brain that has to organize the willing of any act. But humans have created an extra, socialized, level of filtering that all brain planning must pass through before the possible becomes translated into the actual.

References

Aitchison, J. (1994), *Words in the Mind* (Oxford: Basil Blackwell).

Baars, B. (1988), *A Cognitive Theory of Consciousness* (Cambridge: Cambridge University Press).

Bain, A. (1977), *The Senses and the Intellect* and *The Emotions and the Will*, ed. D. Robinson (Washington, DC: University Publications of America).

Bartlett, F. (1932), *Remembering: A Study in Experimental and Social Psychology* (Cambridge: CUP).

Berger, P. and Luckmann, T. (1979), *The Social Construction of Reality* (London: Penguin).

Bickerton, D. (1995), *Language and Human Behaviour* (London: University College London Press).

Boesch, C. (1990), 'First hunters of the forest', *New Scientist*, 19 May, pp. 38–41.

Blackmore, S. (1999), *The Meme Machine* (Oxford: Oxford University Press).

Bloom, P. (1970), *Language Development* (Cambridge, MA: MIT Press).

Burr, V. (1995), *An Introduction to Social Constructionism* (London: Routledge).

Buruma, I. (1984), *A Japanese Mirror* (London: Jonathan Cape).

Carruthers, P. (1996), *Language, Thought and Consciousness* (Cambridge: CUP).

Carruthers, P. and Boucher, J. (1998), *Language and Thought* (Cambridge: CUP).

Chomsky, N. (1965), *Aspects of the Theory of Syntax* (Cambridge, MA: MIT Press).

Clark, A. (1998), 'Magic words: how language augments human computation', in Carruthers and Boucher (1998).

Clark, A. and Thornton, C. (1997), 'Trading spaces: computation, representation and the limits of uninformed learning', *Behavioral and Brain Sciences*, **20**, pp. 57–92.

Condillac, E.B. de (1930), *Treatise on the Sensations*, tr. G. Carr (Los Angeles: Univ. of California Press).

Conway, M. (1990), *Autobiographical Memory* (Milton Keynes: Open University Press).

Cooley, C.H. (1912), *Human Nature and the Social Order* (New York: Charles Scribner).

Coulter, J. (1979), *The Social Construction of Mind* (London: Macmillan).

Damasio, A.R. (1994), *Descartes' Error* (New York: Putnam).

Damasio, H., Grabowski, T.J., Tranel, D., Hichwa, R.D. and Damasio, A.R. (1996), 'A neural basis for lexical retrieval', *Nature*, **380**, pp. 499–505.

Danziger, K. (1997), *Naming the Mind* (London: Sage).

Davidson, D. (1984), *Inquiries into Truth and Interpretation* (Oxford: Clarendon Press).

Dawkins, R. (1993), 'Viruses of the mind', in *Dennett and his Critics*, ed. B. Dahlbom (Oxford: Blackwell).

Deacon, T. (1997), *The Symbolic Species* (London: Allen Lane, Penguin).

Dennett, D. (1991), *Consciousness Explained* (New York: Little, Brown).

Dennett, D. (1998), 'Reflections on language and mind', in Carruthers and Boucher (1998).

Dewart, L. (1989), *Evolution of Consciousness* (Toronto: University of Toronto Press).

Diaz, R.M. and Berk, L.E. (1992), *Private Speech* (Hillsdale, NJ: Lawrence Erlbaum).

Dodds, E.R. (1963), *The Greeks and the Irrational* (Berkeley, CA: University of California Press).

Donald, M. (1991), *Origins of the Modern Mind* (Cambridge, MA: Harvard University Press).

Elman, J., Bates, E., Johnson, M., Karmiloff-Smith, A., Parisi, D. and Plunkett, K. (1996), *Rethinking Innateness* (Cambridge, MA: MIT Press).

Foucault, M. (1990), *The History of Sexuality Vol 3: The Care of the Self* (London: Penguin).

Gergen, K.J. and Davis, K.E. (1985), *The Social Construction of the Person* (New York: Springer-Verlag).

Goffman, E. (1969), *The Presentation of Self in Everyday Life* (London: Penguin).

Gray, J.A., Feldon, J., Rawlins, J.N.P., Hemsley, D.R. and Smith, A.D. (1991), 'The neuropsychology of schizophrenia', *Behavioral and Brain Sciences*, **14**, pp.1–84.

Gray, J.A. (1995), 'The contents of consciousness: a neuropsychological conjecture', *Behavioral and Brain Sciences*, **18**, pp. 659–722.

Graybiel, A.M. (1998), 'The basal ganglia and chunking of action repertoires', *Neurobiology of Learning and Memory*, **70**, pp. 119–36.

Greenberg, J. (1963), *Universals of Language* (Cambridge, MA: MIT Press).

Hampson, N. (1968), *The Enlightenment* (Harmondsworth: Pelican).

Haren, M. (1985), *Medieval Thought* (London: Macmillan).

Harré, R. (1983), *Personal Being* (Oxford: Basil Blackwell).

Harré, R. (1986), *The Social Construction of Emotions* (Oxford: Basil Blackwell).

Harré, R. and Gillett, G. (1994), *The Discursive Mind* (London: Sage).

Hobbes, T. (1951), *Leviathan* (Oxford: Basil Blackwell).

Hume, D. (1967), *A Treatise of Human Nature*, edited by Selby-Bigge, L. (Oxford: Clarendon Press).

Jahoda, G. (1992), *Crossroads Between Culture and Mind* (Hemel Hempstead: Harvester Wheatsheaf).

Jackendoff, R. (1996), 'How language helps us think', *Pragmatics and Cognition*, **4**, pp. 1–34.

James, W. (1981), *The Principles of Psychology* (Cambridge, MA: Harvard University Press).

Johanson, D. and Edey, M. (1982), *Lucy: The Beginnings of Humankind* (New York: Warner Books).

Kety, S.S. and Schmidt, C.E. (1946), 'The determination of cerebral blood flow in man by the use of nitrous oxide in low concentrations', *American Journal of Physiology*, **143**, pp. 53–6.

Kimura, D. (1979), 'Neuromotor mechanisms in the evolution of human communication', in *Neurobiology of Social Communication in Primates*, ed. H. Steklis and M. Raleigh (New York: Academic Press).

Lane, H. (1976), *The Wild Boy of Aveyron* (Cambridge, MA: Harvard University Press).

Lenneberg, E. (1967), *Biological Foundations of Language* (New York: Wiley).

Libet, B. (1985), 'Unconscious cerebral initiative and the role of conscious will in voluntary action', *Behavioral and Brain Sciences*, **8**, pp. 529–66.

Lieberman, P. (1991), *Uniquely Human* (Cambridge, MA: Harvard University Press).

Locke, J. (1975), *An Essay Concerning Human Understanding*, ed. P. Nidditch (Oxford: Clarendon Press).

Luria, A. (1973), *The Working Brain* (London: Penguin).

Luria, A. (1976), *Cognitive Development* (Cambridge, MA: Harvard University Press).

Luria, A. (1982), *Language and Cognition*, ed. J. Wertsch (Chichester: John Wiley).

Luria, A. and Yudovich, F. (1956), *Speech and the Development of Mental Processes in the Child* (London: Penguin).

Lutz, C. (1986), 'The domain of emotion words on Ifaluk', in Harré (1986).

Lutz, C. (1988), *Unnatural Emotions* (Chicago: University of Chicago Press).

Lynn, R. (1966), *Attention, Arousal and the Orientation Response* (Oxford: Pergamon Press).

MacNamara, J. (1977), *Language, Learning and Thought* (New York: Academic Press).

McCrone, J. (1990), *The Ape That Spoke* (London: Macmillan).

McCrone, J. (1993), *The Myth of Irrationality* (London: Macmillan).

McCrone, J. (1999), *Going Inside* (London: Faber and Faber).

Martin, A., Haxby, J.V., Lalonde, F.M., Wiggs, C.L. & Ungerleider, L.G. (1995), 'Discrete cortical regions associated with knowledge of color and knowledge of action', *Science*, **270**, pp. 102–5.

Mason, J.H. (1979), *The Indispensable Rousseau* (London: Quartet).

Mead, G.H. (1934), *Mind, Self and Society* (Chicago: University of Chicago Press).

Mithen, S. (1996), *The Prehistory of the Mind* (London: Thames and Hudson).

Morsbach, H. and Tyler, W.J. (1986), 'A Japanese emotion: Amae', in Harré (1986).

Morton, A. (1980), *Frames of Mind* (Oxford: Oxford University Press).

Mueller, R-A. (1996), 'Innateness, autonomy, universality? Neurobiological approaches to language', *Behavioral and Brain Sciences*, **19**, pp. 611–75.

Müller, M. (1888), *The Science of Thought* (Chicago: Open Court).

Neisser, U. (1967), *Cognitive psychology* (New York: Appleton-Century-Crofts).

Neisser, U. (1976), *Cognition and Reality* (New York: W.H. Freeman).

Nietzsche, F. (1961), *Thus Spake Zarathustra*, trans. R.J. Hollingdale (London: Penguin).

Passingham, R. (1993), *The Frontal Lobes and Voluntary Action* (Oxford: Oxford University Press).

Pinker, S. (1994), *The Language Instinct* (New York: William Morrow).

Posner, M.I. and Rothbart, M.K. (1994), 'Constructing neuronal theories of mind', in *Large-Scale Neuronal Theories of the Brain*, ed. C. Koch and J. Davis (Cambridge, MA: MIT Press).

Pulvermüller, F. (1999), 'Words in the brain's language', *Behavioral and Brain Sciences*, **22**, pp. 253–336.

Rao, R.P.N., and Ballard, D.H. (1999), 'Predictive coding in the visual cortex: a functional interpretation of some extra-classical receptive-field effects', *Nature Neuroscience*, **2**, pp. 79–87.

Ryle, G. (1949), *The Concept of Mind* (London: Hutchinson).

Saffran, J.R., Aslin, R.N. and Newport, E.L. (1996), 'Statistical learning by 8-month-old infants', *Science*, **274**, pp. 1926–8.

de Saussure, F. (1959), *Course in General Linguistics* (New York: McGraw-Hill).

Service, E.R. (1962), *Primitive Social Organisation* (New York: Random House).

Simon, B. (1978), *The Classical Roots of Modern Psychiatry* (Ithaca, NY: Cornell University Press).

Singh, J. and Zingg, R. (1941), *Wolf Children and Feral Man* (New York: Harper).

Sluckin, W. and Herbert, M. (1986), *Parental Behaviour* (Oxford: Basil Blackwell).

Sokolov, A.N. (1972), *Inner Speech and Thought* (New York: Plenum Press).

Sokolov, E. (1963), *Perception and the Conditioned Reflex* (New York: Macmillan).

Sorabji, R. (1993), *Animal Minds and Human Morals* (Ithaca, New York: Cornell University Press).

Spence, S.A., Brooks, D.J., Hirsch, S.R., Liddle, P.F., Meehan, J., Grasby, P.M. (1997), 'A PET study of voluntary movement in schizophrenic patients experiencing passivity phenomena (delusions of alien control)', *Brain*, **120**, pp. 1997–2011.

Thompson, H.S. (1966), *Hell's Angels* (New York: Random House).

Trefil, J. (1997), *Are We Unique?* (New York: Wiley).

Vygotsky, L. (1986), *Thought and Language*, ed. A. Kozulin (Cambridge, MA: MIT Press).

Vygotsky, L. (1978), *Mind in Society*, ed. S. Cole (Cambridge, MA: Harvard University Press).

Vygtotsky, L. and Luria, A. (1994), 'Tool and symbol in child development', in *The Vygotsky Reader*, ed. R. van der Veer and J. Valsiner (Oxford: Basil Blackwell).

de Waal, F. (1982), *Chimpanzee Politics* (London: Jonathan Cape).

Walker, S. (1983), *Animal Thought* (London: Routledge and Kegan Paul).

Wall, P. (1999), *Pain: The Science of Suffering* (London: Weidenfeld and Nicolson).

Wertsch, J. (1991), *Voices of the Mind* (Cambridge, MA: Harvard University Press).

Whitten, W.B. and Leonard, J.M. (1981), 'Directed search through autobiographical memory', *Memory and Cognition*, **9**, pp. 566–79.

Whorf, B. (1956), *Language, Thought and Reality* (Cambridge, MA: MIT Press).

Williams, G.V. and Goldman-Rakic, P.S. (1995), 'Modulation of memory fields by dopamine D1 receptors in prefrontal cortex', *Nature*, **376**, pp. 572–5.

Wittgenstein, L. (1922), *Tractatus Logico-Philosophicus* (London: Routledge and Kegan Paul).

Wittgenstein, L. (1976), *Philosophical Investigations* (Oxford: Basil Blackwell).

Wolpert, D.M., Ghahramani, Z. and Jordan, M.I. (1995), 'An internal model for sensorimotor integration', *Science*, **269**, pp.1880–2.

Zivin, G. (1979), *The Development of Self-Regulation Through Private Speech* (New York: John Wiley).

Zohar, D. (1990), *The Quantum Self* (New York: William Morrow).

Jaron Lanier

And Now a Brief Word From Now

Logical Dependencies Between Vernacular Concepts of Free Will, Time and Consciousness

I: Please Note That 'Now' Is Remarkable

Consider the idea of the present moment in time. This is one of the most imprecise of concepts. Does it last for an instant or for three seconds? Do all the parts of a brain share the same present moment? Is the present moment one is conscious of even coherent enough to compare to the position of the hands of a clock? In a relativistic universe, can it ever be sensible to talk about a present? To the best of our knowledge, the answers to all the above questions must be had at the expense of the integrity of the idea of 'now'. People do not make very good clocks — we are poor at sensing the absolute passage of time, and, even if we were better at it, relativity would only allow us to share a 'now' with compromised accuracy. Despite the looseness of the present moment, the fact that we can talk about it at all, even with imprecision and ambiguity, is an important bit of evidence to keep in mind when considering consciousness.

Let's suppose the universe is, for practical purposes, deterministic. The universe in this case isn't 'doing anything' that can distinguish one moment from another. And yet the human perspective does achieve such a distinction. The vaguely perceived present moment is distinguished from other moments. This human ability reminds one of the old joke about a dancing bear: it's not that the bear dances well, but that he dances at all that charms an audience. The very concept of a present moment is only meaningful to one who is trapped in time by being conscious.

In an earlier article (Lanier, 1995), this author has suggested that the human acquaintance with gross objects such as words and chairs, as opposed to fundamental particles, is the strongest evidence for dualistic consciousness. By what mechanism within the universe could a particular granularity of description be favoured over others? There is none. The present moment is a similar phenomenon. No instrument can detect it. Even the most accurate clock cannot distinguish one moment from another. All clocks are ultimately calibrated to humans who have perceived a present moment, however imprecisely.

It is possible to go down the other path, of course, and investigate the possibility that the universe is non-deterministic. Mere non-determinism is not sufficient to distinguish the present moment, however. A universe that knows the present moment is,

Journal of Consciousness Studies, **6**, No. 8–9, 1999, pp. 261–68

as we shall see, perhaps even spookier than a person who can accomplish the feat. Within the physics community, a discomfort with the present moment has led to a variety of multiple-universe theories (see in particular the recent work of Julian Barbour). Perhaps there is no time flow, but rather a separate universe for each moment complete with an appropriately aged copy of each of us.

So perhaps it is possible to construct a mechanism by which the universe does account for the present moment on its own, even if it requires a rather radical strategy. If a construction like this were to become widely accepted, it would still not address the experience of experience. Consciousness must ultimately remain a secret pleasure for those who have it, and a matter of faith with regard to others. Nonetheless, I present the present moment as an enigma that points out how the best evidence of consciousness is usually too close at hand to notice.

II: Free Will and Consciousness: Strange Bedfellows in the Bed of 'Now'

Although free will and consciousness are sisters in the ontology of folk wisdom beliefs, and are generally dismissed as a pair by contemporary determinists, they are actually somewhat at odds with each other when it comes to 'now'. Consciousness would be a pointless exercise without surprise at the next moment. Free will makes itself known by limiting surprise, by causing a predicted effect. So free will and consciousness, if they exist, are not precisely coincident; they have a give-and-take relationship, like the intertwining of the sensory and motor systems. Free will, to the degree it is a sensible concept, can only be conceived as being dependent on its agent being trapped in a flowing 'now'. Furthermore, if free will is authentic, it cannot take place in a deterministic universe. So free will is dependent on flowing time and non-determinacy. The serious problems with this possibility have been well articulated. A 'Cartesian extension' of some kind is required to hold the mechanism of free will, and this leads to an infinite regress. (Infinite regresses scare me no more than multiple universe hypotheses, but that is perhaps a result of my jaded temperament.) We will return to the relationship of free will and consciousness below, after considering determinism and non-determinism.

III: Visualizing Determinism

Time is hard to think about. Unlike the other, more accommodating dimensions, it seizes us and allows us no opportunity to move about in order to gain perspective. We must resort to imagination in order to attempt to understand our stern captor. One visualization of deterministic time was presented by Kurt Vonnegut in some of his early novels. His alien 'Tralfamadorians' lived a few dimensions up the epistemological ladder from people. They could see time 'from the side', as a panorama stretching from the beginning of the past to the end of the future. To a Tralfamadorian, a person looks like a millipede with baby arms and legs at one end and skeleton limbs at the other. This millipede is seen tangled about the globe of the earth, tracing out the movements of a person in the course of a lifetime. Actually, people are able to pretend to be Tralfamadorians when considering past events. Timeline visualizations have been created by people since ancient times, and the earliest ones often assert a superiority befitting a Tralfamadorian. Rulers of the ancient world created timelines in stone depicting hagiographies of military triumphs. Napoleon went so far as to have just such an artefact created in imitation of ancient Egyptian models.

Timeline visualizations answer a natural desire to step out of time. Alas; this attractive imaginary vista can be deceptive. Such visualizations have been criticized for imposing an arrow of causality in cases where there might not be one. For instance, the palaeontologist Stephen Jay Gould frequently complains about the familiar timeline showing a ramp of progression from crawling ape to upright man. He suggests that this image tells a lie about the degree of order in the process of evolution. Gould prefers an alternative view, in which the sheer amount of increasing diversity in evolution leads to the appearance of odd creatures such as humans.

Whether it is misleading or not, the timeline understanding of time is probably the most common one, and it derives from the time concept of both Newtonian, and a great deal of more recent, physics. Time is treated as another dimension in these disciplines, much like the three dimensions of space. This is true even in a relativistic universe, where time gets bent and stretched along with the other dimensions, but is still just another axis.

Back to Tralfamadorians: These ultimate timeline gazers serve to visualize two important propositions that some might find counter-intuitive. First, they help us to realize how dimensionally impoverished we are. Second, and more to the point for the subject at hand, they ease us into considering the possibility that free will is an illusion. The mere possibility of a Tralfamadorian perspective casts suspicions on the idea of free will. There is a very long-running crisis in theology on this point. God is presumed to be able to see everything a Tralfamadorian can see, so, for God, the book of the future has already been written. A great many thoughtful people have found it hard to see how moral choice can exist for people if the future is already there in some sense.

For readers who are uncomfortable with God or Tralfamadorians, an observer of time 'from the side' can be proposed who is considerably more like everyday people. Suppose a civilization becomes obsessed with recording every event in every person's life. Video cameras are embedded in every surface, and every shirt collar has an ultra-high resolution functional brain scanner. All this data is beamed to computer banks on the moon. After a catastrophic plague has wiped out all but a single survivor, that lonely individual flies to the moon to relive the collective experience of all her ancestors. Here is time 'from the side', once again. As she scans the historical records, she will feel a sense of pathos. All the struggle of her ancestors was in vain, for inevitably their fate, or some other equally claustrophobic one, was written as if in time itself.

What might consciousness comprise in a deterministic universe, such that it can serve as the identifier of the present moment? Not much. To a Tralfamadorian, consciousness might be imagined as being rather like a radio dial moving steadily across its appointed round. This is the most minimal Cartesian extension possible — the 'nanoextension'.

Consciousness without effect, a purely voyeuristic consciousness, is a terrifying image — along the lines of being buried alive. For awareness to be genuine but free will to be an illusion — this prospect is like a debilitating neurological disorder. So, while consciousness might comprise nothing more than the nanoextension, we hope that this is not true. This is the emotional appeal of non-determinism.

IV: Imagining Non-Determinism

A comforting illusion of free will might be possible in a deterministic universe. This is what the mainstream of physicists usually believe — indeed Einstein was an early articulator of this idea. In a deterministic manner, events in the brain should be able to form an illusory perception of free will, just as optical illusions can be perceived deterministically. A case can be made that Illusory Free Will is dependent on consciousness — that is, an illusion ought to be had consciously if we are to give it any notice. Any prospective unconsciously-had illusion can probably be more clearly explained simply as an unconscious process. This judgement seems robust; it should remain true for the various ambiguous uses of the word 'consciousness'. So, if free will sinks, and illusion is asserted, Consciousness swims. Likewise, if consciousness does not exist, free will would provide an alternate mechanism to explain how the present moment could be differentiated from others. If free will is real, the universe, or some part of it like a brain, actually does 'do something' to get from one moment to the next. A more meaty, decision-making Cartesian extension would mark the 'now'. While it would seem like a wasted opportunity, perhaps a free agent could be unconscious (this is a possibility that will be examined below). So if the 'now' can ever be referred to, and consciousness of the 'hard problem' kind does not exist, then free will gains a *raison d'être*.

Free will is dependent on non-determinism, and, as it happens, the scientific community also remains in part dependent on the idea of non-determinism. For example, typical explanations given by determinists for the existence of consciousness are along the lines that it was evolved to focus mental attention in critical circumstances. But such explanations can only make sense if consciousness has an effect. The new breed of mechanist/consciousness-denying authors tends to want to have it both ways. They wish to explain what we call consciousness as an evolutionary adaptation, but then, asserting determinism, also claim that consciousness has no actual effect, which would have made it irrelevant to evolution. This is, of course, merely a bubbling up of the classic ambivalence all scientists are forced into on the question of determinism. Biologists tend to use the language of non-determinism, and it is possible that the reasons for doing so are more than skin deep. Why would the complexity of evolution happen in a deterministic universe? Why would a preset universe bother to contain repeating patterns of competition and adaptation? If the universe is just a deterministic, algorithmic unfolding of a seed of information, there's no particular reason the unfolding should be so consistent. In fact, I'd argue that, all in all, the consistency of evidence for biological evolution argues against fundamental determinism. The Dawkinsian biology of 'ultradarwinism' is only deterministic at a level of high, general description; it is dependent on an underlying stratum of reality that is non-deterministic. Patterns of change might be broadly predictable, but the best explanation for that might be that they actually are driven; that changes have consequences. Here's why: Speaking as a computer scientist, when I program a self-contained but complex deterministic simulation, I have trouble choosing initial states for variables and I get unpredictable results. If, on the other hand, I set up a game of components driven by nearly random number generators, I can get coherence by placing the components in a consistent causal environment. A truly deterministic universe has no reason to be consistent in the 'high level' phenomena it spawns — it could go either way — while a non-deterministic universe will evolve consistent and repeating patterns as high level phenomena interact and inevitably 'compete' in a common environment. I can make a deterministic simulation be as inscrutable as I wish, but an effectively non-deterministic simulation of interacting components tends to turn into a game with scrutable patterns. So high level coherence might be seen as circumstantial evidence of low level non-determinism.

V: Free Will, Hiding in the Shadows

It is quite a leap to get from non-determinism to its *wunderkind* offspring, free will. While non-determinism does not demand the presence of free will, free will does require non-determinism. Could we detect free will empirically if it does exist? Would it be possible to distinguish acts of free will from random outcomes in a non-deterministic universe that obeyed statistical rules? There is the possibility that free will carefully selects which outcome will occur so as to create no observable variation from a predictable random distribution of results. Free will could be sneaking around at low altitudes, not showing statistical effects. Or perhaps free will could be showing effects only at a large scale, in such a way that it would still be impossible to demonstrate causality. In this view, free will would be a nocturnal creature, a paranoid version of Maxwell's demon. There is room for such a demon. To understand how, consider the dilemmas of evolutionary explanation. Random mutations in a system of natural selection can yield what might at first seem to be highly improbable evolutionary adaptations. Evolutionary theorists come up with stories of what might have happened to explain the appearance of specific strange features, but they cannot prove that the causal components of the stories are true. Gould has characterized some of these stories as 'just so'. I once asked Richard Dawkins (in a dialogue that appeared in Psychology Today magazine) what he thought the best explanation was for the vulnerable placement of many mammalian testicles, including those of humans. I compared them to a soldier who must pilot a well-armoured tank through a war zone while he himself is protected only by a balloon attached to the outside of the vehicle. Neither the tank nor the driver would get very far, however effective the armour was. The testicles ought to be better protected than the brain, by vernacular evolutionary reasoning. He replied with a variety of 'just so' stories to explain testicles, but conceded that they all have serious problems. While it is true that the testicles are helpfully cooled by their position, evolution holds all the cards of the game, and could have evolved air conditioners, or different chemistry. After all, testicles are *the* jewels she is protecting. There are also theories concerning male risk-taking as a method of demonstrating or cultivating fitness. But these theories would apply equally well to any vital organ — and the vital organs are all well protected. I certainly hope testicles are not in their compromised position as a result of divine intervention. Their unfortunate position might be a side effect, leftover from other unrelated evolutionary events, what Gould has called a 'spandrel'. Perhaps someday someone will come upon a story that rings true to explain them. Proof will not be forthcoming, however, until we can get confirmation from the Tralfamadorians. A variety of coexisting stories to explain why testicles are not better protected might survive well into the future. I have descended to the level of testicles in order to illustrate that even well-founded theories explaining specific events in complicated systems can leave, at the very least, wiggle room. Evolutionary theorists have shown that evolution can explain what we see in nature, but there is no definitive way to prove that flying saucers, divine intervention, or some other outside force did not have an effect, precisely because it would have been superfluous to what we can measure. In the same way, the subjective experience of free will might well be authentic and correct, and yet not lead to demonstrable results. Or, alternatively, as stated above, free will might not be detectable when it makes individual appearances, but might have a measurable effect at a larger scale.

The case for free will made above is not for the kind of free will we experience in everyday life. For we feel we have measurable effects all the time. Our free will does not slink about in the shadows. Furthermore, if there is a Cartesian extension complicated enough to perform acts of free will, we can know nothing about it. Those hoping to find a confirmation of free will as the bearer of moral agency should take no comfort from the wiggle room afforded to demons by statistics.

VI: Strange Bedfellows, Stranger Binding

Let us return to the question of whether there could be an unconscious form of free will. There is evidence that some philosophers (such as Dennett) do not experience consciousness, and yet do seem to exercise will. Furthermore, patients with certain neurological deficits can exhibit will, but without coherent enough memory formation to have perceived the whole of the act. I have used the term 'will' in the previous two examples, rather than 'free will'; somehow it seems that the vernacular and legal addition of the word 'free' should be taken to imply the presence of consciousness. But consciousness does not sit gracefully with will, whether free or not. The relationship between the two shares features with the much-discussed 'binding problem' of consciousness. I will state the problem in a stronger form than usual: Why would the sensation of consciousness be localized to a particular brain? If consciousness is an effect of organized matter, why do I not share your sensations? Why would I experience my particular molecules and not yours? It has to be pointed out that the binding problem only makes sense to people who experience consciousness — to others who do not share it, it does not seem like a problem, since it cannot be otherwise (empirically) demonstrated. I shall assume the reader is conscious and proceed. Let's try another fantastic construction. As was mentioned above with regard to universes and time in contemporary physics, binding problems can always be addressed by creating unlimited numbers of the entities to be bound. In order to avoid having an unexplained fact, which suggests an awkward Cartesian extension as the source of the fact, all possible alternative facts can be made to coexist concurrently. This strategy shows up in physics repeatedly. The classic example is the original multiple universes hypothesis, in which the universe is constantly splitting apart so that all potential future histories actually exist, even if they have a common point of origin. (In this case a particular consciousness might not just look like a radio dial, but also like a snake that has chosen a particular path through the ever-expanding branches of fate.) More recently, Lee Smolin has suggested a multiple universe model to explain the origin of universal constants. He suggests that there might be many universes in which the constants are different — we happen to be in one in which they are what we have discovered them to be. Following a similar strategy, let us imagine a reality in which binding is not a problem because there are a huge number of consciousnesses to match up with the dizzy superset of all parts and wholes of all brains in combination. Some significant number of them would have experienced the authoring of this paper, each in a slightly different way.

As a simple example of a member of the superset of consciousnesses, imagine a consciousness unperceived by others nearby, who is aware only of hearing — to her, sight is an unconscious process. Sensory modalities can potentially be separated in this way because they are made up to a significant degree of different anatomical portions of the brain, although inevitably there is also some overlap. Now consider sight and sound together, excluding smell. Why would there not be an additional subjective awareness that comprises the union of these two, but no other components? Why should subconcsciousnesses discipline themselves into a clean ontology without overlap? Indeed how could they? If there are any of these subconsciousnesses, there ought to be very many of them. When you observe a person from the outside, each one of your consciousnesses would imagine that there is only one consciousness present in the other, but they would be wrong. In fact, all those consciousnesses would be in the other person, each experiencing his or her own illusion of free will. And make no mistake about it, free will must be illusory for this swarm of souls. If they all were able to exercise authentic free will, they would become aware of each other, since they would inevitably conflict in their intentions. Now it is true that we do experience subjective frustrations — 'I didn't mean to do that!' — but we don't experience enough of them to give credence to the existence of a full-on swarm. So, if consciousness and free will are both real, consciousness must bind itself to the physicality of a brain in a way that minimizes such conflicts — and that is an example of the peculiarity that is the binding problem. Free will can accommodate a few subconsciousnesses, but not enough of them to make the binding problem go away.

There is a curious version of the binding problem that occurs in time rather than space. Let us suppose I have experienced an illusion of free will, where there in fact was determinism. There is a specific duration to the events in the brain that constitute that experience. Suppose, for instance, that I choose to move my hand to the right. I experience a discrete moment of decision, and then action. (This is not to imply that I do not frequently act in a more automatic fashion — only that the possibility of control appears to exist on at least some occasions.) Presumably, we will soon be able to study free will with functional brain imaging, and eventually even more detailed techniques of analysis. We will be able to compare occasions when a person predetermines to move a hand, and when the hand has moved without premeditation. An ontology should become apparent for mental sequences that precede hand motion — some are wilful and some not. Once this research has been done, Will will at last be localized to parts of the brain, and/or to unique sequences of neural events. While the philosophical solution of the binding problem might remain as unresolved as ever, the phenomenology will at least have been clarified. But notice that, during a willed act, consciousness has also spread itself out over a sequence of moments and unified them into a single experience of a moment of will. This is a temporal statement of the binding problem. Consciousness has to be oddly capricious in its binding to time in order to be matched up with free will. If the universe is indeed non-deterministic, there is circumstantial evidence that consciousness is, at least sometimes, connected with the creation of outcomes, because it is often suspiciously well-bound to the timeline in which such outcomes seem to happen.

Conclusion

I have tried to outline some of the logical dependencies between vernacular conceptions of free will, time, and consciousness. These relationships are surprisingly complicated. Once again, a person who experiences neither free will nor consciousness can happily come up with a neurological framework to capture the complex relationship of the two. Perhaps consciousness can be defined as a function of sensory integration, memory, and planning, and free will as a bridge between that and the motor system. These two entities would have to trade off and occasionally be in conflict, while still being dependent on each other, following a pattern of the sort described above. To such a person, the physiological side of the binding problem provides a sufficient explanation — and that person would be correct. No new information is added by the other side of the binding; only experience. To someone who experiences consciousness, however, it remains the only thing that would still be as real if it were shown to be an illusion — in fact that would merely reinforce its reality. To others, it is never real. And this is the dilemma, and why consciousness studies must slink about in the shadows rather like the demons in the examples above.

If I made my living from philosophy, I would choose to ignore consciousness and free will. They make everything too complicated. I would simplify the problem so I could make some progress.

Reference

Lanier, J. (1995), 'You can't argue with a zombie', *Journal of Consciousness Studies*, **2** (4), pp. 333–44.

Whit Blauvelt

Y's Domain

How many hold despairingly yet to the models departed, caste, myths,
obedience, compulsion, and to infidelity,
How few see the arrived models, the athletes, the Western States, or
see freedom or spirituality, or hold any faith in results. . . .

Whitman (1881)

I foresee that mankind will resign itself more and more fully every day to more and more
horrendous undertakings; soon there will be nothing but warriors and brigands. I give
them this piece of advice: *He who is to perform a horrendous act should imagine to himself that it is already done, should impose upon himself a future as irrevocable as the
past.* [italics in original]

Borges (1998)

I

The issue of determinism is well respected by many philosophers I, in turn, respect —
but always for other work, not their treatment of this supposed problem. Personally, I
make no progress on a problem unless I get bothered by it, unless it becomes personally problematic. The claims for thorough going determinism have never bothered
me, in the sense of making me feel there might be some cause to believe them, some
conflict with my knowledge of freedom.

As a computer programmer, I have great faith in the efficacy of cause-and-effect in
constrained realms. And my folk understanding of chaos theory is that it explores
how, traditionally, science played it safe by only studying constrained realms (low
energy, limited variable, simple systems) and then pretending the patterns it found
there obtained everywhere.

The human presence on the landscape is itself one of pockets of constrained realms
— our towns and cities (although as they become larger they often gain a wildness in
their hearts) — set within the richer chaos that is wilderness in all its varieties. We
ourselves, though, have come from the wilderness, and represent it in our cities which
we have striven to render sterile, concrete, and safely predictable. We like predictability. We like it when prejudice suffices for awareness and judgement. It lets us get
on with our ordered activities. So belief in determinability is, in a way, belief in our
own project.

Journal of Consciousness Studies, **6**, No. 8–9, 1999, pp. 269–74

But it is a very limited project — or set of projects — when set against the wilder-nesses (however we have diminished them, they are still considerable) of earth, and space beyond. To read determinism into the larger scheme of existence, can it be more than parochial projection? Isn't the freedom at our own individual cores a most evident proof that well-determined realms are a small subset of the totality of being, and that, even when we engineer them well, we ourselves represent the wilderness within them?

A determinist: is that someone who has never hiked the backwoods, never studied her dreams, never been intoxicated or in love? Someone who has been conditioned to approximate a simple system in someone else's fascistic programme of determining the course of a culture by putting blinders[1] on its members to their full freedom and potential, and who is co-operating with his own psychic executioner by internalizing the rhetoric of his repression?

In other words, can belief in the overarching doctrine of determinism be seen cor-rectly as anything but quaint or psychopathological? Belief in freedom, after all, is essential to our social institutions, with their emphasis on individual responsibility. Belief in determinism, to the extent it undermines that, is nothing but destructive of our social order — despite the attractions of communist, fascist, and religio-fundamentalist (determinist) ideologies for those within their circles.

On the other hand, local conditions can be set up so that determinism works quite amazingly well in ensuring the effective operation of computers and machinery (pro-viding they are constantly attended by skilled technicians — people outside the infor-mation services industry have no idea how many tens of thousands stay up all night tending this stuff, despite the incredible engineering behind it). There is no question that being able to run things through branch structured logic, apply geometries and set theory and so on, is of immense practical value. But experience with how hard it is to maintain realms where this stuff really works supports the realization that this is hardly the overall structure of existence. Even here, the best engineering insights come in flashes of intuition, not merely from blindly grinding causal gears.

To paraphrase Jesus, the truth is, we are free. That was a man who knew the wilder-ness. And the Satan who tempted him there was the same Satan who was previously pitchman for the tree of the knowledge of good and evil, also known as branch-structured, yes/no, deterministic logic. For a society which saw the limitations and dangers in this programme so anciently — if in a bit of a simplistic, yes/no way, ironi-cally enough — we've made remarkably little progress in putting the issue fully in perspective. While such a tree may be well kept and productive in our own garden, we ourselves are eternally creatures of the wild and unpredictable beyond.

As the Buddhists discovered, there is no worse nightmare than that of being caught in an eternal causal chain; and losing that illusion is essential to gaining broad aware-ness and compassionate humanity — which compassion does not extend to playing along with the deterministic delusions of your neighbours.

Is the problem of determinism that there's no real problem to be solved? Is it a false question that deserves to be begged? Can it even make sense to determine to do some-thing without presupposing the freedom to determine? And, in presupposing that freedom, don't we know that determinism cannot, consistently, be an all-

---

[1]   Also called 'blinkers': the flaps placed beside draft horses' eyes to block their view to the side.

encompassing program of explanation? I have often seen this final objection skirted; I have never seen it refuted. The determinists ask us to accept a paradox which is untenable.

II

To fathom the origins of the faith in determinism, we should consider how determination is situated as a human activity. There are at least three major ways in which the term 'determine' can take centre stage:

(1) We can, as we often seek to do, determine what can and will happen in the passive sense of assessment, of investigation. (This also more broadly includes determining what something is, which consists essentially of determining what it can cause to happen, its properties, what role it can play.) Call this determine$_1$.

(2) We can, as we often seek to do, determine what will happen in the active sense of causation, of instigation. Call this determine$_2$.

These first two are closely linked: we want to know what may happen largely because we should like to do something about it. It appears animate life has evolved brains for the first capacity precisely to serve the second capacity.

(3) We also speak, by extension from the first two senses, of a thing, rather than a person, determining$_3$ another thing. That is, when we determine$_1$ from one thing some subsequent thing, we might also speak of the first thing determining$_3$ the subsequent, meaning that we can generally determine$_1$ from the first thing that the second will likely happen. Or we can determine$_2$ the second by causing the first, which we have determined$_1$ will lead to the second. In this case, we also say that the first determines$_3$ the second, and may project onto it an agency derived from our own determination$_2$.[2]

The first two senses, determination$_1$ and determination$_2$, directly involve human beings, as observers and agents respectively. The third is an abstraction or projection in which the human being is left out. To apply these to billiard-ball causation: If I see one ball rolling towards another, and observe it well, I might determine$_1$ (other things being equal) that it will knock the other into the pocket. If I determine$_1$ that setting one ball rolling towards another, at an observed angle, will (other things being equal) knock it into the pocket, I can determine$_2$ to knock it into the pocket by striking the first ball appropriately. In either case I can say, by extension and abstraction from the human determination$_{1or2}$, that the motion of the one ball determines$_3$ (other things being equal) that the second ball will go into the pocket. But this does not literally mean that it determines$_1$ at all, just that we can use our observation of it to determine$_1$. And the only sense in which it determines$_2$ is a metaphorical derivative from — or shorthand for — our own agency; the determination$_2$ accurately belongs to us, not to it.

---

[2] We can tease this out further into determination$_{3a}$ and determination$_{3b}$, where determination$_{3a}$ is an alternate syntax for naming evidence for determination$_1$, while determination$_{3b}$ refers to the intermediate means of a determination$_2$ in progress. This distinction is not so important for the current argument, but shows that in common occurrence even determination$_3$ may be not a simple, pure concept but a conflation.

Does determining$_3$ really have any meaning independent of the human-involved senses of determining$_{1and2}$? For instance, it is commonly held that the proof of scientific knowledge is its predictive utility. From this perspective, whenever we say that one thing determines$_3$ another, the proof of this is that we can determine$_1$ the second's likelihood from the first. In practice in the lab this often means determining$_2$ the first, in order to test whether it determines$_3$ the second. In such a case the proof for determination$_1$ is nothing other than our ability to use it in determination$_2$ — determination$_3$ is a subsidiary concept useful at best for referring to intermediate stages which themselves are ultimately conjectures requiring proof by determinisms$_{1and2}$. Indeed, much of human interest in science is because when we can determine$_1$ things, we can determine$_2$ things — science leads to technology.

Determination$_3$ may have no separate sense or meaning, and be completely parasitic on determination$_1$, with the metaphorical implication of derived agency from its use in association with determination$_2$. Since the evolution of the capability for determination$_1$ would be a *very* hard story to tell in the absence of a real capacity for determination$_2$, there may be no possibility for determination$_3$ existing as a human concept which does not depend on a state of affairs in which determination$_2$ is real.

On the surface, this resembles the anthropic principle in cosmology, the claim that for the universe to exist it must be observable, for which it must be able to support life, for which it must be within certain parameters. But this is a more modest claim: for a creature to exist with a concept of determinism$_3$, it must be the case that the world in which the creature exists is one in which the creature truly has the capacity for determinism$_1$, which, in turn, will only evolve given that determinism$_2$ is a true capability of the creature in that world.

A world describable in terms of determinism$_3$ is often taken to be a world in which there is an absence of real freedom. This may be a mistake arising from confusion of determination$_3$ with the concepts of determination$_{1and2}$ from which it depends. When a human being employs a billiard ball as an agent in order to determine$_2$ where a second ball will go, the first ball as it determines$_3$ the course of the second is, if we have imparted the right impetus to it, the perfect slave of our own determination$_2$, insofar as we can determine$_1$. There is a tendency to work backwards from this to the suspicion that our own determinations$_2$ may be a case of similar perfect slavery to determinations$_3$ which are outside of our conscious selves, the very selves which engage in determinations$_1$ in support of a (real although obviously in some dimensions constrained) range of free choices of what to determine$_2$ to do.

Indeed, in determining$_2$ we often use ourselves instrumentally, and also may employ human as well as mechanical agents beyond ourselves. We have something of a stake in determinism$_3$ being at least a good approximation of an explanation of our human agents' actions — to the extent that if it is not, they have either failed us, or acted as partners in determining$_2$ rather than solely as slaves. So our stake in determinism$_2$ motivates a social reality in which determinism$_3$ can, at times, apply to descriptions of people, considered in the same terms as inanimate objects ('objectified') for the purposes of determining$_{1and2}$ what they will do.

But again, the success of determinism$_3$ here derives from our interest in determinism$_2$, and its approximate truth in this circumstance depends on our human agents' becoming determined$_2$ to accord with our own determination$_2$. Implicit in determining$_2$ is the reality of choice. Choice itself is bound up with the concept of consciousness; to understand this more fully, we will look in the next section at how consciousness, in which we conduct much of our determinism$_{1\,and\,2}$, is itself situated in human experience.

'Will' shares determine's two major senses: we determine$_1$ what will$_1$ (or might$_1$) happen; we also can determine$_2$ what will$_1$ happen, in which case we will$_2$ it (and, if successful, display our might$_2$). There is not, interestingly, a parallel will$_3$. When 'free will' is challenged by 'determinism', it is will$_2$/determinism$_2$ being challenged by either determinism$_3$ — which we have just seen is incoherent — or the theological claim that our own will$_2$/determinism$_2$ is, or should be, pre-empted by a divine will$_2$/determinism$_2$, to which we are, or should be, slaves rather than partners — but this challenge concedes the reality of will$_2$/determinism$_2$, debating instead the location of the nexus to which it is ascribed. The Latinate 'volition' is a simple synonym for will$_2$.

To give the claim a Cartesian flavour: I can determine$_1$, therefore I can determine$_2$ — I have free will. The contrary claim is: I can determine$_1$, therefore everything is determined$_3$ — free will is impossible. The first is a strong claim on evolutionary grounds; while as Hampshire (1971, p. 3) points out, the second is too vague to be a testable, tenable scientific proposition: it is impossible to say what evidence would count against it. The determinist always has the out of claiming the results were fully determined$_3$, but by factors yet to be determined$_1$.

Only the arrogant presumption of an infinite capacity to determine$_1$ requires that everything be determined$_3$, since otherwise our capacity to determine$_1$ must find a degree of limitation when determination$_2$ is at play. It can be said that our history of determining$_1$ is impressive, justifying the presumption of its infinite capacity — but so is our history of determining$_2$. A bias towards determination$_1$'s evidence over determination$_2$'s betrays a membership among thinkers rather than doers, while denying the responsibility of knowledge and speculation in actively shaping the world.

III

As I write, I'm in Brooklyn, with a large statue of a goddess out of the window in the harbour. Famous as Liberty, she is identifiable by her upraised torch as an incarnation of the Greek Hecate. Fittingly the goddess of crossroads and thresholds, she stands guarding the entrance to America, the crossroads of many immigrant journeys. In classical Athens, Hecate's statue was placed in front of most homes, as well as wherever three roads met, where she would be either standing with her torch illuminating the ways, or represented by a pole with three masks on it, each facing down a path from the junction. Often she would be depicted holding a pomegranate, symbol of the many in the one, accompanied by a dog as guide and guardian of the ways and thresholds (Rabinowitz, 1998).

For the Pythagoreans, 'Y' symbolized choice (Patterson, 1991). The image of a 'Y' where paths branch, regularly experienced in a world where travel was often by foot and through wilderness, is foundational both to our notion of freedom and to the progress of science. 'Science' itself comes from a linguistic root meaning 'to see'. Hecate, in the later decline of Greek culture, came to be known as the goddess of witches, our own word for which is based on an Indo-European root for vision that occurs in 'wise', 'wit', 'wizard', 'visionary', and more. Light and the eyes were the symbols of freedom in Greek drama (Patterson, 1991).

The root of 'science' is also the root of 'conscious' and 'conscience', with the prefix of 'con' ('with') added, meaning to 'see with' or 'see together' (similarly, 'intellect' comes from 'gather together'). A possible sense of this is the seeing of two paths together from a junction, as we weigh which way to go ('weigh' and 'way' also being from the same root), taking the ratio between their prospects so as to be 'rational'. Another possible sense is how we fundamentally understand things in terms of each other, by metaphor and analogy, allowing us to abstract basic schemas, such as 'Y' to represent branching paths, from common experience. 'Y' also, stood vertically, represents the branching of a tree. Our words 'tree' and 'true' are also from a common root (the 'Tree of Knowledge' is almost redundant).

'Determinism' itself takes its sense in a context of branching paths, since it means 'identifying the terminus' of a path. A traveller at a crossroads, seeking to determine which road leads to Rome, is aided by a sign saying 'Via Roma'. Roads are often named for the towns they lead to — thenselves most often junctures of ways, but also settings or settlements, typically with defined town lines, even walls around them. The town is a set of sets, a contained community consisting of homes in the local style containing families, also with local resemblance.

These two ancient and common human experiences — of branching paths of travel and contained settings of habitation — provide, in schematic abstraction, not just our capability of mapping our highways and cities, but essential conceptual tools for designing our most sophisticated machinery. Even computer programmers like me, who prefer to write lines of code rather than use visual programming tools, first map out any complex project in diagrams based on these primitive, essential concepts. A program diagram looks like a map of trade routes between towns.

A basic claim for 'free will': We can see various futures, branching paths, consciously comparing, contrasting, anticipating with our various senses, considering how prospects might feel, what we might see in them, what we might hear people say in them; as well as what we might show others, say to others, and cause them to feel; and what further prospects will open out. Then we act in light of our foresight, taking paths that would have been impossible — or forbiddingly improbable — without our conscious consideration.

References

Ayto, John (1990), *Dictionary of Word Origins* (New York: Arcade Publishing).

Borges, Jorge Luis (1998), 'The garden of forking paths', in *Collected Fictions*, tr. Andrew Hurley (New York: Viking Penguin).

Hampshire, Stuart (1971), *Freedom of Mind* (Princeton, NJ: Princeton University Press).

Patterson, Orlando (1991), *Freedom in the Making of Western Culture* (New York: Basic Books).

Rabinowitz, Jacob (1998), *The Rotting Goddess: The origin of the witch in classical antiquity* (Brooklyn, NY: Autonomedia).

Whitman, Walt (1881), *Leaves of Grass* (Boston, MA: James R. Osgood and Co.).

Anthony Freeman

Decisive Action

Personal Responsibility All the Way Down

Colin Blakemore (1988) claims that the human brain is a machine and that all our actions are the products of brain activity. In consequence, he says, it makes no sense (in scientific terms) to distinguish sharply between acts that result from conscious intention and those that are pure reflexes or the outcome of disease or damage to the brain. It may appear to us that some actions are self-willed while others are beyond our control, but in reality that is not the case. All brain activity is physical, and so determined by physical laws, and therefore it makes no sense to distinguish between one set of acts for which someone is personally responsible and another set for which they are not. This being so, it is — according to Blakemore and those determinists who think like him — inappropriate to make personal responsibility the basis of a system of retributive justice. We may need to restrain criminals to prevent them doing harm to themselves and others, but we should not punish them, i.e. exact retribution, for actions they did not freely will.

There are two regular kinds of response to this argument. On the one hand there are libertarians, like David Hodgson (1991). They agree that there can be no responsibility in a deterministic universe, and are then driven by a belief in the reality of moral and legal responsibility to argue that the universe cannot be deterministic. On the other hand there are compatibilists, such as Daniel Dennett, who agree that all human actions are subject to physical determinism, but are still able to declare that 'holding people responsible is the best game in town' (Dennett, 1984, p. 162). My response is a version of compatibilism, but one that turns Blakemore's logic on its head. I accept his contention that actions cannot be divided into some for which we are responsible and some for which we are not, but I draw the opposite conclusion from him. He argues that, since our brains set in train at least some actions for which we cannot possibly be held responsible, therefore we cannot be held responsible for any of our actions. I say that, since there are at least some actions for which we most certainly hold ourselves and others responsible, therefore we must be prepared to accept responsibility for all our actions.

I do not approach the question as a scientist, like Blakemore, or a lawyer, like Hodgson, or philosopher, like Dennett, but as a priest — someone who feels responsible for my own actions and who is called upon to counsel and absolve such as come to me with their shame and their guilt. Should I say that their sense of responsibility is

Journal of Consciousness Studies, **6**, No. 8–9, 1999, pp. 275–8

illusory? Or should I encourage them to accept responsibility, and then to deal with it in the various ways — religious, psychological and practical — that are open to them?

I find myself taking the latter course. I do not say that I choose it, but that I find myself taking it. That is crucial to my approach, which entails distinguishing between responsibility (which I accept) and voluntary choice (which I do not).

Imagine a sliding scale of degrees of choice in the actions that I take. At one end are subconscious actions such as the working of my liver and the production of bone marrow; and at the other, consciously intended actions such as lifting my arm or writing this sentence. The vast majority of the things that I do fall somewhere in between. I pass someone and murmur 'Good day', or I chat inconsequentially with a colleague over coffee, and I am hardly aware of what I am saying — certainly I do not carefully plan my words. It would be too much to say in any strong sense that I 'willed' them. Nonetheless they are voluntary in the sense that I could choose not to say them. Many of my physical movements also fall into this category of semi-automatic actions. Others are completely deliberate, but not totally voluntary. For instance, much of my time is spent editing the *Journal of Consciousness Studies*. I enjoy this and am grateful enough to be employed when many are not, but it is not necessarily what I would do with my time had I no need to earn a living.

Now consider that small number of actions which I think of as being completely voluntary — actions that I carry out with full deliberate desire and intention. Such an action might commonly be supposed to consist of three steps: (A) a decision to act, (B) putting the decision into effect and (C) the consequent action. I shall argue that this model is wrong, that the moment of decision is in fact the moment of action.

The evidence for this claim is partly from third-person science and partly from first-person introspection, both my own and the reports of others. The neuroscientific evidence comes from Benjamin Libet's experimental work (described and referenced in his contribution to this volume). Libet's results suggest that my step (C) above — the physical action, represented by the onset of electrical activity in the brain — occurs before step (A), the mental decision to act, as reported by the subject. In other words, the conscious decision to act follows rather than precedes the action in question, and cannot therefore be its cause. Consequently, it is argued, our impression that we voluntarily will our actions is false; what we experience as a decision is in fact no more than a monitoring of an automatic and physically determined act already under way.

Libet himself accepts the first part of this interpretation, but not the negative consequences for freewill. He draws the conclusion that, while our mental decisions do not initiate actions, that the speed of monitoring leaves open the possibility of a veto being applied. That is, there is enough time between the initiating brain activity and the physical movement for the incipient action to be detected and countermanded. So, according to Libet, while I may not consciously initiate an action, I always have the option of stopping it coming about. By not to stopping it, I freely will it and may properly be taken to be responsible for it. This interpretation has not been fully accepted, but for my purposes it is sufficient that Libet and his critics agree that his results dispose of the simple three-step model of voluntary action with which I started.

Now for the evidence from introspection. It is commonly held to be the strongest card in the hand of those arguing for free will that every one of us has the experience of making free choices. We all make decisions all the time, from little ones like which sock to put on first to momentous ones like whom to marry or whether to run for

President. Well, I am not so sure. In fact I do not believe I have ever taken a positive free-choice decision in my life.[1] By that I mean that I have not carried out a fully voluntary action in the strong sense of being at the far end of the range I set out at the beginning of this paper. Let me illustrate this with the two biggest 'decisions' that I made in my life, and one trivial one.

First, my ordination to the priesthood. My memory of childhood is quite vague, but I can distinctly remember, at the age of eleven, telling the headmaster of my junior school that I wanted to be a priest. I certainly cannot remember deciding it; but I can remember saying it. Over the years I never wavered in my desire for the priesthood. There was a kind of inevitability about it that I did nothing to stop. There is good biblical support for interpreting the matter in this way. In St John's Gospel, Jesus says to his twelve disciples, 'Ye have not chosen me, but I have chosen you, and ordained you' (*John* 15.16) and those words are routinely taken as being applicable to all Christians and especially to ministers. That is why it is known as a vocation — a calling — and not something initiated by the individual from the human end.

Secondly, my marriage. Because from an early age I felt called to the priesthood, and also had strong leanings to the monastic life, I never seriously considered that I should ever marry. But it was inconvenient as a student not to have a girlfriend to take to dances and other social events. I had such a friend, who lived happily with her elder sister and never intended tying herself down to a mere man (as she would put it). But she also wanted a partner for dances. So we both felt safe. Six years on we were aware of a growing love and mutual dependence and it somehow became accepted that we should be married. We were never formally engaged, our two second-hand gold wedding rings cost less than £10 the pair, Jacqueline has never taken my surname . . . but twenty-seven years later our married life together seems to be happier and more stable than that of many contemporary couples, a significant number of whom are no longer together. A satisfying outcome for us, but no major choice, no great decision.

Finally, a trivial example. If you offered me a plate of biscuits with three kinds — chocolate, coconut and plain — and politeness dictated that I only took one, surely then I should have to make a choice? Again, I would say not, at least not in the strong sense of the three-step path to voluntary action. In the first place I do not like coconut. So I would not take one of those. But that is not a free choice. I never chose to dislike coconut, I just don't. That leaves the plain and the chocolate. I enjoy both. Sometimes I feel in the mood for one, and sometimes the other. As the plate comes towards me I might think, 'Yes, a chocolate one today', but I might still end up taking a plain one. Maybe they are closer to me and I am embarrassed to stretch over. Maybe I just change my mind. Or maybe I don't. My point is that it is only when I have the biscuit in my hand that even I will know for certain which one I have chosen.

Being ordained, marrying, taking a biscuit: three examples of what I call decisive action, because it is the action that makes the decision. Until the action is taken, no decision is finally made. Once the action is taken, there is no going back. But — and this is the crucial point — they are my actions and I own them. Determinists argue

---

[1] I was encouraged to explore my own experience in this matter by Sam Harris' trenchant contributions to the jcs-online debate on Free Will at the end of 1998. For example, on November 10 he wrote: 'What compatibilists and libertarians overlook, however, is that free will does not even correspond to any *subjective* fact . . . apparent acts of volition merely arise spontaneously . . . and cannot be traced to a point of origin in the conscious self.'

that because all actions are determined, none is our responsibility. I argue in the opposite direction and extend the scope of responsibility much further in the 'non-voluntary' direction than is normal in legal circles.

I start with certain actions at the extreme positive end of my 'sliding scale' which I cannot help but claim as my own actions willingly undertaken. Yet it appears that even those actions that feel most obviously like 'free choices' can be shown, on both physiological and introspective grounds, to have been initiated other than by conscious choice, and to have been decided upon only in the act of doing them. Do I react by disowning my actions? Not at all. I disown the three-step model, but not my decisive actions. This means taking the actions themselves, rather than the alleged intentions with which they are carried out, as the crucial factor. It means taking the whole embodied person — not some abstracted theoretical mind or soul — as the responsible agent. And that in turn carries the concept of responsibility back along the scale. Not only my fully volitional actions, but my semi-automatic ones, my imposed ones, and even my non-conscious ones, all of them — on this view — become the responsible actions of the embodied person.

Ben Libet remarks — half jokingly — that his experimental results could provide a physiological basis for the doctrine of 'original sin' (this volume, p. 54). My argument here also ties in with Christian understandings of sin, and more importantly of forgiveness, for which accepting of responsibility — repenting — is the necessary first step. Traditionally absolution would have been thought of as God's doing, but as a Christian humanist I interpret the concept of divine forgiveness at the practical level in terms of acceptance within the human community. And therefore I see no problem in principle — indeed I see every advantage — to extending this approach from the religious to the legal sphere as well.

I believe this approach could provide a way out of the impasse between the Hodgsons and the Blakemores. Determinists dislike retribution and believe that showing that people are not responsible for their actions is a necessary gateway to a more compassionate justice. Libertarians fear that a loss of personal responsibility will inevitably lead to a loss of personal rights and eventually of all justice. My approach offers a way to avoid both fears. First, it keeps the concept of responsibility and — if rights and responsibilities go hand in hand — then responsibility 'all the way down' will safeguard human rights 'all the way down' as well. Secondly, by taking such a wide view of responsibility, and severing it from the idea of unfettered choice, this approach (like the doctrine of original sin) will not permit anyone to adopt an attitude of moral superiority. When everyone accepts a share in the responsibility for the state of the world, then justice will surely be tempered with mercy (if not forgiveness, but why not?) and this will be a guard against vengeance.[2]

References

Blakemore, C. (1988), *The Mind Machine* (London: BBC Publications).
Dennett, D.C. (1984), *Elbow Room* (Cambridge, MA: MIT Press).
Hodgson, D. (1991), *The Mind Matters* (Oxford: Oxford University Press).
Libet, B. (1999), 'Do we have free will?', *Journal of Consciousness Studies*, **6** (8–9), pp. 47–57.

---

[2] An earlier version of this article was delivered as a seminar paper at Elizabethtown College, PA, in April 1999. I am grateful to Michael Silberstein for the invitation to speak and for helpful comments from the seminar's participants, especially David Hodgson.

Thomas W. Clark

Fear of Mechanism

A Compatibilist Critique of 'The Volitional Brain'

As several contributions to this volume make clear, the problem of free will engages us deeply because it seems central to our conception of who we are, our place in the world, and our moral intuitions. To take a position on whether we have free will, and what sort of freedom this is, is to take positions on a host of other fundamental and necessarily interlocking issues: what we ultimately consist of as selves, the relation of mind to body, the role of consciousness in behaviour, the proper methods of scientific and phenomenological inquiry, the need for foundations in ethics, and the possibility of the supernatural, among many other questions. To define the will, or volition, and argue that this definition captures the truth of the matter, is to invoke an entire world view, which must stand against its competitors.

And competition there is, since world views have consequences in policy and politics. When U.S. cigarette companies, defending themselves in class action suits, claim that smokers could have chosen to quit at any time, they are appealing to a particular notion of will and its relation to behaviour. As the Truth and Reconciliation Commission completed its work in South Africa, some have questioned whether justice is served by forgoing punishment in return for the true story of one's misdeeds. Shouldn't retribution against the freely willing despot trump the need for social reconstruction? Or, conversely, might not the retributive impulse be softened by understanding the causal histories of political criminals? Such questions inevitably get answered using background assumptions at the heart of the free will debate.

As mentioned in the introduction, the argument over free will is in a very real sense the successor, and to some extent the companion, of the centuries old argument about God. Since the Enlightenment, Western theistic views, placing power and our ultimate fate in the hands of an almighty deity, have to some extent given way to a secularism in which our destiny is understood to lie largely within our own hands. We have usurped God's power, or at least a good share of it, but many continue to believe that the capacity to shape ourselves still supercedes the rest of nature and its physical laws. Free will, on the libertarian, incompatibilist account, in which we are ultimately responsible for ourselves and our acts (see Introduction, p. xiii), makes the self more or less a first cause, an unmoved mover: we could have willed otherwise in the radical sense that the will is *not* the explicable or predictable result of any set of conditions that held at the moment of choice. The question of whether we actually have such free

Journal of Consciousness Studies, **6**, No. 8–9, 1999, pp. 279–93

will thus recapitulates in the domain of human metaphysics the question of the existence of God. That many believe that we stand above nature in some essential respect suggests that the Enlightenment was more successful in its glorification of the individual than in its challenge to the supernatural.[1]

Libertarians tend to suppose that not only do we have such freedom, but that without it our moral intuitions and institutions are at risk. The ultimately responsible, self-originating self — the *causa sui* self, to use Galen Strawson's term (Strawson, 1998) — is thought necessary to ground ethical judgments and social justice, and a fully explanatory and inclusive science of human behaviour threatens the status of such a self. Using the other (Peter) Strawson's typology (Strawson, 1962) such libertarians are *pessimists* regarding the compatibility of (current) science and personal responsibility. On the other hand, compatibilists and determinists such as myself are *optimists*, who cheerfully accept that the will is entirely a function of antecedent conditions, and find that no capacity for ultimate self-determination is either conceivable or necessary to found our moral intuitions.

Peter Strawson's classification cuts across the categories represented here — neuroscience, psychology, physical science, and philosophy — in that scientists such as **Libet** and **Schwartz** and **Stapp** agree with legal philosopher David **Hodgson** that having libertarian free will is an essential aspect of our humanity which may eventually be confirmed by science, perhaps in radical departures from current theory. On the other side, neuroscientists **Ingvar**, **Frith** and **Spence**, are joined by philosopher **Gomes,** psychologist **Claxton,** and polymath **McCrone** in taking more or less the compatibilist position: volition is no more (or less) than the brain in action; it is therefore in principle explicable within our current, more or less deterministic physical understanding (at the neural, cybernetic level, no need for quantum niceties); and that this sort of volition is sufficient for our moral purposes. This last point — the issue of moral foundations and the role of free will — is not addressed in depth in these papers, so will receive more attention from me in what follows (see Waller, 1998; Clark, 1998a).

Benjamin **Libet**'s paper illustrates several key difficulties faced by libertarians as they seek to find free will of the 'ultimate' variety within science. First, it is clear that Libet's research, and more importantly his interpretation of it, is driven by what we might call *fear of mechanism*. He worries that under standard scientific determinism, 'we would be essentially sophisticated automatons, with our conscious feelings and intentions tacked on as epiphenomena with no causal power'. The impression given from the start (and this concern is evident in Stapp's and Hodgson's pieces as well) is that there is a *right answer* to the free will question, one that will secure us from the bogey of mechanism and its pernicious spawn of relativism, fatalism, fascism, puppethood, abuse excuses, and the like. The implicit agenda is: since it's unthinkable that we don't have free will (we don't want to be automatons, do we?) we'd damn well better come up with proof that we do.

While having an agenda works for meetings, companies and political parties, it's out of place in scientific investigations, and in Libet's case the need to find a shred of evidence to support libertarian free will forces him into a strained interpretation of his own data. His main finding, which very much undercuts libertarian free will, is the

---

[1]   I owe this last point to Keith Sutherland.

unsurprising one that conscious acts are invariably preceded by unconscious neural processes which prepare for action. After all, shouldn't we expect consciousness, obviously a brain-based phenomenon, to have causal links with unconscious processes, some of which precede conscious episodes? But Libet, intent on his quest to defeat 'mere' mechanism, gamely tries to make a case that our will resides in the 'conscious veto' that allows us *not* to perform an act after unconscious processes have readied it for expression. The obvious question, to which Libet has only the weakest answer, is whether or not this veto itself has neural antecedents and correlates. If it did, then it would simply be yet another part of a complex physical system (the brain) responding in astonishingly intricate ways to generate appropriate behaviour. He says:

> I propose . . . that the conscious veto may *not* require or be the direct result of preceding unconscious processes. The conscious veto is a *control* function, different from simply becoming aware of the wish to act. There is no logical imperative in any mind-brain theory, even identity theory, that requires specific neural activity to precede and determine the nature of a conscious control function. And there is no experimental evidence against the possibility that the control process may appear without development by prior unconscious processes. (p. 53; original emphasis.)[2]

Libet's case here (and in other sections of his paper) for the independence of the conscious veto from neural activity is not that there is positive evidence for it, but merely that logical and empirical considerations don't rule it out. But even this is too strong a claim, for surely under mind–brain identity theory, any discoverable conscious control function must be neurally instantiated. And evidence acceptable to the neuroscientific community would inevitably show the *connection* of such a control function to other brain functions, whether conscious or unconscious. The startling fact is that Libet wants to find a non-neural, non-physical basis for free will (some sort of mental conscious control over the brain itself) *and* he wants to find it doing research predicated on the assumption of neural cause and effect. Such a research agenda, wedded to the *a priori* goal of defeating mechanism yet rooted in physicalist science, is surely doomed from the outset.

What exactly, one might ask, is the threat of mechanism, that it can so distort normal scientific constraints on what constitutes a plausible hypothesis and that would make proponents of the hypothesis plead that absence of disconfirmation counts as positive evidence? For Libet, as for many others, the underlying concern is that if the self reduces to the brain, and conscious control reduces to a sub-system of the brain, then the individual doesn't have *real*, *contra-causal* free will (as Dennett, 1984, puts it, the type of free will Libet thinks is 'worth wanting') and can't be held responsible:

> We do not hold people responsible for actions performed unconsciously, without the possibility of control. For example, actions by a person during a psychomotor epileptic seizure, or by one with Tourette's syndrome, etc., are not regarded as actions of free will. Why then should an act unconsciously developed by a normal individual, a process over which he also has no conscious control, be regarded as an act of free will? (pp. 52–3.)

Similarly, Stapp warns us that

> It has become now widely appreciated that assimilation by the general public of this 'scientific' view, according to which each human being is basically a mechanical robot,

---

[2] Undated page references are to this volume.

is likely to have a significant and corrosive impact on the moral fabric of society . . . [involving] the growing tendency of people to exonerate themselves by arguing that it is not 'I' who is at fault, but some mechanical process within . . . (pp. 144–5).

Libet thinks that unless conscious control (something brain-independent, remember) plays a role in either generating or vetoing normal behaviour, then normal behaviour is essentially no different from movements resulting from seizures or tics. But clearly we can, without resorting to obscure notions of mental agency, continue to make the distinction between voluntary, deliberate behaviour in which consciousness plays a role and reflexive, involuntary acts. (Gomes in this volume does an excellent job of describing the spectrum of intentional and impulsive behaviour while relating them to neural function, illuminating the territory that Libet must conceal to push his agenda.) With this distinction in hand, we are at least part way to establishing a plausible, albeit compatibilist and non-libertarian, notion of personal responsibility: Individuals who can deliberate, anticipate consequences, recall relevant episodes, and who are otherwise rational are capable of change by virtue of being held responsible, in the sense that the anticipation of being praised and blamed is effective in shaping their voluntary acts (very young children and the mentally incompetent the obvious exceptions). Therefore, we *should* hold them responsible — treat them as moral agents — in order to encourage the sorts of behaviour we want. So even though no individual on this view has anything resembling the ultimate free will or conscious control Libet hopes to find, it makes perfect sense, as well as good interpersonal, social, and legal policy, to suppose we are *justified* in holding most individuals responsible for their voluntary behaviour (Clark, 1998a,b). If this is true, then mechanism (deterministic or incorporating indeterministic elements), even if it penetrates to the core of the self, is no threat to responsibility, morality, or the social order. Having understood this, scientists such as Libet and Stapp and others exploring physical theory such as Hodgson need not beat the bushes quite so hard to discover a basis for 'ultimate' responsibility.

For those of the libertarian persuasion, the first-person phenomenology of choice is all but indisputable evidence for free will. For Libet, the experience of agency is not to be questioned, and any science that fails to validate it is suspect:

> [W]e must recognize that the almost universal experience that we can act with a free, independent choice provides a kind of *prima facie* evidence that conscious mental processes can causatively control some brain processes . . . The phenomenal fact is that most of us feel that we do have free will, at least for some of our actions and within certain limits that may be imposed by our brain's status and by our environment. The intuitive feelings about the phenomenon of free will form a fundamental basis for views of our human nature, and great care should be taken not to believe allegedly scientific conclusions about them which actually depend on hidden ad hoc assumptions. A theory that simply interprets the phenomenon of free will as illusory and denies the validity of this phenomenal fact is less attractive than a theory that accepts or accommodates the phenomenal fact (p. 56).

Let us grant the point (although it's eminently contestable, as Claxton and McCrone show) that most of the world's inhabitants *feel* as if they are free agents in the radical, libertarian sense, able via some mental process to affect their brains without in turn being at the effect of anything else. When conducting science, the validity of such a feeling — whether or not it refers to an actual state of affairs — is exactly the question at issue, one would suppose. Do we in fact exist as something apart from the brain that could manipulate its very neurons, or sub-neural mechanisms? The truth of this proposition presumably gets established by winning scientific consensus via the preponderance of empirical support. But here Libet seems to have things precisely backwards: judge the attractiveness of a theory by how well it conforms to one's subjective experience, which is taken as criterial. As Claxton properly observes, the phenomenology of volition, insofar as it actually feels as Libet supposes, might merely *reflect* the consensual Western 'folk theory' of free will, since 'once such a view has been culturally adopted and become "second nature", then perception itself becomes skewed and selective . . . and persistent interpretations self-reinforcing' (p. 100). The feeling of freedom, therefore, hardly counts as evidence for libertarian free will, nor should the failure of science to validate this feeling reflect upon the adequacy of contrary theories. The methodological point here is the rather prosaic one that first person phenomenology, however widely shared, can at most be the basis for a hunch, which may get lucky and become a plausible hypothesis, which may yet become a full fledged theory, *if* the empirical cards fall in its favor. But feelings or intuitions *per se* never count as self-evident proof of anything.

Like Libet, Jeffery **Schwartz** combines (with difficulty) a practical commitment to neuroscience with a sharp ideological aversion to the notion that the will might be embodied. Unfortunately, the result is that both his science and his philosophy end up compromised. He conceives of human effort — in this instance, the efforts by obsessive-compulsive disorder (OCD) patients to overcome their symptoms — as something categorically non-physical and mental, yet emphasizes 'the critical role of effort as a necessary component for keeping the machinery [of the brain] on track and functioning' (p. 121). This sets up the standard (and usually fatal) problem of dualism: how exactly can something non-physical influence the physical machinery of the brain? Should an interactive mechanism ever get specified, this threatens to absorb the non-physical antecedent into the physical consequent. If it doesn't get specified, then it's mere speculation that the non-physical has such power, and methodologically more circumspect to suppose that physical causes, as yet unknown, are doing the work.

On the one hand, Schwartz is conversant with the neurophysiology underlying the symptoms of OCD, and indeed his main findings are that there are measurable differences in brain metabolism between responders and non-responders to behavioural treatment for OCD (p. 124). On the other hand, he credits the change in metabolism to an entirely obscure, theoretically disconnected (from neuroscience, and hence predictively inert) notion of 'mental force' that 'generates the energy necessary to activate, strengthen, and stabilize [a responder's] new health-giving and life-affirming circuitry' (p. 131).

Schwartz's motive is much the same as Libet's: defend, at all costs, the intuition of mental agency, of an essentially active, willed power independent of the brain and body which can reach down and manipulate the brain itself. And again, the validity of the experience of effort and volition as referring to a categorically *mental*, non-neural phenomenon goes unquestioned. Rather, science must conform to experience and take the verbal reports of patients at face value ('the directly perceived reality of the causal efficacy of volition', p. 138), otherwise we would be 'resorting to reductionist approaches which irrationally prefer materialist as opposed to experiential perspectives' (p. 132). But there is no real conflict between such perspectives, as long as we understand that phenomenology is *data*, just like metre readings, that needs explaining, not the benchmark of empirical truth (see Dennett, 1991, on 'heterophenomenology').

Schwartz's difficulty is that he conflates passivity at the behavioural and neural levels:

> Without reference to a naturally occurring mental force, the observed changes in cerebral energy use . . . would have to be autonomously generated by an entirely *passive* process – but that is plainly inconsistent with a very large amount of clinical data, most especially the verbal reports of patients who have actually undergone these treatments. (p. 132; original emphasis.)

Presumably, patients said such things as 'I really tried hard not to let that obsessive thought run away with me.' But there is nothing inconsistent with the experience of trying hard and having effort itself be a 'passive' process in the rather strained, nonstandard sense that its neural correlates are entrained without benefit of active supervision. In this sense, *all* brain events are passive, since no one supposes we are actually in a position to consciously pick out and activate particular neural bundles or connections. Nevertheless, effortful, deliberate, focussed action arises, distinguished from passive responding not by the additional effort supplied by 'mental force' (which would need explaining in turn), but by the specific sorts of neural networks involved. This distinction, of course, is not enough for Schwartz, since his concern is to buttress 'the age old belief that human beings have in their capacity to act as *genuinely* self-directed agents capable of instituting *real* self-directed change' (p. 138; my emphasis). Mere embodied brains, apparently, can't change on their own in response to social influences like behavioural therapy; they need extra help from the mental force. To which I am tempted to respond: may the force be with *you*, Dr. Schwartz; I have no need of it.

Henry **Stapp** starts by emphasizing the momentousness of the debate on mind/body problem. It is, he says, a 'raging battle' which pits our intuition that conscious thoughts guide behaviour against philosophies which 'proclaim, in the name of science, that we are mechanical systems governed entirely by impersonal laws that operate at the microscopic level of our atomic or cellular components.' Having dealt with the *fear* of mechanism above, I will comment on Stapp's *characterization* of mechanism, which seems simply wrong as applied to ourselves or anything much above a mollusk.

The worst case scenario, for Stapp and other libertarians, is if it turns out there's nothing more to us than deterministically law-governed meat, whether it be bones, brain, muscle or gut. Now the laws governing the meat (that is, the more or less invariable or statistically reliable covariations between states of affairs we call natural laws) are *not* merely at the microscopic atomic or cellular level, as Stapp supposes, but also obtain at successively higher levels of biological and behavioural description, each of which incorporates whatever levels lie beneath it. There are laws, for example, of bipedal locomotion control common to robots and humans (left right, left right) which have little or nothing to do with the instantiating physical substrate. And there are, perhaps, psychological laws having to do with motivation and goal satisfaction (e.g., the conditions which generate 'disappointment') which would obtain for silicon Martians and vaporous Venusians as well as for us protoplasmic Earthlings.

The point, elaborated by Dennett (1987) is that organisms of our complexity (naturally evolved mechanisms amenable to behavioural prediction and control) are intentional systems in which law-governed behaviour is best understood, and practically speaking *only* understood, at the *personal* level of beliefs and desires, not the 'machine' level. But this means that on a materialist functional view of the self, there is no gulf needing to be bridged, nor any conflict, between the impersonal component level and the highest personal level of deliberate choice: true explanations can co-exist at both levels. And descriptions of the functional components of complex, conscious behaviour, linked to the brain's cybernetic control systems, are showing great promise, even in their infancy (see for instance Baars, 1997; Churchland, 1995; Damasio, 1994, Ingvar, this volume).

Stapp rejects this sort of materialism, in particular the notion that conscious experience of the sort commonly associated with our deliberative choices might be identical to some set of neural processes. But, since he believes consciousness must play an important causal role in shaping behaviour (if it didn't, we'd be robots) he must, like Libet and Hodgson (see below), find the physical, or more broadly, the natural correlates of consciousness somewhere else. This is in the interstices of quantum mechanics, of which I know little and on which I will therefore remain silent (see Churchland & Grush, 1995, for an extended critique of quantum theories of consciousness).

Nevertheless, there is a general point to be made relevant to Stapp and others engaged in the quantum quest for consciousness and free will: when you finally pin it down, will it still be what you want? Stapp wants a 'pragmatic theory of the mind/brain that allows our thoughts to be causally efficacious yet not controlled by local-mechanistic laws combined with random chance' (p. 160). But any good scientific theory of thought will of necessity show how thoughts themselves arise within a context, not merely how they cause behaviour. That is, such a theory will place thought, consciousness, the will, mental agency, what have you, within a general, law-invoking explanation in which there are predictable antecedents as well as consequents. But libertarian free will *is precisely that which by definition can't have law-like or predictable antecedents, otherwise it wouldn't be free in the required sense.* So to find it within nature is to destroy it. Since knowledge explodes the causa sui self, its defenders tend to occupy the penumbra of science and psychology, where the light of explanation has yet to penetrate.

Most of the motives and methods critiqued above can be found in **Hodgson**'s sally against mainstream science and philosophy, undertaken for the now familiar reason of defending 'common-sense ideas of responsibility'. Hodgson, like Kane in his 1996 book *The Significance of Free Will* and a recent paper (Kane, 1999), tries to establish the possibility that a person's motives, reasons, and character never necessitate choices, they only *incline* a person in particular directions. It is the sheer 'capacity to choose', the essential, stripped down 'I', not anything distinctive about the person, which finally determines behaviour (p. 209). During the choice process, this I, or what Hodgson calls 'volitional causation', goes about 'adjusting the probabilities of alternatives' (p. 210). In sum,

> The way the agent is, in respect of character and motivation, does not determine what the agent does: it only determines what the alternatives are and how they appeal. The agent is not responsible for having the capacity to choose between these alternatives, but it is not constrained in how that capacity is exercised, *even by the way the agent then is in respect*

of character and motivation; and so the agent (and no-one and nothing else) is responsible for the way that capacity is exercised (p. 212; original emphasis).

The final redoubt of free will is therefore nothing publicly recognizable as me, but something very much like a dispassionate 'soul', operating behind the scene of motivational conflict. But what interests, one might ask, does such a soul-chooser have, that would explain why it adjusts the probabilities of alternatives (the weights of reasons) in one direction rather than another? Apparently none, since the agent, in its capacity as chooser, has no character and motives, rather it operates *over* such mundanities, in which case the adjustments themselves are inexplicable. Nevertheless, they still get chalked up to the responsible agent. The price of ultimate responsibility it seems, is the intelligibility and explicability of freely willed choices. (For a discussion of this point, see Clark, 1996.)

But Hodgson's claim is that our standard notion of explanation, that which seeks a causal context for action, perhaps leavened by various sorts of randomness, is 'Hume's mistake'. Hume, the arch sceptic about folk theories of causation, along with most of the philosophical and scientific community, somehow failed to see there is yet a third alternative beyond chance and deterministic causality, namely 'volitional causation'. However, even if we accept Hodgson's argument that such causation is a conceptual possibility (a stretch by my lights) it's not a *mistake* by Hume and the rest of us compatibilists to spend little time considering it, since *we have no need of such an hypothesis*. That is, since we suppose we have a good account of responsibility and agency of the non-ultimate variety, that does all the work necessary to ground personal, social, and legal practice, it's methodological wisdom not to waste time on what seems *prima facie* a metaphysical non-starter. Hodgson, driven by the libertarian assumption that only a radically free self can be held responsible, must play Don Quixote versus mainstream science and philosophy. (Of course that's how compatibilists feel when taking up the lance *against* this same assumption as it gets expressed in Western culture. For both sides the romance of being the gadfly underdog is irresistible.)

Mohrhoff, in his well-written essay, takes the problem of freedom to be an offshoot of the so-called *hard problem* of consciousness (see Shear, 1998). If, as some contend, consciousness is causally epiphenomenal (the conjoined claims that experience *qua* experience serves no function above and beyond neural functions, *and* that it is not identical with neural functions; see Clark, 1995; Papineau, 1998) and free will is a property or an attribute of consciousness, it looks as though free will might be illusory. Mohrhoff's exposition concentrates on showing that mind–body interactionism of the sort which might confer *causal priority* on the mental — the power to influence without being influenced in turn — is not inconsistent with physical theory. Since I'm not competent to assess Mohrhoff's analyses of physical claims, I will simply comment that his conclusions do not give much comfort to dualists. Mohrhoff admits that

> Although there are no compelling theoretical or experimental reasons why mental events should not be capable of causing departures from physical laws, it may remain difficult for interactionists and proponents of free will, at least for some time, to disabuse the contemporary physicist, biologist, biologist, or philosopher of science of the doctrine of physicalism . . . (p. 182).

The reason for the obduracy of contemporary scientists is simply that although Mohrhoff may have adduced arguments supporting the *consistency* of some vague notion of mental causation with physical theory (e.g., 'modifications, by the conscious self, of the electromagnetic interactions between particles') neither he nor anyone else to date has given a convincing *positive account* of mental causation backed up by scientific findings. Until an experimentally testable model of how a 'self' can modify electromagnetic fields is forthcoming, few scientists are likely to jump on the interactionist bandwagon. However, if research on 'psi' powers or directed prayer (see, e.g., Dossey, 1997) starts to show a robust, replicable effect *and* a testable hypothesis connecting such an effect to the rest of science is forthcoming, then interactionism might get rolling. Until such time, we all would be well advised *not* to disabuse ourselves of physicalism as the methodologically most parsimonious and productive first guess about phenomena.

Wilson usefully discusses the biological mechanisms which a non-physical mind might employ to influence the brain, and concludes (agreeing with Mohrhoff) that any such mechanism must involve violation of basic physical laws such as the conservation of energy, and further that it must involve energy above the quantum mechanical level. Wilson actually gets his feet wet in the biological mind/brain interactive territory where Libet, Schwartz and Stapp fear to tread, which of course is essential if we are to discover a positive account of dualism. But in Wilson's view no such account is forthcoming any time soon, and he summarizes nicely what might be called the *naturalistic challenge* to libertarians:

> For those who believe that free will must be totally independent and free of physical causes, the idea that physical laws must be violated should not be taken as a negative but almost as an expectation, especially to the extent that physical laws appear to specify a universe that is either determined or randomly probabilistic. If a non-physical mind exists, the research project for the next century should be to explore the impact of such non-physical influences — where in the brain does such influence occur and what laws are broken? (p. 196).

The challenge, which I think is insuperable, is to stay within naturalism (i.e., no ad hoc, mysterious, immeasurable, or theoretically disconnected forces or entities such as your typical incubus or angel) and yet find something causally privileged, something that operates as a first cause, unmoved mover, or is self-constructing from the ground up.[3] This indeed is a research project that we should defer until the millenium (starting 2001, remember) if not the following century, or until such time it is shown not to be completely misconceived.

Meanwhile, research on the mind, conceived as more or less the brain in action, proceeds apace. Here David **Ingvar** surveys the literature on brain mapping studies of volition, while Wolfram **Schultz** reports on the activation of single neurons during self-initiated acts. Although the physiological levels investigated could hardly differ more between these two papers (large brain structures vs. individual cells) the implicit assumption common to both is that will, intention, and voluntary control of behaviour are physically instantiated. The will, as quantifiable and locatable, is what

---

[3] Or from the sky down. See Dennett's *Darwin's Dangerous Idea* (1995) for an extended discussion of 'skyhooks': miraculous devices that are brought in to do the heavy explanatory lifting when reductionist explanations are deemed too unpalatable. Libertarian free will seems the paradigm example of a skyhook.

the brain does in translating desire into action, and it arises in the neuronal context of the entire nervous system, from perceptual inputs to motor outputs, which in turn is securely embedded in the physical and social environment. Of course, none of this research has the least relevance for *libertarian* free will, since it's all about how internal cybernetic mechanisms respond, more or less deterministically, to environmental contingencies. (Although it's of interest that Robert Kane thinks that some sort of indeterminism, generated by conflicting neural processes, may turn out to be the basis for a free will incompatible with determinism; see Kane, 1999.) But for compatibilists, for whom the will need not be independent of mechanism, such studies offer the beginnings of evidence that the brain indeed has the neural resources to accomplish what, until recently, only a controlling mental agent was thought capable of.

Although they pretty much take for granted a compatibilist definition of free will, neuroscientists **Spence** and **Frith** are refreshingly non-ideological in their description of the brain systems subserving voluntary behaviour and intention. Without a philosophical axe to grind, they are free simply to describe biology on the one side, and behaviour, including verbal reports, on the other. No mental supervisor is needed, on their account, to help the brain sort through the pressing demands of acting on time-limited opportunities. Instead, attention is focussed, priorities are set, and choices made by various brain sub-systems themselves, interacting with the environment. In particular, Spence and Frith explore the *feeling* of freedom, which is intimately connected with the sense of 'ownership' of one's body and the covariation of intention and action, both of which they show to be matters of neurobiology, not mental agency. The sense of being a particular, freely choosing self is plausibly tied to how our brains and bodies produce unique, character-specific behaviours, rather than to being something like Hodgson's stripped down soul.

In reaching such conclusions, Spence and Frith's paper combines with **Gomes**', **Claxton**'s, and **McCrone**'s contributions to create a formidable rebuttal to mentalistic and dualist theories of free will. **Gomes** digs very deeply and forcefully into Libet's data, recognizing that 'the dualist thesis [Libet's] is of course not a solution to the dilemma' of how to reconcile naturalism with our sense of voluntary agency. Having cut the libertarian knot, Gomes sets out the compatibilist alternative in its methodological context:

> [F]rom the third-person perspective — which is anyway the proper perspective for explanation — there is not so much difficulty in considering choice, decision and action as part of the natural world. .... All we need to suppose is that there is, in human beings, a decision system that can represent actions and action sequences before their performance, that can select among them, and the output of which is not fully determined by its input, but also by its internal state, by its representations of aims to be achieved, by internal criteria that affect its activity (moral and other personal values), and also by a certain degree of randomness (which gives the arbitrary character that our choices often have). (p. 61.)

Given this brain-based decision making system, the next compatibilist move is to *identify* with it. As Gomes goes on to say:

> If the 'I' is such a system as we have roughly described above, we can consider this intuition [that I act freely] to be essentially correct. It all depends on the concept we have of the self, of the 'I'. When we see our actions as determined by ourselves, this [intuition of freedom] can be considered to be right. It is when we consider our self to be pure spontaneity — a being that is not subject to causality — that we are in illusion (p. 62).

Such compatibilism gives Gomes a clear advantage over Libet in making sense of Libet's own data on how readiness potentials precede voluntary, conscious choices. Gomes doesn't have to side-step the obvious interpretation, that consciousness and deliberate acts are, *in toto*, brain-based phenomena. The guiding assumption — that the mind just *is* the brain in action — helps ground Gomes' somewhat tortuous, but ultimately rewarding analysis of intention, consciousness, voluntariness, and deliberation and how these are linked in various ways. He combines careful attention to the phenomenology of choice with a nuanced typology of choice-making acts, concluding that we act with the most (compatibilist) free will when we deliberate — that is, consciously engage our intentions — concerning the real alternatives facing us.

Although **Claxton** certainly agrees with Gomes that we don't have contra-causal, incompatibilist freedom, he might contest the notion that we are most free when carefully deliberating. His aim (largely achieved, I think, but of course I'm very much in his camp) is nothing less than to demolish the myth he sees at the heart of the Western conception of free will: that intentions, generated by an 'instigatory self', cause ensuing behaviour. He makes a plausible case that the virtues of conscious control are overrated, and its influence over voluntary behaviour vastly inflated. Claxton elegantly dissects the phenomenology and metaphysics of choice, exposing the assumption of a supervisory 'I' as a fraud and, occasionally, a positive hindrance to effective behaviour.

What's most striking about Claxton's approach is his painstaking insistence that we call into question our culturally given assumptions about the whole issue of free will. We must, he says quite rightly, be extra vigilant not to imagine that we already know the truth of the matter, since our natural tendency is to confabulate a role for the freely willing self given the least opportunity. If we really pay attention, Claxton says, we will find that thoughts, intentions, and feelings *arise on their own* (for an extended exploration of the personal and social implications of this see Breer, 1989). These arisings are appropriated by the phenomenological *impression* of being an instigatory self, an impression which helps maintain the self/other distinction and the sense of personal continuity, both useful, perhaps, as day-to-day working hypotheses.

But isn't this a dangerous, even unpatriotic, admission: that we're not really in control, that we can't be trusted not to 'run amok'? Yes, if we continue to identify with the now disempowered conscious controller, but emphatically not if instead we take Claxton's recommendation (and Gomes') to identify with the cognitive processes embodied in our brains. (Which are, after all, so idiosyncratically *us*: no two brains are alike; disinterested souls are like peas in a pod.) Brains, suitably connected to bodies, and given the right sorts of upbringing, control themselves quite nicely, it turns out; no nanny necessary. The paralysing effect of excess conscious control might lift, Claxton suggests, should we accept this reality. The only problem, of course, is that brains, unlike souls, don't go to heaven to live the life hereafter, which is perhaps one reason we're not so keen to identify with them. (For materialist reassurances on the fear of death, see Clark, 1994.)

But *are* we just our brains and bodies? In the only classically philosophical essay of this set, **Lowe** argues that the self or person, although physically embodied, cannot be *identified* with the body or any part of it, such as the brain. Furthermore, since Lowe believes the self's mental intentions are categorically *not* physical states, but nonetheless have physical consequences (actions), it must be the case that non-physical states can cause physical events. Although I and many others have sought to undermine the intuition that the mental just can't be the physical (see Clark, 1995; Papineau, 1998), let us grant Lowe his major conclusion: that under his 'naturalistic dualism' non-physical beliefs and desires are essential in causing and explaining human behaviour, and that therefore thoroughgoing physicalism is false. What follows from this regarding free will?

Perhaps libertarians (such as Schwartz, above) will take heart from the fact that the mental does, after all, control the physical. Since it's the sheer physical inexorability of impersonal mechanism that seems so alien to common intuitions of freedom, Lowe's location of causal power within a self's non-physical intentions may buy some sort of psychological relief or cognitive consistency, especially for those who strongly interpret the phenomenology of choice as the mental 'I' controlling the physical body. Well and good, but what about the issue of ultimate freedom? Are intentions any less conditioned by the context in which they arise simply by virtue of their non-physical status? Does the self and its attributes, even if not identical with the brain and body, have a self-constructing freedom independent of its surroundings? It is not clear that it would, short of demonstrating, which Lowe does not, that the non-physical creates itself 'out of context', so to speak. There seems to be no obvious way in which splitting the natural world into two domains, the physical and non-physical, helps to ground libertarian free will.

In his account of free will, **McCrone**, very much like Claxton, seeks to show that our internalized sense of agency is a socially-induced artifact, which can vary tremendously across cultures. The most recent Western version, McCrone suggests, derives from the Romantic rebellion against the Enlightenment, a rebellion which reified the will as a 'pure motive force', something which could counter the constraints of the clockwork universe described by eighteenth-century science. At the close of the millenium, we have the curious paradox that radical individualism, expressed in the ideology of libertarian free will, is itself a culturally reinforced *norm*. And further, McCrone notes, following B.F Skinner's crucial insight from *Beyond Freedom and Dignity*, the norm is actually a *means of control*:

> It is central to the script of modern Western society that moral agency lies within and that this self is essentially free. Even our legal, political and educational systems depend on the assumption that it is fair to treat individuals as point-like moral agents, fully in charge of what comes out their own minds . . . [T]he clear goal is to keep pushing individuals until they can live up to the model of autonomous behaviour set by Western culture . . . [T]he message is to take charge so society can judge you hard for the quality of your self-regulation and decision-making (p. 254).

Here's the irony: the Western myth of the *causa sui* self (Skinner's 'autonomous man') licenses the culture to control behaviour by exacting stiff after-the-fact sanctions against the individual, since, after all, the individual (self-originating first cause, unmoved mover) is alone responsible for authoring acts. By fostering the illusion of free will, the conditions which create individuals and shape choices are largely ignored as factors in behaviour, setting the person up to take the fall, or take all the credit. Now, without disputing the fact that controls are necessary, the question arises as to whether this often punitive, and sometimes disproportionately rewarding system is really the best. Is feeding the fiction of libertarian freedom, and its attendant blindness to causality, any way to run a culture? Although McCrone doesn't take up this question, his (and Claxton's) analysis of the social construction of free will should prompt its reexamination, nearly thirty years after Skinner so impolitely raised it.

Resistance to any reconsideration of free will runs deep, as testified by the libertarian contributions in this volume. Not many, perhaps, are ready to challenge the 'consensual Cartesian trance' (Claxton) and take the heat for daring to suggest that (1) we aren't unmoved movers, and (2) we don't need to be in order to hold people responsible, ground moral judgments, and maintain a just, democratic social order. As mentioned at the start of this commentary, the notion of free will has ramifications for our most fundamental conceptions of self, agency, and responsibility, and to these we are deeply attached. We *do* want credit, we *do* enjoy imposing just deserts, we *can't*, realistically, give up entirely those 'reactive attitudes' (Strawson, 1962) such as gratefulness and resentment which seem to point to the 'instigatory self'. As much as free will exposes us to the threat of unlimited retaliation for wrongdoing, it nevertheless compensates us by making us the lords of our little domains, the micro-gods of our minds. Contra-causal freedom pays us the ultimate compliment, even if sometimes it exacts the ultimate price, by making us finally responsible for ourselves.

There is the truth of the matter about free will, which must be approached with all due humility (again, Claxton eloquently says why), and then there is the practical issue of whether the truth, in this particular case, is something we are ready to face. Some here have argued that freedom is directly perceived in the irrefutable experience of choice, but others, including myself, take the truth about free will to be a matter of where a scientific understanding of ourselves leads, and experience is simply data added to the mix. To decide between these two approaches is to decide between intuitionism and empiricism, or between personal modes of knowing versus collective and experimental modes. I suspect there is no final arbitration of this issue, except to point out that one can pitch intuitionist arguments successfully to those, like much of the public, that are prepared to buy them, but to convince scientists and (most) philosophers, you'd better have a theory linked to some institutional, peer-reviewed wisdom (see Clark, 1992 and 1993). So if libertarians want to get funded for research, they'll have to come up with a plausible naturalistic model for an unmoved mover (not likely) and if compatibilists like myself want to change the public's conception of free will, we first have to change attitudes about what counts as evidence (not likely).

That libertarians search science to confirm their interpretation of the experience of volition indicates that they too feel the empiricist pull. They, just as much as compatibilists, want the satisfying unification of intuition and observation, the personal and the impersonal perspectives. My claim is, however, that as much as libertarians want validation by science, it will never be forthcoming since the very notion of the ultimately responsible self is inherently opposed to scientific objectives of explanation and prediction. In short, there's a conceptual conflict at the deepest level which blocks this sort of cognitive unification for libertarians. And for that reason, I pity them.

They will reject my pity, and reply that I am dangerously confused in supposing that our commonsense concept of personal liberty should evolve to become compatible with determinism. Whatever the truth about free will may be, too much is at stake, in terms of our social and legal institutions, our self-esteem, and our personal power and creativity to relinquish this most central of assumptions: that we alone choose ourselves and our futures. Better to finesse the science indefinitely by clinging to the straw that just because there's no good evidence *for* free will, that doesn't constitute proof that it doesn't exist. Since science can't ever pronounce the definitive death of ultimate freedom, why not persist in our libertarian convictions?

There are many reasons why not, but mere absence of evidence is perhaps the least persuasive reason for those convinced that the *causa sui* self simply *must* exist. First, the fear of mechanism must be diffused, by showing that a causally embedded self *can* be a moral agent, responsive to the value-reinforcing effects of social sanctions and rewards (indeed, *only* such a self is fully responsive; a *causa sui* self is, by definition, not). Responsibility doesn't have to be ultimate to justify praise and blame, which means a causal understanding of voluntary acts isn't tantamount to excusing them, as is often supposed. Nor does the fair application of sanctions need a basis beyond the fact that behaviour is indeed modified by its consequences. Punishing others for my sins is unjust because they are not the ones needing correction; their suffering is undeserved — non-functional and needless — because the punishment fits no crime of theirs that needs extinguishing, in the Skinnerian sense.

Beyond the moral issues, compatibilists must show that determinism is no threat to human efficacy and creativity: our personal power derives not from having some mysterious causal priority over circumstances, but from exploiting the causal context of which we are so inextricably a part. Being ultimate self-choosers would merely tie us in knots, as we tried to discover some basis for taking that first step towards self-definition. Being *proximate* self-choosers, on the other hand, is all we need to fulfil the desires nature and nurture bequeath us in such variety (see Dennett, 1984; Clark, 1999).

And finally, there may well be benefits flowing from a thoroughly naturalistic conception of the self and its choices. The retributive impulse, cut off from its metaphysical justification in free will, might soften, leading to a less punitive culture. More attention might be paid to improving the social conditions shaping individuals, and no longer will policy makers so blithely blame the victim (remember the multitudes in the U.S. who 'chose' to be homeless during the Reagan era?). On the personal level, dethroning the supervisory 'I' might help us become less self-conscious, more playful, and less likely to wallow in excessive self-blame, pride, envy, or resentment (see Breer, 1989).

Might we become less ambitious, once we see that we don't ultimately choose ourselves or our projects, and that our successes (and failures) result from thousands of combining circumstances? Perhaps, but this might be all to the good, given that the unfettered accumulation of wealth seems likely to compromise the long-term sustainability of resources, or at least concentrate them in a very few hands. And after all, we need not worry that putting the self in its natural, causal context will extinguish desire, any more than we need worry that it will undermine our rights and liberties. Our selves, physically embodied, are virtually *constituted* by desire, and real freedom lies in having the opportunity to pursue our motives as we discover them arising in us. Seeing that the self neither has, nor needs, ultimate responsibility for itself may well lead to the more responsible use of such freedom.

Acknowledgements

I wish to thank the editors for the opportunity to comment on the contents of this volume and for their substantive and stylistic suggestions.

References

Baars, B. (1997), 'In the theatre of consciousness', *Journal of Consciousness Studies*, **4** (4), pp. 292–309.

Breer, P. (1989), *The Spontaneous Self: Viable Alternatives to Free Will* (Cambridge, MA: Institute for Naturalistic Philosophy).

Churchland, P.M. (1995), *The Engine of Reason, the Seat of the Soul* (Cambridge, MA: MIT Press).

Churchland, P.S. and Grush, R. (1995) 'Gaps in Penrose's toilings', *Journal of Consciousness Studies* **2** (1), pp. 10–29.

Clark, T. (1990), 'Free choice and naturalism', *The Humanist*, **50** (3), pp. 18–24.

Clark, T. (1992), 'Relativism and the limits of rationality', *The Humanist*, **52** (1), pp. 25–32.

Clark, T. (1993), 'Faith, science and the soul: on the pragmatic virtues of naturalism', *The Humanist*, **53** (3), pp. 7–12.

Clark, T. (1994), 'Death, nothingness, and subjectivity', *The Humanist*, **54**, (6), pp. 15–20.

Clark, T. (1995), 'Function and phenomenology: closing the explanatory gap', *Journal of Consciousness Studies* **2** (3), pp. 241–55. Reprinted in Shear (1998).

Clark, T. (1996), 'The freedom of Susan Smith', *The Humanist*, **56** (2), pp. 8–12.

Clark, T. (1998a), 'Materialism and morality: the problem with Pinker', *The Humanist*, **58** (6), pp. 20–25.

Clark, T. (1998b), 'To help addicts, look beyond the fiction of free will', *The Scientist*, **12** (16), p. 9.

Clark, T. (1999), 'The flaw of fatalism', on the World Wide Web at http://world.std.com/~twc/fatalism.htm.

Damasio, A. (1994), *Descartes' Error* (New York: Putnam).

Dennett, D. (1984), *Elbow Room* (Cambridge, MA: MIT Press).

Dennett, D. (1987), *The Intentional Stance* (Cambridge, MA: MIT Press).

Dennett, D. (1991), *Consciousness Explained* (Boston, MA: Little, Brown).

Dennett, D. (1995), *Darwin's Dangerous Idea* (New York: Simon and Schuster).

Dossey, L. (1997) *Healing Words: The Power of Prayer and the Practice of Medicine* (New York: Harper Collins).

Kane, R. (1996), *The Significance of Free Will* (New York: Oxford University Press).

Kane, R. (1999), 'Responsibility, luck, and chance: reflections on free will and determinism', *Journal of Philosophy*, **XCVI** (5), pp. 217–40.

Papineau, D. (1998) 'Mind the gap', in *Philosophical Perspectives*, **12**: 'Language, Mind and Ontology', ed. James E. Tombelin (Oxford: Blackwell Publishers).

Shear, J. (ed. 1998) *Explaining Consciousness: The Hard Problem* (Cambridge, MA: MIT Press).

Strawson, G. (1998), 'Luck swallows everything', *Times Literary Supplement*, 26 June, pp. 8–10.

Strawson, P. (1962), 'Freedom and resentment', *Proceedings of the British Academy*, **XLVIII**, pp. 1–25.

Waller, B. (1998), *The Natural Selection of Autonomy* (Albany: State University of New York Press).

Index